Guidelines

A Cross-Cultural Reading/Writing Text

Second Edition

RUTH SPACK

Tufts University

ST. MARTIN'S PRESS

New York

To Norman, Rebecca, and Jonathan Spack
with love

Editor: Darcy Meeker
Manager, publishing services: Emily Berleth
Project editor, publishing services: Kalea Chapman
Project management: Julie Sullivan
Production supervisor: Dennis Para
Cover design: Rod Hernandez
Cover photo: Decoding the Invisible Leopard by Laurence M. Gartel. © Laurence M. Gartel "Decoding the Invisible Leopard," 1984, Polaroid SX-70 Mural, Polaroid Corporate Collection, Massachusetts.

Library of Congress Catalog Card Number: 94-80175

Copyright © 1996 by St. Martin's Press, Inc.

All rights reserved. No part of this book may be reproduced, stored in a retrieval system, or transmitted by any form or by any means, electronic, mechanical, photocopying, recording, or otherwise, except as may be expressly permitted by the applicable copyright statutes or in writing by the Publisher.

Manufactured in the United States of America.

0 9 8 7
f e d

For information, write:
St. Martin's Press, Inc.
175 Fifth Avenue
New York, NY 10010

ISBN: 0-312-10152-X

ACKNOWLEDGMENTS

Acknowledgments and copyrights are continued at the back of the book on pages 386–387, which constitute an extension of the copyright page.

Sydney J. Harris, "What True Education Should Do." Copyright © 1994. Reprinted with the permission of the *Chicago Sun-Times*, Inc.
Jacob Neusner, "The Commencement Speech You'll Never Hear" from the *Daily Herald* (1981). Brown University campus newspaper. Reprinted by permission of the author.
James Thomas Jackson, "Waiting in Line at the Drugstore" from *Waiting in Line at the Drugstore and Other Writings of James Thomas Jackson,* published by the University of North Texas Press, 1993. Reprinted by permission.
Anzia Yezierska, "College." Pages 209–220 from *Bread Givers* by Anzia Yezierska. Copyright © 1925 by Doubleday, renewed 1952 by Anzia Yezierska, transferred to Louise Levitas Henriksen 1970. Reprinted by permission of Persea Books, Inc.

Brief Contents

Contents

Preface

Guidelines: A Cross-Cultural Reading/Writing Text, second edition, features a generous selection of thought-provoking classic and contemporary readings. Unique to this text is the integration of readings with essay assignments, emphasizing the connection between reading and writing. With its multicultural and international scope, the text will have considerable appeal to a diverse group of readers.

Guidelines addresses the academic needs of students who can benefit from carefully structured support as they undertake increasingly complex tasks. Building on language resources and knowledge that students already have, guidelines within the text show students ways to integrate new procedures and ideas with previously learned skills and information. In the process, students are challenged to think critically about what they read and to develop analytical and argumentative skills that enable them to present and support ideas.

The Level

Guidelines is designed for composition courses with a cross-cultural emphasis and for advanced ESL programs.

The Structure

Guidelines has four major sections: Part One: Reading, Part Two: Readings and Writing Assignments, Part Three: Academic Reading and Writing Skills, and Part Four: The Editing Process.

Part One: Reading

Part One consists of two chapters that are designed to help students develop effective strategies for reading and responding to what they read.

☐ Chapter 1 describes and demonstrates general strategies for reading and responding to written texts: generating background knowledge, reading, rereading, defining, annotating, and making double-entry notes.

☐ Chapter 2 provides guidelines for keeping a reading/writing journal to record reactions to the readings and to discuss writing progress and ideas. Sample student journal entries are included.

Part Two: Readings and Writing Assignments

Part Two consists of six units of readings and writing assignments directly connected to the readings. Composing strategies—for exploring, focusing, drafting, structuring, giving and receiving feedback, revising, and completing—are demonstrated with student writers' work; a sample student essay completes each unit. Throughout, the text emphasizes flexibility: students are reminded again and again that different reading and writing approaches work for different writers.

☐ The first unit, *Writing from Experience*, includes five reading selections in Chapter 3 that draw upon the writers' own experiences; discussion activities in Chapter 4 that relate to the readings; and guidelines in Chapter 5 for fulfilling an assignment to write from experience.

☐ The second unit, *Writing from Sources: Field Research*, includes five reading selections in Chapter 6 that draw from the writers' field research; discussion activities in Chapter 7 that relate to the readings; and guidelines in Chapter 8 for fulfilling an assignment to write from field research.

☐ The third unit, *Writing from Sources: Essays*, includes five reading selections in Chapter 9 in which the writers argue their viewpoints; discussion activities in Chapter 10 that relate to the readings; and guidelines in Chapter 11 for fulfilling an assignment to write about essays.

☐ The fourth unit, *Writing from Sources: Fiction*, includes five short stories in Chapter 12; discussion activities in Chapter 13 that relate to the stories; and guidelines in Chapter 14 for fulfilling an assignment to write about fiction.

☐ The fifth unit, *Writing from Sources: Poetry*, includes five poems in Chapter 15; discussion activities in Chapter 16 that relate to the poems; and guidelines in Chapter 17 for fulfilling an assignment to compile a poetry anthology.

☐ The sixth unit, *Writing from Sources: Library Research*, includes three chapters. Chapter 18 provides guidelines for exploring a research topic; Chapter 19 provides guidelines for conducting library research; and Chapter 20 provides guidelines for composing a research essay.

Part Three: Academic Writing Conventions

Part Three consists of four chapters that demonstrate skills that can help students write about what they read.

☐ Chapter 21, *Summarizing*, provides general guidelines for summarizing both nonfiction and fiction works.

☐ Chapter 22, *Paraphrasing*, explains the purpose and process of paraphrasing another writer's words.

☐ Chapter 23, *Quoting*, offers suggestions for selecting and incorporating quotations from the reading.

☐ Chapter 24, *Citing and Documenting Sources*, focuses on various ways to cite and document sources.

Part Four: The Editing Process

Part Four consists of three chapters that explain the editing process.

☐ Chapter 25, *Proofreading and Editing,* provides guidelines for proofreading and editing an essay.

☐ Chapter 26, *Causes of Error,* provides a unique approach to editing, asking students to examine and categorize the logic of their errors.

☐ Chapter 27, *A Handbook for Correcting Errors,* provides guidelines for understanding the structure of sentences and for correcting errors. Wherever possible, examples are drawn from the readings in *Guidelines,* to show how language works in context.

☐ Chapter 28, *Manuscript Form for Final Copy,* explains ways to prepare a handwritten, typewritten, or computer-generated paper.

The Readings

The readings offer a wide range of choices in terms of subject, genre, culture, gender, point of view, length, style, and theme, yet lend themselves well to comparison, both within and across genres. Together, the readings deal with thought-provoking and culturally diverse topics such as social and cultural adjustment, school and college life, friendship and cross-cultural communication, teaching and learning, oppression and freedom, and moral dilemmas and life choices. The authors represent several fields, including literature, anthropology, communications, education, biology, psychology, and business.

The readings have the additional advantage of providing a social history, ranging as they do from works published in the 19th century to works published in 1993. The readings cover events such as the dislocation of Native Americans, the Civil War, discrimination against African Americans, the exclusion of Chinese immigrants, the struggle of Jewish immigrants, the changing roles of women and men, World War II, and the plight of refugees and illegal aliens.

Before each reading selection, background information about the author and text includes explanations of culture-specific items, technical terms, and historical references. Explanatory material within the reading selections is kept to a minimum so that students can interact freely with the text.

The Content and Flexibility of the Second Edition

In the process of writing the first edition of *Guidelines,* I captured a moment of time in two decades of teaching. Because I am always experimenting in the classroom, exploring with students new readings and approaches to writing, *Guidelines* has had to change with me. In writing this second edition, guided by reviewers' requests, I tried to save the best of the past and to enrich it with the best of the present.

What remains is a comprehensive textbook that includes clear, purposeful, and sequential guidelines for reading, writing, and editing. As in the first edition, reading and writing are treated as interconnected processes. The readings are those that have consistently appealed to and challenged students and to which they have responded in meaningful ways. The writing assignments are designed so that students can build on what they have learned. Examples of student writers' work make it possible to view writing processes from inception to completion of an assignment. Chapters on summarizing, paraphrasing, quoting, and citing and documenting sources promote students' acquisition of academic ways of analyzing texts.

The second edition of *Guidelines* provides greater flexibility. This edition has many more readings and writing assignments than the first edition, allowing greater choice. Depending on the level and goals of a course, instructors can assign five or fewer reading selections within each unit. Reading assignments can also be made across units, as many common themes reverberate throughout the readings. The number of selections also allows instructors variety from course to course; what is assigned in one class may not be assigned in the next semester.

The major revisions in the second edition include the following:

Readings
Eighteen new reading selections, including five short stories and five poems
More readings that reflect the multiple cultures that compose the United States, including selections by and about Native Americans and Americans of African, Asian, Hispanic, and Jewish descent
New sets of readings that reflect opposing viewpoints
Readings by British writers

Discussion Activities
Separate chapters of discussion activities to accompany each unit of reading selections, which provide guidelines for responding to, summarizing, analyzing, interpreting, and making connections among the readings

Writing Assignments
More writing assignments within each unit
New assignments to conduct field research
New assignments to write about fiction
A new assignment to compile a poetry anthology

Student Writing
Five new student essays, including a sample student anthology that contains eight poems

Editing
Clearer guidelines, with examples drawn from the readings in the book to show how language works in context

Glossary
A new alphabetized list of defined words taken from the readings

An instructor's manual is available.

Acknowledgments

As must be obvious to anyone who reads this book, I rely on the students to whom I teach writing to show me how to teach and how to write. I thank all of them for their willingness to test out materials for *Guidelines* and for the useful feedback they provided.

I have been fortunate to have colleagues with whom I can discuss issues related to teaching and learning, all of whom understand how important the process of talking is to the process of writing. Among those who have most influenced my work are Gay Brookes, Ann Raimes, Catherine Sadow, Roberta Steinberg, Vivian Zamel, and the teaching assistants at Tufts University with whom I work.

Many instructors have been generous in their support of this book. In particular, I would like to thank Catherine Sadow, without whom I could not have developed the unit on library research, and Helen Fragiadakis, who has shared the material she wrote to supplement the first edition of *Guidelines,* some of which appears in this second edition.

I will always be grateful to the following reviewers of the second edition of *Guidelines* for their insightful comments and attention to detail: Melissa Allen, George Mason University; Helen Fragiadakis, Contra Costa College; Margaret Grant, San Francisco State University; Victoria Holder, San Francisco State University; Franklin E. Horowitz, Teachers College, Columbia University; Wendy Levison, San Francisco State University; Jill A. Makegon, Kapi'olani Community College; Beatrice Mikulecky, Bentley College; and Holly Zaitchik, Boston University.

St. Martin's editor Naomi Silverman told me that it would be easy to write a second edition. She was wrong about that. But she was always supportive of my meticulous approach to writing, and I always appreciated her patience, good humor, and friendship. Associate editor Carl Whithaus guided me wisely through the last stages of composing, and I thank him. I am indebted to project manager Julie Sullivan for the role she played in the final design and editing of the book. Finally, I would like to thank Emily Berleth, manager of publishing services, and Sandy Schechter, permissions associate, for their dedication.

Ruth Spack

Reading

Part One consists of two chapters that are designed to help you interact with what you read.

Chapter 1 describes and demonstrates some general strategies for reading and responding to written texts: generating background knowledge, reading, rereading, defining, annotating, and making double-entry notes.

Chapter 2 provides guidelines for keeping a reading/writing journal to record your reactions to what you read and to discuss your writing progress and ideas. Sample student journal entries are included.

CHAPTER 1

Reading Strategies

The guidelines in Chapter 1 are designed to help you develop effective approaches to reading. You may not need to apply every suggested strategy to every selection you read or to follow the order in which they are presented. Your instructor may assign certain tasks for some or all of the reading, or you may discover other strategies that work best for you.

Generating Background Knowledge

You may be able to achieve a deeper understanding of what you read if you have some background knowledge before you begin reading a selection. The following suggestions may provide clues to the context of a reading and may help you plan reading strategies.

Note: Not every suggestion will apply to every reading selection.

GUIDELINES

For Generating Background Knowledge

1. Read the *Write before You Read* activity that precedes a reading selection.
2. Read the *title* of the reading selection.
3. Read the *background information* that precedes each reading.
4. Look at the *length* of the reading.
5. Look at *headings* and *subheadings,* if they are provided.
6. Look for *words in boldface* (darker print) or in *italics*.
7. Look at *charts* and *illustrations,* if they are provided.

A First Reading

The first time you read, you do not need to understand every word or detail. Try to grasp the essence of the selection.

For a First Reading

1. Preview the reading to help predict its content and purpose, adapting the preceding guidelines for generating background knowledge.
2. Read through the selection once, without stopping to use a dictionary.

ACTIVITY

Reading

Adapting the guidelines for a first reading, read "What True Education Should Do" by Sydney J. Harris.

What True Education Should Do

Sydney J. Harris

Sydney J. Harris (1917–1986) was a writer for major newspapers in Chicago, Illinois. His syndicated column, "Strictly Personal," was published weekly throughout the United States and in several other countries.

When most people think of the word "education," they think of a pupil as a sort of animate sausage casing. Into this empty casing, the teachers are supposed to stuff "education."

But genuine education, as Socrates knew more than two thousand years ago, is not inserting the stuffings of information *into* a person, but rather eliciting knowledge *from* him; it is the drawing out of what is in the mind.

"The most important part of education," once wrote William Ernest Hocking, the distinguished Harvard philosopher, "is this instruction of a man in what he has inside of him."

And, as Edith Hamilton has reminded us, Socrates never said, "I know, learn from me." He said, rather, "Look into your own selves and find the spark of truth that God has put into every heart, and that only you can kindle to a flame."

In the dialogue called the "Meno," Socrates takes an ignorant slave boy, without a day of schooling, and proves to the amazed observers that the boy really "knows" geometry—because the principles and axioms of geometry are already in his mind, waiting to be called out.

So many of the discussions and controversies about the content of education are futile and inconclusive because they are concerned with what should "go into" the student rather than with what should be taken out, and how this can best be done.

The college student who once said to me, after a lecture, "I spend so much time studying that I don't have a chance to learn anything," was succinctly expressing his dissatisfaction with the sausage-casing view of education.

He was being so stuffed with miscellaneous facts, with such an indigestible mass of material, that he had no time (and was given no encouragement) to draw on his own resources, to use his own mind for analyzing and synthesizing and evaluating this material.

Education, to have any meaning beyond the purpose of creating well-informed dunces, must elicit from the pupil what is latent in every human being—the rules of reason, the inner knowledge of what is proper for men to be and do, the ability to sift evidence and come to conclusions that can generally be assented to by all open minds and warm hearts.

Pupils are more like oysters than sausages. The job of teaching is not to stuff them and then seal them up, but to help them open and reveal the riches within. There are pearls in each of us, if only we knew how to cultivate them with ardor and persistence. ■

Subsequent Readings

You may achieve a fuller understanding of a reading simply by reading it more than once. But you may be able to generate meaning by making notations as you reread.

Defining Unfamiliar Words

As you reread, underline or in some way make note of unfamiliar words that seem to hold a key to achieving a general understanding of the passages in which they occur.

One way to approach unfamiliar vocabulary is to guess at the general meanings of words, using contextual clues. Context will not always give you precise meaning, but it may give you enough clues to understand a passage.

GUIDELINES

For Using Clues to Guess at Meaning

1. Look at what precedes and follows the word or expression (for example, grammatical forms within the same sentence, other key words or expressions, important ideas, significant scenes, and so on).
2. Try to determine whether the word has a positive or negative connotation.
3. Consider how the word fits into the whole reading.

Guessing Meaning from Context

Working in pairs or a small group, read "What True Education Should Do" by Sydney J. Harris (p. 3).

1. Identify one or two words or expressions whose dictionary definition(s) you may not know precisely.
2. Adapting the guidelines for using context clues to guess at meaning (p. 4), discuss each word to infer its meaning in the sentence in which it occurs.
3. Consult a dictionary or the Glossary (pp. 375–385) to compare the meanings you have arrived at with the dictionary definitions. ■

Annotating

Annotating involves recording your reactions to what you read. You can make notes in the margins of the text, within the text itself, or on a separate sheet of paper. This process may help you interact with the reading and also clarify your understanding.

GUIDELINES

For Annotating

The many possibilities for recording your reactions and clarifying your understanding include these:

1. Express any emotion you feel in response to what you have just read, for example, pleasure, surprise, anger, or confusion.
2. Recall personal associations with actions or conversations that take place in the reading selection.
3. Make connections with something else you have read, heard, or seen.
4. Create headings to identify different sections.
5. Write brief summaries of different sections.
6. Underline or in some way mark a certain passage or scene that you think is significant.
7. Write definitions of unfamiliar words.
8. Ask questions.

Making Double-Entry Notes

Another way to make notations is to write brief *double-entry notes* to reveal a double perspective on the reading: (1) summary and (2) reaction. In other words, separate what you perceive the author is saying (summary) from what you think (reaction).

For Making Double-Entry Notes

To write double-entry notes, you can write (1) in the left and right margins of the reading selection, (2) on the left and right sides of a sheet of paper folded in two lengthwise, or (3) on two separate sheets of paper.

1. On the left side or sheet, write notes that *summarize* the essay you are reading, to help you understand and focus on what the author is saying. This can be done paragraph by paragraph or in larger chunks.
2. On the right side or sheet, write notes that *record your reactions* to what you have just read. This can be done paragraph by paragraph or in larger chunks. For example, you can express pleasure, surprise, disagreement, or anger at what you've just read; recall personal associations; make connections with something else you've read or seen; or ask questions.

ACTIVITY

Making Double-Entry Notes

Adapting the guidelines above, make double-entry notes on "What True Education Should Do" by Sydney J. Harris (p. 3). ∎

A Student Reader at Work

Reprinted below is an example of how one student annotated "What True Education Should Do." Using the double-entry format, she summarized sets of paragraphs in the left margin and recorded her reactions in the right margin.

Read this annotated version of the essay, paying attention to the marginal comments. Compare her impression of the essay with your own, and discuss your responses with the class.

Student Double-Entry Notes

What True Education Should Do

Sydney J. Harris

Summary

Education as sausage casing
Education as drawing out

When most people think of the word "education," they think of a pupil as a sort of animate sausage casing. Into this empty casing, the teachers are supposed to stuff "education."

But genuine education, as Socrates knew more than two thousand years ago, is not inserting the stuffings of information *into* a person, but rather eliciting knowledge *from* him; it is the drawing out of what is in the mind.

Reaction

Am I a sausage?

Nice, but impossible in college

"The most important part of education," once wrote William Ernest Hocking, the distinguished Harvard philosopher, "is this instruction of a man in what he has inside of him."

And, as Edith Hamilton has reminded us, Socrates never said, "I know, learn from me." He said, rather, "Look into your own selves and find the spark of truth that God has put into every heart, and that only you can kindle to a flame."

Knowledge already in ourselves

In the dialogue called the "Meno," Socrates takes an ignorant slave boy, without a day of schooling, and proves to the amazed observers that the boy really "knows" geometry—because the principles and axioms of geometry are already in his mind, waiting to be called out.

So many of the discussions and controversies about the content of education are futile and inconclusive because they are concerned with what should "go into" the student rather than with what should be taken out, and how this can best be done.

The college student who once said to me, after a lecture, "I spend so much time studying that I don't have a chance to learn anything," was succinctly expressing his dissatisfaction with the sausage-casing view of education.

Student stuffed with facts

But how is he going to learn what the professor knows?

He was being so stuffed with miscellaneous facts, with such an indigestible mass of material, that he had no time (and was given no encouragement) to draw on his own resources, to use his own mind for analyzing and synthesizing and evaluating this material.

Education = reason, inner knowledge, sift evidence, come to conclusions

Education, to have any meaning beyond the purpose of creating well-informed dunces, must elicit from the pupil what is latent in every human being—the rules of reason, the inner knowledge of what is proper for men to be and do, the ability to sift evidence and come to conclusions that can generally be assented to by all open minds and warm hearts.

Pupils = oysters
Pupils ≠ sausages

Sounds beautiful. But it's a fairy tale.

Pupils are more like oysters than sausages. The job of teaching is not to stuff them and then seal them up, but to help them open and reveal the riches within. There are pearls in each of us, if only we knew how to cultivate them with ardor and persistence.

CHAPTER 2

Keeping a Reading/Writing Journal

One way to explore and record your thoughts about what you read and write is to make regular entries in a journal.

Depending on what your instructor assigns, your journal may include all or some of the following:

☐ *Responses to the Write before You Read activities.* You may follow some or all of the Write before You Read suggestions that precede most of the reading selections in this book.

☐ *Discussions of your writing plans and progress.* You may write entries in which you describe your essay topic and the progress you are making on the essay.

☐ *Reactions to what you read.* You may explore what you feel and think as you read, or just after you read, a particular selection. The guidelines that follow may help you with those entries.

Making a Journal Entry on a Reading Selection

There are no set rules for what a journal entry should look like. How you respond to what you read depends on how the reading selection is written, its content, its length, its meaning or purpose. Your response also depends on who you are: your background, culture, beliefs, prejudices, and experiences. And, of course, your response is also related to how carefully you have read and how fully you understand the reading. You may have a lot to say, or you may have very little to say.

GUIDELINES

For Making a Journal Entry on a Reading Selection

The possibilities for responses to a reading selection are numerous. You may write whatever you want or choose among the following suggestions.

1. Describe what you think or feel as you read.
2. Explore what you like or what interests you most.
3. Explore what you don't like or find confusing.
4. Explore what you agree or disagree with.
5. Relate your own experiences or background knowledge to the reading.
6. Raise questions if you don't understand all or part of the reading.

To identify exactly what you are referring to, quote relevant passages from the reading—either a few words or one or more sentences (see Chapter 23).

Student Readers at Work

The following journal entries show two students' initial, but different, reactions to Sydney J. Harris's "What True Education Should Do" (p. 3). Read one or both of the entries, and compare what the students have written with your own reactions. Discuss the possible reasons for the different responses.

Note: The students' journal entries are reprinted as they were written, with errors and crossed-out words, so that you can see that a journal entry does not need to be a polished work.

Student Journal Entry on "What True Education Should Do"

"There are pearls in each of us, if only we knew how to cultivate them with ardor and persistence."

Even if I hadn't liked the rest of the reading, this concluding phrase would have changed all my feelings. It is so easy to say it but yet so difficult to understand it or even believe it. Most people judge you ~~from the knowledge that~~ without ever trying to reveal what or who you realy are, What you have inside and what you have to offer. That also occurs ~~here specificaly~~ in school. Bad grades mean you are nothing. Not able to understand math? Then you are not someone ~~to~~ to work with. They (most of the times) do not try to see you as a person. ~~but~~ You are a machine to them. A ~~mach~~ computer where they can typewrite their own thoughts and feelings.

S. D.

Student Journal Entry on "What True Education Should Do"

In this peace of reading there are things that have made me think about different things and aspects about education. I would like to start talking about the comparisson that we find in the beginning between the human brain, or ability of keeping information to a sausage. If a teacher or instructor thinks that our brain is this "sausage", what's going to happen is what this college student said in the middle of the reading—"I spend so much time studying that I don't have a chance to learn anything." This is what would happen to a student if he had a "sausage maker" as a teacher.

In the other hand we can find what Socrates says about eliciting knowledge from a person. Socrates tried to demonstrate that in that dialogue called "Meno". He made a boy with no schooling demonstrate something on geometry. From my point of view we cannot make ourselves Socrates believers because we don't know everything that has happened or it is to come and somebody has to open our "oyster," as the last comparisson made in our reading about our knowledge.

What I would say is that we are not either an oyster or a sausage what we need is somebody to teach us and give us information in a way that we have fun receiving this information and we have this energy to keep learning.

R. D.

ACTIVITY

Reading, Annotating, and Writing a Journal Entry

1. Preview the essay entitled "The Commencement Speech You'll Never Hear" by Jacob Neusner (p. 11) by reading the material that precedes the essay.

2. Read through the essay, without using a dictionary.

3. Reread the essay, making notations (see pp. 4–6).

4. Write a journal entry in which you explore your reactions to the reading (see pp. 8–9).

5. Working in pairs, in a small group, or with the whole class, share your journal responses.

Write before You Read

The following reading selection is entitled "The Commencement Speech* You'll Never Hear." Before reading, think or write for several minutes about the following topic:

> When you attend your own college graduation, what do you expect the commencement speaker to say?

Share what you think with classmates.

The Commencement Speech You'll Never Hear

Jacob Neusner

About the Author   Jacob Neusner was a professor in the Religious Studies Department at Brown University in Providence, Rhode Island, when he wrote the following essay. He is the author of numerous scholarly books in his field.

The Context of the Reading   As the title suggests, the commencement speech was not delivered at the college graduation, but it was published as an essay in the Brown University campus newspaper, the *Daily Herald,* in 1981.

We the faculty take no pride in our educational achievements with you. We have prepared you for a world that does not exist, indeed, that cannot exist. You have spent four years supposing that failure leaves no record. You have learned at Brown that when your work goes poorly, the painless solution is to drop out. But starting now, in the world to which you go, failure marks you. Confronting difficulty by quitting leaves you changed. Outside Brown, quitters are no heroes.

With us you could argue about why your errors were not errors, why mediocre work really was excellent, why you could take pride in routine and slipshod presentation. Most of you, after all, can look back on honor grades for most of what you have done. So, here grades can have meant little in distinguishing the excellent from the ordinary. But tomorrow, in the world to which you go, you had best not defend errors but learn from them. You will be ill-advised to demand praise for what does not deserve it, and abuse those who do not give it.

For years we created an altogether forgiving world, in which whatever slight effort you gave was all that was demanded. When you did not keep appointments, we made new ones. When your work came in beyond the deadline, we pretended not to care.

---

commencement speech: talk given to graduates by an invited speaker

Worse still, when you were boring, we acted as if you were saying something important. When you were garrulous and talked to hear yourselves talk, we listened as if it mattered. When you tossed on our desks writing upon which you had not labored, we read it and even responded, as though you earned a response. When you were dull, we pretended you were smart. When you were predictable, unimaginative and routine, we listened as if to new and wonderful things. When you demanded free lunch, we served it. And all this why?

Despite your fantasies, it was not even that we wanted to be liked by you. It was that we did not want to be bothered, and the easy way out was pretense: smiles and easy Bs.

It is conventional to quote in addresses such as these. Let me quote someone you've never heard of: Prof. Carter A. Daniel, Rutgers University (*Chronicle of Higher Education,* May 7, 1979):

> College has spoiled you by reading papers that don't deserve to be read, listening to comments that don't deserve a hearing, paying attention even to the lazy, ill-informed and rude. We had to do it, for the sake of education. But nobody will ever do it again. College has deprived you of adequate preparation for the last 50 years. It has failed you by being easy, free, forgiving, attentive, comfortable, interesting, unchallenging fun. Good luck tomorrow.

That is why, on this commencement day, we have nothing in which to take much pride.

Oh, yes, there is one more thing. Try not to act toward your coworkers and bosses as you have acted toward us. I mean, when they give you what you want but have not earned, don't abuse them, insult them, act out with them your parlous relationships with your parents. This too we have tolerated. It was, as I said, not to be liked. Few professors actually care whether or not they are liked by peer-paralyzed adolescents, fools so shallow as to imagine professors care not about education but about popularity. It was, again, to be rid of you. So go, unlearn the lies we taught you. To Life! ■

Readings and Writing Assignments

Part 2 consists of six units of readings and writing assignments.

Each of the first five units begins with a chapter of reading selections that may act as stimuli or sources for writing. The next chapter in each of these units provides discussion activities connected to the readings. The final chapter provides guidelines for fulfilling an essay assignment. Composing strategies, with examples of student writers at work, are demonstrated, and a sample student essay completes each unit.

The sixth unit includes three chapters that demonstrate a way to conduct library research. This unit follows a student writer at work to show the process she went through to produce a research essay. Her essay completes the unit.

This unit, Writing from Experience, consists of three chapters that can help you fulfill an assignment to write an essay drawn from experience. By reading and examining your reactions to the readings in Chapter 3, guided by the discussion activities in Chapter 4, you may develop a sense of how a writer can capture and hold a reader's interest. In Chapter 5, you can observe a student writer at work, exploring, focusing, drafting, organizing, receiving feedback, revising, and completing an essay based on his own experience.

Readings

Chapter 3 provides five reading selections drawn from the author's experiences. As you read and reread each selection, you can aim to accomplish the following:

☐ Enter the world of the writer

☐ Reflect on what the writer thinks and feels

☐ Examine your own experience and views

The Reading Selections

The reading selections in this chapter focus on personal experiences, which the writers may have exaggerated or fictionalized for dramatic effect or for other reasons. Together, the readings cover life experiences from childhood through adulthood and deal with personal, philosophical, and political topics.

Write before You Read

The following reading selection is entitled "The School Days of an Indian Girl." Before reading, think or write for several minutes about the following topic:

Describe your first memories of school.

Share your memories with classmates.

The School Days of an Indian Girl

Zitkala-Ša (Gertrude Simmons Bonnin)

About the Author   Zitkala-Ša (1876–1938), also known by the name Gertrude Simmons Bonnin, was born on a reservation in South Dakota to a Sioux mother and white father. Named Gertrude Simmons at birth, she later gave herself the Lakota Sioux name Zitkala-Ša, which means Red Bird. Pressured by missionaries, she chose to study at a Quaker missionary school in Indiana, not knowing that she would not be allowed to return home for three years. She later attended Earlham College and the Boston Conservatory of Music. One of the earliest Native American writers to record the traditions of their people in English, she published most of her work in two books: *Old Indian Legends* (1901) and *American Indian Stories* (1921). In addition to being a writer, she was a teacher, violinist, and an activist for Native American rights.

The Context of the Reading   Before the advent of Euro-Americans, the Sioux (also known as Dakota or Lakota) were hunters who roamed the western plains of what is now the United States. Because of the federal government's growing demand for land in the 19th century, the Sioux (like all other Native American groups) were deprived of their lands through wars, broken treaties, cheap deals, and congressional acts. By the end of the century, Congress had passed laws to confine Native American peoples to reservations and to prevent them from following their customs and religious beliefs. In an attempt to assimilate Native Americans into white society, government authorities often took children from their parents and sent them to schools in distant states, where they were required to speak only English and to ignore their own heritage. Likewise, missionaries, who viewed Native Americans' cultures and beliefs to be inferior and barbaric, attempted to convert them to Christianity.

Zitkala-Ša makes several references to terms used by her people:

- □   *braves:* warriors (males who were old enough to have been initiated into manhood)
- □   *iron horse:* train
- □   *palefaces:* white people
- □   *mother tongue:* the author's first language, Nakota Sioux

"The School Days of an Indian Girl" was first published in 1900 in the *Atlantic Monthly* magazine. Reprinted here are the first three sections of that selection.

The Land of Red Apples

There were eight in our party of bronzed children who were going East with the missionaries. Among us were three young braves, two tall girls, and we three little ones, Judéwin, Thowin, and I.

We had been very impatient to start on our journey to the Red Apple Country, which, we were told, lay a little beyond the great circular horizon of the Western prairie. Under a sky of rosy apples we dreamt of roaming as freely and happily as we had chased the cloud shadows on the Dakota plains. We had anticipated much pleasure from a ride on the iron horse, but the throngs of staring palefaces disturbed and troubled us.

On the train, fair women with tottering babies on each arm, stopped their haste and scrutinized the children of absent mothers. Large men, with heavy bundles in their hands, halted near by, and riveted their glassy blue eyes upon us.

I sank deep into the corner of my seat, for I resented being watched. Directly in front of me, children who were no larger than I hung themselves upon the backs of their seats, with their bold white faces toward me. Sometimes they took their forefingers out of their mouths and pointed at my moccasined feet. Their mothers, instead of reproving such rude curiosity, looked closely at me, and attracted their children's further notice to my blanket. This embarrassed me, and kept me constantly on the verge of tears.

I sat perfectly still, with my eyes downcast, daring only now and then to shoot long glances around me. Chancing to turn to the window at my side, I was quite breathless upon seeing one familiar object. It was the telegraph pole which strode by at short paces. Very near my mother's dwelling, along the edge of a road thickly bordered with wild sunflowers, some poles like these had been planted by white men. Often I had stopped, on my way down the road, to hold my ear against the pole, and, hearing its low moaning, I used to wonder what the paleface had done to hurt it. Now I sat watching for each pole that glided by to be the last one.

In this way I had forgotten my uncomfortable surroundings, when I heard one of my comrades call out my name. I saw the missionary standing very near, tossing candies and gums into our midst. This amused us all, and we tried to see who could catch the most of the sweet-meats. The missionary's generous distribution of candies was impressed upon my memory by a disastrous result which followed. I had caught more than my share of candies and gums, and soon after our arrival at the school I had a chance to disgrace myself, which, I am ashamed to say, I did.

Though we rode several days inside of the iron horse, I do not recall a single thing about our luncheons.

It was night when we reached the school grounds. The lights from the windows of the large buildings fell upon some of the icicled trees that stood beneath them. We were led toward an open door, where the brightness of the lights within flooded out over the heads of the excited palefaces who blocked the way. My body trembled more from fear than from the snow I trod upon.

Entering the house, I stood close against the wall. The strong glaring light in the large whitewashed room dazzled my eyes. The noisy hurrying of hard shoes upon a bare wooden floor increased the whirring in my ears. My only safety seemed to be in keeping next to the wall. As I was wondering in which direction to escape from all this confusion, two warm hands grasped me firmly, and in the same moment I was tossed high in midair. A rosy-cheeked paleface woman caught me in her arms. I was both frightened and insulted by such trifling. I stared into her eyes, wishing her to let me stand on my own feet, but she jumped me up and down with increasing enthusiasm. My mother had never made a plaything of her wee daughter. Remembering this I began to cry aloud.

They misunderstood the cause of my tears, and placed me at a white table loaded with food. There our party were united again. As I did not hush my crying, one of the older ones whispered to me, "Wait until you are alone in the night."

It was very little I could swallow besides my sobs, that evening.

"Oh, I want my mother and my brother Dawée! I want to go to my aunt!" I pleaded; but the ears of the palefaces could not hear me.

From the table we were taken along an upward incline of wooden boxes, which I learned afterward to call a stairway. At the top was a quiet hall, dimly lighted. Many narrow beds were in one straight line down the entire length of the wall. In them lay sleeping brown faces, which peeped just out of the coverings. I was tucked into bed with one of the tall girls, because she talked to me in my mother tongue and seemed to soothe me.

I had arrived in the wonderful land of rosy skies, but I was not happy, as I had thought I should be. My long travel and the bewildering sights had exhausted me. I fell asleep, heaving deep, tired sobs. My tears were left to dry themselves in streaks, because neither my aunt nor my mother was near to wipe them away.

The Cutting of My Long Hair

The first day in the land of apples was a bitter-cold one; for the snow still covered the ground, and the trees were bare. A large bell rang for breakfast, its loud metallic voice crashing through the belfry overhead and into our sensitive ears. The annoying clatter of shoes on bare floors gave us no peace. The constant clash of harsh noises, with an undercurrent of many voices murmuring an unknown tongue, made a bedlam within which I was securely tied. And though my spirit tore itself in struggling for its lost freedom, all was useless.

A paleface woman, with white hair, came up after us. We were placed in a line of girls who were marching into the dining room. These were Indian girls, in stiff shoes and closely clinging dresses. The small girls wore sleeved aprons and shingled hair. As I walked noiselessly in my soft moccasins, I felt like sinking to the floor, for my blanket had been stripped from my shoulders. I looked hard at the Indian girls, who seemed not to care that they were even more immodestly dressed than I, in their tightly fitting clothes. While we marched in, the boys entered at an opposite door. I watched for the three young braves who came in our party. I spied them in the rear ranks, looking as uncomfortable as I felt.

A small bell was tapped, and each of the pupils drew a chair from under the table. Supposing this act meant they were to be seated, I pulled out mine and at once slipped into it from one side. But when I turned my head, I saw that I was the only one seated, and all the rest at our table remained standing. Just as I began to rise, looking shyly around to see how chairs were to be used, a second bell was sounded. All were seated at last, and I had to crawl back into my chair again. I heard a man's voice at one end of the hall, and I looked around to see him. But all the others hung their heads over their plates. As I glanced at the long chain of tables, I caught the eyes of a paleface woman upon me. Immediately I dropped my eyes, wondering why I was so keenly watched by the strange woman. The man ceased his mutterings, and then a third bell was tapped. Every one picked up his knife and fork and began eating. I began crying instead, for by this time I was afraid to venture anything more.

But this eating by formula was not the hardest trial in that first day. Late in the morning, my friend Judéwin gave me a terrible warning. Judéwin knew a few words of English; and she had overheard the paleface woman talk about cutting our long, heavy hair. Our mothers had taught us that only unskilled warriors who were captured had their hair shingled by the enemy. Among our people, short hair was worn by mourners, and shingled hair by cowards!

We discussed our fate some moments, and when Judéwin said, "We have to submit, because they are strong," I rebelled.

"No, I will not submit! I will struggle first!" I answered.

I watched my chance, and when no one noticed I disappeared. I crept up the stairs as quietly as I could in my squeaking shoes—my moccasins had been exchanged for shoes. Along the hall I passed, without knowing whither I was going. Turning aside to an open door, I found a large room with three white beds in it. The windows were covered with dark green curtains, which made the room very dim. Thankful that no one was there, I directed my steps toward the corner farthest from the door. On my hands and knees I crawled under the bed, and cuddled myself in the dark corner.

From my hiding place I peered out, shuddering with fear whenever I heard footsteps near by. Though in the hall loud voices were calling my name, and I knew that even Judéwin was searching for me, I did not open my mouth to answer. Then the steps were quickened and the voices became excited. The sounds came nearer and nearer. Women and girls entered the room. I held my breath, and watched them open closet doors and peep behind large trunks. Some one threw up the curtains, and the room was filled with sudden light. What caused them to stoop and look under the bed I do not know. I remember being dragged out, though I resisted by kicking and scratching wildly. In spite of myself, I was carried downstairs and tied fast in a chair.

I cried aloud, shaking my head all the while until I felt the cold blades of the scissors against my neck, and heard them gnaw off one of my thick braids. Then I lost my spirit. Since the day I was taken from my mother I had suffered extreme indignities. People had stared at me. I had been tossed about in the air like a wooden puppet. And now my long hair was shingled like a coward's! In my anguish I moaned for my mother, but no one came to comfort me. Not a soul reasoned quietly with me, as my own mother used to do: for now I was only one of many little animals driven by a herder.

The Snow Episode

A short time after our arrival we three Dakotas were playing in the snowdrifts. We were all still deaf to the English language, excepting Judéwin, who always heard such puzzling things. One morning we learned through her ears that we were forbidden to fall lengthwise in the snow, as we had been doing, to see our own impressions. However, before many hours we had forgotten the order, and were having great sport in the snow, when a shrill voice called us. Looking up, we saw an imperative hand beckoning us into the house. We shook the snow off ourselves, and started toward the woman as slowly as we dared.

Judéwin said: "Now the paleface is angry with us. She is going to punish us for falling into the snow. If she looks straight into your eyes and talks loudly, you must wait until she stops. Then, after a tiny pause, say, 'No.' " The rest of the way we practiced upon the little word "no."

As it happened, Thowin was summoned to judgment first. The door shut behind her with a click.

Judéwin and I stood silently listening at the keyhole. The paleface woman talked in very severe tones. Her words fell from her lips like crackling embers, and her inflection ran up like the small end of a switch. I understood her voice better than the things she was saying. I was certain we had made her very impatient with us. Judéwin heard enough of the words to realize all too late that she had taught us the wrong reply.

"Oh, poor Thowin!" she gasped, as she put both hands over her ears.

Just then I heard Thowin's tremulous answer, "No."

With an angry exclamation, the woman gave her a hard spanking. Then she stopped to say something. Judéwin said it was this: "Are you going to obey my word the next time?"

Thowin answered again with the only word at her command, "No."

This time the woman meant her blows to smart, for the poor frightened girl shrieked at the top of her voice. In the midst of the whipping the blows ceased abruptly, and the woman asked another question: "Are you going to fall in the snow again?"

Thowin gave her bad password another trial. We heard her say feebly, "No! No!"

With this the woman hid away her half-worn slipper, and led the child out, stroking her black shorn head. Perhaps it occurred to her that brute force is not the solution for such a problem. She did nothing to Judéwin nor to me. She only returned to us our unhappy comrade, and left us alone in the room.

During the first two or three seasons misunderstandings as ridiculous as this one of the snow episode frequently took place, bringing unjustifiable frights and punishments into our little lives.

Within a year I was able to express myself somewhat in broken English. As soon as I comprehended a part of what was said and done, a mischievous spirit of revenge possessed me. One day I was called in from my play for some misconduct. I had disregarded a rule which seemed to me very needlessly binding. I was sent into the kitchen to mash the turnips for dinner. It was noon, and steaming dishes were hastily carried into the dining room. I hated turnips, and their odor which came from the brown jar was offensive to me. With fire in my heart, I took the wooden tool that the paleface woman held out to me. I stood upon a step, and, grasping the handle with both hands, I bent in hot rage over the turnips. I worked my vengeance upon them. All were so busily occupied that no one noticed me. I saw that the turnips were in a pulp, and that further beating could not improve them; but the order was, "Mash these turnips," and mash them I would! I renewed my energy; and as I sent the masher into the bottom of the jar, I felt a satisfying sensation that the weight of my body had gone into it.

Just here a paleface woman came up to my table. As she looked into the jar, she shoved my hands roughly aside. I stood fearless and angry. She placed her red hands upon the rim of the jar. Then she gave one lift and a stride away from the table. But lo! the pulpy contents fell through the crumbled bottom to the floor! She spared me no scolding phrases that I had earned. I did not heed them. I felt triumphant in my revenge, though deep within me I was a wee bit sorry to have broken the jar.

As I sat eating my dinner, and saw that no turnips were served, I whooped in my heart for having once asserted the rebellion within me.

Write before You Read

The following reading selection is entitled "Waiting in Line at the Drugstore." Before reading, think or write for several minutes about the following topic:

> Describe circumstances in which you had to wait in line. Discuss the reasons why you had to wait and how you felt about it.

Share your experience with classmates.

Waiting in Line at the Drugstore

James Thomas Jackson

About the Author   James Thomas Jackson (1925–1985) was born in the United States, in Texas. After he became a member of a writers' workshop, he published his work in a variety of newspapers and journals. His writing chronicles his childhood, his years in the U.S. Army in Europe, and his later years during which he practiced his craft.

The Context of the Reading   Even after slavery was abolished in the United States (1865), African Americans faced discrimination. Legislators enacted laws that restricted where and how African Americans could live, eat, go to school, and travel. Many were segregated into poor sections of cities known as *ghettos.* They were not granted full civil rights until the 1960s.

Jackson refers to a number of authors in this essay. Four of the authors were white (*Jan Valtin, William Ernest Henley, John Steinbeck, Erskine Caldwell*) and six were black (*Countée Cullen, Charles W. Chestnutt, Walter White, Frederick Douglass, Paul Laurence Dunbar, Jean Toomer*).

"Waiting in Line at the Drugstore" was originally published in the *Los Angeles Times* newspaper in 1975.

I am black. I am a writer and I want to place full credit where it belongs for the direction my life has taken: on a photography studio and a drugstore on Main Street in Houston, Texas.

When I was thirteen, I dropped out of school, bought a bike for $13 (secondhand and innately durable) and went to work as a messenger for the Owl Foto Studio. Each day we processed film which I picked up as raw rolls on my three routes. That was great: a bike and job are supreme joys to a thirteen-year-old.

The Owl Studio, on a nondescript street named Brazos (very Texan), was located in a white stucco building that blended unobtrusively into the rest of the neighborhood, which was mostly residential. The area was predominantly white, and though it did not smack of affluence, it was not altogether poverty stricken either. Six blocks away was the drugstore, where I had to go first thing each morning for coffee, cakes, doughnuts, jelly rolls, milk, cigarettes, whatever—anything the folks at the Owl wanted. My trip amounted to picking up "breakfast" for a crew of six: three printer-developers, one wash-dry man, the roll-film man and the foreman. The drugstore was the biggest challenge of my young life. Being thirteen is doubtless bad enough for white male youths, but for blacks—me in particular—it was pure dee hell. Going to this drugstore each morning was part of my job; it was required of me. <u>With my dropping out of school and all, my parents would have whipped my behind till it roped like okra if I had tried</u> to supply them with reasons for not wanting to go. So, I gritted my teeth and, buoyed by the power of my Western Flyer, rode on down there.

The place had your typical drugstore look: sundries, greeting cards, cosmetics, women's "things," pharmaceuticals—but most instantly fetching was the large, U-shaped lunch counter. White-uniformed waitresses dispensed eats and sweet drinks of varying kinds: from cakes, donuts and pies to cups of the freshest smelling, strongest tasting coffee one could ask for. In the morning, there were countless servings of ham, bacon, sausages and eggs and mounds of hash-brown potatoes. At lunch there was a "Blue Plate Special"—three vegetables and a meat dish. Oh, they were together, no doubt about that.

My beef was that I was forbidden to sit at that counter. If any black wanted service whether for himself or, like me, for those he worked for—he simply had to stand and wait until all the white folks were served. Those blacks who went contrary to this were worked over something fierce, often by those mild-mannered Milquetoasts who looked as if they wouldn't hurt a fly. A fly, no; but an uppity nigger, in a minute.

I had once witnessed the beating of a black brother at the drugstore and heard tales of other beatings elsewhere. Clean and sanitary as the drugstore was, I preferred the ghetto (though we didn't call it that then). There, at least, we had the freedom to roam all over our stretch of black territory and could shuck our feelings of enforced inferiority as soon as we were on common ground.

Yet I went to the drugstore each morning with my order of coffee, cakes and whatever, written out and clutched firmly in my hand. And each time I was confronted with rows of white folks, seated at the counter and clamoring for attention. I did what I was expected to do: I waited, all the while hating it.

Especially that kind of waiting. As those white faces stared at my black face, I stood conspicuously in a spot near the counter, wanting not to be there, to be somewhere else.

My film pickups were not like this at all. I simply went in a store, picked up a small sack of roll film and split. After all, we provided twenty-four-hour service, and every son-of-a-buck and his brother wanted to see how his pictures came out. It was only the drugstore bit that bugged me.

While waiting near the counter one morning, I realized that I was leaning on a bookcase. I had seen it before but had ignored it because I was in a hurry to get served and get the hell out of there. The case was about four feet high and held perhaps six rows of hardcover books. The sign said "Lending Library." I began looking idly at the books, studying the titles and names of authors, so many unfamiliar to me. But the jackets were impressive, alluring, eye-catching.

One book caught my fancy: *Out of the Night,* the bestseller by Jan Valtin. I opened it, glanced at the fly pages and came across a poem by William Ernest Henley:

> Out of the night that covers me
> Black as the pit from pole to pole
> I thank whatever gods may be
> For my unconquerable soul.

Then I turned to the beginning of Valtin's narrative, read that first page, and then the second. Eleven pages later, going on twelve, hoping to get to thirteen, I heard the white waitress call my name. My order was ready. I folded a corner of the page and tried to hide the book so no one would take it before I could get back the next day.

I picked up the food and wheeled back to the studio—slowly. My mind was a fog—I had never begun a real book before. All the way back, I felt different from before. Something was happening to me, and I didn't quite know what to make of it. Somehow I didn't feel the "badness" that I usually felt when I returned from the drugstore.

The next day, my usual waiting was not the same. I went from page thirteen to page twenty-seven . . . twenty eight, pinned a corner down, returned to the studio, delivered my routes, went home, thought and wondered. God, I wondered, when would tomorrow come? The promise of tomorrow, of course, was the difference.

Many mornings later I finished reading Valtin's book. But there was another that looked interesting: *The Grapes of Wrath* by John Steinbeck. (We weren't as poor, I discovered, as those people.) Then *Tobacco Road* by Erskine Caldwell.

A year passed, and I discovered a black library branch at Booker T. Washington High. An elderly friend of mine in the ghetto who had noticed the change in me made a list of things to ask for: Countée Cullen's poem "Heritage," Charles W. Chestnutt's "The Wife of His Youth," Walter White's "Fire in the Flint"; also Frederick Douglass, Paul Laurence Dunbar, Jean Toomer—how was I to read them all?

Find a way, my friend said.

All the while I kept going to the drugstore each morning. I must have read every worthwhile book on that "Lending Library" shelf. But during this period, something strange happened: my waiting time got shorter and shorter each morning. I could hardly get five pages read before my order was handed to me with—of all things—a sense of graciousness from the waitresses. I didn't understand it.

Later on I went off to World War II. My mind and attitudes were primed for the books yet to come and for the words that were to come out of me. I was eighteen then and a drop-out, but I was deep into the wonderful world of literature and life. I found myself, and my niche, in the word. Who would have thought that a drugstore could provide such a vista for anyone? And my waits at the counter? I keep wondering: which way would I have gone had I not waited?

Good question.

Write before You Read

The following reading selection is entitled "College." Before reading, think or write for several minutes about one of the following topics:

☐ Discuss your initial expectations of college.

☐ Describe your first impressions of college life.

Share your thoughts with classmates.

College
Anzia Yezierska

About the Author   Anzia Yezierska (1883?–1970) was born in Russia and emigrated to the United States as a young girl. Like many immigrants of that time, she lived in poverty in New York City. She left home at the age of 17, later received a college diploma, and became a best-selling writer. One of her stories won the O. Henry Prize for the best short story of 1919. Among her works are the collection *Hungry Hearts* (1920) and her memoir *Red Ribbon on a White Horse* (1950).

The Context of the Reading   In the latter part of the 19th century, hundreds of thousands of Jewish people fled eastern Europe to escape religious persecution and poverty. Most came to America with little money and had to struggle to survive. Many lived in crowded sections of big cities called *ghettos,* in run-down buildings known as *tenements,* and eked out a living selling cheap goods from *pushcarts* (two-wheeled wooden vehicles pushed by hand) or working in factories. Education was the route out of poverty and toward Americanization.

In the opening paragraph, Yezierska makes two references to U.S. history:

☐ *(Christopher) Columbus* (1451–1506): the Italian explorer who has been mythologized as the discoverer of America

☐ *the pilgrim fathers:* the Puritans who left England to seek a new life and religious freedom in North America and who founded the colony of Plymouth in Massachusetts in 1620

The author later refers to two streets—Grand Street and Hester Street—in New York City's Lower East Side, the center of immigrant Jewish life.

"College" is taken from Yezierska's autobiographical novel *Bread Givers* (1925).

That burning day when I got ready to leave New York and start out on my journey to college! I felt like Columbus starting out for the other end of the earth. I felt like the pilgrim fathers who had left their homeland and all their kin behind them and trailed out in search of the New World.

I had stayed up night after night, washing and ironing, patching and darning my things. At last, I put them all together in a bundle, wrapped them up with newspapers, and tied them securely with the thick clothes line that I had in my room on which to hang out my wash. I made another bundle of my books. In another newspaper I wrapped up my food for the journey: a loaf of bread, a herring, and a pickle. In my purse was the money I had been saving from my food, from my clothes, a penny to a penny, a dollar to a dollar, for so many years. It was not much but I counted out that it would be enough for my train ticket and a few weeks' start till I got work out there.

It was only when I got to the train that I realized I had hardly eaten all day. Starving hungry, I tore the paper open. *Ach!* Crazy-head! In my haste I had forgotten even to cut up the bread. I bent over on the side of my seat, and half covering myself with a newspaper, I pinched pieces out of the loaf and ripped ravenously at the herring. With each bite, I cast side glances like a guilty thing; nobody should see the way I ate.

After a while, as the lights were turned low, the other passengers began to nod their heads, each outsnoring the other in their thick sleep. I was the only one on the train too excited to close my eyes.

Like a dream was the whole night's journey. And like a dream mounting on a dream was this college town, this New America of culture and education.

Before this, New York was all of America to me. But now I came to a town of quiet streets, shaded with green trees. No crowds, no tenements. No hurrying noise to beat the race of the hours. Only a leisured quietness whispered in the air: Peace. Be still. External time is all before you.

Each house had its own green grass in front, its own free space all around, and it faced the street with the calm security of being owned for generations, and not rented by the month from a landlord. In the early twilight, it was like a picture out of fairyland to see people sitting on their porches, lazily swinging in their hammocks, or watering their own growing flowers.

So these are the real Americans, I thought, thrilled by the lean, straight bearing of the passers-by. They had none of that terrible fight for bread and rent that I always saw in New York people's eyes. Their faces were not worn with the hunger for things they never could have in their lives. There was in them that sure, settled look of those who belong to the world in which they were born.

The college buildings were like beautiful palaces. The campus stretched out like fields of a big park. Air—air. Free space and sunshine. The river at dusk. Glimmering lights on passing boats, the floating voices of young people. And when night came, there were the sky and the stars.

This was the beauty for which I had always longed. For the first few days I could only walk about and drink it in thirstily, more and more. Beauty of houses, beauty of streets, beauty shining out of the calm faces and cool eyes of the people! Oh—too cool. . . .

How could I most quickly become friends with them? How could I come into their homes, exchange with them my thoughts, break with them bread at their tables? If I could only lose myself body and soul in the serenity of this new world, the hunger and the turmoil of my ghetto years would drop away from me, and I, too, would know the beauty of stillness and peace.

What light-hearted laughing youth met my eyes! All the young people I had ever seen were shut up in factories. But here were young girls and young men enjoying life, free from the worry for a living. College to them was being out for a good time, like to us in the shop a Sunday picnic. But in our gayest Sunday picnics there was always the under-feeling that Monday meant back to the shop again. To these born lucky ones joy seemed to stretch out for ever.

What a sight I was in my gray pushcart clothes against the beautiful gay colours and the fine things those young girls wore. I had seen cheap, fancy style, Five- and Ten-Cent Store finery. But never had I seen such plain beautifulness. The simple skirts and sweaters, the stockings and shoes to match. The neat finished quietness of their tailored suits. There was no show-off in their clothes, and yet how much more pulling to the eyes and all the senses than the Grand Street richness I knew.

And the spick-and-span cleanliness of these people! It smelled from them, the soap and the bathing. Their fingernails so white and pink. Their hands and necks white like milk. I wondered how did those girls get their hair so soft, so shiny, and so smooth about their heads. Even their black shoes had a clean look.

Never had I seen men so all shaved up with pink, clean skins. The richest store-keepers in Grand Street shined themselves up with diamonds like walking jewellery stores, but they weren't so hollering clean as these men. And they all had their hair clipped so short; they all had a shape to their heads. So ironed out smooth and even they looked in their spotless, creaseless clothes, as if the dirty battle of life had never yet been on them.

I looked at these children of joy with a million eyes. I looked at them with my hands, my feet, with the thinnest nerves of my hair. By all their differences from me, their youth, their shiny freshness, their carefreeness, they pulled me out of my senses to them. And they didn't even know I was there.

I thought once I got into the classes with them, they'd see me and we'd get to know one another. What a sharp awakening came with my first hour!

As I entered the classroom, I saw young men and girls laughing and talking to one another without introductions. I looked for my seat. Then I noticed, up in front, a very earnest-faced young man with thick glasses over his sad eyes. He made me think of Morris Lipkin, so I chose my seat next to him.

"What's the name of the professor?" I asked.

"Smith," came from his tight lips. He did not even look at me. He pulled himself together and began busily writing, to show me he didn't want to be interrupted.

I turned to the girl on my other side. What a fresh clean beauty! A creature of sunshine. And clothes that matched her radiant youth.

"Is this the freshman class in geometry?" I asked her.

She nodded politely and smiled. But how quickly her eyes sized me up! It was not an unkind glance. And yet, it said more plainly than words, "From where do you come? How did you get in here?"

Sitting side by side with them through the whole hour, I felt stranger to them than if I had passed them in Hester Street. Wasn't there some secret something that would open us toward one another?

In one class after another, I kept asking myself, "What's the matter with me? Why do they look at me so when I talk with them?"

Maybe I'd have to change myself inside and out to be one of them. But, how?

The lectures were over at four o'clock. With a sigh, I turned from the college building, away from the pleasant streets, down to the shabby back alley near the post office, and entered the George Martin Hand Laundry.

Mr. Martin was a fat, easy-going, good-natured man. I no sooner told him of my experience in New York than he took me on at once as an ironer at fifty cents an hour, and he told me he had work for as many hours a day as I could put in.

I felt if I could only look a little bit like other girls on the outside, maybe I could get in with them. And that meant money! And money meant work, work, work!

Till eleven o'clock that night, I ironed fancy white shirtwaists.

"You're some busy little worker, even if I do say so," said Mr. Martin, good-naturedly. "But I must lock up. You can't live here."

I went home, aching in every bone. And in the quiet and good air, I so overslept that I was late for my first class. To make matters worse, I found a note in my mailbox that puzzled and frightened me. It said, "Please report at once to the dean's office to explain your absence from Physical Education I, at four o'clock."

A line of other students was waiting there. When my turn came I asked the secretary, "What's this physical education business?"

"This is a compulsory course," he said. "You cannot get credit in any other course unless you satisfy this requirement."

At the hour when I had intended to go back to Martin's Laundry, I entered the big gymnasium. There was a crowd of girls dressed in funny short black bloomers and rubber-soled shoes.

The teacher blew the whistle and called harshly, "Students are expected to report in their uniforms."

"I have none."

"They're to be obtained at the bookstore," she said, with a stern look at me. "Please do not report again without it."

I stood there dumb.

"Well, stay for to-day, and exercise as you are," said the teacher, taking pity on me.

She pointed out my place in the line, where I had to stand with the rest like a lot of wooden soldiers. She made us twist ourselves around here and there. "Right face!" "Left face!" "Right about face!" I tried to do as the others did, but I felt like a jumping-jack being pulled this way and that way. I picked up dumbbells and pushed them up and down and sideways until my arms were lame. Then she made us hop around like a lot of monkeys.

At the end of the hour, I was so out of breath that I sank down, my heart pounding against my ribs. I was dripping with sweat worse than Saturday night in the steam laundry. What's all this physical education nonsense? I came to college to learn something, to get an education with my head, and not monkeyshines with my arms and legs.

I went over to the instructor. "How much an hour do we get for this work?" I asked her, bitterly.

She looked at me with a stupid stare. "This is a two-point course."

Now I got real mad. "I've got to sweat my life away enough only to earn a living," I cried. "God knows I exercised enough, since I was a kid—"

"You properly exercised?" She looked at me from head to foot. "Your posture is bad. Your shoulders sag. You need additional corrective exercises outside the class."

More tired than ever, I came to the class next day. After the dumb-bells, she made me jump over the hurdles. For the life of me, I couldn't do it. I bumped myself and scratched my knees on the top bar of the hurdle, knocking it over with a great clatter. They all laughed except the teacher.

"Repeat the exercise, please," she said, with a frozen face.

I was all bruises, trying to do it. And they were holding their sides with laughter. I was their clown, and this was their circus. And suddenly, I got so wild with rage that I seized the hurdle and right before their eyes I smashed it to pieces.

The whole gymnasium went still as death.

The teacher's face was white. "Report at once to the dean."

The scared look on the faces of the girls made me feel that I was to be locked up or fired.

For a minute when I entered the dean's grand office, I was so confused I couldn't even see.

He rose and pointed to a chair beside his desk. "What can I do for you?" he asked, in a voice that quieted me as he spoke.

I told him how mad I was, to have piled on me jumping hurdles when I was so tired anyway. He regarded me with that cooling steadiness of his. When I was through, he walked to the window and I waited, miserable. Finally he turned to me again, and with a smile! "I'm quite certain that physical education is not essential in your case. I will excuse you from attending the course."

After this things went better with me. In spite of the hard work in the laundry, I managed to get along in my classes. More and more interesting became the life of the college as I watched it from the outside.

What a feast of happenings each day of college was to those other students. Societies, dances, letters from home, packages of food, midnight spreads and even birthday parties. I never knew that there were people glad enough of life to celebrate the day they were born. I watched the gay goings-on around me like one coming to a feast, but always standing back and only looking on.

One day, the ache for people broke down my feelings of difference from them. I felt I must tear myself out of my aloneness. Nothing had ever come to me without my going out after it. I had to fight for my living, fight for every bit of my education. Why should I expect friendship and love to come to me out of the air while I sat there, dreaming of it?

The freshman class gave a dance that very evening. Something in the back of my head told me that an evening dress and slippers were part of going to a dance. I had no such things. But should that stop me? If I had waited till I could afford the right clothes for college, I should never have been able to go at all.

I put a fresh collar over my old serge dress. And with a dollar stolen from my eating money, I bought a ticket to the dance. As I peeped into the glittering gymnasium, blaring with jazz, my timid fears stopped the breath in me. How the whole big place sang with their light-hearted happiness! Young eyes drinking joy from young eyes. Girls, like gay-coloured butterflies, whirling in the arms of young men.

Floating ribbons and sashes shimmered against men's black coats. I took the nearest chair, blinded by the dazzle of the happy couples. Why did I come here? A terrible sense of age weighed upon me; yet I watched and waited for someone to come and ask me to dance. But not one man came near me. Some of my classmates nodded distantly in passing, but most of them were too filled with their own happiness even to see me.

The whirling of joy went on and on, and still I sat there watching, cold, lifeless, like a lost ghost. I was nothing and nobody. It was worse than being ignored. Worse than being an outcast. I simply didn't belong. I had no existence in their young eyes. I wanted to run and hide myself, but fear and pride nailed me against the wall.

A chaperon must have noticed my face, and she brought over one of those clumsy, backward youths who was lost in a corner by himself. How unwilling were his feet as she dragged him over! In a dull voice, he asked, "May I have the next dance?" his eyes fixed in the distance as he spoke.

"Thank you. I don't want to dance." And I fled from the place.

I found myself walking in the darkness of the campus. In the thick shadows of the trees I hid myself and poured out my shamed and injured soul to the night. So, it wasn't character or brains that counted. Only youth and beauty and clothes—things I never had and never could have. Joy and love were not for such as me. Why not? Why not? . . .

I flung myself on the ground, beating with my fists against the endless sorrows of my life. Even in college I had not escaped from the ghetto. Here loneliness hounded me even worse than in Hester Street. Was there no escape? Will I never lift myself to be a person among people?

I pressed my face against the earth. All that was left of me reached out in prayer. God! I've gone so far, help me to go on. God! I don't know how, but I must go on. Help me not to want their little happiness. I have wanted their love more than my life. Help me be bigger than this hunger in me. Give me the love that can live without love. . . .

Darkness and stillness washed over me. Slowly I stumbled to my feet and looked up at the sky. The stars in their infinite peace seemed to pour their healing light into me. I thought of the captives in prison, the sick and the suffering from the beginning of time who had looked to these stars for strength. What was my little sorrow to the centuries of pain which those stars had watched? So near they seemed, so compassionate. My bitter hurt seemed to grow small and drop away. If I must go on alone, I should still have silence and the high stars to walk with me.

Write before You Read

The following reading selection is entitled "Shooting an Elephant." Before reading, think or write for several minutes about the following topic:

> Discuss whatever comes into your mind as you contemplate shooting an elephant.

Share your thoughts with classmates.

Shooting an Elephant

George Orwell

About the Author   George Orwell (1903–1950) was born Eric Blair in Bengal to British parents. After finishing high school in England, he went to Burma (today known as Myanmar) and served five years in the Imperial Police. After his return to England, he became a prolific and famous writer. Among his many works are *Animal Farm* (1945) and *Nineteen Eighty-Four* (1949).

The Context of the Reading   The British Empire, consisting of the British Isles and overseas territories, was established over three centuries. At its height in the late 19th and early 20th centuries, it included 25 percent of the world's population and area. During three Anglo-Burman wars in the 19th century, Burma was annexed piece by piece to British India and did not receive limited self-government until 1937.

References to Great Britain and Burma include the following Hindi words:

- *Raj:* rule; dominion
- *mahout:* the keeper and driver of an elephant
- *coolie:* an unskilled laborer
- *sahib:* master; lord; ruler; the formal title used by colonized people to address the colonizers
- *dahs:* heavy knives

"Shooting an Elephant," originally published in the British journal *New Writing* in 1936, draws on Orwell's experience as a British police official in Burma ten years earlier.

In Moulmein, in lower Burma, I was hated by large numbers of people—the only time in my life that I have been important enough for this to happen to me. I was sub-divisional police officer of the town, and in an aimless, petty kind of way anti-European feeling was very bitter. No one had the guts to raise a riot, but if a European woman went through the bazaars alone somebody would probably spit betel juice over her dress. As a police officer I was an obvious target and was baited whenever it seemed safe to do so. When a nimble Burman tripped me up on the football field and the referee (another Burman) looked the other way, the crowd yelled with hideous laughter. This happened more than once. In the end the sneering yellow faces of young men that met me everywhere, the insults hooted after me when I was at a safe distance, got badly on my nerves. The young Buddhist priests were the worst of all. There were several thousands of them in the town and none of them seemed to have anything to do except stand on street corners and jeer at Europeans.

All this was perplexing and upsetting. For at that time I had already made up my mind that imperialism was an evil thing and the sooner I chucked up my job and got out of it the better. Theoretically—and secretly, of course—I was all for the Burmese and all against their oppressors, the British. As for the job I was doing, I hated it more bitterly than I can perhaps make clear. In a job like that you see the dirty work of Empire at close quarters. The wretched prisoners huddling in the stinking cages of the lock-ups, the gray, cowed faces of the long-term convicts, the scarred buttocks of the men who had been flogged with bamboos—all these oppressed me with an intolerable sense of guilt. But I could get nothing into perspective. I was young and ill educated and I had had to think out my problems in the utter silence that is imposed on every Englishman in the East. I did not even know that the British Empire is dying, still less did I know that it is a great deal better than the younger empires that are going to supplant it. All I knew was that I was stuck between my hatred of the empire I served and my rage against the evil-spirited little beasts who tried to make my job impossible. With one part of my mind I thought of the British Raj as an unbreakable tyranny, as something clamped down, *in saecula saeculorum*, upon the will of prostrate peoples; with another part I thought that the greatest joy in the world would be to drive a bayonet into a Buddhist priest's guts. Feelings like these are the normal by-products of imperialism; ask any Anglo-Indian official, if you can catch him off duty.

One day something happened which in a roundabout way was enlightening. It was a tiny incident in itself, but it gave me a better glimpse than I had had before of the real nature of imperialism—the real motives for which despotic governments act. Early one morning the sub-inspector at a police station the other end of the town rang me up on the 'phone and said that an elephant was ravaging the bazaar. Would I please come and do something about it? I did not know what I could do, but I wanted to see what was happening and I got on a pony and started out. I took my rifle, an old .44 Winchester and much too small to kill an elephant, but I thought the noise might be useful *in terrorem*. Various Burmans stopped me on the way and told me about the elephant's doings. It was not, of course, a wild elephant, but a tame one which had gone "must." It had been chained up, as tame elephants always are when their attack of "must" is due, but on the previous night it had broken its chain and escaped. Its mahout, the only person who could manage it when it was in that state, had set out in pursuit, but had taken the wrong direction and was now twelve hours' journey away, and in the morning the elephant had suddenly reappeared in the town. The Burmese population had no weapons and were quite helpless against it. It had already destroyed somebody's bamboo hut, killed a cow and raided some fruit-stalls and devoured the stock; also it had met the municipal rubbish van and, when the driver jumped out and took to his heels, had turned the van over and inflicted violences upon it.

The Burmese sub-inspector and some Indian constables were waiting for me in the quarter where the elephant had been seen. It was a very poor quarter, a labyrinth of squalid bamboo huts, thatched with palm-leaf, winding all over a steep hillside. I remember that it was a cloudy, stuffy morning at the beginning of the rains. We began questioning the people as to where the elephant had gone and, as usual, failed to get any definite information. That is invariably the case in the East; a story always sounds clear enough at a distance, but the nearer you get to the scene of events the vaguer it becomes. Some of the people said that the elephant had gone in one direction, some said that he had gone in another, some professed not even to have heard of any elephant. I had almost made up my mind that the whole story was a pack of lies, when we heard yells a little distance away. There was a loud, scandalized cry of "Go away, child! Go away this instant!" and an old woman with a switch in her hand came round the corner of a hut, violently shooing away a crowd of naked children. Some more women followed, clicking their tongues and exclaiming; evidently there was something that the children ought not to have seen. I rounded the hut and saw a man's dead body sprawling in the mud. He was an Indian, a black Dravidian coolie, almost naked, and he could not have been dead many minutes. The people said that the elephant had come suddenly upon him round the corner of the hut, caught him with its trunk, put its foot on his back and ground him into the earth. This was the rainy season and the ground was soft, and his face had scored a trench a foot deep and a couple of yards long. He was lying on his belly with arms crucified and head sharply twisted to one side. His face was coated with mud, the eyes wide open, the teeth bared and grinning with an expression of unendurable agony. (Never tell me, by the way, that the dead look peaceful. Most of the corpses I have seen looked devilish.) The friction of the great beast's foot had stripped the skin from his back as neatly as one skins a rabbit. As soon as I saw the dead man I sent an orderly to a friend's house nearby to borrow an elephant rifle. I had already sent back the pony, not wanting it to go mad with fright and throw me if it smelt the elephant.

The orderly came back in a few minutes with a rifle and five cartridges, and meanwhile some Burmese had arrived and told us that the elephant was in the paddy fields below, only a few hundred yards away. As I started forward practically the whole population of the quarter flocked out of the houses and followed me. They had seen the rifle and were all shouting excitedly that I was going to shoot the elephant. They had not shown much interest in the elephant when he was merely ravaging their homes, but it was different now that he was going to be shot. It was a bit of fun to them, as it would be to an English crowd; besides they wanted the meat. It made me vaguely uneasy. I had no intention of shooting the elephant—I had merely sent for the rifle to defend myself if necessary—and it is always unnerving to have a crowd following you. I marched down the hill, looking and feeling a fool, with the rifle over my shoulder and an ever-growing army of people jostling at my heels. At the bottom, when you got away from the huts, there was a metalled road and beyond that a miry waste of paddy fields a thousand yards across, not yet ploughed but soggy from the first rains and dotted with coarse grass. The elephant was standing eight yards from the road, his left side toward us. He took not the slightest notice of the crowd's approach. He was tearing up bunches of grass, beating them against his knees to clean them, and stuffing them into his mouth.

I had halted on the road. As soon as I saw the elephant I knew with perfect certainty that I ought not to shoot him. It is a serious matter to shoot a working elephant—it is comparable to destroying a huge and costly piece of machinery—and obviously one ought not to do it if it can possibly be avoided. And at that distance, peacefully eating, the elephant looked no more dangerous than a cow. I thought then and I think now that his attack of "must" was already passing off; in which case he would merely wander harmlessly about until the mahout came back and caught him. Moreover, I did not in the least want to shoot him. I decided that I would watch him for a little while to make sure that he did not turn savage again, and then go home.

But at that moment I glanced round at the crowd that had followed me. It was an immense crowd, two thousand at the least and growing every minute. It blocked the road for a long distance on either side. I looked at the sea of yellow faces above the garish clothes—faces all happy and excited over this bit of fun, all certain that the elephant was going to be shot. They were watching me as they would watch a conjurer about to perform a trick. They did not like me, but with the magical rifle in my hands I was momentarily worth watching. And suddenly I realized that I should have to shoot the elephant after all. The people expected it of me and I had got to do it; I could feel their two thousand wills pressing me forward, irresistibly. And it was at this moment, as I stood there with the rifle in my hands, that I first grasped the hollowness, the futility of the white man's dominion in the East. Here was I, the white man with his gun, standing in front of the unarmed native crowd—seemingly the leading actor of the piece; but in reality I was only an absurd puppet pushed to and fro by the will of those yellow faces behind. I perceived in this moment that when the white man turns tyrant it is his own freedom that he destroys. He becomes a sort of hollow, posing dummy, the conventionalized figure of a sahib. For it is the condition of his rule that he shall spend his life in trying to impress the "natives," and so in every crisis he has got to do what the "natives" expect of him. He wears a mask, and his face grows to fit it. I had got to shoot the elephant. I had committed myself to doing it when I sent for the rifle. A sahib has got to act like a sahib; he has got to appear resolute, to know his own mind and do definite things. To come all that way, rifle in hand, with two thousand people marching at my heels, and then to trail feebly away, having done nothing—no, that was impossible. The crowd would laugh at me. And my whole life, every white man's life in the East, was one long struggle not to be laughed at.

But I did not want to shoot the elephant. I watched him beating his bunch of grass against his knees with that preoccupied grandmotherly air that elephants have. It seemed to me that it would be murder to shoot him. At that age I was not squeamish about killing animals, but I had never shot an elephant and never wanted to. (Somehow it always seems worse to kill a *large* animal.) Besides, there was the beast's owner to be considered.

Alive, the elephant was worth at least a hundred pounds; dead, he would only be worth the value of his tusks, five pounds, possibly. But I had got to act quickly. I turned to some experienced-looking Burmans who had been there when we arrived, and asked them how the elephant had been behaving. They all said the same thing: he took no notice of you if you left him alone, but he might charge if you went too close to him.

It was perfectly clear to me what I ought to do. I ought to walk up to within, say, twenty-five yards of the elephant and test his behavior. If he charged, I could shoot; if he took no notice of me, it would be safe to leave him until the mahout came back. But also I knew that I was going to do no such thing. I was a poor shot with a rifle and the ground was soft mud into which one would sink at every step. If the elephant charged and I missed him, I should have about as much chance as a toad under a steam-roller. But even then I was not thinking particularly of my own skin, only of the watchful yellow faces behind. For at that moment, with the crowd watching me, I was not afraid in the ordinary sense, as I would have been if I had been alone. A white man mustn't be frightened in front of "natives"; and so, in general, he isn't frightened. The sole thought in my mind was that if anything went wrong those two thousand Burmans would see me pursued, caught, trampled on, and reduced to a grinning corpse like that Indian up the hill. And if that happened it was quite probable that some of them would laugh. That would never do. There was only one alternative. I shoved the cartridges into the magazine and lay down on the road to get a better aim.

The crowd grew very still, and a deep, low, happy sigh, as of people who see the theater curtain go up at last, breathed from innumerable throats. They were going to have their bit of fun after all. The rifle was a beautiful German thing with cross-hair sights. I did not then know that in shooting an elephant one would shoot to cut an imaginary bar running from ear-hole to ear-hole. I ought, therefore, as the elephant was sideways on, to have aimed straight at his ear-hole; actually I aimed several inches in front of this, thinking the brain would be further forward.

When I pulled the trigger I did not hear the bang or feel the kick—one never does when a shot goes home—but I heard the devilish roar of glee that went up from the crowd. In that instant, in too short a time, one would have thought, even for the bullet to get there, a mysterious, terrible change had come over the elephant. He neither stirred nor fell, but every line of his body had altered. He looked suddenly stricken, shrunken, immensely old, as though the frightful impact of the bullet had paralyzed him without knocking him down. At last, after what seemed a long time—it might have been five seconds, I dare say—he sagged flabbily to his knees. His mouth slobbered. An enormous senility seemed to have settled upon him. One could have imagined him thousands of years old. I fired again into the same spot. At the second shot he did not collapse but climbed with desperate slowness to his feet and stood weakly upright, with legs sagging and head drooping. I fired a third time. That was the shot that did for him. You could see the agony of it jolt his whole body and knock the last remnant of strength from his legs. But in falling he seemed for a moment to rise, for as his hind legs collapsed beneath him he seemed to tower upward like a huge rock toppling, his trunk reaching skyward like a tree. He trumpeted, for the first and only time. And then down he came, his belly toward me, with a crash that seemed to shake the ground even where I lay.

I got up. The Burmans were already racing past me across the mud. It was obvious that the elephant would never rise again, but he was not dead. He was breathing very rhythmically with long rattling gasps, his great mound of a side painfully rising and falling. His mouth was wide open—I could see far down into caverns of pale pink throat. I waited a long time for him to die, but his breathing did not weaken. Finally I fired my two remaining shots into the spot where I thought his heart must be. The thick blood welled out of him like red velvet, but still he did not die. His body did not even jerk when the shots hit him, the tortured breathing continued without a pause. He was dying, very slowly and in great agony, but in some world remote from me where not even a bullet could damage him further. I felt that I had got to put an end to that dreadful noise. It seemed dreadful to see the great beast lying there, powerless to move and yet powerless to die, and not even to be able to finish him. I sent back for my small rifle and poured shot after shot into his heart and down his throat. They seemed to make no impression. The tortured gasps continued as steadily as the ticking of a clock.

In the end I could not stand it any longer and went away. I heard later that it took him half an hour to die. Burmans were bringing dahs and baskets even before I left, and I was told they had stripped his body almost to the bones by the afternoon.

Afterward, of course, there were endless discussions about the shooting of the elephant. The owner was furious, but he was only an Indian and could do nothing. Besides, legally I had done the right thing, for a mad elephant has to be killed, like a mad dog, if its owner fails to control it. Among the Europeans opinion was divided. The older men said I was right, the younger men said it was a damn shame to shoot an elephant for killing a coolie, because an elephant was worth more than any damn Coringhee coolie. And afterwards I was very glad that the coolie had been killed; it put me legally in the right and it gave me a sufficient pretext for shooting the elephant. I often wondered whether any of the others grasped that I had done it solely to avoid looking a fool.

Write before You Read

The following selection is entitled "The Rewards of Living a Solitary Life." Before reading, think or write for several minutes about one of the following topics:

☐   Look at the photograph of May Sarton on the following page, along with the excerpt from one of her poems. Explore your reaction to what you see and read.
☐   Discuss the negative and positive aspects of being alone.

Share your ideas with classmates.

The Rewards of Living a Solitary Life

May Sarton

About the Author   May Sarton (1912–1995) was born in Belgium and came to the United States with her family when World War I began. She worked as a writer in residence and lectured at a number of universities and colleges. An essayist, novelist, and poet, her many books include *A Reckoning* (1978) and *Endgame: Journal of the Seventy-Ninth Year* (1992).

The Context of the Reading   Sarton makes several references to North American culture:

☐   *Whitney:* an art museum in New York City
☐   *"Music I heard with you was more than music":* first line of an untitled poem by U.S. poet Conrad Aiken (1889–1973)
☐   *till death do us part:* part of the marriage vows spoken by a couple at their wedding ceremony

"The Rewards of Living a Solitary Life" was originally published in 1974 in the *New York Times* newspaper.

The other day an acquaintance of mine, a gregarious and charming man, told me he had found himself unexpectedly alone in New York for an hour or two between appointments. He went to the Whitney and spent the "empty" time looking at things in solitary bliss. For him it proved to be a shock nearly as great as falling in love to discover that he could enjoy himself so much alone.

What had he been afraid of, I asked myself? That, suddenly alone, he would discover that he bored himself, or that there was, quite simply, no self there to meet? But having taken the plunge, he is now on the brink of adventure; he is about to be launched into his own inner space, space as immense, unexplored and sometimes frightening as outer space to the astronaut. His every perception will come to him with a new freshness and, for a time, seem startlingly original. For anyone who can see things for himself with a naked eye becomes, for a moment or two, something of a genius. With another human being present vision becomes double vision,

I moved into my house one day
In a downpour of leaves and rain,
"I took possession," as they say,
With solitude for my domain. . . .

I moved into my life one day
In a downpour of leaves in flood,
I took possession as they say,
And knew I was alone for good.

Excerpt from "Moving In," from *Collected Poems* (1930–1973), p. 210.
(Photograph of May Sarton reprinted by permission of Seacoast Life Magazine)

inevitably. We are busy wondering, what does my companion see or think of this, and what do I think of it? The original impact gets lost, or diffused.

"Music I heard with you was more than music." Exactly. And therefore music *itself* can only be heard alone. Solitude is the salt of personhood. It brings out the authentic flavor of every experience.

"Alone one is never lonely: the spirit adventures, walking/In a quiet garden, in a cool house, abiding single there."

Loneliness is most acutely felt with other people, for with others, even with a lover sometimes, we suffer from our differences of taste, temperament, mood. Human intercourse often demands that we soften the edge of perception, or withdraw at the very instant of personal truth for fear of hurting, or of being inappropriately present, which is to say naked, in a social situation. Alone we can afford to be wholly whatever we are, and to feel whatever we feel absolutely. That is a great luxury!

For me the most interesting thing about a solitary life, and mine has been that for the last twenty years, is that it becomes increasingly rewarding. When I can wake up and watch the sun rise over the ocean, as I do most days, and know that I have an entire day ahead, uninterrupted, in which to write a few pages, take a walk with my dog, lie down in the afternoon for a long think (why does one think better in a horizontal position?), read and listen to music, I am flooded with happiness.

I am lonely when I am overtired, when I have worked too long without a break, when for the time being I feel empty and need filling up. And I am lonely sometimes when I come back home after a lecture trip, when I have seen a lot of people and talked a lot, and am full to the brim with experience that needs to be sorted out.

Then for a little while the house feels huge and empty, and I wonder where my self is hiding. It has to be recaptured slowly by watering the plants, perhaps, and looking again at each one as though it were a person, by feeding the two cats, by cooking a meal.

It takes a while, as I watch the surf blowing up in fountains at the end of the field, but the moment comes when the world falls away, and the self emerges again from the deep unconscious, bringing back all I have recently experienced to be explored and slowly understood, when I can converse again with my hidden powers, and so grow, and so be renewed, till death do us part.

Discussion Activities

The discussion activities in Chapter 4 are designed to help you become engaged in the processes of reading and responding to the reading selections in Chapter 3. They are not meant to be rigid instructions that you must follow. Ideally, the activities will lead you to think through what you have read and come to your own conclusions about what is significant.

Working with a partner, in a small group, or with the whole class, decide which material to cover and the amount of time to spend on each section. Allow for different responses to the various aspects of the reading.

Write after You Read: Making a Journal Entry

Writing about a selection just after reading it may help you remember and reflect on your reading experience. You can explore your response by recording your reactions in a journal entry, adapting the guidelines on page 9. Share what you have written.

Summarizing

Your goal in summarizing a reading selection based on experience can be to retell what is happening and/or what thoughts are going through the writer's mind. Sometimes writers whose work is based on experience directly state a message or an insight. When they do not state their ideas directly, readers often infer meaning from the details of the central experience(s) described.

To summarize, you can answer questions such as these:

☐ What is the subject of the reading selection?

☐ Why is the writer focusing on this subject?

☐ What is the writer's attitude toward or conclusion about the central experience(s) of the reading selection?

Share your summary with one or more classmates. Discuss the reasons for the differences in your summaries.

Note: Further guidelines for summarizing can be found in Chapter 21.

Analyzing

To analyze a reading, you can break it down into parts to examine those parts and their relationship.

The following suggestions are designed to help you analyze readings based on experience. As you make observations about the various elements of a reading selection, identify or read aloud corresponding passages.

Note: Not every suggestion will apply to every selection you read.

1. Discuss what you learn or find significant about the writer and the other people in the reading selection. For example, you can focus on the following details:

   □ their outward appearance and behavior

   □ their spoken words and inner thoughts

   □ their interaction with one another

   □ their inner qualities and values

   □ their conflicts (internal or external)

   □ the choices they make

   □ the changes they undergo—or do not undergo

   Note ways in which the writer contrasts people with one another (for example, note differences in culture, socioeconomic level, religion, gender, race).

2. Discuss what you learn or find significant about the setting. For example, you can focus on the following details:

   □ place: where the events take place

   □ time: when and over what period of time the events take place

   □ social environment: the manners, customs, or codes of behavior of the society in which the events take place

   □ physical environment: nature, objects, buildings, clothing, sounds, and so on

   □ images: details that appeal to your senses of sight, smell, taste, touch, or sound

   Note details that offer contrasts with other details (for example, country versus city, poverty versus wealth, light versus darkness, nature versus machine-made products).

3. Discuss passages that strike you for some reason. For example, you can focus on the following material:

   □ passages that you like

   □ passages that you find difficult to understand

   □ passages that you think reveal an important message or insight

4. Discuss what you learn or find significant about the examples the writer provides to illustrate or support a point. For example, you can focus on the following material:

□ examples that you think effectively clarify a point

□ examples that you find convincing

□ examples that you find unconvincing

Note examples that offer contrasts with other examples (for example, contrasts between lifestyles, relationships, or attitudes).

5. Discuss what you learn or find significant about how the writer has structured the selection. For example, you can focus on the following material:

□ information or ideas provided in the opening paragraph(s)

□ information or ideas provided in the middle paragraphs

□ information or ideas provided in the ending

□ transitions from one paragraph to the next

Making Connections

Making connections between a reading selection and something outside a reading selection—such as another reading or your own experience—can help uncover meanings.

1. Explore the similarities and differences between one reading selection and another. Identify or read aloud relevant passages. The many comparisons you can make include the following:

□ The experience of being in an unfamiliar or unfriendly environment in "The School Days of an Indian Girl," "Waiting in Line at the Drugstore," and/or "College"

□ The experience of being alone in "The Rewards of Living a Solitary Life" and "College"

□ The experience of being white in "Shooting an Elephant," "The School Days of an Indian Girl," and/or "Waiting in Line at the Drugstore"

□ The experience of oppression in "The School Days of an Indian Girl," "Waiting in Line at the Drugstore," "Shooting an Elephant," and/or "Still I Rise" (p. 220)

2. Examine the relationship between the experiences and ideas in the reading and your own experiences and attitudes. Identify or read aloud relevant passages.

□ Explore whether the writer's generalizations, theories, or experiences support or contradict what you have learned from experience.

□ Explore whether the writer's generalizations, theories, or experiences help you make sense of your own life.

Guidelines for Writing from Experience

Chapter 5 provides guidelines for fulfilling an assignment to write an essay in which you write from experience. The strategies in this chapter are designed to help you in your exploration and composing; they are not meant to be taken as rigid instructions that you must follow.

The writing of one student, Rolando Niella, is included to show some of the strategies he used to write an essay based on his own experience.* His completed essay, "Barriers," can be found on pages 59–61.

Note: Since all writers use different strategies, the approaches that worked well for Rolando may not work as well for you. Rolando's work was selected as an example; it is not presented as a model to imitate.

SUGGESTED ESSAY ASSIGNMENTS

Select or adapt one of the following assignments, or devise your own assignment in consultation with your instructor.

1. Write an essay in which you draw from your own experience to express a personal viewpoint. Include a detailed description of an event or experience (or series of events or experiences) that has led you to learn, believe, or understand something.
2. Write an essay in the form of a letter to someone who can benefit from hearing your views about an important issue or relationship. Include a detailed description of your experience with the issue or relationship so that the recipient of the letter can understand how your viewpoint evolved.
3. Write an essay in the form of a letter from you to the author of one of the reading selections, to share your viewpoint about what you have read. You may describe your own experience(s) as well as the author's.
4. Write an essay based on one of the suggestions for Making Connections on page 42.

Note: To fulfill the third or fourth assignment, you might want to consult Chapter 11 and/or Chapters 21–23.

---

*Rolando made many language errors as he wrote; they have been edited for this book so that you can focus on the development of his ideas.

Exploring a Topic

The strategies that follow represent a way of thinking on paper. Use only those that you find useful for your own writing, or devise your own strategies. Since exploratory writing is primarily for your own eyes, you do not need to be overly concerned with grammatical correctness at this stage.

Making a List

Making a list can be a valuable first step in writing. If it works for you, it can help you find a topic that you can write about in detail.

GUIDELINES

For Making a List

1. Make a list of possible topics for an essay (for example, a time when you confronted a problem or challenge, made an important choice or decision, or came to a significant realization).
2. Choose one of the listed topics, and then make a list of details. For example, the details may include the following:

   □ Indication of where, when, why, and over what period of time events took place
   □ Description of the people involved
   □ Description of your and other people's actions
   □ Description of the physical environment: objects, buildings, clothing, nature scenes, and so on
   □ Excerpts from conversations that you remember

A Student Writer at Work

In preparation for his essay, Rolando made a list of several problems he had experienced or was experiencing. He put a check mark next to the topics he thought he might want to write about.

Rolando's List of Topics

○ Culture shock ✓
○ Making friends ✓
○ Problems in my family
○ Problems in adolescence
○ Defining my friends ✓
○ Taking tests
○ Christian problem
○ Good problems

Freewriting

*Freewriting** is an activity in which you write whatever comes into your mind about a topic. In other words, you talk to yourself on paper. This technique is one way to get started on your writing and to find something to say about your topic. If it works for you, it can help you find out what is really on your mind.

GUIDELINES

For Freewriting

1. Write a topic at the top of a blank sheet of paper.
2. Write for several minutes on the topic.
3. Write whatever comes into your mind about the topic.
4. Don't focus on grammar, punctuation, or spelling.

A Student Writer at Work

Even after he had made his list of topics, Rolando was still not sure what to write about in his essay. He began to freewrite to try to discover which problem was most important to him. As you will see, the problem of culture shock emerges as the most important thing on his mind.

Rolando's Freewriting

I have to start writing. I just thought . . . I don't have other problems. There must be some other problems that I'm not aware of, but I can't think. I think it's because there is one problem that takes so much time and space in my head. THE CULTURE SHOCK. Well that's a problem, to have a problem that goes around your head night and day and wears your brain away. What to do. I don't know. Well, there are some problems in my family, but they are so complicated. I have to look for some other problem not so complicated—what could it be? I don't really know. What else is a problem in the past, problem in the past . . . define my friends . . . problem in the past was to . . . I don't know. Well, I guess I'm running out of ideas about problems. Come on problems, come to my mind. I don't know. What a problem not to know.

Looping

---

*This discussion is based on the work of Peter Elbow.

Looping is a writing activity in which you loop (join together) two or more freewriting passages and reflect on what you have written. If this technique works for you, it can help you explore a topic in some depth.

GUIDELINES

For Looping

1. Freewrite on a topic for several minutes.
2. Stop.
3. Read what you have just written.
4. Find an idea in your freewriting that you want to pursue.
5. Write that idea in a new sentence.
6. Freewrite on that idea.
7. Repeat steps 2–6 once or twice.

A Student Writer at Work

After his freewriting (p. 45), Rolando realized that the number one problem in his mind was the culture shock he was experiencing by living in the United States. He began to explore this subject by looping.

Rolando's Looping

1. Rolando wrote freely for several minutes, using the word *problem* as his topic:

   I have of course many problems in my life like everybody has, but right now I am feeling new problems like the cultural shock. I got out of my country and came to study in the U.S.A. One of the biggest problems is to make friends, to make or have the good old friends I have back home. It's so hard here—you don't know how to act, whether you should ask them their telephone number or wait for them to do it, whether you should call them very often or not. Are they bothered by my language problem? Can they not carry on a conversation with me because they always talk about local or national subjects about which I am not informed? This is really hard and sometimes makes me feel like a stranger in a group where everybody is laughing and talking and they supposedly were my friends.

2. Rolando then stopped writing,
3. He read what he had just written.
4. He found an idea he wanted to pursue.
5. He wrote that idea in a new sentence:

   Sometimes I feel like a stranger.

6. He began to freewrite on the idea in that sentence:

   Yes, this is true, so I start wondering if my feelings are part of my imagination or not. I try to put myself into the same position—my having a foreign kid as a friend in Paraguay—and I realize that sometimes you just can't explain everything even though you still care for the person. I really care about my friends. I mean, whenever they know I like to be their friend, I care a lot about them. But I wonder, are these new friends like that? Is that the way they act but not what they mean? I know what the solution is: get together with the Latin people; but I don't want that. I don't want to be part of a minority and limit my circle of friends. I want to meet a lot of people.

7. Rolando then repeated steps 2–4 and came up with a new idea he wanted to pursue, this time creating two sentences:

I don't want to limit my circle of friends. I want to meet a lot of people.

8. He then began to freewrite on the idea:

This is a hard experience. I don't know the solution for this problem. Otherwise I would have solved it already. But it seems to me that the only thing I can do is keep trying—try to get close to people very carefully—try to learn, not only the way they act, but their language and their culture. But there is so much to learn. I have to wait—I think waiting is the best thing—and be very observant and careful. But I have to watch out and not become paranoid and over-analyze every single aspect of what happens between me and my friends. I don't know if I am going to write about this problem. It seems so confusing that I don't even know if a good paper will come out of it. The least it could show is the total confusion I have in my head.

9. Rolando read over everything that he had written and decided that the problem that most affected him was communicating in a second language, because it interfered with his ability to make new friends.

Cubing

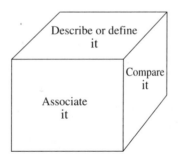
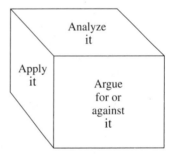

*Cubing** is a writing activity that allows you to explore a specific topic from six different perspectives. Imagine that your topic is inside a cube and that you are looking at it through each of the six sides. Move quickly from one viewpoint to another, writing down whatever each perspective suggests to you about your subject. If this technique works for you, it can help you find a way to approach your topic.

*This discussion is based on the work of Elizabeth Cowan.

GUIDELINES

For Cubing

Explore a topic through these six perspectives:

1. *Description or Definition:* Describe or define it. What is it?
2. *Comparison and Contrast:* Compare and contrast it. What is it similar to? What is it different from?
3. *Association:* Associate it. What does it remind you of? And what other associations come to mind?
4. *Analysis:* Analyze it. What parts can it be broken down into? What is their relationship?
5. *Application:* Apply it. What can you do with it? How can it be applied?
6. *Argument:* Argue for *and* against it. Why are you in favor of it? Why are you against it?

A Student Writer at Work

To explore his topic, which he now called "The Language Barrier," Rolando used cubing.

Note: Rolando underlined certain sentences *after* he finished this writing activity. These were the ideas he decided to focus on in his essay.

Rolando's Cubing

Topic: The Language Barrier

1. Rolando first described his topic:

   The language barrier is the idealistic or imaginary barrier that you feel in a country or groups of people that speak a different language than you do. You feel that barrier because even though you can speak the language and you can make yourself understand, you can't get your ideas across. You are speaking but you <u>feel your words disintegrate before reaching their effect.</u> You feel continually that <u>you have to think about every word you are saying when the natural thing is just to let your spirit express without thinking. You doubt yourself;</u> you feel <u>insincere;</u> you feel <u>insecure;</u> you feel <u>false</u> because you are choosing your words so much. But when you use them just like that you are misunderstood.

2. Then he compared it with other things:

   It is hard to compare, but it is like you reach a point where you feel you are in a theater rehearsing where everybody is talking in a way that deep inside is not natural, that all talking doesn't belong to reality. It's like seeing a poem but you don't know its meaning. It's like when you have to write a letter and you don't have the paper to write on, or even you write but you don't know the zip code so you don't send your letter. It's like talking to yourself.

3. Then he made associations:

It reminds me of reading a very hard book and not understanding the meaning but yes the words. It's like being in a band and not singing with the group. Every time I feel the barrier of language, I feel how far I am from home and how necessary are cultures. Feeling the language barrier is like when I play tennis. I can't get a serve in and sometimes I can't even answer the ball. You don't know how to say what you want to say. Pain. Frustration.

4. Then he analyzed it:

Well . . . there are two sides, and you are trying to go over it, to make your ball go over the net . . . There are two parts: (a) Make yourself understood and (b) understand the others.

   a. You are always choosing the words.
      You don't know the words.
      You just shut up.

   b. They talk and you can't understand them because of so many reasons. So they give up or they tell you "forget it," "it doesn't matter." This is the terrible part because these are the things that really enable you to participate, share, that make you feel part of the team, of a system of that "functioning" or "belongness" you were used to.

5. Then he tried to apply it:

What do you mean by "apply it"? It [the language barrier] is applied to me by force, because of you.

  ○ When they tell jokes
  ○ When they talk slowly
  ○ When they say something good to you, and you have to ask again
  ○ When they complain to you
  ○ When they give "trivial comments" that will help you
  ○ When you want to express your inner feelings, being mean but nice, etc.

6. Finally he argued for and against it:

  ○ *For:* because it makes you aware of everything, of every word; develops your senses; gives you an idea of how important language is
  ○ *Against:* frustrated, bad complex, unhappiness, paranoia, anxiety, wastes your time

After Rolando had covered all of the perspectives, he read what he had written. He decided that he would try to write an essay comparing learning how to play tennis with learning a new language.

Clustering

Clustering is a technique that enables you to create a visual pattern of ideas and details. If it works for you, it can help you focus on a topic and see significant relationships between abstract ideas and concrete details.

GUIDELINES

For Clustering

1. Choose a word or expression that might become the central subject of your essay.
2. Write that word or expression in the center of a blank page, and circle it.
3. Write down any word or expression that is associated in your mind with the topic. The word or expression may be an image, an action, an abstract idea, a quotation, an example, a detail, and so on.
4. Circle the words you have written, draw lines and/or arrows from the central word to each of the new words, and draw lines and/or arrows between words that seem to connect.
5. If something new occurs to you, add the word, circle it, and connect it to relevant words.

Sample Cluster

In the following example, the central expression is *language barrier;* all of the other words are taken from Rolando's exploratory writing.

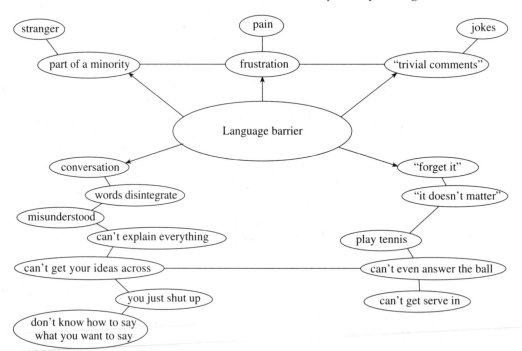

Focusing

When you do exploratory writing, you generate ideas to develop your own understanding of your subject. When you write an essay, you share your understanding with others, bringing your thoughts into focus for readers.

For Focusing

1. Reread whatever you have written up to this point: annotations, journal entries, exploratory writing, class notes. Make note of ideas that you want to explore further.
2. Then ask yourself, "What do I want to show in my essay?" You might try to answer this question by writing a sentence that can act as a focal point, to indicate what your essay will be about.
3. To further shape your ideas, explain your focus to one or more classmates to see if they understand what your essay will cover.

A Student Writer at Work

Rolando had generated many ideas about the language barrier in his exploratory writing. He now needed to turn the topic into a focused idea that he could share with readers. Rolando started several different sentences until he settled on one:

☐   Problems . . .

☐   Language play . . .

☐   Learning to use . . .

☐   Learning how to use a foreign language is like a tennis . . .

☐   Learning a foreign language as a means of integration into a new culture is like learning how to play tennis.

As you can see by looking at his final essay (pp. 59–61), Rolando did not repeat the exact wording of this sentence in his essay. But this sentence did act as a focal point to guide him as he drafted his essay.

If you are not yet ready to establish a focal point, turn to the next section, which discusses writing a trial draft.

Writing a Trial Draft

This section provides guidelines for moving toward the essay-writing stage by writing a *trial draft*. *Trial* refers to the process of testing or trying. A *draft* is a preliminary essay. When you write a trial draft, you can test out the ideas you have generated in exploratory writing to see how they will work together.

For Writing a Trial Draft

☐   Don't try to write the perfect paper now.
☐   Focus on the development of ideas rather than on grammar or spelling.
☐   If you can't think of a beginning, start in the middle.
☐   If you can't think of an ending, just stop.

If you are a writer who needs a more structured approach to writing a draft, turn to the next section for guidelines on organizing an essay based on experience.

Structuring the Entire Essay

There is no rigid formula that you must follow to organize an essay based on experience, as you can see from the reading selections in Chapter 3.

Nevertheless, you can establish an overall organizational goal: to move readers toward some sort of understanding or insight. And there is a basic, three-part organizational framework that might help you develop your essay: a *beginning,* a *middle,* and an *ending.*

As you plan your essay, you can consider a variety of organizational patterns. You can use the drafting process to experiment with organization; your early efforts can be revised later.

Organizational Patterns

The following patterns represent three possible ways to structure an essay based on experience.

Organizational Pattern 1

Beginning: Retell the first stage of an experience.

↓

Middle: Continue describing the experience.

↓

Ending: Discuss your view of the experience. *Note:* The ending does not have to express a "lesson learned" or a moral.

Organizational Pattern 2

Beginning: Provide background information and the main point (or message or insight) of the essay.

↓

Middle: Describe an experience or experiences related to the point made in the beginning.

↓

Ending: Reflect on the experience, for example, by discussing its significance, implications, irony, and/or contradictions.

Organizational Pattern 3

Beginning: Provide background information and raise a question about your topic.

Middle: Describe an experience or experiences related to your topic.

Ending: Answer the question you raised in the beginning, or explain why the question cannot be answered.

Writing an Interim Draft

For many writers, composing an essay involves going through a drafting process, that is, writing more than one version of the essay. This section provides advice for writing an interim draft: a draft that is written between the first and final stages of composing. As you read the advice, remember that writing a draft may be a messy process. You may be pausing to reread, rethink, cross out, and/or rewrite certain sections before you reach the end.

GUIDELINES

For Writing an Interim Draft

1. *Reflect on the assignment.* Consider its purpose, its requirements, and the needs and expectations of readers.
2. *Set aside some uninterrupted time, and start to write.* You may have to force yourself to begin. But once you get started, your writing may begin to flow.
3. *Devise a tentative organizational plan for the essay.* Try to follow the organizational pattern you have planned, but be flexible in your approach. If the plan doesn't work, allow another organizational pattern to emerge from your material.
4. *Begin by introducing your topic.* You do not have to write a "perfect" beginning at this point. Move on to the middle of your essay if you feel stuck. You can go back to the beginning later.
5. *Continue with the middle of the essay.* Provide whatever material can support or illustrate any points you have made or will make in the essay (examples, explanations, quotations, and so on).
6. *Finish by reflecting on or raising questions about what you have written.* If you do not have much to say at this point, write only one or two sentences. You can return to the ending later.
7. *Create a title.* The title can reflect the subject matter and/or point of view of the essay.
8. *Prepare a legible copy of the essay.*
Note: Identify any sources you have consulted (see Part Three).

A Student Writer at Work

While drafting his essay, Rolando erased and crossed out many words, and he threw a lot of paper into the wastebaskets. Part of his interim draft is included in the "Revising" section (pp. 58–59).

Giving and Receiving Feedback

By sharing your work in progress with others, you can become aware of how readers react to your writing. Asking other writers questions about their drafts can lead you to become a critical reader of your own work.

To prepare for giving and receiving feedback, read the recommendations on page 55. The recommendations are printed as they appear in a book on problem solving entitled *The Revised All New Universal Traveler.* To get their points across, the authors humorously refer to problem solving as a journey, and they give advice in the form of tips for travelers.

Use this opportunity to express your concerns and to ask questions about feedback.

Note: The feedback form on page 56 is based on the recommendations on page 55 and can act as a guide as you respond to someone else's writing.

GUIDELINES

For Giving and Receiving Feedback

Feedback can be provided in pairs, groups, or with the whole class.

1. Exchange drafts and read silently, or take turns reading your own drafts aloud.
2. Use the feedback form on page 56 and/or the suggestions for summarizing and analyzing in the Discussion Activities chapter, or raise your own questions. Your instructor will help you decide whether to provide written as well as oral feedback.
3. Discuss the responses to each draft, helping the writer understand what is effective in the paper and what might be done to strengthen it.
4. After the discussion of your draft, write a note to yourself or to your instructor, explaining what you may do to strengthen the paper.

HOW TO CRITICIZE PAINLESSLY

The need for assertive criticism often emerges in the realm of conscious problem-solving.

Here is a fool-proof method for telling yourself or someone else that something is wrong without fear of losing a friendship or of starting a battle.

The trick is to place the criticism within a context of positive reinforcements . . . just simple diplomacy.

1. BEGIN WITH TWO POSITIVE REINFORCEMENTS
   "You really are a well-seasoned traveler."
   "You have all of the best gear for hiking."

2. INSERT YOUR CRITICISM
   "I wish we could stay in step when we hike together."

3. ADD ONE MORE POSITIVE REINFORCEMENT
   "I notice that you can adapt easily to most things."

4. FINISH WITH A RAY OF HOPE
   "If we work on this together, I'm sure we'll be able to get harmony into our stride."

Now you try it!

HOW TO ACCEPT CRITICISM

It is easier to feel a discontent than it is to accept the challenge of constructively improving the situation. And it is also easier, as the old saying goes, "to give criticism than it is to receive it." Being "defensive" of our position, which we imagine to be under attack from outside, is wasted motion. But it is also far more normal than an outlook of receptive self-improvement.

Be *abnormal*. Instead of wasting time with defenses and soothing self-inflicted, imaginary hurts, get procedural. *Accept* the comments for further ANALYSIS and DEFINITION. If the criticism then seems appropriate, "try it on for size." If not, discard it as irrelevant and the matter is finished.

Feedback Form

Writer's name: _____   Reader's name: _____

Directions:

Read the paper completely before making a response. Unless errors interfere with your ability to understand what the writer is saying, read for meaning only. Your goal can be to help the writer discover what works and what doesn't work and to find ways of strengthening the paper.

1. *Begin with positive reinforcement.* Tell the writer what you like about the paper and what you think should not be changed.

2. *Insert your criticism.* Tell the writer what confused you, misled you, bothered you, or left you wanting more. Be specific.

3. *Finish with a ray of hope.* Give the writer helpful suggestions. Be specific. If you were the writer of this paper, what would you do to strengthen it?

Revising

By now, one or more students and/or your instructor may have commented on your paper. Now you can revise the paper to meet your own goals and your readers' needs and expectations.

There can be no hard-and-fast rules for revision, of course, because each of you has a different paper and different reviewer responses. But the following questions may help you sift through the criticism you have received.

GUIDELINES

For Revising

Revise your paper by asking questions such as these:

☐ What should I keep?
☐ What should I add?
☐ What should I delete?
☐ What should I change?
☐ What should I rearrange?
☐ What should I rethink?

What Should I Keep?

Reread your reviewers' comments and/or your own notes to remember what readers like about your paper. Though it may not be possible to save everything that appeals to them, you can keep their positive impressions in your mind as you rewrite.

What Should I Add?

Reread the comments and/or notes to discover whether more details and examples or other evidence are needed to illustrate or support points you have made. It might be helpful at this point to look at some passages of the reading selections to see how the published authors achieved detailed writing. Exploratory activities may be useful in helping you generate new points or examples (see pp. 44–50).

What Should I Delete?

A reader might suggest that you used too much detail or included too much information. This is especially difficult criticism to hear because this reader may be recommending deletion of some of your favorite parts. Before you take anything out, remember that this is one reader's reaction. As with all feedback, you might determine that the suggestion is not appropriate and decide to keep the material in your revision. However, if more than one reader made the same comment, this might be advice worth taking.

What Should I Change?

If a reader expresses confusion, make note of the section(s) of your draft that has caused the problem. You may be able to solve the problem just by explaining what you meant to say. As you rewrite the confusing section, you may want to experiment with one or two versions. Read them aloud to yourself, or show them to a classmate or your instructor; they can help you determine which version is clearer.

What Should I Rearrange?

If a reader says that your paper needs a more logical development, it might be a good idea to outline your draft briefly, paragraph by paragraph, summarizing each paragraph. Then look at your outline to see where the logic of the organization breaks down. Revise the outline to reflect a better organization. Then rearrange the material in your draft.

What Should I Rethink?

You may not have clearly indicated your point of view about your topic. Reconsider what you have written. Try an exploratory strategy such as looping on your topic (see pp. 45–46), or discuss your topic with a classmate or your instructor to find what is important to you about this topic.

A Student Writer at Work

After he received comments and suggestions from his classmates and instructor, Rolando began to rewrite his draft. One of the responses he received and the changes he made are reprinted below.

Opening Paragraphs of Rolando's Interim Draft

I've been in the States for two months now and even though my English is good enough to make myself understand, trying to communicate with people in a language that is not mine is a problem.

Whenever I talk to someone, I feel like I'm playing tennis. In tennis as in English, I am a novice. I know how to hold the racket and how to hit the ball, but that's not enough to carry on a complete game and enjoy it.

Reader's Comments on the Opening Paragraphs

I think your comparison with tennis is unique. But I think you need more background information about your experience with tennis before you talk about language. Now, the first sentence of the second paragraph is too confusing, too abrupt.

Rolando's Revision of the Opening Paragraphs

A few months ago I decided that I wanted to learn how to play tennis. Today, after much practice and a few classes, I know how to hold the racket and basically how to hit the ball; however, I still can't say that I actually play tennis. It is taking me so long to learn, and it is so difficult! It didn't look that hard when I saw my friends playing it so gracefully. Even so, I am still giving it a try. But to play a sport that I cannot master is becoming a pain. I feel so frustrated sometimes, that I consider forgetting all about tennis. It is hurting my pride.

Today, tennis is not the main source of my frustrations. I have another problem that generates feelings and puts me into moods very similar to those that I experience when I play it. This is daily conversation with people. It may sound bizarre, but it is not. I am a foreign student, and in playing tennis as in speaking English, I am still in the learning process. That is why the best way I can explain these complex feelings created by my communication problem is by associating them with tennis.

Completing the Essay

Once you have revised the draft, you can complete the essay by following these guidelines:

GUIDELINES

For Completing the Essay

1. *Evaluate the essay as a whole.*
2. *Proofread and edit the essay.* Turn your attention to grammar, punctuation, spelling, and mechanics. Give your essay a final check to catch any errors you might have made (see Chapter 25).
3. *Adapt the guidelines for preparing a final manuscript* (see Chapter 28).

Student Essay

Barriers

Rolando Niella

About the Author   Rolando Niella was born and raised in Paraguay. He studied English for several years in Paraguay, for one year as an exchange student in junior high school in the United States, and for a summer just prior to entering college in the United States. He now runs his own business in New York.

The Context of the Reading   "Barriers" was written to fulfill a writing assignment for a college composition course. References to the game of tennis include the following:

- □ *service* or *serve:* act of putting the ball into play
- □ *ace:* a serve the opponent fails to return
- □ *volley:* hitting of the tennis ball before it touches the ground
- □ *forehand shot:* stroke of the racket made with the hand moving palm forward
- □ *backhand shot:* stroke of the racket made with the back of the hand facing outward

  Note: This essay has been edited for publication in this book.

A few months ago I decided that I wanted to learn how to play tennis. Today, after much practice and a few classes, I know how to hold the racket and basically how to hit the ball; however, I still can't say that I actually play tennis. It is taking me so long to learn, and it is so difficult! It didn't look that hard when I saw my friends playing it so gracefully. Even so, I am still giving it a try. But to play a sport that I cannot master is becoming a pain. I feel so frustrated sometimes that I consider forgetting all about tennis. It is hurting my pride.

Today, tennis is not the main source of my frustrations. I have another problem that generates feelings and puts me in moods very similar to those that I experience when I play it. This is daily conversation with people. It may sound bizarre, but it is not. I am a foreign student, and in playing tennis, as in speaking English, I am still in the learning process. That is why the best way I can explain these complex feelings created by my communication problem is by associating them with tennis.

One of the most common situations I find myself in, when I play tennis, is that people, either conscious or unconscious of my level, will start the game with a strong service or will answer my weak service with a fast ball which I cannot possibly hit back. Comparable examples are the ladies at the cafeteria telling me about the menu, while speaking at an incredible speed. This is often worsened by their personal style, the Somerville accent. I also encounter the same problem when my roommate speaks with his heavy Massachusetts accent. He is from Peabody, or "PEEb'dy."

Experiences like these are likely to happen when I speak to someone for the first time. Usually, however, once they realize my level, most of them will not "serve for the ace." But with those who still do, it is a different story. If, after asking them to repeat their serves many times, and, after repeatedly failing to return their balls, I don't give up, they will find an excuse to leave the court immediately, or they will simply tell me to "forget it." In daily conversation, even my friends will use this phrase when they give up trying to make their point, or to understand my point. I do not blame them sometimes, but this little phrase is one of the most frustrating ones I have heard. It can take away my desire to talk, and discourage me in my efforts to get my ideas across—making me leave the court frustrated and angry. I then isolate myself or look for a friend with whom I can speak a language I don't have to concentrate on, and at which I am very good: Spanish. In like manner, when I am tired of tennis and still want to do some sport, I jog alone or play soccer.

Once a person is aware of my level and tries to go at my pace, I still confront some problems. First, in tennis, if you are a fairly experienced player, you should be familiar with some basic game plans. The way your opponents are sending the balls may lead you to realize which plan they are using to score upon you. In the same way, if in a language you have experience with the cultural patterns of expressing feelings and moods, and you distinguish the different connotations of words, you may understand the point the speaker is trying to make to you. In tennis, I am not very good at predicting what play my opponent is trying to use; and when I do, it is usually too late. Likewise, in conversation, I usually don't react to a joke until it is too late. I also have a hard time realizing how annoyed my roommate gets, because he selects words to make his point; but the connotations of some of them sometimes don't reach me because of my inexperience. I don't know exactly which is worse to him, "mad," "angry," "disturbed," or "pissed off."

Second, in tennis, by observing your opponents' movements, you improve your chances to return the ball and prolong the volley. The swing of their rackets, the way they hit the balls, and their position in relation with the net are good hints for predicting the direction and the power of the ball. I still can't tell precisely how fast the ball is coming, or if I have to return it with a forehand or a backhand shot just by watching my opponent. It is not only that I am unfamiliar with these movements, but I also am too busy analyzing the movements I have done, and the ones I am about to do. At the same time, my opponent can tell very little about my next shot by observing me, because my style is very awkward. When talking to people I also feel the necessity to be familiar with the nonverbal language of Americans. Yesterday, for example, the guy across the hall asked me to turn down my stereo. By the time I had understood what he had said, he was gone. I wasn't sure what his talking from the doorway and the tone of his voice meant. Everything happened so fast, just like a crosscourt backhand. I didn't feel happy with my vague answer, and I am sure he didn't either.

Playing tennis, for me, in general is an uncomfortable situation. I waste too much energy and attention on every single movement of my hand, my racket, my feet, etc., and besides I also have to watch the player at the other side of the net; then I don't enjoy the game. In everyday conversation, it is also very annoying to pay so much attention to things that should be automatic and to give as much thought to almost every word I and the other person are using.

Exposed to so many unfamiliar rules and ways, I easily lose the train of thought in my conversation. I feel that I am not being natural and start questioning the way I communicate and relate with people. I worry so much about the "how to" that conversation is not always as relaxing as it should be. This is a problem from which the only way to escape is by fully experiencing it. As in any sport, if you want to enjoy it, you have to practice until you master it.

So, if you happen to be talking to a foreigner, be aware of this problem. If you are a foreign student yourself, do not feel depressed. I believe that in the long run there will be a reward, a better understanding of ourselves and the vital phenomenon of communication.

Write after You Read

Explore your response to "Barriers" by recording your reactions in a journal entry, adapting the guidelines on page 9.

ACTIVITY

For Class Discussion

Working with a partner, in a small group, or with the whole class, engage in some or all of the following activities. Decide the order in which to cover the material and the amount of time to spend on each activity. Allow for different reactions to and interpretations of the various aspects of the reading.

1. Share the reactions to ''Barriers'' that you have recorded in your journal entry.

2. Examine ''Barriers'' closely, using the suggestions for summarizing and analyzing on pages 40–42.

3. Compare the experiences and ideas in ''Barriers'' with your own experiences and attitudes.

■

FIELD RESEARCH

This unit, Writing from Sources: Field Research, consists of three chapters that can help you fulfill an assignment to write an essay based on your own field research, drawn from conversations, observations, interviews, and/or surveys.

Chapter 6 includes readings that go beyond personal experience to draw from the writers' research on their subjects. By reading and examining your reactions to these works, guided by the discussion activities in Chapter 7, you may develop a sense of how a writer can present a researched subject in a meaningful way. In Chapter 8, guidelines explain some ways to gather material, interview, observe, conduct a survey, and organize an essay based on your own field research. A sample student essay is included.

Readings: Field Research

Chapter 6 provides five reading selections based on field research. The writers go beyond personal experience, drawing ideas and information from conversations, observations, surveys, interviews, and other sources.

As you read and reread each selection, you can aim to accomplish the following:

☐ Understand the findings of the research

☐ Evaluate the evidence provided to support points made about the subject

☐ Question what you are reading

☐ Examine your own views on the subject

The Reading Selections

The reading selections in this chapter cover several subjects, including friendship, cross-cultural communication, and teaching and learning. They were written by professionals in the fields of journalism, psychology, communications, and education.

The selections follow different formats because the writers published their work in different publications; each is directed toward a different audience.

☐ Articles or other writings intended for an academic reading audience include careful documentation of sources. Footnotes and bibliographies reveal to readers the writer's knowledge of other research in the field. In addition, they provide resources for other researchers who may wish to locate the sources themselves to investigate the same subject.

☐ Writers whose articles are intended for a general audience do not have the same obligation to cite and document sources. Although they must be honest in giving credit to ideas taken from other writers, they do not necessarily provide bibliographic information. General audiences usually are more interested in gaining knowledge from the writer than in pursuing the research themselves.

Write before You Read

The following reading selection is entitled "Friends, Good Friends—and Such Good Friends." Before reading the selection, interview a classmate to discover that classmate's view on the difference between a "friend" and a "good friend." Write down the responses.

Share with the whole class what you have found. As a class, discuss the differences between "friends" and "good friends," based on the material from the interviews.

Friends, Good Friends—and Such Good Friends

Judith Viorst

About the Author   Judith Viorst was born in the United States, in New Jersey. She is a poet, journalist, and the author of several books of fiction and nonfiction for children and adults. Among her works are *Necessary Losses* (1988) and *Murdering Mr. Monti* (1994).

The Context of the Reading   Based on personal experience and conversations with women, "Friends, Good Friends—and Such Good Friends" first appeared in 1977 in *Redbook,* a magazine at that time directed primarily toward an audience of nonworking women.

The author's use of informal language includes the following word:

□   *un-Brooklyned:* a word made up by the author, referring to Brooklyn, a section of New York City whose residents' strong accents are easily recognized

Women are friends, I once would have said, when they totally love and support and trust each other, and bare to each other the secrets of their souls, and run—no questions asked—to help each other, and tell harsh truths to each other (no, you can't wear that dress unless you lose ten pounds first) when harsh truths must be told.

Women are friends, I once would have said, when they share the same affection for Ingmar Bergman, plus train rides, cats, warm rain, charades, Camus, and hate with equal ardor Newark and Brussel sprouts and Lawrence Welk and camping.

In other words, I once would have said that a friend is a friend all the way, but now I believe that's a narrow point of view. For the friendships I have and the friendships I see are conducted at many levels of intensity, serve many different functions, meet many different needs and range from those as all-the-way as the friendship of the soul sisters mentioned above to that of the most nonchalant and casual playmates.

Consider these varieties of friendship:

1. Convenience friends. These are women with whom, if our paths weren't crossing all the time, we'd have no particular reason to be friends: a next-door neighbor, a woman in our car pool, the mother of one of our children's closest friends or maybe some mommy with whom we serve juice and cookies each week at the Glenwood Co-op Nursery.

Convenience friends are convenient indeed. They'll lend us their cups and silverware for a party. They'll drive our kids to soccer when we're sick. They'll take us to pick up our car when we need a lift to the garage. They'll even take our cats when we go on vacation. As we will for them.

But we don't, with convenience friends, ever come too close or tell too much; we maintain our public face and emotional distance. "Which means," says Elaine, "that I'll talk about being overweight but not about being depressed. Which means I'll admit being mad but not blind with rage. Which means that I might say that we're pinched this month but never that I'm worried sick over money."

But which doesn't mean that there isn't sufficient value to be found in these friendships of mutual aid, in convenience friends.

2. Special-interest friends. These friendships aren't intimate, and they needn't involve kids or silverware or cats. Their value lies in some interest jointly shared. And so we may have an office friend or a yoga friend or a tennis friend or a friend from the Women's Democratic Club.

"I've got one woman friend," says Joyce, "who likes, as I do, to take psychology courses. Which makes it nice for me—and nice for her. It's fun to go with someone you know and it's fun to discuss what you've learned, driving back from the classes." And for the most part, she says, that's all they discuss.

"I'd say that what we're doing is *doing* together, not being together," Suzanne says of her Tuesday-doubles friends. "It's mainly a tennis relationship, but we play together well. And I guess we all need to have a couple of playmates."

I agree.

My playmate is a shopping friend, a woman of marvelous taste, a woman who knows exactly *where* to buy *what,* and furthermore is a woman who always knows beyond a doubt what one ought to be buying. I don't have the time to keep up with what's new in eyeshadow, hemlines and shoes and whether the smock look is in or finished already. But since (oh shame!) I care a lot about eyeshadows, hemlines and shoes, and since I don't *want* to wear smocks if the smock look is finished, I'm very glad to have a shopping friend.

3. Historical friends. We all have a friend who knew us when . . . maybe way back in Miss Meltzer's second grade, when our family lived in that three-room flat in Brooklyn, when our dad was out of work for seven months, when our brother Allie got in that fight where they had to call the police, when our sister married the endodontist from Yonkers and when, the morning after we lost our virginity, she was the first, the only, friend we told.

The years have gone by and we've gone separate ways and we've little in common now, but we're still an intimate part of each other's past.

And so whenever we go to Detroit we always go to visit this friend of our girlhood. Who knows how we looked before our teeth were straightened. Who knows how we talked before our voice got un-Brooklyned. Who knows what we ate before we learned about artichokes. And who, by her presence, puts us in touch with an earlier part of ourself, a part of ourself it's important never to lose.

"What this friend means to me and what I mean to her," says Grace, "is having a sister without sibling rivalry. We know the texture of each other's lives. She remembers my grandmother's cabbage soup. I remember the way her uncle played the piano. There's simply no other friend who remembers those things."

4. Crossroads friends. Like historical friends, our crossroads friends are important for *what was*—for the friendship we shared at a crucial, now past, time of life. A time, perhaps, when we roomed in college together; or worked as eager young singles in the Big City together; or went together, as my friend Elizabeth and I did, through pregnancy, birth and that scary first year of new motherhood.

Crossroads friends forge powerful links, links strong enough to endure with not much more contact than once-a-year letters at Christmas. And out of respect for those crossroads years, for those dramas and dreams we once shared, we will always be friends.

5. Cross-generational friends. Historical friends and crossroads friends seem to maintain a special kind of intimacy—dormant but always ready to be revived—and though we may rarely meet, whenever we do connect, it's personal and intense. Another kind of intimacy exists in the friendships that form across generations in what one woman calls her daughter-mother and her mother-daughter relationships.

Evelyn's friend is her mother's age—"but I share so much more than I ever could with my mother"—a woman she talks to of music, of books and of life. "What I get from her is the benefit of her experience. What she gets—and enjoys—from me is a youthful perspective. It's a pleasure for both of us."

I have in my own life a precious friend, a woman of 65 who has lived very hard, who is wise, who listens well; who has been where I am and can help me understand it; and who represents not only an ultimate ideal mother to me but also the person I'd like to be when I grow up.

In our daughter role we tend to do more than our share of self-revelation; in our mother role we tend to receive what's revealed. It's another kind of pleasure—playing wise mother to a questioning younger person. It's another very lovely kind of friendship.

6. Part-of-a-couple friends. Some of the women we call our friends we never see alone—we see them as part of a couple at couples' parties. And though we share interests in many things and respect each other's views, we aren't moved to deepen the relationship. Whatever the reason, a lack of time or—and this is more likely—a lack of chemistry, our friendship remains in the context of a group. But the fact that our feeling on seeing each other is always, "I'm *so* glad she's here" and the fact that we spend half the evening talking together says that this too, in its own way, counts as a friendship.

(Other part-of-a-couple friends are the friends that came with the marriage, and some of these are friends we could live without. But sometimes, alas, she married our husband's best friend; and sometimes, alas, she *is* our husband's best friend. And so we find ourselves dealing with her, somewhat against our will, in a spirit of what I'll call *reluctant friendship*.)

7. Men who are friends. I wanted to write just of women friends, but the women I've talked to won't let me—they say I must mention man-woman friendships too. For these friendships can be just as close and as dear as those that we form with women. Listen to Lucy's description of one such friendship:

"We've found we have things to talk about that are different from what he talks about with my husband and different from what I talk about with his wife. So sometimes we call on the phone or meet for lunch. There are similar intellectual interests—we always pass on to each other the book that we love—but there's also something tender and caring too."

In a couple of crises, Lucy says, "he offered himself for talking and for helping. And when someone died in his family he wanted me there. The sexual, flirty part of our friendship is very small—but *some*—just enough to make it fun and different." She thinks—and I agree—that the sexual part, though small, is always *some*, is always there when a man and a woman are friends.

It's only in the past few years that I've made friends with men, in the sense of a friendship that's *mine*, not just part of two couples. And achieving with them the ease and the trust I've found with women friends has value indeed. Under the dryer at home last week, putting on mascara and rouge, I comfortably sat and talked with a fellow named Peter. Peter, I finally decided, could handle the shock of me minus mascara under the dryer. Because we care for each other. Because we're friends.

8. There are medium friends, and pretty good friends, and very good friends indeed, and these friendships are defined by their level of intimacy. And what we'll reveal at each of these levels of intimacy is calibrated with care. We might tell a medium friend, for example, that yesterday we had a fight with our husband. And we might tell a pretty good friend that this fight with our husband made us so mad that we slept on the couch. And we might tell a very good friend that the reason we got so mad in that fight that we slept on the couch had something to do with that girl who works in his office. But it's only to our very best friends that we're willing to tell all, to tell what's going on with that girl in his office.

The best of friends, I still believe, totally love and support and trust each other, and bare to each other the secrets of their souls, and run—no questions asked—to help each other, and tell harsh truths to each other when they msut be told.

But we needn't agree about everything (only 12-year-old girl friends agree about *everything*) to tolerate each other's point of view. To accept without judgment. To give and to take without ever keeping score. And to *be* there, as I am for them and as they are for me, to comfort our sorrows, to celebrate our joys.

Write before You Read

The following reading selection is entitled "Myth, Reality and Shades of Gray: Comparing Same-Sex Friendships." Before reading, interview a classmate, and ask the classmate to describe a typical friendship with a person of the same gender. Write down the response.

Share what you have found with the whole class. As a class, compare the differences between male and female relationships, based on the material gathered from the interviews.

Myth, Reality and Shades of Gray: Comparing Same-Sex Friendships

Joel D. Block

About the Author   Joel D. Block is a diplomate of the American Board of Professional Psychology and is on the staff of a hospital in New York. He is the author of several books including *The Other Man, The Other Woman* (1978) and *Women and Friendship* (1985), coauthored with Diane Greenley.

The Context of the Reading   "Myth, Reality and Shades of Gray: Comparing Same-Sex Friendships" is a complete chapter from Block's book *Friendship* (1980), the result of three years of research. The book is based on 500 interviews, previously published research on friendship, and a national survey questionnaire completed by over 2,000 people representative of what Block calls the "American middle class." The questionnaire consisted of 52 questions, beginning with basic personal information and following with friendship experiences in five stages of life: the preteen years, adolescence, adulthood, marriage, and divorce.

Among the references Block makes are the following:

☐ *Margaret Mead:* U.S. cultural anthropologist (1901–1978)
☐ *Equal Rights Amendment:* In 1972, Congress passed an amendment to the U.S. Constitution, prohibiting discrimination on the basis of gender. After considerable debate, the amendment failed to obtain the necessary ratification of 38 states by 1982.
☐ *James Bond:* character developed in a series of books by Ian Fleming, made famous in a series of action movies.

The physical differences between men and women are obvious and universal. As for differences related to sex roles, each society varies in this, as Margaret Mead has convincingly demonstrated. Dr. Mead showed that in three New Guinea tribes, there was considerable difference from tribe to tribe in masculine and feminine behavior. In one group, the Arapesh, men and women alike were passive, "maternal," cooperative and nonaggressive. In the Mundugumor, a tribe in geographic proximity to the Arapesh, men and women alike were fierce, cruel and aggressive. A third tribe, the Tchambuli, showed yet another pattern of sex typing. The men were passive, dependent individuals who spent their time cultivating the arts while the women took the more active, assertive role of provider.

In America, most researchers concede that boys and girls are brought up in divergent ways, taught different skills, rewarded for diverse acts. Women, it is agreed, excel at certain tasks, men at others. There is little argument that some personality traits appear more dominant in one sex than the other. All of this notwithstanding, sex differences are a hotly contested issue—from occupational controversy to debates about the Equal Rights Amendment—masculine and feminine behavior is very much in the media these days. Since the rise of the women's movement, sex-role behavior has come under closer scrutiny. How has this affected friendship? How do the sexes differ in their friendship relations? Drawing from the findings of the two preceding chapters,* some dimensions of the same-sex friendship experience are compared below.

Early Impressions

Most preteen children have a best friend who is usually someone of the same sex and similar age. Both sexes share an essentially positive recollection of these childhood friendships; they do not differ in this respect. However, the type of play engaged in during these early friendships is telling of the divergence to come: Boys tend to form play groups that are competitive in nature; girls' groups more frequently revolve around cooperative enterprises. Thus, at an early age, boys become concerned with trying hard and winning while girls, by contrast, play house and school, engaging in roles that require complementary support.

Speaking of their childhood, men recall being highly responsive to and aware of the sex-role opinions of other boys. Girls in preteen years appear to be less susceptible to sex-role pressure. While "sissy" is the most powerful charge against the young male ego, prior to puberty girls do not report sensitivity to accusations that they are being unfeminine. It is not until the dating years, when competition for boys becomes an issue, that women report being concerned with feminine behavior. Males, for the most part, are responsive to the suggestion that their behavior is unmanly at almost any age.

These early attitudes, reinforced by social conditioning, continue to play an active part in the friendships of both sexes during adolescence. This is a period when the majority of males once again report a close alliance with same-sex friends but now, with heightened intensity, considerable energy is devoted to jockeying for position and a definite undercurrent of competition pervades the relationship. Although in dissimilar fashion, females share equally fragile relationships at this age. For them the bond of loyalty extends only to the line of romantic involvement. This is most apt to be the case in late adolescence, when dating and relationships with boys take sharp precedence over sisterhood. Actually, dating dilutes the intensity of same-sex friendships for men also. For the majority of us—men and women alike—the moment we begin to date seriously, there is a competition between romance and friendship. Add to this career strivings and family obligations, and close friendships move to the back burner. It isn't until our third decade that they are once again revived.

---

*The two preceding chapters were separate discussions of female friendships and male friendships.

Getting Personal

Male friendships revolve almost exclusively around work and play: The office or the assembly line, the hobby or sports activity, these are the focal areas of friendship talk. Most notable about male friendships is that they rarely include personal, confidential exchanges. Men who have known each other for years may not know anything about each other's family crises or problems.

Women, unlike men, do use their friendships to share difficult times and to ask for help. Their friendships have a decidedly personal flavor; women are nearly three times more likely than men to have a close confidante. Even though self-disclosure is an infrequent occurrence, it is clear that men desire others with whom to share problems and personal experiences. Those men who do fulfill this longing are more likely to turn to a woman or a stranger than to each other. Women, on the other hand, practically always choose a same-sex friend. Individuals of either sex who have a trusted friend to whom they can express thoughts, feelings and opinions honestly are less likely to report symptoms of depression and loneliness than those who do not have the benefit of this experience.

This is not to say that the sheer amount of self-disclosure that goes on between friends is an index of the health of the relationship or of the persons. There are such factors as timing, interest of the other person, appropriateness and the effects of the disclosures on either party which also must be considered. If a relationship exists between self-disclosure and factors of psychological health, research trends suggest it is curvilinear, not linear; that is, too much disclosure and too little disclosure may be associated with undesirable symptoms, while some intermediate amount, under appropriate conditions, is related to a sense of well-being.

While very high self-disclosure is not necessarily a blessing, as a general principle most of us agree that never knowing what a companion really thinks, feels and wants is distressing and quite unpleasant. This guardedness is a dominant theme in male interaction; it is, by comparison, a minor issue among women. In short, women as a group demonstrate substantially more trust than do men.

Attractions and Hazards

Such qualities of a relationship as openness, compassion and mental stimulation are of concern to most of us regardless of sex, but—judging from the questionnaire response—they are more important to women than to men. Asked to consider the ingredients of close friendship, women rated these qualities above all others. Men assigned a lower priority to them in favor of similarity in interests, selected by seventy-seven percent of men, and responsiveness in a crisis, chosen by sixty-one percent of male respondents. Mental stimulation, ranked third in popularity by men as well as women, was the only area of overlap. Among men, only twenty-eight percent named openness as an important quality; caring was picked by just twenty-three percent.

It is evident by their selections that when women speak of close friendships they are referring to emotional factors, while men emphasize the pleasure they find in a friend's company. That is, when a man speaks of "a friend" he is likely to be talking about someone he does things with—a teammate, a fellow hobbyist, a drinking buddy. These activities are the fabric of the friendship; it is a "doing" relationship in which similarity in interests is the key bond. This factor was a consideration of a meager eleven percent of women. Women opt for a warm, emotional atmosphere where communication flows freely; activity is mere background.

Lastly, men, as we have seen, have serious questions about each other's loyalty. Perhaps this is why they placed such strong emphasis on responsiveness in a crisis—"someone I can call on for help." Women, as their testimonies indicate, are generally more secure with each other and consequently are more likely to treat this issue lightly. In follow-up interviews this was confirmed numerous times as woman after woman indicated that "being there when needed was taken for granted."

As for the hazards of friendship, more than a few relationships have been shattered because of cutthroat competition and feelings of betrayal. This applies to both men and women, but unequally. In comparison, nearly twice as many men complained about these issues as women. Further, while competition and betrayal are the main thorns to female friendship, men are plagued in almost equal amounts by two additional issues: guardedness (lack of candor) and a fear of appearing unmanly. Obviously, for a man, a good friendship is hard to find.

Friendships: Desire, Quality, and Source

The literature on sex differences is replete with discussions of the greater affiliative and nurturant needs of women and the greater male needs for independence, achievement and aggression. Curiously enough, although men and women do react to the friendship experience differently, their desires for companionship are of similar intensity. As mentioned earlier, both men and women in their twenties consider friendship to play a relatively minor role in their lives. This, as might be predicted, is less true for single individuals than it is for those who are married. Nonetheless, there is no significant distinction to be made with regard to males and females. The friendship desires of men and women beyond the late twenties are once again congruent but are increased in comparison to their younger counterparts—sixty-two percent of men and sixty-seven percent of women over age twenty-nine consider friendship to play a moderately important part in their lives, as compared to twenty-eight percent of younger men and thirty-one percent of younger women.

Men and women may assess the role of friendship in their lives similarly, but the extent of their actual friendships varies considerably. Among my respondents, adult women (over age twenty) were at least twice as likely as adult men to have a close friend. The conventional belief that of the two sexes, men have the richer friendships is simply untrue. The only exception to this may be in regard to mentor relationships in the work setting. Although the questionnaire did not cover this topic, interview impressions are that women as a group have less mentor relationships than men. The scarcity of women in high-level positions possibly accounts for this. In general, though, women as a group are less frustrated, more in tune with their friendship goals than are men. Other friendship researchers agree: Dr. Alan Booth of the University of Nebraska studied the friendship patterns of eight hundred adults in two major cities and found that both working-class and middle-class women had more solid and emotionally satisfying friendships than did working-class and middle-class men. In another investigation, Dr. Mirra Komarovsky scrutinized a number of blue-collar marriages and found that six out of every ten wives she interviewed, but only two out of every ten husbands, enjoyed close nonfamilial relationships.

Just as the extent and quality of close friendships differ between the sexes, so do their sources of friendship. Employed activity attracts many women as much for the companionship and friendship to be found on the job as for the work or money earned. Men, more influenced by on-the-job competition, avoid friendships in this setting. Instead, they form relationships with persons in similar work but different organizations or through mutual recreational interests and men's clubs. Men more than women are apt to be the same ages and, as already noted, have the same interests. Single men are more likely than single women to join company exclusively with other singles. Men more than women have educational backgrounds in common with their friends.

Implications

Clearly, the two sexes travel a different friendship path. If an atmosphere of discovery and delight pervades many female friendships, an atmosphere of ambivalence is the most generous characterization that can be ascribed to the state of male relationships. Because they have been exposed to sex roles that are constraining and dysfunctional, men have allowed themselves precious few options for friendship. Generation upon generation of boys (and girls) have been presented with male role models who have an inexhaustible capacity to withstand not only adversity and pain, but any feeling.

From Hercules to James Bond, the heroic man is presented as impenetrable. Witness some discriminating reactions to male and female children: A shy little girl is considered cute; a shy boy is thought of as a sissy. A frightened girl is comforted; a boy is admonished to act like a man. Girls are allowed comfortably to kiss each other and to cry openly without shame; boys who even touch each other had better be "horsing around," and crying is done only at the expense of sheer ridicule.

These behavioral distinctions, which may seem extreme to some, were confirmed in a recent study commissioned by the United States government. It was revealed that the majority of tested parents would not hug or cuddle their sons (after the average age of five) as often as they did their daughters (regardless of age), would not kiss male children at all after a certain age (usually the onset of adolescence), and would discourage boys as young as four years old from sobbing by calling them crybabies or telling them to "act their age." When asked to explain, the most common response from the parents was: "I don't want my son to grow up to be a sissy."

Without doubt, women have also had their difficulties with rigid sex-role training. If men have been told that rough and tough is masculine, women have been told that soft and sweet is feminine. Rather than seeing themselves as full human beings capable of versatile roles, many women have confined themselves to one dimension: Mother, Companion, Follower, Bitch, Homemaker, Whore, Glamor Girl. Unrealistic views such as these wreak havoc on friendship relations.

It may come down to this: When men or women confine themselves exclusively to either "masculine" or "feminine" behavior, they are being incomplete human beings. The inevitable result is that their friendships prove to be unsatisfactory. The psychologically healthy individual, one who is able to develop satisfying, nurturing relationships, must be nonconforming in this respect. He or she is a person who takes the relatively fixed sex roles in our society and redefines them in ways that dovetail better with his or her needs. Consequently, he or she has greater freedom to express and act out a wider range of feelings and behavior. The benefits that men derive from sharing office or hobby interests could well be of value to women, while men could profit by learning to confide in each other about problems they find emotionally baffling. Healthy men and women can do many things that might be deemed "out of role" by some, and yet they need not experience any threat to their humanity—nor to their femininity or masculinity. They may cry, be tender, touch, ask for help as well as be independent, assertive and ambitious.

Bibliography

Booth, Alan. "Sex and Social Participation." *American Sociological Review* 37 (1972): 183–192.

Komarovsky, Mirra. *Blue Collar Marriage.* New York: Random House, 1962.

Mead, Margaret. *Male and Female.* New York: Morrow, 1949.

Write before You Read

The following reading selection, "Intercultural Communication Stumbling Blocks," is a report of research on cross-cultural communication. Before reading, fill out the following questionnaire.

Purpose of survey: To gather information about cross-cultural experiences

☐ Please check the appropriate category:

female _____ male_____

freshman _____ sophomore _____ junior _____ senior _____ graduate student _____ exchange student_____

☐ Please fill in your age:_____

☐ Please briefly describe an experience you have had when one of the following categories caused a problem (humorous or otherwise) communicating with someone from a culture or country other than your own.

1. Language
2. Nonverbal signs (for example, hand motions, facial expressions, pace of life, punctuality)
3. Preconceptions or stereotypes (either those you had about other people or those that others had about you or your culture or country)
4. Tendency to judge values (for example, when you or someone else had a negative attitude toward someone's religion, politics, family values, and/or way of life)
5. Anxiety

Share what you have written with classmates.

Intercultural Communication Stumbling Blocks

LaRay M. Barna

About the Author   LaRay M. Barna, a professor in the Department of Speech Communication at Portland State University in Oregon, wrote "Intercultural Communication Stumbling Blocks" to report on her classroom research with U.S. and international students.

The Context of the Reading   "Intercultural Communication Stumbling Blocks" was originally published in 1976 in *Kentucky Speech Arts Journal,* a journal for professionals in the field of communications.

Barna makes reference to some political and historical events:

☐ *"We'll bury you":* These words of Nikita Khrushchev, leader of the Soviet Union from 1953 to 1964, were directed to the people of the United States. He was referring to *economic* competition with the West, but it was misunderstood as a *military* boast.

□ *Paris Peace talks:* Held between Vietnamese and U.S. representatives in the early 1970s, these negotiations strove to end the Vietnam War.

□ *Nixon's historic visit:* U.S. president Richard Nixon visited the People's Republic of China in 1972, the first U.S. president to do so.

· *Note:* Because this article was written for a professional audience, it contains a number of technical terms; they are explained in footnotes.

Introduction

There are many viewpoints regarding the practice of intercultural communication but a familiar one is that "people are people," basically pretty much alike; therefore increased interaction through travel, student exchange programs, and other such ventures should result in more understanding and friendship between nations. Others take a quite different view, particularly those who have done research in the field of speech communication and are fully aware of the complexities of interpersonal interaction, even *within* cultural groups. They do not equate contact with communication, do not believe that the simple experience of talking with someone insures a successful transfer of meanings and feelings. Even the basic commonalities of birth, hunger, family, death, are perceived and treated in vastly different ways by persons with different backgrounds.[1] If there *is* a universal, it might be that each has been so subconsciously influenced by his own cultural upbringing that he assumes that the needs, desires, and basic assumptions of others are identical to his own.[2]

It takes a long time of noninsulated living* in a new culture before a foreigner can relax into new perceptions and nonevaluative thinking so that he can adjust his reactions and interpretations to fit what's happening around him. The few who achieve complete insight and acceptance are outstanding by their rarity. After nine years of monitoring dyads[†] and small group discussions between U.S. and international students, this author, for one, is inclined to agree with Charles Frankel, who says: "Tensions exist within nations and between nations that never would have existed were these nations not in such intense cultural communication with one another."[3] The following typical reactions of three foreign students to one nonverbal behavior that most Americans expect to bridge gaps—the smile—may serve as an illustration:

> Japanese student: On my way to and from school I have received a smile by nonacquaintance American girls several times. I have learned they have no interest for me; it means only a kind of greeting to a foreigner. But if someone smiles at a stranger in Japan, especially a girl, she can assume he is either a sexual maniac or an impolite person.

noninsulated living: participating socially
[†]*dyads:* groups of two people

Korean student: An American visited me in my country for one week. His inference was that people in Korea are not very friendly because they didn't smile or want to talk with foreign people. That's true because most Korean people take time to get to be friendly with people. We never talk or smile at strangers.

Vietnamese student: The reason why certain foreigners may think that Americans are superficial—and they are, some Americans even recognize this—is that they talk and smile too much. For people who come from placid cultures where nonverbal language is more used, and where a silence, a smile, a glance have their own meaning, it is true that Americans speak a lot. The superficiality of Americans can also be detected in their relations with others. Their friendships are, most of the time, so ephemeral compared to the friendships we have at home. Americans make friends very easily and leave their friends almost as quickly, while in my country it takes a long time to find out a possible friend and then she becomes your friend—with a very strong sense of the term. Most Americans are materialistic and once they are provided with necessities, they don't feel the need to have a friend. Purposes of their friendships are too clear, and you can hardly find a friendship for friendship's sake.

An American girl in the same class gives her view:

In general it seems to me that foreign people are not necessarily snobs but are very unfriendly. Some class members have told me that you shouldn't smile at others while passing them by on the street. To me I can't stop smiling. It's just natural to be smiling and friendly. I can see now why so many foreign people stick together. They are impossible to get to know. It's like the Americans are big bad wolves. How do Americans break this barrier? I want friends from all over the world but how do you start to be friends without offending them or scaring them off—like sheep?[4]

One reason for the long delay in tackling the widespread failure to achieve understanding across cultures might be that it is not readily apparent when there has been miscommunication at the interpersonal level. Unless there is overt reporting of assumptions* such as in the examples above, which seldom happens in normal settings, there is no chance for comparing impressions. The foreign visitor to the United States nods, smiles, and gives affirmative comments, which the straightforward, friendly American confidently translates as meaning that he has informed, helped, and pleased the newcomer. It is likely, however, that the foreigner actually understood very little of the verbal and nonverbal content and was merely indicating polite interest or trying not to embarrass himself or his host with verbalized questions. The conversation may even have confirmed his stereotype that Americans are insensitive and ethnocentric.

---

*overt reporting of assumptions: open explanations of basic beliefs and practices

In a university classroom U.S. students often complain that the international members of a discussion or project seem uncooperative or uninterested. The following is a typical statement from the international point of view:

> I had difficulty with the opinion in the class where peoples in group discuss about subject. I was surrounded by Americans with whom I couldn't follow their tempo of discussion half of the time. I have difficulty to listen and speak, but also with the way they handle the group. I felt uncomfortable because sometimes they believe their opinion strongly. I had been very serious about the whole subject but I was afraid I would say something wrong. I had the idea but not the words.[4]

Typically, the method used to improve chances for successful intercultural communication is to gather information about the customs of the other country and a smattering of the language. The behaviors and attitudes are sometimes researched, but almost always from a secondhand source. The information is seldom sufficient and may or may not be helpful. Knowing "what to expect" too often blinds the observer to all but what is confirmatory to his image or preconception. Any contradictory evidence that does filter through is likely to be treated as an exception.[5]

A better approach is to study the history, political structure, art, literature, and language of the country if time permits. But more important, one should develop an investigative nonjudgmental attitude* and a high tolerance for ambiguity†—which means lowered defenses. Margaret Mead suggests sensitizing persons to the kinds of things that need to be taken into account instead of developing behavior and attitude stereotypes, mainly because of the individual differences in each encounter and the rapid changes that occur in a culture pattern.[6] Edward Stewart concurs with this view.[7]

The Stumbling Blocks

Language

One way to reach an improved state of awareness and sensitivity to what might go wrong is to examine five variables in the communication process that seem to be major stumbling blocks when the dyad or small group is cross-cultural. The first is so obvious it hardly needs mentioning—*language*. Vocabulary, syntax, idioms, slang, dialects, and so on, all cause difficulty, but the person struggling with a different language is at least aware when he's in this kind of trouble. A worse language problem is the tenacity with which someone will cling to *"the"* meaning of a word or phrase in the new language once he has grasped one, regardless of connotation or context. The infinite variations, especially of English, are so impossible to cope with that they are waved aside. The reason the problem

---

investigative nonjudgmental attitude: the objective position a researcher attempts to take toward the research subject
†*high tolerance for ambiguity:* willingness to accept uncertainty and complexity

is "worse" is because each thinks he understands. The nationwide misinterpretation of Khrushchev's sentence "We'll bury you" is a classic example. Even "yes" and "no" cause trouble. When a Japanese hears, "Won't you have some tea?" he listens to the literal meaning of the sentence and answers, "No," meaning that he wants some. "Yes, I won't" would be a better reply because this tips off the hostess that there may be a misunderstanding. In some cultures, also, it is polite to refuse the first or second offer of refreshment. Many foreign guests have gone hungry because their U.S. hostess never presented the third offer.

Nonverbal Signs and Symbols

Learning the language, which most foreign visitors consider their *only* barrier to understanding, is actually only the beginning. As Frankel says, "To enter into a culture is to be able to hear, in Lionel Trilling's phrase, its special 'hum and buzz of implication.' "[8] This brings in *nonverbal areas* and the second stumbling block. People from different cultures inhabit different nonverbal sensory worlds. Each sees, hears, feels, and smells only that which has some meaning or importance for him. He abstracts whatever fits into his personal world of recognitions and then interprets it through the frame of reference* of his own culture.

An Oregon girl in an intercultural communication class asked a young man from Saudi Arabia how he would signal nonverbally that he liked her. His response was to smooth back his hair which, to her, was just a common nervous gesture signifying nothing. She repeated her question three times. He smoothed his hair three times and, finally realizing that she was not recognizing this movement as his reply to her question, automatically ducked his head and stuck out his tongue slightly in embarrassment. This behavior *was* noticed by the girl, and she interpreted it as the way he would express his liking for her.

The lack of comprehension of obvious nonverbal signs and symbols such as gestures, postures, and vocalizations† is a definite communication barrier, but it is possible to learn the meaning of these messages (once they are perceived) in much the same way as a verbal language is learned. It is more difficult to correctly note the unspoken codes of the other culture that are further from awareness, such as the handling of time and spatial relationshps, subtle signs of respect or formality, and many others.

Preconceptions and Stereotypes

The third stumbling block is the presence of *preconceptions* and *stereotypes*. If the label "inscrutable" has preceded the Japanese guest, it is thus we explain his constant and inappropriate smile. The stereotype that Arabs are "inflammable" causes U.S. students to keep their distance when an animated and noisy group from Libya is enjoying lunch in the cafeteria. A professor who "knows" of the bargaining habits of natives of certain countries may unfairly interpret a hesitation by one of his foreign students as a move to "squirm out" of a commitment. Stereotypes help do

---

*frame of reference: a set or system of beliefs against which other ideas are tested
†vocalizations: sounds made with the voice

what Ernest Becker[9] says the anxiety-prone human race *must* do, and that is to reduce the threat of the unknown by making the world predictable. Indeed, this is one of the basic functions of culture: to lay out a predictable world in which the individual is firmly oriented. Stereotypes are overgeneralized beliefs that provide conceptual bases from which to "make sense" out of what goes on around us. In a foreign land they increase our feeling of security and are psychologically necessary to the degree that we cannot tolerate ambiguity or the sense of helplessness resulting from inability to understand and deal with people and situations beyond our comprehension.

Stereotypes are stumbling blocks for communicators because they interfere with objective viewing of stimuli.* Unfortunately, they are not easy to overcome in others or in ourselves by demonstrations of the "truth," hoping to teach a lesson of tolerance or cultural relativity.† They persist because they sometimes rationalize prejudices or are firmly established as myths or truisms by one's own national culture. They are also sustained and fed by the tendency to perceive selectively only those pieces of new information that correspond to the image. The Asian or African visitor who is accustomed to privation and the values of denial and self-help cannot fail to experience American culture as materialistic and wasteful. The stereotype for him turns into a concrete reality.

The Tendency to Evaluate

Another deterrent to an understanding between persons of differing cultures or ethnic groups is the *tendency to evaluate,* to approve or disapprove, the statements and actions of the other person or group rather than to try to completely comprehend the thoughts and feelings expressed. Each person's culture, his own way of life, always seems right, proper, and natural. This bias prevents the open-minded attention needed to look at the attitudes and behavior patterns from the other's point of view. A midday siesta changes from a "lazy habit" to a "pretty good idea" when someone listens long enough to realize the midday temperature in that country is 115° Fahrenheit.

The communication cut-off caused by immediate evaluation is heightened when feelings and emotions are deeply involved; yet this is just the time when listening with understanding is most needed. It takes both awareness of the tendency to close our minds and courage to risk change in our own values and perceptions to dare to comprehend why someone thinks and acts differently from us. As stated by Sherif, Sherif, and Nebergall, "A person's commitment to his religion, politics, values of his family, and his stand on the virtue of his way of life are ingredients in his self-picture—intimately felt and cherished."[10] It is very easy to dismiss strange or different behaviors as "wrong," listen through a thick screen of value judgments, and therefore fail miserably to receive a fair understanding. The impatience of the American public over the choice of the shape of the

---

objective viewing of stimuli: the ability to look at things without making judgments about them
†*cultural relativity:* the evaluation of a custom in relation to other customs of a particular group

conference table at the Paris Peace talks and their judgment of a "poor reception" for the President of the United States because there were no bands or flag-waving throngs waiting for Nixon as he was driven through towns in New China on his historic visit are two examples.

The following paragraph written by an international student from Korea illustrates how a clash in values can lead to poor communication and result in misunderstanding and hurt feelings:

> When I call on my American friend, he had been studying his lesson. Then I said, "May I come in?" He said through window, "I am sorry. I have no time because of my study." Then he shut the window. I thought it over and over. I couldn't understand through my cultural background. In our country, if someone visits other's house, house owner should have welcome visitor whether he likes or not and whether he is busy or not. Then next, if the owner is busy, he asks to visitor, "Would you wait for me?" Also the owner never speaks without opening his door.[11]

This example also illustrates how difficult it is to bring one's own cultural norm* into awareness. It is unlikely the "American friend" ever knew that he insulted the young Korean.

High Anxiety

The fifth stumbling block is *high anxiety,* separately mentioned for the purpose of emphasis. Unlike the other four (language, illusive nonverbal cues, preconceptions and stereotypes, and the practice of immediate evaluation), the stumbling block of anxiety is not distinct but underlies and compounds the others. The presence of high anxiety/tension is very common in cross-cultural experiences because of the uncertainties present. An international student says it well:

> During those several months after my arrival in the U.S.A., every day I came back from school exhausted so that I had to take a rest for a while, stretching myself on the bed. For all the time, I strained every nerve in order to understand what the people were saying and make myself understood in my broken English. When I don't understand what American people are talking about and why they are laughing, I sometimes have to pretend to understand by smiling, even though I feel alienated, uneasy and tense.
>
> In addition to this, the difference in culture or customs, the way of thinking between two countries, produces more tension because we don't know how we should react to totally foreign customs or attitudes, and sometimes we can't guess how the people from another country react to my saying or behavior. We always have a fear somewhere in the bottom of our hearts that there are much more chances of breakdown in intercultural communication than in communication with our own fellow countrymen.[12]

---

cultural norm: standard regarded as typical or appropriate for a specific cultural group

The native of the country is uncomfortable when talking with a foreigner because he cannot maintain the normal flow of verbal and non-verbal interaction to sustain the conversation. He is also threatened by the unknown other's knowledge, experience, and evaluation—the visitor's potential for scrutiny and rejection of himself and his country. The inevitable question, "How do you like it here?" which the foreigner abhors, is the host's quest for reassurance, or at least the "feeler" that reduces the unknown and gives him ground for defense if that seems necessary.

The foreign member of the dyad is under the same threat, with the added tension of having to cope with the differing pace, climate, and culture. The first few months he feels helpless in coping with messages that swamp him and to which his reactions may be inappropriate. His self-esteem is often intolerably undermined when he employs such defenses as withdrawal into his own reference group* or into himself, screening out or misperceiving stimuli, rationalizing, overcompensating, even hostility—none of which leads to effective communication.

Conclusion

Since all of the communication barriers mentioned are hard to remove, the only simple solution seems to be to tell everybody to stay home. This advice obviously is unacceptable, so it is fortunate that a few paths are being laid around the obstacles. Communication theorists are continuing to offer new insights and are focusing on problem areas of this complex process.[13] Educators and linguists are improving methods of learning a second language. The nonverbal area, made familiar by Edward T. Hall in his famous books *The Silent Language* and *The Hidden Dimension,* is getting a singular amount of attention.[14] The ray of hope offered by Hall and others is that nonverbal cues, culturally controlled and largely out-of-awareness, can be discovered and even understood when the communicator knows enough to look for them, is alert to the varying interpretations possible, and is free enough from tension and psychological defenses to notice them.

In addition, textbooks are appearing and communication specialists are improving means for increasing sensitivity to the messages coming from others in an intercultural setting.[15] Professional associations are giving increased amounts of attention to intercultural communication, and new societies such as the Society for Intercultural Education, Training and Research are being developed. The International and Intercultural Communication Annual[16] has a complete listing of these.

What the interpersonal intercultural communicator must seek to achieve can be summarized by two quotations. The first is by Roger Harrison, who says:

> The communicator cannot stop at knowing that the people he is
> working with have different customs, goals, and thought patterns
> from his own. He must be able to feel his way into intimate contact

reference group: the group of people with whom one has something in common, such as nationality or native language

with these alien values, attitudes, and feelings. He must be able to work with them and within them, neither losing his own values in the confrontation nor protecting himself behind a wall of intellectual detachment.[17]

Robert T. Oliver phrases it thus: "If we would communicate across cultural barriers, we must learn what to say and how to say it in terms of the expectations and predispositions of those we want to listen."[18]

References

1. Marshall R. Singer, "Culture: A Perceptual Approach," in *Readings in Intercultural Communication.* Vol. I (Regional Council for International Education, University of Pittsburgh), and Edward T. Hall, *The Hidden Dimension* (New York: Doubleday and Company, Inc., 1966), p. 2.

2. Edward T. Hall, *The Silent Language* (Greenwich, Conn.: Fawcett Publications, Inc., 1959).

3. Charles Frankel, *The Neglected Aspect of Foreign Affairs* (Washington, D.C.: Brookings Institution, 1965), p. 1.

4. Taken from student papers in a course in intercultural communication taught by the author.

5. For one discussion of this concept, see Daryl J. Bem, *Beliefs, Attitudes, and Human Affairs* (Belmont, Calif.: Brooks/Cole Publishing Co., 1970), p. 9.

6. Margaret Mead, "The Cultural Perspective," in *Communication or Conflict,* ed. Mary Capes (Association Press, 1960).

7. Edward C. Stewart, *American Cultural Patterns: A Cross-cultural Perspective* (Pittsburgh, Pa.: Regional Council for International Education, University of Pittsburgh, April 1971), p. 14.

8. Frankel, *The Neglected Aspect of Foreign Affairs,* p. 103.

9. Ernest Becker, *The Birth and Death of Meaning* (New York: Free Press, 1962), pp. 84–89.

10. Carolyn W. Sherif, Musafe Sherif, and Roger E. Nebergall, *Attitude and Attitude Change* (Philadelphia: W.B. Saunders Co., 1965), p. vi.

11. &12. Taken from a student's paper in a course in intercultural communication taught by the author.

13. An early book, now in its second edition, which adapted the language of information theory to communication and stressed the influence of culture, remains one of the best sources: *Communication: The Social Matrix of Psychiatry* by Jurgen Ruesch and Gregory Bateson (New York: W. W. Norton & Co., 1968).

14. See, for example, *Silent Messages* by Albert Mehrabian (Belmont, Calif.: Wadsworth Publishing Co., 1971).

15. Sources include: Edward D. Stewart, "The Simulation of Cultural Differences," *The Journal of Communication,* Vol. 16, December 1966; Alfred J. Kraemer, *The Development of Cultural Self-awareness Design of a Program of Instruction* (George Washington University, Human Resources Research Office, Professional Paper 27–69, August 1969); David Hoopes, Ed., *Readings in Intercultural Communication,* Vols. I–IV. (Regional Council for International Education, University of Pittsburgh).

16. *International and Intercultural Communication Annual,* Vol. 1, December 1974, published by Speech Communication Association, Statler Hilton Hotel, New York.

17. Roger Harrison, "The Design of Cross-cultural Training: An Alternative to the University Model," in *Explorations in Human Relations Training and Research* (Bethesda, Md.: National Training Laboratories, 1966), NEA No. 2, p. 4.

18. Robert T. Oliver, *Culture and Communication: The Problem of Penetrating National and Cultural Boundaries* (Springfield, Ill.: Charles C. Thomas, 1962), p. 154.

Write before You Read

The following reading selection is entitled "Social Time: The Heartbeat of Culture." Before reading, observe people's sense of time by arriving early to one of your classes and noting what time the instructor and students arrive and how they behave at the moment of arrival. Record your observations in detail.

Share with classmates what you have observed. Discuss what you have all discovered.

Social Time: The Heartbeat of Culture

Robert Levine, with Ellen Wolff

About the Authors   Robert Levine, professor of psychology at California State University at Fresno, collaborated with Ellen Wolff, a freelance writer, to write "Social Time: The Heartbeat of Culture."

The Context of the Reading   "Social Time: The Heartbeat of Culture" was originally published in 1985 in *Psychology Today,* a monthly magazine that makes research findings accessible to a nonprofessional audience.

Levine uses the following Portuguese expressions:

☐ *Hola:* Hi
☐ *Tudo bem?:* Is everything okay?
☐ *Manhã:* shortened form of the word *amanhã,* which means "tomorrow"

"If *a man does not keep pace with his companions, perhaps it is because he hears a different drummer."* This thought by Thoreau strikes a chord in so many people that it has become part of our language. We use the phrase "the beat of a different drummer" to explain any pace of life unlike our own. Such colorful vagueness reveals how informal our rules of time really are. The world over, children simply "pick up" their society's time concepts as they mature. No dictionary clearly defines the meaning of "early" or "late" for them or for strangers who stumble over the maddening incongruities between the time sense they bring with them and the one they face in a new land.

I learned this firsthand, a few years ago, and the resulting culture shock led me halfway around the world to find answers. It seemed clear that time "talks." But what is it telling us?

My journey started shortly after I accepted an appointment as visiting professor of psychology at the federal university in Niteroi, Brazil, a midsized city across the bay from Rio de Janeiro. As I left home for my first day of class, I asked someone the time. It was 9:05 A.M., which allowed me time to relax and look around the campus before my 10 o'clock lecture. After what I judged to be half an hour, I glanced at a clock I was passing. It said 10:20! In panic, I broke for the classroom, followed by gentle calls of

New York, New York: pounding the pavement at a pretty pace.

"Hola, professor" and "Tudo bem, professor?" from unhurried students, many of whom, I later realized, were my own. I arrived breathless to find an empty room.

Frantically, I asked a passerby the time. "Nine forty-five" was the answer. No, that couldn't be. I asked someone else. "Nine fifty-five." Another said: "Exactly 9:43." The clock in a nearby office read 3:15. I had learned my first lesson about Brazilians: Their timepieces are consistently inaccurate. And nobody minds.

My class was scheduled from 10 until noon. Many students came late, some very late. Several arrived after 10:30. A few showed up closer to 11. Two came after that. All of the latecomers wore the relaxed smiles that I came, later, to enjoy. Each one said hello, although a few apologized briefly, none seemed terribly concerned about lateness. They assumed that I understood.

The idea of Brazilians arriving late was not a great shock. I had heard about "manhã," the Portuguese equivalent of "mañana" in Spanish. This term, meaning "tomorrow" or "the morning," stereotypes the

Brazilian who puts off the business of today until tomorrow. The real surprise came at noon that first day, when the end of class arrived.

Back home in California, I never need to look at a clock to know when the class hour is ending. The shuffling of books is accompanied by strained expressions that say plaintively, "I'm starving. . . . I've got to go to the bathroom. . . . I'm going to suffocate if you keep us one more second." (The pain usually becomes unbearable at two minutes to the hour in undergraduate classes and five minutes before the close of graduate classes.)

When noon arrived in my first Brazilian class, only a few students left immediately. Others slowly drifted out during the next 15 minutes, and some continued asking me questions long after that. When several remaining students kicked off their shoes at 12:30, I went into my own "starving/bathroom/suffocation" routine.

I could not, in all honesty, attribute their lingering to my superb teaching style. I had just spent two hours lecturing on statistics in halting Portuguese. Apparently, for many of my students, staying late was simply of no more importance than arriving late in the first place. As I observed this casual approach in infinite variations during the year, I learned that the "manhã" stereotype oversimplified the real Anglo/Brazilian differences in conceptions of time. Research revealed a more complex picture.

With the assistance of colleagues Laurie West and Harry Reis, I compared the time sense of 91 male and female students in Niteroi with that of 107 similar students at California State University in Fresno. The universities are similar in academic quality and size, and the cities are both secondary metropolitan centers with populations of about 350,000.

We asked students about their perceptions of time in several situations, such as what they could consider late or early for a hypothetical lunch appointment with a friend. The average Brazilian student defined lateness for lunch as 33½ minutes after the scheduled time, compared to 19 minutes for the Fresno students. But Brazilians also allowed an average of about 54 minutes before they'd consider someone early, while the Fresno students drew the line at 24.

Are Brazilians simply more flexible in their concepts of time and punctuality? And how does this relate to the stereotype of the apathetic, fatalistic and irresponsible Latin temperament? When we asked students to give typical reasons for lateness, the Brazilians were less likely to attribute it to a lack of caring than the North Americans were. Instead, they pointed to unforeseen circumstances that the person couldn't control. Because they seemed less inclined to feel personally responsible for being late, they also expressed less regret for their own lateness and blamed others less when they were late.

We found similar differences in how students from the two countries characterized people who were late for appointments. Unlike their North American counterparts, the Brazilian students believed that a person who is consistently late is probably more successful than one who is consistently on time. They seemed to accept the idea that someone of status is expected to arrive late. Lack of punctuality is a badge of success.

Tokyo, Japan: Lead, follow or get out of the way.

Even within our own country, of course, ideas of time and punctuality vary considerably from place to place. Different regions and even cities have their own distinct rhythms and rules. Seemingly simple words like "now," snapped out by an impatient New Yorker, and "later," said by a relaxed Californian, suggest a world of difference. Despite our familiarity with these homegrown differences in tempo, problems with time present a major stumbling block to Americans abroad. Peace Corps volunteers told researchers James Spradley of Macalester College and Mark Phillips of the University of Washington that their greatest difficulties with other people, after language problems, were the general pace of life and the punctuality of others. Formal "clock time" may be a standard on which the world agrees, but "social time," the heartbeat of society, is something else again.

How a country paces its social life is a mystery to most outsiders, one that we're just beginning to unravel. Twenty-six years ago, anthropologist Edward Hall noted in *The Silent Language* that informal patterns of time "are seldom, if ever, made explicit. They exist in the air around us. They are either familiar and comfortable, or unfamiliar and wrong." When we realize we are out of step, we often blame the people around us to make ourselves feel better.

Appreciating cultural differences in time sense becomes increasingly important as modern communications put more and more people in daily contact. If we are to avoid misreading issues that involve time perceptions, we need to understand better our own cultural biases and those of others.

Florence, Italy: living at a leisurely pace, particularly at the post office.

When people of different cultures interact, the potential for misunderstanding exists on many levels. For example, members of Arab and Latin cultures usually stand much closer when they are speaking to people than we usually do in the United States, a fact we frequently misinterpret as aggression or disrespect. Similarly, we assign personality traits to groups with a pace of life that is markedly faster or slower than our own. We build ideas of national character, for example, around the traditional Swiss and German ability to "make the trains run on time." Westerners like ourselves define punctuality using precise measures of time: 5 minutes, 15 minutes, an hour. But according to Hall, in many Mediterranean Arab cultures there are only three sets of time: no time at all, now (which is of varying duration) and forever (too long). Because of this, Americans often find difficulty in getting Arabs to distinguish between waiting a long time and a very long time.

According to historian Will Durant, "No man in a hurry is quite civilized." What do our time judgments say about our attitude toward life? How can a North American, coming from a land of digital precision, relate to a North African who may consider a clock "the devil's mill"?

Each language has a vocabulary of time that does not always survive translation. When we translated our questionnaires into Portuguese for my Brazilian students, we found that English distinctions of time were not readily articulated in their language. Several of our questions concerned how long the respondent would wait for someone to arrive, as compared with when they hoped for arrival or actually expected the person

Solo, Indonesia: Volleyball, anyone? There's always time for a friendly game.

would come. In Portuguese, the verbs "to wait for," "to hope for" and "to expect" are all translated as "esperar." We had to add further words of explanation to make the distinction clear to the Brazilian students.

To avoid these language problems, my Fresno colleague Kathy Bartlett and I decided to clock the pace of life in other countries by using as little language as possible. We looked directly at three basic indicators of time: the accuracy of a country's bank clocks, the speed at which pedestrians walked and the average time it took a postal clerk to sell us a single stamp. In six countries on three continents, we made observations in both the nation's largest urban area and a medium-sized city: Japan (Tokyo and Sendai), Taiwan (Taipei and Tainan), Indonesia (Jakarta and Solo), Italy (Rome and Florence), England (London and Bristol) and the United States (New York City and Rochester).

What we wanted to know was: Can we speak of a unitary concept called "pace of life"? What we've learned suggests that we can. There appears to be a very strong relationship (see chart on p. 90) between the accuracy of clock time, walking speed and postal efficiency across the countries we studied.

We checked 15 clocks in each city, selecting them at random in downtown banks and comparing the time they showed with that reported by the local telephone company. In Japan, which leads the way in accuracy, the clocks averaged just over half a minute early or late. Indonesian clocks, the least accurate, were more than three minutes off the mark.

I will be interested to see how the digital-information age will affect our perceptions of time. In the United States today, we are reminded of the exact hour of the day more than ever, through little symphonies of beeps emanating from people's digital watches. As they become the norm, I fear our sense of precision may take an absurd twist. The other day, when I asked for the time, a student looked at his watch and replied, "Three twelve and eighteen seconds."

"'Will you walk a little faster?' said a whiting to a snail. 'There's a porpoise close behind us, and he's treading on my tail.'"

So goes the rhyme from *Alice in Wonderland,* which also gave us that famous symbol of haste, the White Rabbit. He came to mind often as we measured the walking speeds in our experimental cities. We clocked how long it took pedestrians to walk 100 feet along a main downtown street during business hours on clear days. To eliminate the effects of socializing, we observed only people walking alone, timing at least 100 in each city. We found, once again, that the Japanese led the way, averaging just 20.7 seconds to cover the distance. The English nosed out the Americans for second place—21.6 to 22.5 seconds—and the Indonesians again trailed the pack, sauntering along at 27.2 seconds. As you might guess, speed was greater in the larger city of each nation than in its smaller one.

Our final measurement, the average time it took postal clerks to sell one stamp, turned out to be less straightforward than we expected. In each city, including those in the United States, we presented clerks with a note in the native language requesting a common-priced stamp. . . . They were also handed paper money, the equivalent of a $5 bill. In Indonesia, this procedure led to more than we bargained for.

At the large central post office in Jakarta, I asked for the line to buy stamps and was directed to a group of private vendors sitting outside. Each of them hustled for my business: "Hey, good stamps, mister!" "Best stamps here!" In the smaller city of Solo, I found a volleyball game in progress when I arrived at the main post office on Friday afternoon. Business hours, I was told, were over. When I finally did get there during business hours, the clerk was more interested in discussing relatives in America. Would I like to meet his uncle in Cincinnati? Which did I like

□□□ **The Pace of Life in Six Countries**			
	Accuracy of Bank Clocks	**Walking Speed**	**Post Office Speed**
Japan	1	1	1
United States	2	3	2
England	4	2	3
Italy	5	4	6
Taiwan	3	5	4
Indonesia	6	6	5

Numbers (1 is the top value) indicate the comparative rankings of each country for each indicator of time sense.

better: California or the United States? Five people behind me in line waited patiently. Instead of complaining, they began paying attention to our conversation.

When it came to efficiency of service, however, the Indonesians were not the slowest, although they did place far behind the Japanese postal clerks, who averaged 25 seconds. That distinction went to the Italians, whose infamous postal service took 47 seconds on the average.

"A man who wastes one hour of time has not discovered the meaning of life. . . ."

That was Charles Darwin's belief, and many share it, perhaps at the cost of their health. My colleagues and I have recently begun studying the relationship between pace of life and well-being. Other researchers have demonstrated that a chronic sense of urgency is a basic component of the Type A, coronary-prone personality. We expect that future research will demonstrate that pace of life is related to rate of heart disease, hypertension, ulcers, suicide, alcoholism, divorce and other indicators of general psychological and physical well-being.

As you envision tomorrow's international society, do you wonder who will set the pace? Americans eye Japan carefully, because the Japanese are obviously "ahead of us" in measurable ways. In both countries, speed is frequently confused with progress. Perhaps looking carefully at the different paces of life around the world will help us distinguish more accurately between the two qualities. Clues are everywhere but sometimes hard to distinguish. You have to listen carefully to hear the beat of even your own drummer.

Write before You Read

The following reading selection is entitled "Creativity in the Classroom." Before reading, observe one of your own classroom settings. Take notes on the instructor's teaching style. Does the instructor lecture? ask questions? lead discussions? sit? stand? move around? (Additionally or alternatively, you may want to note the students' classroom behavior.)

Share with classmates what you have observed.

Creativity in the Classroom

Ernest L. Boyer

About the Author   Ernest L. Boyer is the president of the Carnegie Foundation for the Advancement of Teaching and senior fellow at the Woodrow Wilson School of Public and International Affairs, Princeton University. A former U.S. commissioner of education, he is a highly regarded educational researcher.

The Context of the Reading   "Creativity in the Classroom" is the first section of the ninth chapter of Boyer's book *College: The Undergraduate Experience in America* (1987). The book is a report based on research done by a team of 16 observer-reporters sponsored by the Carnegie Foundation for the Advancement of Teaching. The team visited 29 four-year public and private colleges and universities during a fall semester. The observers spent approximately two weeks at each institution, interviewing officials, faculty, and students and observing classrooms and other activities. In addition, researchers conducted a national survey with 5,000 faculty members and 4,500 undergraduates to discover their attitudes toward teaching and learning.

At a freshman psychology lecture we attended, 300 students were still finding seats when the professor started talking. "Today," he said into the microphone, "we will continue our discussion of learning." He might as well have been addressing a crowd in a Greyhound bus terminal. Like commuters marking time until their next departure, students in this class alternately read the newspaper, flipped through a paperback novel, or propped their feet on the chairs ahead of them, staring into space. Only when the professor defined a term which, he said, "might appear on an exam" did they look up and start taking notes.[1]

What we found in many classrooms was a mismatch between faculty and student expectations, a gap that left both parties unfulfilled. Faculty, concerned with scholarship, wanted to share ideas with students, who were expected to appreciate what professors do. This appreciation might exist in graduate or upper-division courses, where teachers and students have overlapping interests, but we found that often this was not the case in lower-division courses.

"If you're batting .666 in attendance, you're doing well," one faculty member complained, implying that if only two out of three students attend a class, it was a success. Another asserted: "Students don't seem to have the attention span they used to. It's hard to hold their interest. You practically have to do a song and dance, and I won't do that." An English teacher described the learning climate on his campus as one of "intellectual meekness."[2]

As for students, they are remarkably conscious of grades, willing to conform to the formula for success. A sophomore in a pre-med program said she wanted her courses to be spelled out "with no surprises. My goal is to get a good background so I can pass the MCAT [Medical College Admission Test] and I'm not interested in hearing about the professor's Ph.D. dissertation."[3]

"A college degree isn't enough," said one honors student. "You've got to have a good GPA to get into graduate school, or get a first-rate job." Another commented: "People at this college are very résumé-conscious. Undergraduates are afraid of controversy. They hesitate to participate in vigorous give and take on any topic. The main thing is to prepare for the exam."[4]

If faculty and students do not see themselves as having important business to do together, prospects for effective learning are diminished. If students view teachers as distant and their material as irrelevant, what could be a time of exciting exploration is reduced to a series of uninspired routines.

The most discouraging comment came from a professor who said he *liked* the passivity of students. "With these students, not everything has to be proven. . . . Some people say this is a return to the fifties. Perhaps, and that isn't all bad. . . . We didn't feel we knew it all and neither do they. For the first time in a while, I don't feel a generation gap."[5]

This "no hassle" attitude was vividly revealed in the classroom at a prestigious Northeast college. Students in a Gothic fiction course had been asked to read all of Peter Straub's novel *Ghost Story*. When they assembled the following Monday morning, only six of the sixty students in a large lecture hall raised their hands when asked who had done the reading. A few volunteered that they were halfway through the novel, but most admitted that they hadn't cracked the book. The professor then took all of his ninety-minute lecture to review the plot. Some students took notes. At the end of class he apologized: "I'm sorry if I spoiled the finish for those of you who haven't gotten there yet." But no one looked disappointed. They'd just received all the information they needed for an upcoming test and wouldn't have to read.[6]

A science professor stated this frustration: "How am I to cover difficult and important material when students are unwilling to really work? Sure, they'll cram for tests but they want to be spoon-fed, and when I try to get them interested in more substantial matters only a few respond. I'm pretty discouraged with students."[7]

Students are just as quick to switch the blame to their professors. One student said, "Why should I be interested in the class if the professor acts bored?" Another student agreed and added, "There's nothing worse than my biology professor, who acts as though he's doing us a big favor by teaching us about photosynthesis. Believe me, he's not doing me a favor." Still another student said, "Most of my professors are great. But I have one who makes it clear that he'd rather be in his laboratory conducting research than standing in front of two hundred students."[8]

At a large university with many teaching assistants who handle labs and discussion sections, students resent the lack of attention from the professor, suspecting (correctly) that only the T.A. will see and grade their work during the course of the quarter. In particular departments, foreign teaching assistants are a problem. Mathematicians, according to the arts and science dean, are "hard to hire in this city, unless they're foreign students who can barely speak English."[9]

Students are quick to praise their teachers, too. One said, "I love my history professor. I don't even like history but he makes it so interesting that I really want to go to class." Another said, "I like the professors who have a sense of humor. They come into class, joke around a little, and then start the lecture." Students also praise their professors for being available after class. Another student: "The professors here will go out of their way to find time to see if you need help or want to discuss something." Said another: "This college has a good academic reputation. So, I knew the classes were going to be hard. I didn't know they were going to be as hard as they are, though. Still, that's why I'm here!"[10]

One sophomore said, "My biology teacher is the worst. He is all biology. He comes in and starts talking. It's like he's not even human." She continued, "But my French teacher is great. He comes into class, talks informally with us before he begins the lecture. I feel like he really gets to know his students." A senior engineering major said, "The best teachers are those that really care about their students. I've never had a professor who wouldn't find time to talk with you after class, but some professors really make an effort to get to know their students. I also like professors who act like they're interested in what they're teaching."[11]

This mixed response, the ambivalence we found to teaching and learning, was reinforced in our national survey. Most students are quite satisfied with the teaching on their campus, but the pressure to get good grades diminishes their enthusiasm. Almost two thirds say they are under great pressure to get high grades; about one third feel it is difficult to get good grades and still "really learn something." Forty-three percent of today's undergraduates also say that many students at their institutions succeeded by "beating the system" rather than by studying (Table 1). The cheating on assignments, the term papers students buy, the shortcuts to duplicating homework assignments—all enhance the cynicism of students and erode the quality of education.

Do professors take a personal interest in the academic progress of their students? At liberal arts colleges 73 percent of the students feel they do. The proportion dropped to 59 percent when all institutions were counted. On the matter of classroom participation, we found that 81 percent of liberal arts college students feel they are encouraged to "discuss their feelings about important issues"; but that's true for only 66 percent of the total sample. Students at liberal arts colleges are also far more

□□□ **Table 1. Student Attitudes toward Course Grades, 1976 and 1984 (percent who agree)**

1984: By Type of Institution

	All Institutions 1976	All Institutions 1984	Public	Private	Research University	Doctorate-Granting University	Comprehensive College	Liberal Arts College
I am under a great deal of pressure to get high grades.	58	64	66	59	71	62	63	55
It is difficult both to get good grades and really learn something.	36	34	35	31	41	33	31	32
Many successful students at my college make it by "beating the system" rather than by studying.	50	43	44	37	43	43	44	36

Source: The Carnegie Foundation for the Advancement of Teaching, National Survey of Undergraduates, 1976 and 1984.

satisfied with the teaching they receive. And a higher percentage of these students believe their teachers look out for their interests.

On a nonacademic level, students at liberal arts colleges are more inclined to seek personal advice from professors than are students at all institutions. When asked whether professors encourage them to participate in classroom discussion, 91 percent of the students at liberal arts colleges said yes—10 percent more than undergraduates at all colleges and universities (Table 2).

Class size, like so many other aspects of teaching and learning, varies from one type of institution to another. Twenty-nine percent of the students at research universities report that "most" or "all" of their classes have more than one hundred students enrolled; at liberal arts colleges only 1 percent of the students report having most or all classes of this size. At the other end, only 5 percent of students at research universities said they had *no* classes larger than one hundred students. At liberal arts colleges, it was 80 percent (Table 3).

We also discovered that, for most undergraduates, the freshman and sophomore classes (often the general education sections) are the ones most likely to be overloaded. Further, we found that at large institutions these classes are often taught by graduate assistants or junior professors. Forty-one percent of the students we surveyed report that "general education courses are rarely taught by the best faculty members in the departments in which they are given." And 37 percent said, "General education courses reflect the interests of the faculty" rather than of the students (Table 4).

We concluded that one important way to measure a college's commitment to undergraduate education is to look at class size in general education. Do these courses enroll hundreds of students? Are they taught by senior professors? Do students have an opportunity to meet with their teachers? A college or university that does not give top priority to the basic undergraduate courses is not fully committed to excellence in education.

A significant number of students we interviewed said they had no objection to being in a large lecture course; others, however, strongly favored small classes that allow discussion. A math professor in a small university went so far as to say that if he had been introduced to mathematics in the kind of large, distracting lecture hall he himself was teaching in, he would never have continued to study the subject.[12] We strongly urge, therefore, that the finest teachers should teach freshmen, and that undergraduate classes should be small enough for students to have lively intellectual interaction with teachers and fellow students.

In the early American college the primary method of instruction was recitation, a process in which students repeated from memory, often verbatim, textbook assignments. For disputation, students defended or attacked a proposition in Latin, the required language both in and out of class.[13] By the mid–eighteenth century, the lecture by teachers occasionally supplemented student recitations. Lectures were, however, a talking textbook as instructors read slowly and students copied down what was said, word for word.

□□□ **Table 2. Students' Appraisal of Their College Professors and Teaching, 1976 and 1984** (percent who agree)

	All Institutions		1984: By Type of Institution					
	1976	1984	Public	Private	Research University	Doctorate-Granting University	Comprehensive College	Liberal Arts College
Overall, I am satisfied with the teaching I have received.	69	71	68	81	68	68	71	85
There are professors at my college who take a personal interest in my academic progress.	63	59	57	68	52	56	61	73
Professors at my college encourage students to discuss their feelings about important issues.	NA	66	63	74	59	63	67	81
On the whole, I trust the faculty here to look out for students' interests.	75	75	72	84	71	72	75	88
There are professors at my college whom I feel free to turn to for advice on personal matters.	53	39	36	49	30	37	41	54
Most of my professors encourage students to actively participate in classroom discussion.	NA	81	79	88	74	79	83	71

NA: Question not asked in 1976.
Source: The Carnegie Foundation for the Advancement of Teaching, National Survey of Undergraduates, 1976 and 1984.

Table 3. Frequency of Classes Larger than 100 Students (percent of undergraduates reporting)

1984: By Type of Institution

	All Institutions 1976	All Institutions 1984	Public	Private	Research University	Doctorate-Granting University	Comprehensive College	Liberal Arts College
All	1	1	2	1	3	2	1	1
Most	9	11	13	4	26	14	4	0
Several/few	54	52	58	28	66	68	46	19
None	36	36	27	67	5	16	49	80

Source: The Carnegie Foundation for the Advancement of Teaching, National Survey of Undergraduates, 1976 and 1984.

Table 4. Students' Evaluation of General Education at Their College (percent who agree)

1984: By Type of Institution

	Total	Public	Private	Research University	Doctorate-Granting University	Comprehensive College	Liberal Arts College
General education courses are rarely taught by the best faculty members in the departments in which they are given.	41	43	32	47	45	39	28
General education courses reflect the interests of the faculty and departments rather than broad student interests.	37	38	35	34	35	41	31

Source: The Carnegie Foundation for the Advancement of Teaching, National Survey of Undergraduates, 1984.

The lecture slowly replaced recitation and disputations. There was new knowledge to be conveyed, and it became more difficult to call on all students in the enlarged classes. Another sign of the times: The blackboard was first used by a teacher at Bowdoin College in about 1823.[14] And experiments with the seminar, a German import, were introduced in the mid–nineteenth century. According to Arthur Levine, in his significant *Handbook on Undergraduate Curriculum,* it was in 1869 that Charles Kendall Adams tried the seminar at The University of Michigan. "Seven years later it became a staple in the curriculum at Johns Hopkins. . . . A discussion class, designed to supplement lecture instruction originally called the 'conference quiz section,' was created at Harvard in 1904."[15]

Today, the lecture method is preferred by most professors. With few exceptions, when we visited classes, the teacher stood in front of rows of chairs and talked most of the forty-five or fifty minutes. Information was presented that often students passively received. There was little opportunity for positions to be clarified or ideas challenged.

There are times, of course, when lecturing is necessary to convey essential issues and ideas and also to handle large numbers of students. At other times, such a procedure seems inappropriate, especially when the class is small and much of the material being presented is available in the text.

When discussion did occur in classes we visited, a handful of students, usually men, dominated the exchange. We were especially struck by the subtle yet significant differences in the way men and women participated in class. This situation persists despite the ascendancy of female enrollments on most campuses.

Women now make up over half of all undergraduate enrollments and they get the majority of bachelor's and master's degrees. In 1963 about half of all women undergraduates majored in education. In 1983 only 15 percent were doing so. They receive 32 percent of the academic doctorates awarded, 25 percent of those in medicine, and 33 percent in law.[16]

Still, in many classrooms women are overshadowed. Even the brightest women students often remain silent. They may submit excellent written work, and will frequently wait until after class to approach a teacher privately about issues raised in the discussion. But it is the men who seem most often to be recognized and talk most in class. Not only do men talk more, but what they say often carries more weight. This pattern of classroom leaders and followers is set very early in the term.[17]

We agree with Mortimer Adler's conclusion that "all genuine learning is active, not passive. It involves the use of the mind, not just the memory. It is a process of discovery in which the student is the main agent, not the teacher."[18] And all students, not just the most aggressive or most verbal, should be actively engaged. It is unacceptable for a few students to participate in the give and take with teachers while others are allowed to be mere spectators.

On a related matter, we frequently were struck by the competitive climate in the classroom. Since as a democracy we are committed to equality of opportunity, and since in a vital society we need some way of bringing talent forward, we use, both on and off the campus, the calculus of competition to stimulate ambition and achievement. We must do this, or else we lack essential leadership in all areas of life.

However, if democracy is to be well served, cooperation is essential too. And the goal of community, which is threaded throughout this report, is essentially related to the academic program, and, most especially, to procedures in the classroom. We urge, therefore, that students be asked to participate in collaborative projects, that they work together occasionally on group assignments, that special effort be made, through small seminar units within large lecture sections, to create conditions that underscore the point that cooperation is as essential as competition in the classroom.

The undergraduate experience, at its best, means active learning and disciplined inquiry that leads to the intellectual empowerment of students. Professor Carl Schorske, at Princeton University, says that the test of a good teacher is "Do you regard 'learning' as a noun or a verb? If as a noun, as a thing to be possessed and passed along, then you present your truths, neatly packaged, to your students. But if you see 'learning' as a verb!—the process is different."[19]

While the college teaching we observed was often uninspired, we still found exciting examples of outstanding teaching at many institutions. One professor of English spoke to our site visitor as follows: "At this college there's a lot of emphasis on teaching and there's a lot of good teaching. I like that because teaching is my real vocation. I feel most strongly about that." Another professor also enthusiastically endorsed his role as teacher: "This college is not filled with many academic bright lights. Students work hard and they really care about their studies. The fact that many are 'average' doesn't bother me. My favorite image of a teacher is that of the midwife encouraging students, coaching them. What you really do in the classroom is help students come to know their own mind—become independent thinkers. These students have potential, but they have to have more confidence academically. It's our job to bring it out of them."[20]

One Monday morning, at a New England college, we visited an "Introduction to Philosophy" course. The subject for the day was a problem from Thomas Aquinas: If God is all-powerful and all-good, how can there be evil in the world? The students offered answers: because salvation must be achieved through suffering, because Adam's sin produced suffering, because God just set the world in motion and didn't know how everything would turn out. "You're revising the premise," the professor responded to the last answer. "Your God is not all-powerful, he's only good-intentioned."[21]

A student asked: "Why would you worship a God who is not all-powerful?" "Why not?" asked another. And so it went, with many hands raised and ideas flowing so fast that the professor had to intervene often to sort out key points and keep the discussion on course. "Today's students are poorly equipped to deal with questions about ethics," he told us later. "I think they're unaccustomed to reasoning." Yet, he persisted in engaging students in active forms of inquiry, providing them experience in addressing questions of ethics and challenging them to learn.[22]

At a public institution in the West, we visited a mid-afternoon class in European history, with about one hundred students. The day's lecture was on the influence of the writings of the French philosophers on the enlightened despots of the eighteenth century. "Did Voltaire and Diderot favor a radical reconstruction of society?" the professor asked.

"No, they just wanted to reform society in some ways," a student answered.

"What ways?" the professor probed.

"To make it more rational."

"How can people be made more rational?"

"Through education."

"Did the Enlightenment writers want to introduce mass public education?"

"No, they still favored the aristocracy."

"Why was that?"

This exchanged continued through a discussion of how uniform legal codes developed. The professor lectured briefly, highlighting key themes, but he never stopped asking penetrating questions—and expecting thoughtful answers.[23]

In an upper-division Constitutional law class the professor used the "case method." Each student had been assigned to read summaries of a series of cases dealing with the president, Congress, and the courts. Guiding the discussion, the teacher would name a case and tell a student to give him "the principles we can take from this example." The classroom discussion was lively, with the instructor making it a point to call on different students instead of waiting for them to respond. He occasionally digressed from the set format with interesting historical asides, discussing, for example, Earl Warren's role in the internment of Japanese citizens during World War II. He also tried, when possible, to tell students what was going on in the Supreme Court right now that related to the issues and cases they discussed.[24]

In a class in the history of modern music, we watched the instructor, through a combination of knowledge, enthusiasm, humor, recordings, and exercises, keep the class engaged—even excited—through a ninety-minute session on the early technique in the music of Arnold Schönberg.[25] In a freshman chemistry class, the professor spent the entire period on problem-solving techniques, hoping to break students of the habit of "looking for plug-in formulas" to solve problems.[26]

In a seminar called "Women in Literature," some students who were obviously not impressed with *Jane Eyre* were kept intellectually engaged through a compelling and at times humorous lecture style. "So she faints. Why? Look, you can't have a nineteenth-century novel without somebody fainting. All right? All right." Then: "Okay, let's go through some of your objections to the novel. The diction is first on the list, right?"[27]

At a New England college, we visited a course in French literature conducted entirely in French. The seventeen students enrolled had read Rousseau's *Discourse on the Origin of Inequality* for homework. In class, the professor asked questions about the style and substance of the work: What does Rousseau say is the basis of human inequality? How would people label Rousseau were he to present his ideas today? What was the source of evil for Rousseau? For whom was he writing? What was his tone? Students seemed generally comfortable with discussing the work in French and were able to pinpoint passages from the text to illustrate their answers.[28]

The professor corrected their grammar and pronunciation from time to time. One student, for example, spoke as if *l'amour du bien-être*—love of comfort—were the same as *l'amour*—love. The professor asked her to translate the words literally into English, and she figured out her mistake for herself. But the professor's main emphasis was at least as much on creativity, on original thinking, as on the mastery of French.[29]

The central qualities that make for successful teaching can be simply stated: command of the material to be taught, a contagious enthusiasm for the play of ideas, optimism about human potential, the involvement with one's students, and—not least—sensitivity, integrity, and warmth as a human being. When this combination is present in the classroom, the impact of a teacher can be powerful and enduring.

References

1. The Carnegie Foundation for the Advancement of Teaching, College Visits, 1984–85.
2. Ibid.
3. Ibid.
4. Ibid.
5. Quoted in Elaine Yaffe, "What Are Today's Students Really Like?" *Colorado College Bulletin,* February 1985, p. 7.
6. The Carnegie Foundation for the Advancement of Teaching, College Visits, 1984–85.
7. Ibid.
8. Ibid.
9. Ibid.
10. Ibid.
11. Ibid.
12. Ibid.
13. Arthur Levine, *Handbook on Undergraduate Curriculum* (San Francisco: Jossey-Bass, 1978), p. 171.
14. Ibid., p. 173.
15. Ibid., p. 173.
16. Andrew Hacker, "The Decline of Higher Learning," *New York Review of Books,* February 13, 1986, p. 7.
17. See the excellent discussion in Roberta M. Hall and Bernice R. Sandler, *The Classroom Climate: A Chilly One for Women?* (Washington, D.C.: Association of American Colleges, February 1982), pp. 7–8.

18. Mortimer J. Adler, *The Paideia Proposal: An Educational Manifesto* (New York: Macmillan, 1982), p. 23.

19. Quoted in William McCleery, *Conversations on the Character of Princeton* (Princeton, New Jersey: Princeton University Press, 1986), p. 106.

20. The Carnegie Foundation for the Advancement of Teaching, College Visits, 1984–85.

21. Ibid.

22. Ibid.

23. Ibid.

24. Ibid.

25. Ibid.

26. Ibid.

27. Ibid.

28. Ibid.

29. Ibid.

CHAPTER 7

Discussion Activities: Field Research

The discussion activities in Chapter 7 are designed to help you become engaged in the processes of reading and responding to the reading selections in Chapter 6. They are not meant to be rigid instructions that you must follow. Ideally, the activities will lead you to think through what you have read and to come to your own conclusions about what is significant.

Working with a partner, in a small group, or with the whole class, decide which material to cover and the amount of time to spend on each section. Allow for different responses to the various aspects of the reading.

Write after You Read: Making a Journal Entry

Writing about a selection just after reading it may help you remember and reflect on your reading experience. You can explore your response by recording your reactions in a journal entry, adapting the guidelines on page 9. Share what you have written.

Summarizing

Your goal in summarizing a reading based on field research can be to discover (1) the findings of the research and (2) what conclusions the author(s) draw(s) from the findings.

In a summary, you can describe the method as well as the results of the research by answering questions such as these:

☐ How was information gathered?

☐ What are the findings of the research?

☐ What conclusion is reached by the researcher(s)?

Share your summary with one or more classmates. Discuss the reasons for the differences in your summaries.

Note: Further guidelines for summarizing can be found in Chapter 21.

Analyzing

To analyze a reading, you can break it down into parts to examine those parts and their relationship.

The following suggestions are designed to help you analyze readings based on field research. As you make observations about the various elements of a reading selection, identify or read aloud corresponding passages.

Note: Not every suggestion will apply to every research article you read.

1. Discuss what you learn and find significant about how the research was conducted and explained (you may need to consult the background information about the reading). For example, you can focus on the following details:

   □ place, people, and time: where, with whom, and over what period of time the research took place

   □ methods used to gather information: conversations, observations, interviews, surveys, and so on

   □ the reason the research was done

2. Discuss passages that struck you for some reason. For example, you can focus on the following material:

   □ passages that you like

   □ passages that you find difficult to understand

   □ passages that you think reveal an important message or insight

3. Discuss what you learn and find significant about the evidence the writer provides to illustrate or support points: original observations, statistics, quotations, examples, facts, opinions, theories, definitions, references to other works, and so on. For example, you can focus on the following material:

   □ evidence that you think effectively clarifies complex points

   □ evidence that you find convincing

   □ evidence that you find unconvincing

4. Discuss counterarguments or evidence that might challenge the writer's conclusions.

5. Discuss what you learn or find significant about how the writer has structured the article. For example, you can focus on the following material:

   □ information or ideas provided in the opening paragraph(s)

   □ information or ideas provided in the middle paragraphs

   □ information or ideas provided in the ending

   □ transitions from one paragraph to the next

Making Connections

Making connections between a reading selection and something outside a reading selection—such as another reading or your own experience—can help uncover meanings.

1. Explore similarities and differences between one reading selection and another. Identify or read aloud relevant passages. The many comparisons you can make include the following:

   □ Compare experiences of and attitudes toward friendship in "Friends, Good Friends—and Such Good Friends" and "Myth, Reality and Shades of Gray: Comparing Same-Sex Friendships."

   □ Compare discussions of cross-cultural communication in "Intercultural Communication Stumbling Blocks" and "Social Time: The Heartbeat of Culture."

   □ Test the theories and generalizations in LaRay M. Barna's "Intercultural Communication Stumbling Blocks" against the experiences discussed in one or more of the readings based on experience: "The School Days of an Indian Girl" (p. 16), "College" (p. 25), and/or "Barriers" (p. 59).

   □ Compare discussions of college classrooms in "Creativity in the Classroom" and "The Commencement Speech You'll Never Hear" (p. 11).

2. Test the truth or validity of the evidence against your own experience and background knowledge. Identify or read aloud relevant passages.

   □ Explore whether the generalizations, theories, or experiences in the reading support or contradict what you have learned from experience.

   □ Explore whether the generalizations, theories, or experiences in the reading help you make sense of your own experience.

Guidelines for Writing from Field Research

Chapter 8 provides guidelines for fulfilling an assignment to write an essay based on your own field research.

The writing of one student, Ayse Yeyinmen, is included to show some of the strategies she used to conduct and write up her research. Her completed essay, "The Relationship between International and U.S.-born Students: Two Perspectives," is reprinted on pages 118–120. Ayse's work was selected as an example; it is not presented as a model to imitate.

SUGGESTED ESSAY ASSIGNMENTS

Select or adapt one of the following assignments, or devise your own assignment in consultation with your instructor.

1. Write an essay based on an interview with one person—or on conversations or interviews with several people—on a topic covered in a reading selection in this book or on another topic you want to learn more about. Adapt the guidelines for interviewing on pages 108–109.
2. Write an essay based on your observations of an activity on campus or in the community. Adapt the guidelines for observing on page 109.
3. Write an essay based on your own survey research on a topic covered in a reading selection in this book or on another topic you want to learn more about. Adapt the guidelines for constructing and distributing a questionnaire on pages 109–111. Allow sufficient time to design, distribute, collect, and analyze responses to the questionnaire.
4. Using yourself as the object of your research, write an essay in which you test against your own experience the theories or research findings discussed in a reading selection. Consider the ways in which the reading fits or helps you make sense of your experience—or does not.

   Note: You may want to consult Chapter 11, which provides guidelines for writing about essays, and/or Chapters 21–23, which provide guidelines for summarizing, paraphrasing, and quoting.

Note: The guidelines for different ways of conducting research are presented separately, for clarity. In the course of doing the research, however, you may want to combine strategies: observe *and* interview, conduct a survey *and* interviews, and so on. The strategies are designed to help you in your research and composing; they are not meant to be taken as rigid instructions that you must follow.

Gathering Materials

One way to conduct field research is to gather materials from a variety of places. You can collect pamphlets, catalogs, documents, or other literature on your subject from various departments, organizations, and institutions. Which organizations you choose are, of course, dependent on your topic. A partial list of potential places on campus to contact are given in the following list.

☐ *Academic departments:* Administrators or secretaries in various academic departments can provide information about courses and faculty experts. Once you have become somewhat informed about your topic, you can consult a faculty member who is knowledgeable about your research area.

☐ *Offices:* Various officials, such as those in Admissions or a Dean's office can provide information.

☐ *Organizations:* Many organizations on campus, run by professionals or students, specialize in specific areas of interest.

☐ *Libraries:* Conduct research in a library on your campus (see pp. 244–256).

Interviewing

Speaking directly with someone who has expertise in the area you want to learn more about is a fundamental way of conducting research. That person can provide information, clarify issues, suggest related areas for exploration, or provide research sources. Alternatively, that person may be the subject of your interview, for example, if you are interviewing someone to learn more about that person's work.

You can also interview people who have experience with your topic, for example, other students.

Consult with your instructor to determine the most appropriate person or persons to interview for your particular project.

For Conducting an Interview

1. Contact the person you wish to interview, explain your research project, and ask for an appointment. Set a specific time span and place for the interview.
2. Prepare an interview guide, a list of questions about your topic.
3. Be flexible with your questions. One good general opening question may be all you need. Let the interviewee talk.
4. Use a tape recorder, if you have permission to do so, and/or take notes.
5. Right after the interview, find a quiet spot to reflect on what you have just learned. Spend some time writing and adding to your notes.

Observing

One basic way to conduct field research is to observe, that is, to place yourself somewhere relevant to your research and analyze what is happening in that place.

For Observing

1. *Decide what to observe.* Select a site that is relevant to your research.
2. *Determine the objectives of your research.* Deciding what you are looking for can help you limit what you watch. For example, if you are researching eating patterns in the cafeteria, your objective might be to observe how much food students take versus how much they actually eat.
3. *Devise a consistent method for recording your observations.* Plan how you will record and categorize the information. For example, if you are researching eating patterns in the cafeteria, you can record in detail what and how much food a certain number of students takes and what and how much food they actually eat. If you are comparing male and female patterns of eating, you should record which students are male and which are female.
4. *Interpret your findings.* Be careful to separate *what you actually see* with your own eyes (for example, a student took two hot dogs and ate only half of one) from your *interpretation* of what you see (for example, the student is wasting food). Remember that another researcher might have a different interpretation of the same observation (for example, the food may have been improperly cooked). You may include multiple interpretations.

Conducting a Survey

One way to conduct field research is to obtain information from many different people by conducting a *survey*. An efficient way to obtain that information is to construct a *questionnaire* and distribute it to a large number of people (respondents) in a short period of time.

Note: This assignment assumes that you are a novice researcher, and it is therefore designed primarily to teach you ways of obtaining information about a subject other than simply reading about it. You are not expected to produce professional survey research.

GUIDELINES

For Constructing a Questionnaire

1. Put some or all of this information at the top:

☐ A statement of the purpose of the survey
☐ A brief explanation of how the information will be used
☐ Assurance of anonymity, if possible
☐ The estimated time it will take to complete the questionnaire

2. Begin with questions that enable the respondent to check off a choice or fill in an objective answer, for example:

☐ *Gender:* male _____ female _____
☐ *Age:* _____
☐ *Year of graduation:* _____
☐ *Number of times you have [done something]:*
   never _____
   once or twice _____
   three or four times _____
   five times or more _____
☐ *Do you agree or disagree with this statement? [State something related to your research.]*
   agree _____
   disagree _____

3. Place open-ended questions toward the end of the questionnaire. You might want to have only one or two such questions, for example:

☐ *Please describe your experience with [something specific related to the research topic].*
☐ *Please use this space to share any additional comments you may have on this topic.*

4. At the end, indicate when and where to return the completed questionnaire.

Testing and Revising a Questionnaire

With the aid of your instructor, construct a questionnaire that will help you gather information for your research project (see above). To test the questionnaire, ask a small group of people (preferably with similarities to the group you plan to survey) to fill out the questionnaire. After they have filled it out, ask them for suggestions as to how it can be improved. Examine their answers, and determine if other questions might have produced clearer or more useful answers. Revise the questionnaire accordingly.

Distributing and Collecting a Questionnaire

With the aid of your instructor, determine the number of people you want to survey and the best way to distribute the questionnaire. You may want to hand out each copy individually, bring or send copies to a class or club meeting of students on campus, or leave copies at an appropriate place on campus (for example, the library, the computer room), with the permission of the person in charge of the area.

Note: Be sure that the respondents know when and where to return the completed questionnaires. The higher the percentage of return, the more valuable the research results.

Analyzing the Results

After you have collected the questionnaires, you might want to number them for easy reference. To summarize information about the respondents (the number of females, and so on), you can total the answers to the checklist and objective questions. You can figure percentages from the data (for example, "10 percent think that the social life is different"), but this is not the only approach. For the open-ended questions, you can look for patterns in the responses. You might want to highlight, underline, or copy what you perceive to be significant comments. You can also create categories to label answers (see below and p. 112).

A Student Writer at Work

Ayse's composition instructor showed the class a list of actual research questions provided to the class by different departments, offices, and programs at the university. Her instructor gave the students the option of selecting one of the solicited questions or developing their own research question.

Ayse chose to research questions provided by the director of the International Center concerning the cultural adjustment of international students. At first, she worked in a team and met with the director of the International Center, who explained why she wanted this research done and who provided the team with some articles related to the topic. Ayse and her teammates then divided the project so that each one covered a different aspect of the issue.

With her instructor's and classmates' help, Ayse wrote and revised a questionnaire and distributed it on campus, in classrooms and in dormitories. She then collected the questionnaires and analyzed the results (see below and pp. 112–114).

Categorizing Research Data

Once you have gathered research data through interviews, observations, and/or questionnaires, you need to create some order out of the material. The following guidelines suggest one way to make sense of the information. As with all aspects of research and analysis, this process may continue into the writing stage.

GUIDELINES

For Categorizing Research Data

1. Reread the research information you have obtained.
2. Note words, phrases, patterns of behavior, or ways of thinking that are repeated.
3. Create categories or codes to label what you have seen or heard.
4. Group the categories in some order that is logical to you.

A Student Writer at Work

After she collected the completed questionnaires, Ayse underlined what she perceived to be key words or phrases. In the left margin, she wrote words to categorize what the respondents had said (see pp. 113–114). She then could look down the margins quickly to see repeated or similar categories.

Sample Completed Questionnaire with Ayse's Marginal Notes and Underlining

Questionnaire for International Students

Gender: male ✓_____   female_____
Year of graduation from college:_'97_
Are you living on campus? (check one) yes _✓_   no_____
Age:_19_
How long have you been in the U. S.? _____ 3 months _____
What country do you come from?_____ Hong Kong _____

1. How does the life in your country differ from your life here?

    choice

    DIVERSITY   We have a <u>more diverse</u> ~~choose~~ of everything, food, clothes, etc.

    SPEED   Since HK is a very small place, we go from 1 place to another a lot <u>faster</u> than in here

2. What kinds of problems do you face regarding your background, your values, your customs?

    (VALUES)   The difference between our <u>moral values</u> is very big. Well, at least my own ~~culture~~ moral.

3. What are the attitudes of U.S.-born undergraduate students toward you?

    "NICE"
    (CULTURAL
    DIFFERENCES)
    MAKE FUN
        Some of them are really <u>nice</u> but some could <u>not understand the cultural difference</u> and sometimes they <u>make fun</u> of me.

4. How comfortable do you feel with Americans? Is it easier to get along with international students? Why, or why not?

    (INTERNAT'L
    EASIER)
    "depends"
        I think it's <u>easier to get along with some international students</u>, but it <u>depends on our background, our values, our customs</u>. I get along with some local students just fine.

5. What do you think the International Club accomplishes?

    NO CONTACT   I don't have any contact with I. club.

6. What should you and other students (U.S.-born and international) do to understand one another better?

    CLUBS   I was looking for an answer to that question too, but I couldn't find one. Well, at least by <u>joining different culture club</u> would help.

Sample Completed Questionnaire with Ayse's Marginal Notes and Underlining

Questionnaire for International Students

Gender: male ✓_____   female_____
Year of graduation from college: _'95_
Are you living on campus? (check one) yes _____   no ✓_____
Age: _22_
How long have you been in the U. S.? _____ 2 years _____
What country do you come from? _____ Former USSR _____

1. How does the life in your country differ from your life here?

COMPLETELY
DIFFERENT

   Completely, nothing in common.

2. What kinds of problems do you face regarding your background, your values, your customs?

(VALUES)
(DIFFERENCES)
(meanings,
education)

   Difference attitudes to life and its values. Sometime do not understand people, because of different meanings about the same subject, totally different system of education.

3. What are the attitudes of U.S.-born undergraduate students toward you?

NO CLUE

   I have no clue! I hope it is alright.

4. How comfortable do you feel with Americans? Is it easier to get along with international students? Why, or why not?

"NEVER RELAX"
(INTERNAT'L)
(EASIER)
"COMMON
LANGUAGE"

   I do not feel at ease with Americans, I feel, never relax. It is easy for me to find understanding and get along with international students, because we all from different background and in our relations we are trying to find "common language" in understanding.

5. What do you think the International Club accomplishes?

UNDERSTANDING/
RELATIONSHIPS

   Each other understanding more better relationships between students of different backgrounds.

6. What should you and other students (U.S.-born and international) do to understand one another better?

MEETINGS/
FRIENDS

   More intercultural meetings, trying to find more friends among international and American students.

Structuring the Entire Essay

Perhaps the most difficult part of research is organizing all the information you have gathered. The following chart provides an overall view of how an essay based on field research can be developed. It by no means represents a rigid formula.

Purpose of the Research Project

How did the project originate?
What questions are to be answered by the project?
Why were these questions chosen?

↓

Methods

What techniques did you use to gather information?
Over what period of time did the study take place?
How did you determine which people or places to question or observe?
How many people or places did you question or observe?

↓

Presentation of the Research Findings

What was said or done?
What patterns, themes, and tendencies emerge from the information you gathered?
Which responses or behaviors were unusual?

↓

Conclusion and/or Recommendation

↓

Appendix

Materials used in research (for example, interview guide, questionnaire)

Developing the Introduction: Purpose and Methods

The introduction to an essay based on field research can reveal the purpose and methodology of the research project. Among the many items you can include are the following:

☐ A discussion of the assignment that you are fulfilling

☐ Questions that the research is designed to answer

☐ General background information on the topic

☐ A description of the methods you used to conduct the research (for example, the techniques you used to gather information, the time period in which the research took place, the number and type of people you observed, interviewed, and/or surveyed, and so on)

☐ An explanation of your relationship with the people and/or places you are researching.

A Student Writer at Work

In her first draft, Ayse did not mention that she herself was an international student because she wanted her essay to sound objective. She referred to international students as "they" and "them." After consultation with her instructor, she decided it would make more sense to identify herself as an international student, partly because her primary readers (her classmates, her instructor, and the director of the International Center) already knew her identity and partly to show how invested she was in the topic. Her revised introduction can be found on page 118.

Developing the Body: Presenting Research Data

The core of the essay includes the data you have collected through observation, interview, and/or survey. How you organize this material depends on what you perceive to be significant. The many ways to structure the body include the following:

1. *Discuss ideas that have emerged from the data in order of importance (according to your view of what is important).* You may begin with what you think is the less or least important idea and end with the most important, or vice versa.

   ☐ State the idea that you will discuss.

   ☐ Provide evidence (details, examples, quotations) from your data to support or illustrate that idea.

   ☐ Repeat this procedure for each idea you want to discuss.

2. *Discuss your research findings according to categories that emerge from the data.* For example, your categories may reflect repeated patterns of behavior, words, phrases, and/or ways of thinking. Analyze and interpret the data where appropriate.

   ☐ Identify a category of responses or observations.

   ☐ Provide evidence (details, examples, quotations) to show that this category reflects a pattern.

   ☐ Move on to the next category, and provide evidence to show that this category reflects a pattern.

   ☐ Repeat this procedure for every category you want to present.

3. *Present the data in chronological order.* This organizational pattern may work best with events or activities that you have observed or that someone has described in an interview.

   ☐ Begin with what happened first. You may include details, examples, quotations, explanations, and/or analysis.

   ☐ Continue to tell a story in the order that events happened, analyzing and interpreting the data when appropriate.

Developing the Conclusion

The conclusion can present your point of view about the research subject. For example, you can include all or any of the following:

☐ An analysis or explanation of the data

☐ A recommendation based on what you learned

☐ A question or series of questions that emerge from the research

Drafting

Prepare a draft of your essay, adapting the guidelines for writing an interim draft on page 53 and for structuring the entire essay on pages 115–117.

Giving and Receiving Feedback

Exchange drafts with one or more classmates, adapting the guidelines for giving and receiving feedback on page 53. Review one another's work by examining (1) what you like about a paper and (2) what you think can be done to strengthen it. Use the feedback form on page 56 and/or the suggestions for summarizing and analyzing on pages 104–105, or raise your own questions.

Revising

You can revise your paper by answering questions such as these (see pp. 57–58 for a fuller discussion):

☐ What should I keep?

☐ What should I add?

☐ What should I delete?

☐ What should I change?

☐ What should I rearrange?

☐ What should I rethink?

Completing

Once you have revised the draft, you can complete the essay by following these guidelines:

☐ Evaluate the essay as a whole.

☐ Proofread and edit the essay (see Chapter 25).

☐ Prepare a neat final manuscript to hand in for evaluation (see Chapter 28).

The Relationship between International and U.S.-Born Students: Two Perspectives

Ayse Yeyinmen

About the Author   Ayse Yeyinmen was in her first semester of college when she wrote this essay to fulfill an assignment for a composition course. She had a special interest in this topic because she herself was an international student from Turkey.

The Context of the Essay   The research took place on the campus of a four-year private university in the United States. At the time Ayse conducted the research, international students represented 15 percent of the student population.
   Note: This essay has been edited for publication in this book.

Introduction

International students like myself generally enjoy studying abroad, even though we face problems. We know that people can have problems wherever they are. Fortunately, on this campus, the International Center is involved with the lives of international students and tries to help us experience as few difficulties as possible. As a way of assisting students further, the center director asked our class to research the international students who attend the college and the variables that affect their adjustment. This paper is based on two questions provided by the director: How do students from other countries think they are perceived by U.S.-born students? How can the entire college community learn to understand their background and culture better?

   The answers to these questions can provide insight into the problems that international students face and the reasons for these problems. They also can lead the International Center to find different ways to welcome future international students in a more congenial atmosphere, to make them feel more at ease in college, and to improve conditions for them.

   Over 475,000 students from other countries are in the United States to get a college education. This statistical report is drawn from the special *Almanac* issue of *The Chronicle of Higher Education,* which offers tables and charts providing a broad view of higher education in the fifty states and the District of Columbia, along with narrative summaries for each state. Despite that large number of students, there are not many accessible articles concerning these students and their problems. My major source for this research was a questionnaire completed by twenty-nine international (see Appendix A) and six U.S.-born students (see Appendix B).

Responses of International Students

The twenty-nine international students who completed the questionnaire are from Asia (14), Europe (9), South America (4), and the West Indies (2). Nine are female and twenty are male. There are seventeen freshmen, five sophomores, four juniors, and three seniors. Their time spent in the United States ranges from three months to sixteen years, averaging two and one-third years. Eighty-three percent of the students live on campus.

Among the differences students notice are the weather, the food, the dinner time, the quantity of work, and a more competitive atmosphere. Twenty percent of the students say that the education, moral values, and attitudes are totally different in their countries and that these differences are the source of misunderstandings and disagreements. However, 16 percent of them say that their life differs only in meeting people from all over the world. Independence is the newest experience for 13 percent of these students. Ten percent think that the social life is limited, and another 10 percent find everything the same as in their country.

Most of the internationals agree that they do not face many serious problems. The reason for this could be that most of them hang out with people speaking their native language. They complain mostly about the different version of friendship that the Americans* conceive. They notice that everybody is friendly with each other while keeping a distance, without a classification of best friend, treating everyone equally. This makes them feel that friendship is less important in the United States because they are not used to calling someone a friend when they just say "hi" to her or him. Internationals have a much deeper concept of friendship.

The general opinion about the relationship between American and international students is that it is easier for the internationals to become friends with other international students. Fifty percent explain that internationals are more alike since they have more things in common such as being abroad, facing the same problems due to their different backgrounds, being more "open-minded to differences" in others, and being "used to making adjustments." The language is the major problem in hanging out with Americans: it is hard for them to participate in a conversation when they cannot speak as fast. Unfortunately, clinging to friends from their native countries prevents these internationals from making an effort to communicate with Americans.

Twenty percent of internationals say that making friendships depends on the personality, regardless of nationality and native language. Twenty-three percent consider that the Americans are friendly toward them and treat them as any U.S.-born student. International students who have a lot of American friends, 16 percent, think that Americans are open-minded and interested in different cultures. Ten percent agree on the preference of U.S.-born friends among the Americans. Another 10 percent think that Americans are "nice" but at the same time say they can be "indifferent" and "intolerant" toward them. "Focused on their rights," "liberal," "respectful to others," and "outgoing" are some of the

*The word *Americans* refers to U.S.-born students.

other descriptive words given by the international students for Americans. Thus there is no single, common description of U.S.-born students.

When asked what the International Club accomplishes, 33 percent say they have no idea about it. Twenty-six percent think it accomplishes nothing much but parties. Ten percent see the International Club as a good place to meet people. Another 10 percent believe that it is a useful organization in helping students adapt and trying to bring people together. However, some of them think it creates a gap between U.S.-born and international students.

Responses of U.S.-Born Students

Of the six U.S.-born students who completed the questionnaire, all are female; five are freshmen, one is a sophomore; and all live on campus.

The opinions given by these six U.S.-born students about studying with international students show that they are open-minded and interested in different cultures. They enjoy studying in a cosmopolitan atmosphere. They do not see any disadvantages. However, they think internationals segregate themselves. These Americans want to have more connection between themselves and students from other countries. All of them like learning about others' lives and appreciate cultural opportunities at the college due to its diversity. Like internationals, they agree that misunderstandings may occur because of the language and the lack of a common background.

Conclusion

Just as LaRay Barna suggests in her article "Intercultural Communication Stumbling Blocks," tolerance, open-mindedness, and patience are the key words to a better relationship between international and U.S.-born students. More intercultural meetings and activities can help to make life easy for us. Wide exposure of multiple cultures is necessary to break walls between students. Doing more things together, sharing, and accepting that others can be different are important factors in the adjustment issue. To make everything better and easier, both international and U.S.-born students should make an attempt to take people as they are. In order for these friendships to form, the International Center should sponsor more activities and address issues that would bring the two groups together.

Works Cited

The Almanac of Higher Education. Chicago: University of Chicago Press, 1992.

Barna, LaRay M. "Intercultural Communication Stumbling Blocks." *Guidelines: A Cross-Cultural Reading/Writing Text.* Ruth Spack (Ed.), New York: St. Martin's P, 1990. 78–87.

Appendix A: Questionnaire for International Students

Gender: male _____   female_____
Year of graduation from college:_____
Are you living on campus? (check one) yes _____   no_____
Age:_____
How long have you been in the U. S.? _____
What country do you come from?_____

1. How does the life in your country differ from your life here?

2. What kinds of problems do you face regarding your background, your values, your customs?

3. What are the attitudes of U.S.-born undergraduate students toward you?

4. How comfortable do you feel with Americans? Is it easier to get along with international students? Why, or why not?

5. What do you think the International Club accomplishes?

6. What should you and other students (U.S.-born and international) do to understand one another better?

Appendix B: Questionnaire for U.S.-Born Students

Gender: male _____   female_____
Year of graduation from college:_____
Are you living on campus? (check one) yes _____   no_____
Age:_____

1. What are your feelings about studying in college with international students?

2. What are the advantages? What are the disadvantages?

Write after You Read

Explore your response to "The Relationship between International and U.S.-born Students: Two Perspectives" by recording your reactions in a journal entry, adapting the guidelines on page 9.

ACTIVITY

For Class Discussion

Working with a partner, in a small group, or with the whole class, engage in some or all of the following activities. Decide the order in which to cover the material and the amount of time to spend on each activity. Allow for different reactions to and interpretations of the various aspects of the reading.

1. Share reactions to "The Relationship between International and U.S.-born Students: Two Perspectives" that you have recorded in your journal entry.

2. Examine the essay closely, using the suggestions for summarizing and analyzing on pages 104–105.

3. Compare the experiences and ideas in the essay with your own experiences and attitudes. ∎

ESSAYS

This unit, Writing from Sources: Essays, consists of three chapters that can help you fulfill an assignment to write an essay based on reading.

By reading and examining your reactions to the essays in Chapter 9, guided by the discussion activities in Chapter 10, you may develop a sense of how a writer can persuade readers to believe something or to recognize the importance of a particular issue. In Chapter 11, guidelines are provided for writing about reading. A sample student essay is included.

CHAPTER 9

Readings: Essays

Chapter 9 provides five reading selections referred to in this book as argumentative essays. In an argumentative essay, a writer often aims to prove something, for example:

□ That a condition exists

□ That something is true

□ That one thing is more desirable than another

□ That a change should be instituted

As you read and reread an essay, you can aim to accomplish the following:

□ Understand the overall argument

□ Evaluate the evidence provided to support the argument

□ Question what you are reading

□ Examine your own views on the subject

The Reading Selections

The essays in this chapter were written by a businessperson and by educators from the fields of religion, literature, education, and biology. Each writer argues a particular position related to the issue of education, sometimes acknowledging the validity of other positions and often challenging arguments on the opposing side.

Write before You Read

The following reading selection is entitled "We Should Cherish Our Children's Freedom to Think." Before reading, take the following quiz to test your knowledge.

Briefly identify the following:

1. Mussolini
2. Dostoevski
3. Belgrade
4. Prague
5. Kabul
6. Karachi
7. Hamlet
8. Buenos Aires
9. tacos
10. two rivers in Brazil
11. the author of *The Canterbury Tales*
12. Romeo and Juliet
13. Donkey Kong
14. Shakespeare
15. Lyndon Johnson
16. Ho Chi Minh
17. Hirohito
18. Periodic Table
19. Richard Pryor
20. Ku Klux Klan

Compare your results with those of classmates. What do the results reveal about the knowledge level of the class? To answer this question, you might try to classify the material according to categories such as geography, literature, history, and popular culture. Then determine which categories the class knows best or least, and try to explain why this is so.

We Should Cherish Our Children's Freedom to Think

Kie Ho

About the Author   Kie Ho was born and raised in Indonesia and became a business executive in California.

The Context of the Reading   "We Should Cherish Our Children's Freedom to Think" originally appeared in the *Los Angeles Times* newspaper in 1983.

Americans who remember "the good old days" are not alone in complaining about the educational system in this country. Immigrants, too, complain, and with more up-to-date comparisons. Lately I have heard a Polish refugee express dismay that his daughter's high school has not taught her the difference between Belgrade and Prague. A German friend was furious when he learned that the mathematics test given to his son on his first day as a freshman included multiplication and division. A Lebanese boasts that the average high-school graduate in his homeland can speak fluently in Arabic, French and English. Japanese businessmen in Los Angeles send their children to private schools staffed by teachers imported from Japan to learn mathematics at Japanese levels, generally considered at least a year more advanced than the level here.

But I wonder: If American education is so tragically inferior, why is it that this is still the country of innovation?

I think I found the answer on an excursion to the Laguna Beach Museum of Art, where the work of schoolchildren was on exhibit. Equipped only with colorful yarns, foil paper, felt pens and crayons, they had transformed simple paper lunch bags into, among other things, a waterfall with flying fish, Broom Hilda the witch and a house with a woman in a skimpy bikini hiding behind a swinging door. Their public school had provided these children with opportunities and direction to fulfill their creativity, something that people tend to dismiss or take for granted.

When I was 12 in Indonesia, where education followed the Dutch system, I had to memorize the names of all the world's major cities, from Kabul to Karachi. At the same age, my son, who was brought up a Californian, thought that Buenos Aires was Spanish for good food—a plate of tacos and burritos, perhaps. However, unlike his counterparts in Asia and Europe, my son had studied *creative* geography. When he was only 6, he drew a map of the route that he traveled to get to school, including the streets and their names, the buildings and traffic signs and the houses that he passed.

Disgruntled American parents forget that in this country their children are able to experiment freely with ideas; without this they will not really be able to think or to believe in themselves.

In my high school years, we were models of dedication and obedience: we sat to listen, to answer only when asked, and to give the only correct answer. Even when studying word forms, there were no alternatives. In similes, pretty lips were *always* as red as sliced pomegranates, and beautiful eyebrows were *always* like a parade of black clouds. Like children in many other countries in the world, I simply did not have a chance to choose, to make decisions. My son, on the contrary, told me that he got a good laugh—and an A—from his teacher for concocting "the man was as nervous as Richard Pryor at a Ku Klux Klan convention."

There's no doubt that American education does not meet high standards in such basic skills as mathematics and language. And we realize that our youngsters are ignorant of Latin, put Mussolini in the same category as Dostoevski, cannot recite the Periodic Table by heart. Would we, however, prefer to stuff the developing little heads of our children with hundreds of geometry problems, the names of rivers in Brazil and 50 lines from *The Canterbury Tales?* Do we really want to retard their impulses, frustrate their opportunities for self-expression?

When I was 18, I had to memorize Hamlet's "To be or not to be" soliloquy flawlessly. In his English class, my son was assigned to write a love letter to Juliet, either in Shakespearean jargon or in modern lingo. (He picked the latter; his Romeo would take Juliet to an arcade for a game of Donkey Kong.)

Where else but in America can a history student take the role of Lyndon Johnson in an open debate against another student playing Ho Chi Minh? It is unthinkable that a youngster in Japan would dare to do the same regarding the role of Hirohito in World War II.

Critics of American education cannot grasp one thing, something that they don't truly understand because they are never deprived of it: freedom. This most important measurement has been omitted in the studies of the quality of education in this century, the only one, I think, that extends even to children the license to freely speak, write and be creative. Our public education certainly is not perfect, but it is a great deal better than any other.

Write before You Read

The following reading selection is entitled "Teach Knowledge, Not 'Mental Skills.'" Before reading, think or write for several minutes about the following topic:

What do you perceive to be the difference between *knowledge* and *skills?*

Share your thoughts with classmates.

Teach Knowledge, Not "Mental Skills"

E. D. Hirsch

About the Author   E. D. (Eric Donald) Hirsch is a professor of English at the University of Virginia. Among his many books are *The Aims of Interpretation* (1976) and *The Dictionary of Cultural Literacy* (1993).

The Context of the Reading   Already a respected literary theorist, Hirsch gained fame when his book *Cultural Literacy: What Every American Needs to Know* was published in 1987. In it, he claimed that U.S. students do not learn well because the schools emphasize skills (for example, how to read maps and how to think) over content; and therefore students do not know enough essential facts. Hirsch later founded the Core Knowledge Foundation, which develops programs that provide a body of knowledge for students to learn.

Hirsch begins "Teach Knowledge, Not 'Mental Skills' " with a discussion of a public school located in the South Bronx in New York City.

The essay originally appeared in the *New York Times* newspaper in 1993. William Jefferson Clinton had recently been elected president of the United States.

Note: Public schools in the United States provide free lunch to poor children.

The children at Public School 67 in the South Bronx are all African-American or Hispanic, and all are poor enough to qualify for free lunch. In the late 80's, the school was so ineffective that the district board was about to shut it down.

But in 1991 a new principal, Jeff Litt, introduced a grade-by-grade "core knowledge" curriculum. The students' academic performance has risen so dramatically—their reading scores, for instance, were up 13.5 percent last year—that Mr. Litt has had to limit the flow of curious visitors to his school.

The curriculum was developed by the Core Knowledge Foundation, a nonprofit group I founded that advises public schools free of charge. Mr. Litt became an enthusiast of the grade-by-grade sequence after visiting the Three Oaks School in Lee County, Fla., the country's first core-knowledge school. This year the Bronx will get two more core-knowledge schools, joining about 100 others across the nation.

What's the secret of their success? About 50 percent of classroom time is spent teaching each student a core of knowledge that is the same material offered to every other child in the same grade throughout the school.

To understand why this plan has contributed to strong academic improvement, consider how rare such common sense is.

Typically, school guidelines are couched in terms of learning skills, rather than the content of learning. For example, school guidelines might say, "First graders develop map skills" and "learn about plants." In contrast, the Core Knowledge guidelines specify that first graders will "identify the seven continents" and "learn the difference between evergreen and deciduous trees."

Because guidelines are so vague in skill-oriented curriculums, huge variations occur in the content of what is learned from one class to another. A Connecticut mother wrote me that her young twins, who were in separate classrooms at the same school, were learning totally different things.

Because there's no consistency in what children were taught in previous grades, teachers have to make a disastrous compromise: either they fill in knowledge gaps for all students in the class, making progress excruciatingly slow, or they go forward at a pace suited to the more prepared students, leaving others behind.

Such a hit-or-miss approach does the most harm to disadvantaged students, who usually depend on school alone for access to academic knowledge. But even advantaged students are hurt by being left with huge knowledge gaps or by being bored with repetition.

That problem is avoided in the best and fairest school systems in Europe and Asia, which offer programs similar to the core-knowledge schools. Since students have learned the same things, teachers can build on that shared foundation and bring the whole class forward.

It is a promising sign that the Clinton Administration's new education bill employs the resonant new phrase "content standards." Nonetheless, most educational reformers continue to emphasize skills and scornfully dismiss the teaching of "mere facts," which they claim are destined for quick obsolescence.

Hearing few contrary voices, well-intentioned philanthropists and politicians echo such slogans as "learning-to-learn skills," "critical-thinking skills" and "problem-solving skills."

Yes, problem-solving skills are necessary. But they depend on a wealth of relevant knowledge. Meanwhile, street-smart children in the Bronx and elsewhere demonstrate outside school that they already possess higher-order thinking skills. As Jeff Litt has shown, what these students lack is not critical thinking but academic knowledge.

Contrary to proponents' claims, emphasizing all-purpose mental skills to "prepare children for the 21st century" is not new. The tired slogans have dominated U.S. educational discourse for over 40 years, and are a chief cause of the curricular chaos.

Leaving such slogans behind, and following the lead of effective systems in Europe and Asia, P.S. 67 demonstrates how we can achieve excellence and fairness for all.

Write before You Read

The following reading selection is entitled "The Farce Called 'Grading.'" Before reading, think or write for several minutes about one or both of the following topics:

☐ Describe a negative experience you have had regarding grades in school.

☐ Describe a positive experience you have had regarding grades in school.

Share your experience(s) with classmates.

The Farce Called "Grading"
Arthur E. Lean

About the Author   Arthur E. Lean, a professor at Southern Illinois University at Carbondale at the time he wrote this essay, is an educational philosopher. He is coeditor of *John Dewey and the World View* (1964) and coauthor of *Education or Catastrophe?* (1990).

The Context of the Reading   "The Farce Called 'Grading'" is taken from Lean's book entitled *And Merely Teach: Irreverent Essays on the Mythology of Education* (1976). In the essay, Lean quotes four educators: Louis T. Benezet, Ernest O. Melby, William Clark Trow, and Thomas J. Fleming.

A sustained effort should be made to throw out false inducements to learning. In one way or another most of these refer to our obsession with grades. A few colleges that have ended the grading system, like those truly brave ones that have thrown out faculty ranks, have shown what can be done. It is possible to interest students in intrinsic learning, once we rid ourselves of the ancient hobby of making book on each performance. Grades may be useful for checking the memory of items of fact or the solving of pat mathematical problems. As a system for evaluating attainment of broad educational aims, it remains a failure. Few teachers have any systematic idea of how to grade fairly. Grading is also the chief villain behind the scandal of college cheating.

Louis T. Benezet

I have long ago reached the conclusion that the marking system itself is damaging in its impact on the education of our children and youth, and that it should go the way of the hickory stick and dunce caps. It should be abandoned at all levels of education.

Ernest O. Melby

Of all the common practices in our schools, doubtless the most tyrannical and indefensible is our insistence on attempting to evaluate students' performance through a system of grades or "marks." The harm done by this practice is incalculable, but we persistently cling to it in spite of its obvious unworkability. Every person who has ever gone to school can cite numerous instances of unfairness and injustice caused by grading systems and practices, but for some strange reason we seem to assume it to be necessary and intrinsic to the process of formal education.

Some years ago, when numerical grading on a percentage basis was more common than today, several experiments were conducted in an attempt to determine how precisely teachers could evaluate students' written work. In one well-known study, in order to "prejudice the garden to roses" an *exact* subject was chosen—mathematics, of course, because in that field, as everybody knows, things are either right or wrong—and a panel of experienced mathematics teachers, recognized by their peers for their competence, was assembled to do the evaluating. Student papers in plane geometry were graded by these expert teachers, each using an identical copy so as to eliminate any persuasive effect of extraneous factors such as neatness. The result was, of course, that the grades assigned to exactly the same paper ranged all the way from the 90s down to the 40s and 50s. And this in an *exact* subject where answers are "either right or wrong"! Similar results were obtained in other comparable studies.

The shift to letter-grading with fewer distinctions (the familiar A, B, C, D, with either E or F to designate failure) has not really solved the problem; it has merely reduced the number of categories (whereupon, of course, we promptly proceed recidivistically to attach plus and minus signs—multiple ones if single ones will not suffice). And of course we *must* have an equivalency table to indicate that A includes the range 93–100 or 90–100, B 85–92 or 80–89, and so on down, refusing in our obstinacy to recognize the fatal inconsistency involved: is A 93 or 100 or something in between? How about 95? 98? 96.123456789?

During the hectic post–World War II days I was pressed into service to teach Freshman Composition (Expository Writing) at a large university. There were more than a hundred sections of this course, each with a maximum of twenty-five students. We used a book of readings as a basis for class discussion and weekly themes. In addition to class sessions, each student had a short fortnightly conference with his instructor to go over his work and discuss ways of improving his written expression.

One of the "full" professors in the English department was in charge of all the teaching in this course, and he regularly convened the instructors—some seventy or eighty of us—for purposes of coordination and standardization of instruction. Usually at these sessions we were given identical copies of an actual student theme which had been selected at random and duplicated exactly as originally submitted. We took thirty to forty minutes to read and evaluate this short theme, whereupon we wrote on it a grade and an evaluative comment. Having listed our names alphabetically on the blackboard, the professor in charge then called them one by one, and each instructor responded to his name by stating the grade he had assigned to that theme. This grade was inscribed after his name on the blackboard.

Invariably the assigned grades on the same theme ranged all the way from A (excellent) to E (failure). Those instructors who judged that theme to be in either of those extreme categories were then called upon to stand up and justify their grades. This they usually did with great earnestness and sincerity, albeit with increasing reluctance, for in the process their own personal biases, prejudices, and confusions were soon revealed for all to see. (It quickly became obvious to many neophyte instructors that C-minus was an inconspicuous, colorless grade which would not require them to expose themselves to the public justification-humiliation process.) Most of the assigned grades tended, of course, to cluster in the middle of the scale, but there were almost always some on the extremes. But not once did we stop to consider the *student* who must maintain a certain minimum grade-average to stay in school, and whose mark on that theme might be A or E depending on which instructor he has!

All of us are familiar with the classic examples of students' submitting the same paper to different instructors (or even to the same instructor at different times!) and getting widely varying grades, of handing in obscure works of famous authors and getting them back marked "failure," and so on.

Grading tends to stigmatize and punish the less able student, who may be trying very hard but, through no fault of his own, simply did not inherit much in the way of native intelligence.

In spite of the staggering amount of incontrovertible evidence that grading not only does not accomplish its purpose but in reality inhibits and injures the educative process, we obstinately continue with this perverted practice.

After all, what is a "grade" supposed to be and do? Perhaps we could get general agreement on the statement that it is a symbol purporting to express a measurement of academic achievement—an evaluation of the quality and quantity of learning. Now, in order to measure anything, we need a standard such as a ruler or tapeline for linear measurement, a scale for measuring weight, and so on. By using such standards I can determine that the desk at which I sit is thirty inches high, and that its surface measures twenty-eight inches by twenty inches. I put my portable typewriter on a scale and determine its weight to be nine pounds. I look at the thermometer on the wall and discover that room temperature is sixty-eight degrees Fahrenheit. Other people using the same standards would arrive at the same results; any variations would be infinitesimal and certainly negligible for practical purposes.

If all this be so, then what sense does it make for us to speak of "giving" a grade to a student, or of his "earning" or "deserving" it? Do I "give" my desk a height of thirty inches? Does my typewriter "earn" a weight of nine pounds? Does this room "deserve" a temperature of sixty-eight degrees? Arrant nonsense, of course, but this ridiculous absurdity is exactly what we constantly do with our grading systems.

Compounding our criminal practices, we use grades for reward and punishment. Recently a coed sued her university because she claimed that her failing grade in one course was "unfair" and resulted from an attempt "to discipline and punish her" for alleged wrongful conduct. She asserted that she had been found innocent by the university's disciplinary committee, but that the instructor and administrative superiors to whom she had appealed had refused to "raise the grade" to the B which she said she had "merited." And this occurred in an institution of what we fancifully call "higher learning"!

When students disobey instructions or otherwise transgress (often unintentionally) we say to them, "Because of this, I am lowering your grade five points (or one letter)." Such behavior is surely the epitome of cynicism, and if our students display disquieting evidence of becoming increasingly cynical, we have ourselves and our indefensible practices largely to blame. With grades, we *teach* them cynicism, to say nothing of lying, cheating, competitive throat-cutting, and other reprehensible practices.

"But," objects somebody, "after all, a grade is just a sort of *estimate,* and most teachers try to be fair and accurate in their estimates." Yes; most teachers try to be fair and accurate, but all the time they know—at least, those who are honest with themselves know—that they are attempting the impossible. No self-respecting teacher ever rests peacefully the night after turning in a set of grades, for he knows that the "system" has made a charlatan of him and he goes to bed hating himself for it. And as for the estimate, let us not disregard the fact that an *absolute* pass-or-fail system has no place for estimates. Is that 87 on your test paper an estimate? If it is, then mightn't it really be 88, or 86, or something else? Is that B-minus an estimate? No, indeed; when the reports come out, when the averages and grade-points are computed, when the failures are determined, when you are called in and told that you've flunked out of school, there is no room for estimates—this is a very *absolute* decision.

Incidentally, no teacher I know—myself included, God wot—can explain the precise difference between a B-minus and a C-plus, to say nothing of 60 and 59—or, for that matter, 60 and 59.999999999999.

"But," objects somebody else, "if grades are eliminated, what can we substitute for them?" This inevitable question reminds me of the books that have been written on the subject of how to stop smoking. Such a book can be written in one word: Quit!

We have had this asinine practice of grading in schools for so long that we unconsciously assume it to be necessary to the learning process, but this is a manifestly false assumption. Grades are one aspect of the artificial paraphernalia which we have deliberately superimposed upon education—along with courses, academic credit, "promotion," degrees, diplomas, certificates, commencement exercises, graduation, faculty rank, and so on *ad infinitum, ad nauseam.*

We hold these minatory requirements over the students because we assume that most of them are naturally lazy, stupid dolts who must somehow be coerced, cajoled, persuaded, threatened, strong-armed into learning what we have decided is "good for them." Much of this required material is dull, boring, meaningless, and will be forgotten almost immediately; and the way it is taught is even worse, but students realize that they must perforce jump through the hoops in order to emerge finally with that coveted degree, that beribboned diploma upon which our society places such high value. What we invariably seem to forget is that this superimposed academic apparatus is not at all intrinsic to learning—not at all a *sine qua non* of education, formal or informal. *It is there because we put it there.* Just because we're accustomed to it, let us not delude ourselves into assuming that it is essential, organic or integral; it isn't. But once it becomes an established system, students often shift their motivations and values and begin to "work for grades." And when we talk to them about "earning" and "deserving" marks, we are only compounding this felony.

There have been successful attempts to eliminate marks. The Danish Folk High Schools and other brave experimental schools have gotten along very well without them. In place of report cards or transcripts covered with cabalistic symbols, written reports and parent-teacher (or parent-teacher-student) conferences are sometimes used to facilitate communication and understanding. For example, employers of young people find descriptive comments about such traits as dependability, resourcefulness, intelligence, honesty, ability to get along with others, and so on, much more meaningful than the conventional academic transcripts of prospective employees. If you were such an employer, would you prefer, on the one hand, a thoughtful evaluation from adults who have observed the young people closely over a period of time, or, on the other hand, an official piece of paper informing you about a C-minus in English history and a B-plus in college algebra?

Students themselves are so conditioned to grading that they soon become willing dupes of the system. They go to their instructors and ask, "How am I doing in this course?" But in most cases they already *know* how they are doing—better than the instructor does—and the fact that they ask the question demonstrates the unreliability of the system.

Some years ago I found a small midwestern town in which the editor of the local weekly newspaper regularly printed on its front pages the complete names and marks of all the children in that town's schools each time report cards were issued. This editor was obviously a sick man who needed immediate confinement in an institution, but his problem is illustrative of the pathology endemic to the practice of grading. Its elimination is more than I dare hope for in my lifetime.[1] But until the cancer is rooted out and destroyed we can hope for little real improvement in American education.

---

[1]As William Clark Trow observes, "Marks . . . deserve to be abolished. Anyone who has not lived his life in the ivory tower, however, knows that trying to abolish them would be like trying to abolish money."

Thomas J. Fleming notes that "the colossal confusion currently reigning in American education in regard to what teachers call 'evaluating pupil performance' and what more down-to-earth parents and kids call *marks* is our number-one school scandal."

Write before You Read

The following reading selection is entitled "Grades and Self-Esteem." Before reading, think or write for several minutes about the following topic:

What do you think is the relationship between grades and self-esteem?

Share your thoughts with classmates.

Grades and Self-Esteem

Randy Moore

About the Author   Randy Moore, a botanist, is a professor of biology at Baylor University in Waco, Texas, and the editor of the journal *The American Biology Teacher*. He has published numerous scientific articles and is the author of *The Living Desert* (1991).

The Context of the Reading   "Grades and Self-Esteem" first appeared in 1993 as an editorial in the journal *The American Biology Teacher,* which is aimed at teachers of high school and undergraduate students. Moore makes reference to literature and popular culture:

☐   *Wizard of Oz:* a novel by L. Frank Baum (later made into a popular film) in which a fake wizard gives a cowardly lion a badge to show he is brave, a tin man a "heart" to show he is kind, and a scarecrow a "diploma" to show he is smart

☐   *Lake Wobegon:* a fictional town created by popular radio show host and author Garrison Keillor

---

If you're around teachers long enough, the conversation will inevitably get around to "today's under-prepared students." We complain endlessly that students don't know anything, don't *want* to know anything, can't write well and can't think critically. Our complaints are supported by much evidence, including firsthand observations and declining scores on objective tests (e.g., SAT, ACT). Indeed,

☐   Only 11% of eighth-graders in California's public schools can solve seventh-grade math problems.
☐   More than 30% of U.S. 17-year-olds don't know that Abraham Lincoln wrote the Emancipation Proclamation. Almost half do not know who Josef Stalin was, and 30% can't locate Britain on a map of Europe.

Employers echo our complaints: 58% of Fortune 500 companies cannot find marginally competent workers, and the CEOs of major companies report that four of 10 entry-level workers cannot pass seventh-grade exams. Does all of this make a difference? Yes. For example, several major corporations now ship their paperwork to countries such as Ireland because U.S. workers "make too many mistakes."

We have many prepackaged excuses for our failures, some of which are partly valid and others that are self-delusion. I argue that a major reason for our failures is that the primary mission of many schools has shifted from education to "building self-esteem."

Disciples of the self-esteem mission for schools preach that we should take seriously—even praise—all self-expression by students, regardless of its content, context, accuracy or worth. This, the disciples claim, "humanizes" education and makes our courses "nonjudgmental." Everyone is right! Everyone's opinion has equal value! I'm OK, you're OK! Don't worry about learning, thinking or communicating; the important thing is to feel good about ourselves.

Of course, when we assign grades we become *very* judgmental. This upsets teachers who feel bad about holding students accountable to any kind of grading standards. To avoid feeling bad, these teachers lower their standards so that virtually all students meet them, regardless of the students' performance. There are many subtle examples of this: eliminating (or not recording) failing grades, allowing students to withdraw from courses when faced with making a poor grade, "dumbing down" our courses so that everyone "earns" an A or B, and renaming sub-remedial courses to make them appear to be academically viable. All of this produces grade inflation. Consider these facts:

- ☐ In 1966, high school teachers gave twice as many C's as A's. By 1978, the proportion of A's exceeded that of C's. In 1990, more than 20% of all students entering college had an A *average* for their entire high school career.
- ☐ In the 1980s, almost three-fourths of grades at Amherst, Duke, Hamilton, Haverford, Pomona, Michigan, North Carolina and Wisconsin were A or B. At Harvard, the average grade is now B − ; at Princeton, 80% of undergraduates get *only* A's or B's.
- ☐ In some colleges, the *average* undergraduate is an "honors" student.

Many teachers have lowered their standards so far that most of their students—the same ones we claim cannot think critically and who employers know are unprepared for entry-level jobs—are A or B students. These teachers apparently think that our students, like the children at Lake Wobegon, are all above average.

The belief that self-esteem is a precondition to learning is now dogma that few teachers question. However, this confuses cause and effect. Granted, people who excel at what they do usually feel better about themselves than do frauds or convicted felons. But does high self-esteem *cause* success? To many educators, it apparently does: These people claim that self-esteem precedes performance, not vice versa. I argue that self-esteem is *earned* and that schools, despite their good intentions, cannot dispense it as a prepackaged handout. We should avoid the "Wizard of Oz" syndrome in which we merely dispense substitutes for brains, bravery and hearts. We should insist on the real thing.

Despite having lowered our standards to new depths, many self-esteem crusaders claim that we've not lowered our standards far enough. For example, high school seniors in some states must pass a ninth-grade-level test before they can get their diploma. When some students failed the test repeatedly and were told they would not graduate, the self-esteem gurus immediately jumped to their defense. "Outrageous!" they claimed. "If students failed, the tests must be flawed!" One educator even proclaimed that the students "would be stigmatized the rest of their lives because they don't have a diploma." Of course, asking the students to work harder, repeat a grade or achieve a meaningful goal is out of the question because such requests could damage the students' self-esteem. The result? Students who could not pass the ninth-grade test "graduated" and received a "diploma of attendance" (ironically, the fact that many of the students *didn't* attend classes was the basis for their problem). I'm sure that employers—people who care less about "self-esteem" than integrity and productivity— will be *very* impressed by a "diploma of attendance."

The delusion that results from our current emphasis on self-esteem rather than education is best shown by the results of an international study of 13-year-olds that found that Koreans ranked first in math and Americans ranked last. Only 23% of Korean youngsters claimed that they were "good at mathematics," as compared to a whopping 68% of U.S. youngsters. Apparently, self-esteem has little to do with one's ability to do math.

The products of our current emphasis on "self-esteem"—that is, grade inflation, lowered standards, meaningless diplomas and an ignorance of important skills—greatly compromise our work: We cheat students out of a quality education and give parents false hopes about their child's intellectual skills. Moreover, our teaching convinces students that achievement is an entitlement that is given, not earned. Luckily, life is not that way.

We cannot continue to equate higher self-esteem with lowered standards. If we do, we'll not only produce students who can't think, but also students who don't know what thinking *is*. At that point, self-esteem won't matter all that much.

We'll improve students' self-esteem most by helping and motivating our students to exceed *higher* standards. Only then will our students have accomplished something meaningful and will we have excelled at our work.

Write before You Read

The following reading selection is entitled "College Pressures." Before reading, think or write for several minutes about the following topic:

> Look at the picture on page 139. Then speculate on what the student in the picture may be experiencing, thinking, and feeling.

Share your ideas with classmates.

College Pressures
William Zinsser

About the Author   William Zinsser is a writer, professor, and film critic. His many books include *On Writing Well* (1976). In the 1970s, Zinsser taught writing at Yale University in New Haven, Connecticut.

The Context of the Reading   The monetary figures mentioned in the reading (such as college tuition costs) reflect 1979 statistics and information. As you read, you can increase Zinsser's figures to match today's numbers. Even though the numbers have changed, the basic economic problem that Zinsser discusses continues today and affects students in both private and public colleges.

In the essay, Zinsser refers to three Yale graduates:

☐   *Potter Stewart:* a former Supreme Court justice of the United States
☐   *Kingman Brewster:* a former president of Yale University
☐   *William F. Buckley, Jr.:* an influential journalist

"College Pressures" was originally published in the magazine *Blair and Ketchum's Country Journal* in 1979. This publication, which provides information on country living, has a national readership.

Dear Carlos: I desperately need a dean's excuse for my chem midterm which will begin in about 1 hour. All I can say is that I totally blew it this week. I've fallen incredibly, inconceivably behind.

Carlos: Help! I'm anxious to hear from you. I'll be in my room and won't leave it until I hear from you. Tomorrow is the last day for . . .

Carlos: I left town because I started bugging out again. I stayed up all night to finish a take-home make-up exam & am typing it to hand in on the 10th. It was due on the 5th. P.S. I'm going to the dentist. Pain is pretty bad.

Carlos: Probably by Friday I'll be able to get back to my studies. Right now I'm going to take a long walk. This whole thing has taken a lot out of me.

Carlos: I'm really up the proverbial creek. The problem is I really *bombed* the history final. Since I need that course for my major . . .

Carlos: Here follows a tale of woe. I went home this weekend, had to help my Mom & caught a fever so didn't have much time to study. My professor . . .

Carlos: Aargh! Trouble. Nothing original but everything's piling up at once. To be brief, my job interview . . .

Hey Carlos, good news! I've got mononucleosis.

Who are these wretched supplicants, scribbling notes so laden with anxiety, seeking such miracles of postponement and balm? They are men and women who belong to Branford College, one of the twelve residential colleges at Yale University, and the messages are just a few of hundreds that they left for their dean, Carlos Hortas—often slipped under his door at 4 A.M.—last year.

But students like the ones who wrote those notes can also be found on campuses from coast to coast—especially in New England and at many other private colleges across the country that have high academic standards and highly motivated students. Nobody could doubt that the notes are real. In their urgency and their gallows humor they are authentic voices of a generation that is panicky to succeed.

My own connection with the message writers is that I am master of Branford College. I live in its Gothic quadrangle and know the students well. (We have 485 of them.) I am privy to their hopes and fears—and also to their stereo music and their piercing cries in the dead of night ("Does anybody *ca-a-are?*"). If they went to Carlos to ask how to get through tomorrow, they come to me to ask how to get through the rest of their lives.

Mainly I try to remind them that the road ahead is a long one and that it will have more unexpected turns than they think. There will be plenty of time to change jobs, change careers, change whole attitudes and approaches. They don't want to hear such liberating news. They want a map—right now—that they can follow unswervingly to career security, financial security, Social Security and, presumably, a prepaid grave.

What I wish for all students is some release from the clammy grip of the future. I wish them a chance to savor each segment of their education as an experience in itself and not as a grim preparation for the next step. I wish them the right to experiment, to trip and fall, to learn that defeat is as instructive as victory and is not the end of the world.

My wish, of course, is naive. One of the few rights that America does not proclaim is the right to fail. Achievement is the national god, venerated in our media—the million-dollar athlete, the wealthy executive—and glorified in our praise of possessions. In the presence of such a potent state religion, the young are growing up old.

I see four kinds of pressure working on college students today: economic pressure, parental pressure, peer pressure, and self-induced pressure. It is easy to look around for villains—to blame the colleges for charging too much money, the professors for assigning too much work, the

© 1989 Judy Gelles

parents for pushing their children too far, the students for driving them-selves too hard. But there are no villains: only victims.

"In the late 1960s," one dean told me, "the typical question that I got from students was 'Why is there so much suffering in the world?' or 'How can I make a contribution?' Today it's 'Do you think it would look better for getting into law school if I did a double major in history and political science, or just majored in one of them?' " Many other deans confirmed this pattern. One said: "They're trying to find an edge—the intangible something that will look better on paper if two students are about equal."

Note the emphasis on looking better. The transcript has become a sacred document, the passport to security. How one appears on paper is more important than how one appears in person. *A* is for Admirable and *B* is for Borderline, even though, in Yale's official system of grading, *A* means "excellent" and *B* means "very good." Today, looking very good is no longer good enough, especially for students who hope to go on to law school or medical school. They know that entrance into the better schools will be an entrance into the better law firms and better medical practices where they will make a lot of money. They also know that the odds are harsh. Yale Law School, for instance, matriculates 170 students from an applicant pool of 3,700; Harvard enrolls 550 from a pool of 7,000.

It's all very well for those of us who write letters of recommendation for our students to stress the qualities of humanity that will make them good lawyers or doctors. And it's nice to think that admission officers are

really reading our letters and looking for the extra dimension of commitment or concern. Still, it would be hard for a student not to visualize these
officers shuffling so many transcripts studded with *A*s that they regard a
B as positively shameful.

The pressure is almost as heavy on students who just want to
graduate and get a job. Long gone are the days of the "gentleman's *C*,"
when students journeyed through college with a certain relaxation, sam-
pling a wide variety of courses—music, art, philosophy, classics, anthropology, poetry, religion—that would send them out as liberally educated
men and women. If I were an employer I would rather employ graduates
who have this range and curiosity than those who narrowly pursued safe
subjects and high grades. I know countless students whose inquiring
minds exhilarate me. I like to hear the play of their ideas. I don't know if
they are getting *A*s or *C*s, and I don't care. I also like them as people. The
country needs them, and they will find satisfying jobs. I tell them to relax.
They can't.

Nor can I blame them. They live in a brutal economy. Tuition, room,
and board at most private colleges now comes to at least $7,000, not
counting books and fees. This might seem to suggest that the colleges are
getting rich. But they are equally battered by inflation. Tuition covers only
60 percent of what it costs to educate a student, and ordinarily the remainder comes from what colleges receive in endowments, grants, and gifts.
Now the remainder keeps being swallowed by the cruel costs—higher
every year—of just opening the doors. Heating oil is up. Insurance is up.
Postage is up. Health-premium costs are up. Everything is up. Deficits are
up. We are witnessing in America the creation of a brotherhood of pau-
pers—colleges, parents, and students, joined by the common bond of debt.

Today it is not unusual for a student, even if he works part time at
college and full time during the summer, to accrue $5,000 in loans after
four years—loans that he must start to repay within one year after graduation. Exhorted at commencement to go forth into the world, he is already behind as he goes forth. How could he not feel under pressure
throughout college to prepare for this day of reckoning? I have used "he,"
incidentally, only for brevity. Women at Yale are under no less pressure to
justify their expensive education to themselves, their parents, and society.
In fact, they are probably under more pressure. For although they leave
college superbly equipped to bring fresh leadership to traditionally male
jobs, society hasn't yet caught up with this fact.

Along with economic pressure goes parental pressure. Inevitably,
the two are deeply intertwined.

I see many students taking pre-medical courses with joyless tenacity. They go off to their labs as if they were going to the dentist. It saddens
me because I know them in other corners of their life as cheerful people.

"Do you want to go to medical school?" I ask them.

"I guess so," they say, without conviction, or "Not really."

"Then why are you going?"

"Well, my parents want me to be a doctor. They're paying all this money and . . ."

Poor students, poor parents. They are caught in one of the oldest webs of love and duty and guilt. The parents mean well; they are trying to steer their sons and daughters toward a secure future. But the sons and daughters want to major in history or classics or philosophy—subjects with no "practical" value. Where's the payoff on the humanities? It's not easy to persuade such loving parents that the humanities do indeed pay off. The intellectual faculties developed by studying subjects like history and classics—an ability to synthesize and relate, to weigh cause and effect, to see events in perspective—are just the faculties that make creative leaders in business or almost any general field. Still, many fathers would rather put their money on courses that point toward a specific profession—courses that are pre-law, pre-medical, pre-business, or, as I sometimes heard it put, "pre-rich."

But the pressure on students is severe. They are truly torn. One part of them feels obligated to fulfill their parents' expectations; after all, their parents are older and presumably wiser. Another part tells them that the expectations that are right for their parents are not right for them.

I know a student who wants to be an artist. She is very obviously an artist and will be a good one—she has already had several modest local exhibits. Meanwhile she is growing as a well-rounded person and taking humanistic subjects that will enrich the inner resources out of which her art will grow. But her father is strongly opposed. He thinks that an artist is a "dumb" thing to be. The student vacillates and tries to please everybody. She keeps up with her art somewhat furtively and takes some of the "dumb" courses her father wants her to take—at least they are dumb courses for her. She is a free spirit on a campus of tense students—no small achievement in itself—and she deserves to follow her muse.

Peer pressure and self-induced pressure are also intertwined, and they begin almost at the beginning of freshman year.

"I had a freshman student I'll call Linda," one dean told me, "who came in and said she was under terrible pressure because her roommate, Barbara, was much brighter and studied all the time. I couldn't tell her that Barbara had come in two hours earlier to say the same thing about Linda."

The story is almost funny—except that it's not. It's symptomatic of all the pressures put together. When every student thinks every other student is working harder and doing better, the only solution is to study harder still. I see students going off to the library every night after dinner and coming back when it closes at midnight. I wish they would sometimes forget about their peers and go to a movie. I hear the clacking of typewriters in the hours before dawn. I see the tension in their eyes when exams are approaching and papers are due: *Will I get everything done?*

Probably they won't. They will get sick. They will get "blocked." They will sleep. They will oversleep. They will bug out. *Hey Carlos, help!*

Part of the problem is that they do more than they are expected to do. A professor will assign five-page papers. Several students will start writing ten-page papers to impress him. Then more students will write ten-page papers, and a few will raise the ante to fifteen. Pity the poor student who is still just doing the assignment.

"Once you have twenty or thirty percent of the student population deliberately overexerting," one dean points out, "it's bad for everybody. When a teacher gets more and more effort from his class, the student who is doing normal work can be perceived as not doing well. The tactic works, psychologically."

Why can't the professor just cut back and not accept longer papers? He can, and he probably will. But by then the term will be half over and the damage done. Grade fever is highly contagious and not easily reversed. Besides, the professor's main concern is with his course. He knows his students only in relation to the course and doesn't know that they are also overexerting in their other courses. Nor is it really his business. He didn't sign up for dealing with the student as a whole person and with all the emotional baggage the student brought along from home. That's what deans, masters, chaplains, and psychiatrists are for.

To some extent this is nothing new: a certain number of professors have always been self-contained islands of scholarship and shyness, more comfortable with books than with people. But the new pauperism has widened the gap still further, for professors who actually like to spend time with students don't have as much time to spend. They also are overexerting. If they are young, they are busy trying to publish in order not to perish, hanging by their fingernails onto a shrinking profession. If they are old and tenured, they are buried under the duties of administering departments—as departmental chairmen or members of committees—that have been thinned out by the budgetary axe.

Ultimately it will be the students' own business to break the circles in which they are trapped. They are too young to be prisoners of their parents' dreams and their classmates' fears. They must be jolted into believing in themselves as unique men and women who have the power to shape their own future.

"Violence is being done to the undergraduate experience," says Carlos Hortas. "College should be open-ended: at the end it should open many, many roads. Instead, students are choosing their goal in advance, and their choices narrow as they go along. It's almost as if they think that the country has been codified in the type of jobs that exist—that they've got to fit into certain slots. Therefore, fit into the best-paying slot.

"They ought to take chances. Not taking chances will lead to a life of colorless mediocrity. They'll be comfortable. But something in the spirit will be missing."

I have painted too drab a portrait of today's students, making them seem a solemn lot. That is only half of their story; if they were so dreary I wouldn't so thoroughly enjoy their company. The other half is that they are easy to like. They are quick to laugh and to offer friendship. They are not introverts. They are usually kind and are more considerate of one another than any student generation I have known.

Nor are they so obsessed with their studies that they avoid sports and extracurricular activities. On the contrary, they juggle their crowded hours to play on a variety of teams, perform with musical and dramatic groups, and write for campus publications. But this in turn is one more cause of anxiety. There are too many choices. Academically, they have 1,300 courses to select from; outside class they have to decide how much spare time they can spare and how to spend it.

This means that they engage in fewer extracurricular pursuits than their predecessors did. If they want to row on the crew and play in the symphony they will eliminate one; in the '60s they would have done both. They also tend to choose activities that are self-limiting. Drama, for instance, is flourishing in all twelve of Yale's residential colleges as it never has before. Students hurl themselves into these productions—as actors, directors, carpenters, and technicians—with a dedication to create the best possible play, knowing that the day will come when the run will end and they can get back to their studies.

They also can't afford to be the willing slave of organizations like the *Yale Daily News*. Last spring at the one-hundredth anniversary banquet of that paper—whose past chairmen include such once and future kings as Potter Stewart, Kingman Brewster, and William F. Buckley, Jr.—much was made of the fact that the editorial staff used to be small and totally committed and that "newsies" routinely worked fifty hours a week. In effect they belonged to a club: Newsies is how they defined themselves at Yale. Today's student will write one or two articles a week, when he can, and he defines himself as a student. I've never heard the word Newsie except at the banquet.

If I have described the modern undergraduate primarily as a driven creature who is largely ignoring the blithe spirit inside who keeps trying to come out and play, it's because that's where the crunch is, not only at Yale but throughout American education. It's why I think we should all be worried about the values that are nurturing a generation so fearful of risk and so goal-obsessed at such an early age.

I tell students that there is no one "right" way to get ahead—that each of them is a different person, starting from a different point and bound for a different destination. I tell them that change is a tonic and that all the slots are not codified nor the frontiers closed. One of my ways of telling them is to invite men and women who have achieved success outside the academic world to come and talk informally with my students during the year. They are heads of companies or ad agencies, editors of magazines, politicians, public officials, television magnates, labor leaders, business executives, Broadway producers, artists, writers, economists, photographers, scientists, historians—a mixed bag of achievers.

I ask them to say a few words about how they got started. The students assume that they started in their present profession and knew all along that it was what they wanted to do. Luckily for me, most of them got into their field by a circuitous route, to their surprise, after many detours. The students are startled. They can hardly conceive of a career that was not preplanned. They can hardly imagine allowing the hand of God or chance to nudge them down some unforeseen trail.

CHAPTER 10

Discussion Activities: Essays

The discussion activities in Chapter 10 are designed to help you become engaged in the processes of reading and responding to essays. They are not meant to be rigid instructions that you must follow. Ideally, the activities will lead you to think through what you have read and to come to your own conclusions about what is significant.

Working with a partner, in a small group, or with the whole class, decide which material to cover and the amount of time to spend on each section. Allow for different responses to the various aspects of the reading.

Write after You Read: Making a Journal Entry

Writing about a selection just after reading may help you remember and reflect on your reading experience. You can explore your response to a reading selection by recording your reactions in a journal entry, adapting the guidelines on page 9. Share what you have written.

Summarizing

Your aim in summarizing an essay can be to uncover what you perceive to be the writer's stance toward the subject of the essay.

In some essays, a main idea may be clearly stated in the introduction. When this is not the case, you may need to read all of the points the writer makes in the essay to determine what you perceive to be the writer's point of view. You can ask questions such as these:

□ What is the most important issue to this writer?

□ Which major point covers all of the points made in the essay?

□ What is the writer's position toward the subject of this essay?

Share your summary with one or more classmates. Discuss the reasons for the differences in your summaries.

Note: Further guidelines for summarizing can be found in Chapter 21.

Analyzing

To analyze a reading, you can break it down into parts to examine the parts and their relationship.

The following suggestions are designed to help you analyze essays. As you make observations about the various elements of a reading selection, identify or read aloud corresponding passages.

Note: Not every suggestion will apply to every essay you read.

1. Discuss what you learn and find significant about the writer. For example, you can focus on the following details:
    - the writer's position or career
    - the writer's background
    - the writer's gender

2. Discuss passages that struck you for some reason. For example, you can focus on the following material:
    - passages that you like
    - passages that you find troubling or difficult to understand
    - passages that you think reveal an important message or insight

3. Examine and evaluate how effectively the writer uses evidence to illustrate or support points: quotations, examples, facts, opinions, statistics, original observations, explanations, theories, definitions, references to other works, and so on. For example, you can focus on the following material:
    - evidence that you think effectively clarifies complex points
    - evidence that you find convincing
    - evidence that you find unconvincing

4. Discuss counterarguments or evidence that might challenge the writer's interpretation or argument.

5. Discuss the effect of the writer's use of language on the primary audience. You may need first to decide who that audience might be (for example, people who agree or who disagree with the writer; people who are similar to or who are different from the writer; people who have more power or who have less power than the writer; people who are concerned about the topic or who do not give much consideration to the topic). For example, you can focus on the following details:
    - expressions that produce positive or sympathetic reactions
    - expressions that produce negative or resistant reactions

6. Discuss what you learn or find significant about how the writer has structured the essay. For example, you can focus on the following material:
    - information or ideas provided in the opening paragraph(s)
    - information or ideas provided in the middle paragraphs
    - information or ideas provided in the ending
    - transitions from one paragraph to the next

Making Connections

Making connections between a reading selection and something outside the reading selection—such as another reading or your own experience—can help uncover meanings.

1. Explore similarities and differences between one reading selection and another. Identify or read aloud relevant passages. The many comparisons you can make include the following:

   ☐ Compare attitudes toward the importance of factual knowledge in "We Should Cherish Our Children's Freedom to Think" and "Teach Knowledge, Not 'Mental Skills.' "

   ☐ Compare attitudes toward grading in "The Farce Called 'Grading,' " "Grades and Self-Esteem," "College Pressures," and/or "The Commencement Speech You'll Never Hear" (p. 11).

   ☐ Compare attitudes toward college students and academic life in "College Pressures" and "The Commencement Speech You'll Never Hear" (p. 11).

   ☐ Apply the research findings and recommendations of "Creativity in the Classroom" (p. 92) to "The Farce Called 'Grading,' " "College Pressures," and/or "The Commencement Speech You'll Never Hear" (p. 11).

2. Test the truth or validity of the arguments against your own experience and background knowledge. Identify or read aloud relevant passages.

   ☐ Explore whether the generalizations, theories, or experiences in the reading support or contradict what you have learned from experience.

   ☐ Explore whether the generalizations, theories, or experiences in the reading help you make sense of your own experience.

   ☐ Explore whether you agree or disagree with—or take a mixed position toward—some idea(s) or issue(s) raised in the reading.

Guidelines for Writing about Essays

Chapter 11 provides guidelines for fulfilling an assignment to write about one or more reading selections.

The composing strategies in this chapter are designed to help you develop your response and analysis; they are not meant to be taken as rigid instructions that you must follow.

To show different stages of the composing process, the writing of one student, Sophia Skoufaki, is included. Her completed essay, "Is Creativity Suppressed by Knowledge?" can be found on pages 163–165. Sophia's work was selected as an example; it is not presented as a model to imitate.

As you develop this essay, you can work concurrently with Chapters 21–24 in Part 3 to summarize, paraphrase, quote, and document what you read.

SUGGESTED ESSAY ASSIGNMENTS*

Select or adapt one of the following assignments, or devise your own assignment in consultation with your instructor. Whichever topic you choose, adapt these guidelines:

☐ Establish your own position, for example, by agreeing or disagreeing with—or taking a mixed position toward—an author's ideas.
☐ Use details and quotations from the reading to introduce or support your ideas (see Chapters 21–23).
☐ Include examples and ideas from your own experience, background knowledge, reading, and/or research to support your ideas.

1. Write an essay in which you respond to one reading selection.
2. Write an essay in which you compare and contrast two reading selections that deal with the same or a similar subject.
3. Write an essay in which you analyze the way several reading selections deal with the same or a similar subject.
4. Write an essay based on one of the suggestions for Making Connections on page 147.

*These assignments can be adapted for many of the reading selections in this book.

Selecting a Reading

The first step in writing about reading is usually to decide which reading to write about. To determine which reading selection(s) you would like to explore further, review all the writing you have done so far about the readings: annotations, journal entries, and any notes you might have taken during class discussions. If you still cannot decide, reread the selections, or discuss choices with a classmate or with your instructor.

A Student Writer at Work

After completing several assigned readings, Sophia decided she would write an essay about Kie Ho's "We Should Cherish Our Children's Freedom to Think" (p. 125). In her journal entry on this reading selection, she wrote about why she liked it.

Note: Mechanical errors in the entry have been corrected.

Excerpt from Sophia's Journal Entry on "We Should Cherish Our Children's Freedom to Think"

This is one of the most successful essays I've read till today. The essay is mainly personal experiences of Ho—experiences that he had as a student in Indonesia and as a father of a student in California. What I like most in this essay is that it talks about a specific difference between educational systems that is probably the most important. I have heard a lot of times complaints of foreign people and natives about school here. All of them concern the exact same problems of American students compared to international students. None of the essays I had read before Ho's had so specifically and correctly pointed out the difference of the high school education between the U.S. and other countries.

Rereading to Understand the Writer's Ideas

Reread the reading you have selected to gain a fuller understanding of the writer's ideas. One or more of these strategies may be helpful:

1. *Make additional annotations.* Identify what you perceive to be significant passages in the reading by marking (for example, underlining, circling) or copying them.

2. *Take notes.* Decide what you think is the writer's position toward the subject of the essay. Then look for supporting points and the evidence given to support each point. You may find it useful to outline the essay.

3. *Cluster ideas and facts.* Use a clustering technique (see pp. 49–50) to examine the various ideas and facts in the reading. The following example shows how material from the article "Intercultural Communication Stumbling Blocks" by LaRay M. Barna (p. 75) can be clustered:

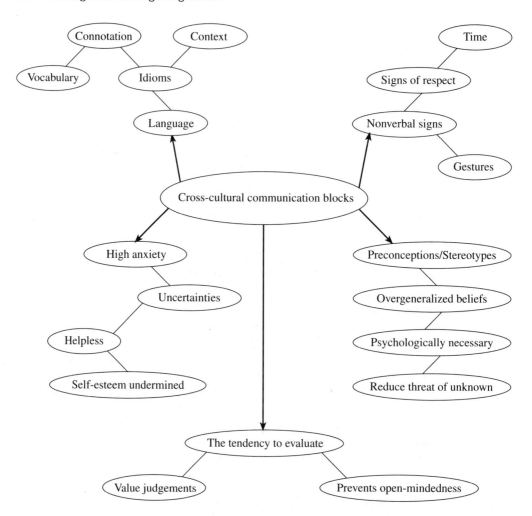

4. *Look up unfamiliar words.* Use the Glossary or a dictionary. Write the meaning above the word in the text, or list words and their meanings in a notebook or in a blank, alphabetized address book.

Identifying Points of Agreement and Disagreement

Reread the source again, this time to focus on your own reactions. For example, you can do the following:

1. Make separate lists of points of agreement and points of disagreement, and/or experiences that match your experience or that contradict your experience.

2. Then review your lists to see if you can find a pattern in your reactions. For example, you may discover one of the following patterns:

   □ Disagree with everything the writer says

   □ Agree on one key point but disagree on other points

☐ Agree and disagree on an equal number of points

☐ Agree with the writer's view completely but disapprove of the way the writer has presented it

Recognizing a pattern in your response might help you organize your essay later.

Selecting Evidence for Critical Analysis of a Reading

You can explain your reaction to and assessment of a reading by giving examples, relating experiences, and referring to other readings or information that you know (either through previous education or research). One of the following suggestions may be useful in helping you recall experiences, ideas, and information.

1. *Review the guidelines for analyzing reading selections in the chapter entitled Discussion Activities*. Write down responses that may help you develop your essay.

2. *Use one or more of the exploratory strategies described in Chapter 5*. Strategies such as making a list, freewriting, looping, cubing, clustering—or others that you find productive—may help generate ideas and uncover experiences that you can write about in your essay.

3. *Discuss the reading with a classmate or group of friends*. By engaging in conversation about the writer's experiences and ideas, you might find reasons why you believe as you do and also get some fresh ideas.

Focusing

When you take notes or engage in exploratory writing, you generate ideas to develop your own understanding of a subject. When you write an essay, you share your understanding with others, bringing your thoughts into focus for readers. Each reading selection allows for many possible focal points. The area you focus on depends upon what you find significant in the reading.

GUIDELINES

For Developing a Focal Point

1. *Review all that you have written in response to the reading.*
2. *Decide what topic you might want to focus on.*
3. *Reread the reading selection(s) to find material related to your topic.*
4. *Group the details under specific categories.*
5. *Look for a pattern in the details.*
6. *Analyze those details to reveal their significance.*
7. *Express in one or two sentences what you find to be the most significant point(s) to make or question(s) to raise about your chosen topic.*

Whatever process you undergo to develop a focal point, remember that at this stage, the focus is tentative. As you move through several stages of writing, your thinking may undergo several changes.

If you are not yet ready to establish a focal point, turn to the section on structuring the essay.

Structuring the Entire Essay

A carefully structured essay can help communicate ideas effectively to readers.

The following chart provides an overall view of how an essay about reading can be developed. It by no means represents a rigid formula. The various parts of this chart are discussed at length in the sections that follow on the introduction, body, and conclusion of an essay.

Introduction
☐ Focus on a particular topic related to the reading.
☐ Ask or imply a question about the topic, or state your position concerning the topic.

↓

Body
Provide supporting points and evidence to develop the topic.

Paraphrases
Quotations
Explanations
Details
Examples
Experiences
Facts
Opinions
Theories
Statistics

↓

Conclusion
Reflect on or explain your position concerning the idea(s) in the reading(s).

↓

Developing the Introduction

The purpose of an introduction can be to focus on the topic: to tell readers what the essay is about. Such an introduction serves to involve readers in your perspective or stance (attitude, position) concerning the topic and can include information that will help them understand the purpose of the essay. This is usually accomplished in one or two paragraphs.

You can choose from a variety of approaches to involve your readers in the topic at the beginning of your essay. For example, you can do one or more of the following:

- Provide background information on your topic (see Barna, p. 76).
- Quote a famous saying (see Levine and Wolff, p. 84).
- Tell a brief story or anecdote (see Sarton, p. 37).
- Make a shocking or unexpected statement (see Neusner, p. 11).
- Ask a question that invites your readers to reconsider their position on the subject or identify with the material you are about to present (see Ho, pp. 125–126).

The introduction is flexible. Its content and form are dependent on your subject matter and individual writing style. But there are features readers usually will need and expect in an introduction to an essay about what you have read.

Note: If the following guidelines do not suit your essay, discuss alternatives with your instructor.

GUIDELINES

For Writing an Introduction

An introduction to an essay about reading can accomplish these goals, though not necessarily in this order and not necessarily in separate sentences:

1. Identify the reading(s) by *title* (within quotation marks) and *author* (full name).
2. Provide a *summary* of the key idea(s) from the reading(s) that you will discuss in your essay.
3. Indicate the *focus* of your essay, for example, in one of these ways:

   - State directly your stance toward the key idea(s) of the reading(s), for example, whether you agree or disagree with—or take a mixed position toward—the writer's ideas.
   - Raise or imply one or more questions about the idea(s) discussed in the reading(s).

A Student Writer at Work

Sophia wrote different versions of her introduction. The first draft is reprinted here; it was almost exactly what she had written in her journal entry (see p. 149).

Note: Errors have been corrected.

Introduction to Sophia's First Draft

One of the most successful essays I have ever read is "We Should Cherish Our Children's Freedom to Think" by Kie Ho, whose purpose is to compare the education of the United States with that of Indonesia and other places in the world. The essay consists mainly of personal experiences of Ho, experiences that he had as a student in Indonesia and as a father of a student in California. What I like most in this essay is that it is about a specific difference between educational systems. I have often heard complaints about the schools in the States. All of them concern the problems of American students as compared to international students. None of the essays I had read before Ho's had so specifically and correctly pointed out the difference of the education between the U.S. and other countries.

Title
Author's name
Author's purpose

Reason for
liking the essay

After consultation with her instructor and two classmates, Sophia decided to eliminate the discussion of why she liked the reading and to get to the heart of the matter by stating what she perceived to be Ho's key points and her own stance concerning Ho's position. Two drafts later, the following one-paragraph introduction emerged.

Note: Errors have been corrected.

Introduction to Sophia's Final Essay

In his essay "We Should Cherish Our Children's Freedom to Think," Kie Ho supports the American system of education. He expresses disappointment with the Indonesian way of teaching that he had experienced. As he points out, American schools tend to teach students how to develop their creativity more, rather than try to stuff their heads with knowledge. Ho always had to memorize things and to acquire as much knowledge as he could from books, while his son in California learned practical things through experience. Ho admires the approach of his son's school. But I hesitate to endorse it.

Title
Author's name
Author's position

Sophia's stance
toward author's
idea

Developing the Body

The body of the paper is its longest section. In several paragraphs, you can supply evidence that supports your position or answers the question(s) you raised in the introduction.

GUIDELINES

For Developing Body Paragraphs

1. For each paragraph or set of paragraphs, you can provide at least one supporting point that relates to and expands on the topic that you focused on in the introduction.
2. Within each paragraph, include explanations, details, examples, and quotations that serve as evidence to substantiate the supporting point. The material from the reading may be presented in the form of paraphrase or quotation (see Chapters 22 and 23). Other evidence can be drawn from your own experience, background knowledge, reading, and/or research.
3. Use appropriate formats for citing sources (see Chapter 24).

Structuring the Body

None of the following patterns represents a rigid formula. You may try variations on these structures or devise another structure that suits your topic. You can use the drafting process to experiment with organization; these first attempts can later be revised.

1. *Explore one major idea from the reading.*

   □ State one major idea from the reading.

   □ Explain the writer's point.

   □ In several paragraphs, provide evidence—this can include your own experience and background knowledge—to support or challenge that idea. Refer periodically to the reading through paraphrase and quotation.

2. *Explore several ideas from the reading one by one, in order of importance, devoting at least one paragraph to each idea.* You may begin with what you think is the less or least important idea and end with the most important, or vice versa.

   □ State an idea from the reading; your statement can appear at the beginning of a new paragraph.

   □ Explain the writer's point.

   □ Provide evidence— this can include your own experiences and background knowledge—to support or challenge that idea. Refer periodically to the reading through paraphrase and quotation.

   □ Repeat this procedure for each idea you want to discuss.

3. *Explore a topic by comparing and contrasting ideas in one or more readings.*

   First half:

   □ State an idea from the reading that you agree with.

   □ Explain the idea.

   □ Provide evidence—this can include your own experience or background knowledge—to support that idea.

   □ Repeat this procedure for each idea you agree with.

Second half:

- ☐ State an idea from the reading that you disagree with.
- ☐ Explain the idea.
- ☐ Provide evidence—this can include your own experience or background knowledge—to challenge that idea.
- ☐ Repeat this procedure for each idea you disagree with.

4. Explore several ideas from the reading, and then explore one or more ideas that the reading does not develop enough or neglects altogether.

First half:

- ☐ State an idea from the reading that you will discuss; your statement can appear at the beginning of a paragraph.
- ☐ Explain the writer's point.
- ☐ Provide evidence—this can include your own experience or background knowledge—to support or challenge that idea.
- ☐ Repeat this procedure for each idea you want to discuss. Refer periodically to the reading.

Second half:

- ☐ State an idea that the reading ignores.
- ☐ Provide evidence—this can include your own experience or background knowledge—to explain why that idea is important to consider.
- ☐ Repeat this procedure for each idea you want to discuss.

A Student Writer at Work

Sophia organized the body of her essay primarily by beginning with ideas of Ho's that she agreed with and then by discussing ideas that she partially or completely disagreed with. The second and third paragraphs of Sophia's essay are reprinted below. In each paragraph, Sophia discusses a different aspect of her topic and supports each point with evidence. Paragraph 2 reveals her agreement with Ho's view; paragraph 3 reveals her disagreement.

Paragraphs 2 and 3 of Sophia's Essay

Ho connects this focus on creativity and practicality with the country's strength. He asks why so many people complain about the American education system, since America is "the country of innovation" (p. 126). This innovativeness is tied to the fact that the public schools provide children with the opportunity to be creative:

Explanation of author's view; evidence provided through paraphrase and quotation

> I think I found the answer on an excursion to the Laguna Beach Museum of Art, where the work of schoolchildren was on exhibit . . . they had transformed simple paper lunch bags into, among other things, a waterfall with flying fish (p. 126).

I have to agree that Ho's observation is true. The opportunity for creativity impressed me, too, when I first went to an American high school. I admired how much attention the teachers gave to students' work and talents. I was impressed by the programs the school offered, the many different opportunities they gave students to do whatever they wanted, no matter how different and unique it was. I noticed that the students were always involved in activities, competitions, and exhibitions that are connected with their classes at school. That is a way of learning that Ho supports.

Agreement; evidence provided from personal experience

However, I don't agree that this is the best way to educate students. Ho wonders if we would "prefer to stuff the developing little heads of our children with hundreds of geometry problems, the names of rivers in Brazil, and 50 lines from *The Canterbury Tales*" (p. 126). He believes that by asking them to acquire much knowledge and take memorization seriously, we really "retard" the impulses of the students, "frustrate their opportunities for self-expression" (p. 126). While I agree that experimentation, free expression of one's self and creativity, and innovation are important, I don't think that by learning geography, history, and math or by studying literature, students underdevelop their impulses. I think that these impulses develop in life by themselves and that knowledge, even that boring, awful memorizing of cities and names of rivers, helps expand one's horizons and enlarge one's perspectives. Besides this, there are some things students have to learn the way they are because, otherwise, they are misunderstood and mixed up. It is not flattering at all for America that "our youngsters . . . put Mussolini in the same category as Dostoevski" (p. 126).

Disagreement Explanation of author's view; evidence provided through paraphrase and quotation

Partial agreement

Disagreement; explanation of viewpoint

Starting a New Paragraph

The paragraph can be an important signaling system. The sight of a newly indented paragraph can send a message to readers that the writer is introducing a new aspect of the topic or is shifting emphasis. The initial sentence of a new paragraph may help readers connect what they have just read with what they are about to read.

To gain an understanding of how paragraphs can function, read the eighth and ninth paragraphs of LaRay M. Barna's "Intercultural Communication Stumbling Blocks," reprinted here. Paragraph 8 makes a point about the importance of nonverbal cues in communication and then provides evidence to support that point. Paragraph 9 simply provides an example to illustrate the point made in the previous paragraph.

Learning the language, which most foreign visitors consider their *only* barrier to understanding, is actually only the beginning. As Frankel says, "To enter into a culture is to be able to hear, in Lionel Trilling's phrase, its special 'hum and buzz of implication.'" This brings in *nonverbal areas* and the second stumbling block. People from different cultures inhabit different nonverbal sensory words. Each sees, hears, feels, and smells only that which has some meaning or importance for him. He abstracts whatever fits into his personal world of recognitions and then interprets it through the frame of reference of his own culture.

First sentence makes a point related to the previous paragraph, which discusses language.

An Oregon girl in an intercultural communication class asked a young man from Saudi Arabia how he would signal nonverbally that he liked her. His response was to smooth back his hair which, to her, was just a common nervous gesture signifying nothing. She repeated her question three times. He smoothed his hair three times and, finally realizing that she was not recognizing this movement as his reply to her question, automatically ducked his head and stuck out his tongue slightly in embarrassment. This behavior *was* noticed by the girl, and she interpreted it as the way he would express his liking for her.

First sentence introduces an example that illustrates the point made in the previous paragraph.

These two paragraphs could have been combined into one paragraph. The writer chose to create two paragraphs. One reason for that choice might have been to break up a paragraph that seemed too long; another might have been to allow readers to absorb the generalizations before they read the specifics.

ACTIVITY

Analyzing the Function of the First Sentence of a Paragraph

1. The eighth paragraph and the first three sentences of the ninth paragraph of William Zinsser's "College Pressures" are reprinted here. Discuss how the first sentence of the ninth paragraph (underlined) might help readers connect what they have just read (in the eighth paragraph) with what they are about to read.

"In the late 1960s," one dean told me, "the typical question that I got from students was 'Why is there so much suffering in the world' or 'How can I make a contribution?' Today it's 'Do you think it would better for getting into law school if I did a double major in history and political science, or just majored in one of them?'" Many other deans confirmed this pattern. One said: "They're trying to find an edge—the intangible something that will look better on paper if two students are about equal."

Note the emphasis on looking better. The transcript has become a sacred document, the passport to security. How one appears on paper is more important than how one appears in person. . . .

2. The fourth paragraph and the first three sentences of the fifth paragraph of Joel D. Block's ''Myth, Reality and Shades of Gray: Comparing Same-Sex Friendships'' are reprinted here. Discuss how the first sentence of the fifth paragraph (underlined) might help readers connect the material in the fourth paragraph with the material in the fifth paragraph.

> Speaking of their childhood, men recall being highly responsive to and aware of the sex-role opinions of other boys. Girls in preteen years appear to be less susceptible to sex-role pressure. While ''sissy'' is the most powerful charge against the young male ego, prior to puberty girls do not report sensitivity to accusations that they are being unfeminine. It is not until the dating years, when competition for boys becomes an issue, that women report being concerned with feminine behavior. Males, for the most part, are responsive to the suggestion that their behavior is unmanly at almost any age.
> <u>These early attitudes, reinforced by social conditioning, continue to play an active part in the friendships of both sexes during adolescence.</u> This is a period when the majority of males once again report a close alliance with same-sex friends but now, with heightened intensity, considerable energy is devoted to jockeying for position and a definite undercurrent of competition pervades the relationship. Although in dissimilar fashion, females share equally fragile relationships at this age. . . . ■

Synthesizing References to Two or More Readings

Writing about more than one reading usually entails taking material from the sources and *synthesizing* it: combining it with your own ideas. Each paragraph of synthesis can contain not only ideas from the readings but also an idea that demonstrates your understanding of ways in which the different readings handle the same subject.

GUIDELINES

For Synthesizing

1. Select one or more readings that deal with the same or a similar subject.
2. Note similarities and differences in the way the readings handle the subject matter or in what they say about the subject. You might want to make separate lists of these similarities and differences.
3. Select a particular aspect of the subject you want to discuss. Create a sentence that reveals your understanding of the ways in which the different readings handle this aspect.
4. Select ideas from the readings to illustrate or support the point you are making. The material in the readings may be presented in the form of summary, paraphrase, or quotation (see Chapters 21–23).
5. Use appropriate expressions to reveal the relationship between ideas in the readings, for example, to show if they are similar or different (see Transitions, pp. 325–327).
6. Identify your sources clearly (see Chapter 24).

Sample Syntheses

The following three examples of synthesis show three different ways in which a writer can make the same point, using the same two readings. The first sentence in each paragraph represents the writer's idea. The next sentences support that idea, using material from Sydney J. Harris's essay "What True Education Should Do" (p. 3) and Kie Ho's essay "We Should Cherish Our Children's Freedom to Think" (p. 125).

Note: The sentences containing expressions used to reveal the relationship between ideas in the readings are in italics.

1. Students should be allowed to be creative and not just memorize. According to Sydney J. Harris, the author of "What True Education Should Do," students are like oysters that have richness within them. And teachers are to help them open and reveal their minds, not to "stuff" them with something outside them, as sausages are stuffed. *Kie Ho has the same opinion as Harris.* In "We Should Cherish Our Children's Freedom to Think," Ho compares his son with himself when he was his son's age. He says his son is very creative and can do many things by himself. But Ho had to memorize things his teachers told him to, and he feels that he is less creative.

2. Students should be allowed to be creative and not just memorize. In other words, we should give the opportunity to students to fulfill their creativity. As Kie Ho says in his essay "We Should Cherish Our Children's Freedom to Think," children will not really be able to think or believe in themselves without experimenting freely with ideas. He also claims that if we force children to memorize, we will "retard their impulses" and prevent them from self-expression. *Sydney J. Harris, in "What True Education Should Do," makes the same point.* According to Harris, the best way to educate is to elicit knowledge, not "stuff" it into a person's head.

3. Students should be allowed to be creative and not just memorize. Indeed, memorization is necessary, but not as important as creativity. In his essay "What True Education Should Do," Sydney J. Harris states that a student should not be "stuffed with miscellaneous facts, with such an indigestible mass of material, that he has no time to draw on his own resources, to use his own mind for analyzing and synthesizing and evaluating this material." Harris means that mere memorization is futile. *Similarly, Kie Ho in "We Should Cherish Our Children's Freedom to Think" insists that creativity helps elicit knowledge from students.*

ACTIVITY

Synthesizing Sources

Find passages in two or more readings that cover related issues. The authors do not necessarily have to agree on the issue. Then write a paragraph of synthesis, adapting the guidelines on page 159. For example, you can choose from the following readings, listed by the author's last name:

☐ Neusner (p. 11), Zinsser (p. 138), Harris (p. 3)

- □ Ho (p. 125), Hirsch (p. 128), Moore (p. 135)
- □ Lean (p. 130), Moore (p. 135), Zinsser (p. 138)
- □ Barna (p. 75), Levine and Wolff (p. 84), Niella (p. 59)
- □ Viorst (p. 65), Block (p. 69)
- □ Zitkala-Ša (p. 16), Yezierska (p. 25)   ■

Developing the Conclusion

The conclusion, usually one to two paragraphs, grows out of the rest of the essay. Having introduced and provided evidence about a topic, you can now discuss the implications of what you have written. There are several strategies you can use to bring your essay to its end. Which approach you choose will depend on your topic and purpose.

Note: If none of the following suggestions suits your topic and purpose, discuss alternatives with your instructor.

GUIDELINES

For Writing a Conclusion

In concluding an essay, you can use one or more of these strategies:

1. Emphasize the importance of the topic and/or explain your own position on the topic.
2. Persuade readers to reject a writer's arguments in favor of your own.
3. Propose a better or different way to view the topic from the way presented in the reading.
4. Connect the topic to your own life.
5. Invite readers to apply the knowledge or insight that you gained from your reading and writing to their own lives.
6. Predict future experiences, or state hope for the future.
7. Raise questions about the topic.
8. Discuss the effect that your reading and writing have had on your outlook on the topic or on your life.

A Student Writer at Work

Sophia had difficulty deciding how to end her essay. After consulting with her instructor, she understood that it was acceptable not to take sides. Her conclusion is reprinted here.

Conclusion of Sophia's Final Essay

Ho was raised by having to memorize things and learn by heart information that he may never have used in his life. His son grew up in a school system where practical information is more desirable than any other

Review of Ho's idea

kind of information. "Our public education certainly is not perfect, but it is a great deal better than any other" is the conclusion of Ho's essay (p. 127). It is clear that Ho has a definite opinion about the system he prefers. I am not able to do that. On the one hand, I believe in memorizing things, in having to learn history, in having to know geography and literature, because these subjects not only serve as the tools people need to face life in a more global way, but they also sharpen the mind and expand points of view. On the other hand, I think that schools should provide students with challenges, competition, and opportunities for creativity. Schools that lack these stimuli should develop them; students need opportunities to get involved in things they may be good at but they never had the chance to discover.

Explanation of her own position toward the topic

Drafting

Prepare a draft of your essay adapting the guidelines for writing an interim draft on page 53 and for structuring the entire essay on pages 152–162.

Giving and Receiving Feedback

Exchange drafts with one or more classmates, adapting the guidelines for giving and receiving feedback on page 54. Review one another's work by examining (1) what you like about a paper and (2) what you think can be done to strengthen it. Use the feedback form on page 56 and/or the suggestions for summarizing and analyzing on pages 145–146, or raise your own questions.

Revising

You can revise your draft by answering questions such as these (see pp. 57–58 for a fuller discussion):

- □ What should I keep?
- □ What should I add?
- □ What should I delete?
- □ What should I change?
- □ What should I rearrange?
- □ What should I rethink?

Completing

Once you have revised the draft, you can complete the essay by adapting these guidelines:

- □ Evaluate the essay as a whole.
- □ Proofread and edit the essay (see Chapter 25).
- □ Prepare a neat final manuscript to hand in for evaluation (see Chapter 28).

Is Creativity Suppressed by Knowledge?

Sophia Skoufaki

About the Author Sophia Skoufaki wrote the following essay in her first semester of college to fulfill an assignment for a composition course. She was educated in Greece until she came to the United States as a high school student.
Note: This essay has been edited for publication in this book.

In his essay "We Should Cherish Our Children's Freedom to Think," Kie Ho supports the American system of education. He expresses disappointment with the Indonesian way of teaching that he had experienced. As he points out, American schools tend to teach students how to develop their creativity more, rather than try to stuff their heads with knowledge. Ho always had to memorize things and to acquire as much knowledge as he could from books, while his son in California learned practical things through experience. Ho admires the approach of his son's school. But I hesitate to endorse it.

Ho connects this focus on creativity and practicality with the country's strength. He asks why so many people complain about the American education system, since America is "the country of innovation" (p. 126). This innovativeness is tied to the fact that the public schools provide children with the opportunity to be creative:

> I think I found the answer on an excursion to the Laguna Beach Museum of Art, where the work of schoolchildren was on exhibit. . . . they had transformed simple paper lunch bags into, among other things, a waterfall with flying fish (p. 126).

I have to agree that Ho's observation is true. The opportunity for creativity impressed me, too, when I first went to an American high school. I admired how much attention the teachers gave to students' work and talents. I was impressed by the programs the school offered, the many different opportunities they gave students to do whatever they wanted, no matter how different and unique it was. I noticed that the students were always involved in activities, competitions, and exhibitions that are connected with their classes at school. That is a way of learning that Ho supports.

However, I don't agree that this is the best way to educate students. Ho wonders if we would "prefer to stuff the developing little heads of our children with hundreds of geometry problems, the names of rivers in Brazil, and 50 lines from *The Canterbury Tales*" (p. 126). He believes that by asking them to acquire much knowledge and take memorization seriously, we really "retard" the impulses of students and "frustrate their opportunities for self-expression'' (p. 126). While I agree that experimentation, free expression of one's self and creativity, and innovation are important, I don't think that by learning geography, history, and math or by studying literature, students underdevelop their impulses. I think that these impulses develop in life by themselves and that knowledge, even that boring, awful memorizing of cities and names of rivers, helps expand one's horizons and enlarge one's perspectives. Besides this, there are some things students have to learn the way they are because, otherwise, they are misunderstood and mixed up. It is not flattering at all for America that ''our youngsters . . . put Mussolini in the same category as Dostoevski'' (p. 126).

Nevertheless, Ho believes that the knowledge his son got in school was more useful than what he himself got in the Indonesian school. He writes:

> unlike his counterparts in Asia and Europe, my son had studied *creative* geography. When he was only 6, he drew a map of the route that he traveled to get to school, including the streets and their names, the buildings and traffic signs and the houses that he passed (p. 126).

What Ho names ''*creative* geography,'' I would call development of common sense, which is, of course, important. But wouldn't students have a better sense of orientation if they studied world maps and knew where their country is located and where other countries, which they hear about every day, are in respect to their country? Isn't it sad that Ho's son thought that ''Buenos Aires was Spanish for good food—a plate of tacos and burritos, perhaps'' (p. 126) and that that doesn't sound strange to Ho? If students know history, if they memorize names, places, and facts, they give themselves material with which to think, criticize, evaluate, and draw conclusions about social and economic conditions. For example, the invasion of Iraq into Kuwait had a lot of impact on other countries. If someone does not know the geography or the history of these places and the relationship of the rival countries with other nations, that person cannot fully understand the influence the event had on the world and on his or her own country at the same time.

The focus on using imagination can have negative consequences. In my Chemistry class in an American high school, for example, our teacher gave us a limited number of instructions and expected us to do everything else needed to conduct the experiment. Students who had never had Chemistry before did the chemical experiments with more ease than I did, due to their imagination and previous experience in other experimental classes. However, they did not know why things happened the way they did, because they did not have enough chemistry background to understand and interpret the results of the experiments. If all classes were like that, then the only thing students would gain is a lot of dispersed, unorganized, and superficial information and not real knowledge.

Ho was raised by having to memorize things and learn by heart information that he may never have used in his life. His son grew up in a school system where practical information is more desirable than any other kind of information. "Our public education certainly is not perfect, but it is a great deal better than any other" is the conclusion of Ho's essay (p. 127). It is clear that Ho has a definite opinion about the system he prefers. I am not able to do that. On the one hand, I believe in memorizing things, in having to learn history, in having to know geography and literature, because these subjects not only serve as the tools people need to face life in a more global way, but they also sharpen the mind and expand points of view. On the other hand, I think that schools should provide students with challenges, competition, and opportunities for creativity. Schools that lack these stimuli should develop them; students need opportunities to get involved in things they may be good at but they never had the chance to discover.

Write after You Read

Explore your response to "Is Creativity Suppressed by Knowledge?" by recording your reactions in a journal entry, adapting the guidelines on page 9.

ACTIVITY

For Class Discussion

Working with a partner, in a small group, or with the whole class, engage in some or all of the following activities. Decide the order in which to cover the material and the amount of time to spend on each activity. Allow for different reactions to and interpretations of the various aspects of the reading.

1. Share the reactions to "Is Creativity Suppressed by Knowledge?" that you have recorded in your journal entry.

2. Examine the essay closely, using the suggestions for summarizing and analyzing on pages 145–146.

3. Compare the experiences and ideas in the essay with your own experiences and ideas. ∎

FICTION

This unit, Writing from Sources: Fiction, consists of three chapters that can help you fulfill an assignment to write an essay in response to fiction. By reading and examining your reactions to short stories in Chapter 12, guided by the discussion activities in Chapter 13, you may develop a sense of how language can be used both to compose and to comprehend a work of fiction. In Chapter 14, guidelines are provided for analyzing and interpreting a literary work. A sample student essay is included.

CHAPTER 12

Readings: Fiction

Chapter 12 presents five works of fiction: short stories.

As you read and reread a short story, you can aim to accomplish the following:

☐ Enter the world of the story

☐ Experience or feel what the characters experience or feel

☐ Examine your own experience and views

The Reading Selections

The reading selections in this chapter are complete and unabridged short stories written by writers from North America and Great Britain. Spanning over one hundred years, the stories reflect a sense of social history as they reveal some of the individual concerns, cultural experiences, and political and social issues of the times.

The Ingrate

Paul Laurence Dunbar

About the Author   Paul Laurence Dunbar (1872–1906) was born in the United States, in Dayton, Ohio, the son of former slaves. After graduating from high school, he could find work only as an elevator operator. Already a published poet, he continued to read extensively and began to write and publish fiction as well as poetry. Widely admired, he was the first African American to make a living as a professional writer. Among his many books are the novels *The Uncalled* (1898) and *The Sport of the Gods* (1902).

The Context of the Reading   "The Ingrate" was originally published in 1900. The story begins in a southern state in the United States just before the Civil War (which began in 1861) between northern and southern states. At that time, slavery was still legal in the South but no longer in the North. Most slaves were treated brutally. In 1863, President Abraham Lincoln signed the Emancipation Proclamation, freeing slaves in certain southern states. After the war ended in 1865, slavery was abolished.

The following references to that time period are used in the reading:

- *Yankee:* native or inhabitant of a northern state
- *abolitionist:* person who wants to end slavery
- *the underground railway:* organization that provided hiding places and transportation for slaves, helping them escape to the North
- *Quaker:* a member of the Religious Society of Friends, which was active in the abolitionist movement (Quakers used the word *thee* for *you* and *thy* for *your*.)
- *(Charles) Sumner, (Wendell) Phillips, (Frederick) Douglass, (William) Garrison:* American abolitionists (Douglass was a runaway slave.)
- *Lucretia Mott:* American social reformer
- *Harriet Beecher Stowe:* American novelist and reformer, author of *Uncle Tom's Cabin* (1852), which was influential in promoting the abolitionist movement

1

Mr. Leckler was a man of high principle. Indeed, he himself had admitted it at times to Mrs. Leckler. She was often called into counsel with him. He was one of those large-souled creatures with a hunger for unlimited advice, upon which he never acted. Mrs. Leckler knew this, but like the good, patient little wife that she was, she went on paying her poor tribute of advice and admiration. Today her husband's mind was particularly troubled—as usual, too, over a matter of principle. Mrs. Leckler came at his call.

"Mrs. Leckler," he said, "I am troubled in my mind. I—in fact, I am puzzled over a matter that involves either the maintaining or relinquishing of a principle."

"Well, Mr. Leckler?" said his wife interrogatively.

"If I had been a scheming, calculating Yankee, I should have been rich now; but all my life I have been too generous and confiding. I have always let principle stand between me and my interests." Mr. Leckler took himself all too seriously to be conscious of his pun, and went on: "Now this is a matter in which my duty and my principles seem to conflict. It stands thus: Josh has been doing a piece of plastering for Mr. Eckley over in Lexington, and from what he says, I think that city rascal has misrepresented the amount of work to me and so cut down the pay for it. Now, of course, I should not care, the matter of a dollar or two being nothing to me; but it is a very different matter when we consider poor Josh." There was deep pathos in Mr. Leckler's tone. "You know Josh is anxious to buy his freedom, and I allow him a part of whatever he makes; so you see it's he that's affected. Every dollar that he is cheated out of cuts off just so much from his earnings, and puts further away his hope of emancipation."

If the thought occurred to Mrs. Leckler that, since Josh received only about one tenth of what he earned, the advantage of just wages would be quite as much her husband's as the slave's, she did not betray it, but met the naïve reasoning with the question, "But where does the conflict come in, Mr. Leckler?"

"Just here. If Josh knew how to read and write and cipher—"

"Mr. Leckler, are you crazy!"

"Listen to me, my dear, and give me the benefit of your judgment. This is a very momentous question. As I was about to say, if Josh knew these things, he could protect himself from cheating when his work is at too great a distance for me to look after it for him."

"But teaching a slave—"

"Yes, that's just what is against my principles. I know how public opinion and the law look at it. But my conscience rises up in rebellion every time I think of that poor black man being cheated out of his earnings. Really, Mrs. Leckler, I think I may trust to Josh's discretion and secretly give him such instructions as will permit him to protect himself."

"Well, of course, it's just as you think best," said his wife.

"I knew you would agree with me," he returned. "It's such a comfort to take counsel with you, my dear!" And the generous man walked out onto the veranda, very well satisfied with himself and his wife, and prospectively pleased with Josh. Once he murmured to himself, "I'll lay for Eckley next time."

Josh, the subject of Mr. Leckler's charitable solicitations, was the plantation plasterer. His master had given him his trade, in order that he might do whatever such work was needed about the place; but he became so proficient in his duties, having also no competition among the poor whites, that he had grown to be in great demand in the country thereabout. So Mr. Leckler found it profitable, instead of letting him do chores and field work in his idle time, to hire him out to neighboring farms and planters. Josh was a man of more than ordinary intelligence; and when he asked to be allowed to pay for himself by working overtime, his master readily agreed— for it promised more work to be done, for which he could allow the slave just what he pleased. Of course, he knew now that when the black man began to cipher this state of affairs would be changed; but it would mean such an increase of profit from the outside that he could afford to give up his own little peculations. Anyway, it would be many years before the slave could pay the two thousand dollars, which price he had set upon him. Should he approach that figure, Mr. Leckler felt it just possible that the market in slaves would take a sudden rise.

When Josh was told of his master's intention, his eyes gleamed with pleasure, and he went to his work with the zest of long hunger. He proved a remarkably apt pupil. He was indefatigable in doing the tasks assigned him. Even Mr. Leckler, who had great faith in his plasterer's ability, marveled at the speed which he had acquired the three R's. He did not know that on one of his many trips a free negro had given Josh the rudimentary tools of learning, and that ever since the slave had been adding to his store of learning by poring over signs and every bit of print that he could spell out. Neither was Josh so indiscreet as to intimate to his benefactor that he had been anticipated in his good intentions.

It was in this way, working and learning, that a year passed away, and Mr. Leckler thought that his object had been accomplished. He could safely trust Josh to protect his own interests, and so he thought that it was quite time that his servant's education should cease.

"You know, Josh," he said, "I have already gone against my principles and against the law for your sake, and of course a man can't stretch his conscience too far, even to help another who's being cheated; but I reckon you can take care of yourself now."

"Oh, yes, suh, I reckon I kin," said Josh.

"And it wouldn't do for you to be seen with any books about you now."

"Oh, no, suh, su't'n'y not." He didn't intend to be seen with any books about him.

It was just now that Mr. Leckler saw the good results of all he had done, and his heart was full of a great joy, for Eckley had been building some additions to his house and sent for Josh to do the plastering for him. The owner admonished his slave, took him over a few examples to freshen his memory, and sent him forth with glee. When the job was done, there was a discrepancy of two dollars in what Mr. Eckley offered for it and the price which accrued from Josh's measurements. To the employer's surprise, the black man went over the figures with him and convinced him of the incorrectness of the payment—and the additional two dollars were turned over.

"Some o' Leckler's work," said Eckley, "teaching a nigger to cipher! Close-fisted old reprobate—I've a mind to have the law on him."

Mr. Leckler heard the story with great glee. "I laid for him that time—the old fox." But to Mrs. Leckler he said, "You see, my dear wife, my rashness in teaching Josh to figure for himself is vindicated. See what he has saved for himself."

"What did he save?" asked the little woman indiscreetly.

Her husband blushed and stammered for a moment, and then replied, "Well, of course, it was only twenty cents saved to him, but to a man buying his freedom every cent counts; and after all, it is not the amount, Mrs. Leckler, it's the principle of the thing."

"Yes," said the lady meekly.

2

Unto the body it is easy for the master to say, "Thus far shalt thou go, and no farther." Gyves, chains, and fetters will enforce that command. But what master shall say unto the mind, "Here do I set the limit of your acquisition. Pass it not"? Who shall put gyves upon the intellect, or fetter the movement of thought? Joshua Leckler, as custom denominated him, had tasted of the forbidden fruit, and his appetite had grown by what it fed on. Night after night he crouched in his lonely cabin, by the blaze of a fat pine brand, poring over the few books that he had been able to secure and smuggle in. His fellow servants alternately laughed at him and wondered why he did not take a wife. But Joshua went on his way. He had no time for marrying or for love; other thoughts had taken possession of him. He was being swayed by ambitions other than the mere fathering of slaves for his master. To him his slavery was deep night. What wonder, then, that he should dream, and that through the ivory gate should come to him the forbidden vision of freedom? To own himself, to be master of his hands, feet, of his whole body—something would clutch at his heart as he thought of it, and the breath would come hard between his lips. But he met his master with an impassive face, always silent, always docile; and Mr. Leckler congratulated himself that so valuable and intelligent a slave should be at the same time so tractable. Usually intelligence in a slave meant discontent; but not so with Josh. Who more content than he? He remarked to his wife: "You see, my dear, this is what comes of treating even a nigger right."

Meanwhile the white hills of the North were beckoning to the chattel, and the north winds were whispering to him to be a chattel no longer. Often the eyes that looked away to where freedom lay were filled with a wistful longing that was tragic in its intensity, for they saw the hardships and the difficulties between the slave and his goal and, worst of all, an iniquitous law—liberty's compromise with bondage, that rose like a stone wall between him and hope—a law that degraded every free-thinking man to the level of a slave catcher. There it loomed up before him, formidable, impregnable, insurmountable. He measured it in all its terribleness, and paused. But on the other side there was liberty; and one day when he was away at work, a voice came out of the woods and whispered to him "Courage!"—and on that night the shadows beckoned him as the white hills had done, and the forest called to him, "Follow."

"It seems to me that Josh might have been able to get home tonight," said Mr. Leckler, walking up and down his veranda, "but I reckon it's just possible that he got through too late to catch a train." In the morning he said, "Well, he's not here yet; he must have had to do some extra work. If he doesn't get here by evening, I'll run up there."

In the evening, he did take the train for Joshua's place of employment, where he learned that his slave had left the night before. But where could he have gone? That no one knew, and for the first time it dawned upon his master that Josh had run away. He raged; he fumed; but nothing could be done until morning, and all the time Leckler knew that the most valuable slave on his plantation was working his way toward the North and freedom. He did not go back home, but paced the floor all night long. In the early dawn he hurried out, and the hounds were put on the fugitive's track. After some nosing around they set off toward a stretch of woods. In a few minutes they came yelping back, pawing their noses and rubbing their heads against the ground. They had found the trail, but Josh had played the old slave trick of filling his tracks with cayenne pepper. The dogs were soothed and taken deeper into the wood to find the trail. They soon took it up again, and dashed away with low bays. The scent led them directly to a little wayside station about six miles distant. Here it stopped. Burning with the chase, Mr. Leckler hastened to the station agent. Had he seen such a negro? Yes, he had taken the northbound train two nights before.

"But why did you let him go without a pass?" almost screamed the owner.

"I didn't," replied the agent. "He had a written pass, signed James Leckler, and I let him go on it."

"Forged, forged!" yelled the master. "He wrote it himself."

"Humph!" said the agent. "How was I to know that? Our niggers round here don't know how to write."

Mr. Leckler suddenly bethought him to hold his peace. Josh was probably now in the arms of some northern abolitionist, and there was nothing to be done now but advertise; and the disgusted master spread his notices broadcast before starting for home. As soon as he arrived at his house, he sought his wife and poured out his griefs to her.

"You see, Mrs. Leckler, this is what comes of my goodness of heart. I taught that nigger to read and write, so that he could protect himself—and look how he uses his knowledge. Oh, the ingrate, the ingrate! The very weapon which I give him to defend himself against others he turns upon me. Oh, it's awful—awful! I've always been too confiding. Here's the most valuable nigger on my plantation gone—gone, I tell you—and through my own kindness. It isn't his value, though, I'm thinking so much about. I could stand his loss, if it wasn't for the principle of the thing, the base ingratitude he has shown me. Oh, if I ever lay hands on him again!" Mr. Leckler closed his lips and clenched his fist with an eloquence that laughed at words.

Just at this time, in one of the underground railway stations, six miles north of the Ohio, an old Quaker was saying to Josh, "Lie still—thee'll be perfectly safe there. Here comes John Trader, our local slave catcher, but I will parley with him and send him away. Thee need not fear. None of thy brethren who have come to us have ever been taken back to bondage—Good evening, Friend Trader!" and Josh heard the old Quaker's smooth voice roll on, while he lay back half smothering in a bag, among other bags of corn and potatoes.

It was after ten o'clock that night when he was thrown carelessly into a wagon and driven away to the next station, twenty-five miles to the northward. And by such stages, hiding by day and traveling by night, helped by a few of his own people who were blessed with freedom, and always by the good Quakers wherever found, he made his way into Canada.

And on one never-to-be-forgotten morning he stood up, straightened himself, breathed God's blessed air, and knew himself free!

3

To Joshua Leckler this life in Canada was all new and strange. It was a new thing for him to feel himself a man and to have his manhood recognized by the whites with whom he came into free contact. It was new, too, this receiving the full measure of his worth in work. He went to his labor with a zest that he had never known before, and he took a pleasure in the very weariness it brought him. Ever and anon there came to his ears the cries of his brethren in the South. Frequently he met fugitives who, like himself, had escaped from bondage; and the harrowing tales that they told him made him burn to do something for those whom he had left behind him. But these fugitives and the papers he read told him other things. They said that the spirit of freedom was working in the United States, and already men were speaking out boldly in behalf of the manumission of the slaves; already there was a growing army behind that noble vanguard, Sumner, Phillips, Douglass, Garrison. He heard the names of Lucretia Mott and Harriet Beecher Stowe, and his heart swelled, for on the dim horizon he saw the first faint streaks of dawn.

So the years passed. Then from the surcharged clouds a flash of lightning broke, and there was the thunder of cannon and the rain of lead over the land. From his home in the North he watched the storm as it raged and wavered, now threatening the North with its awful power, now hanging dire and dreadful over the South. Then suddenly from out the fray came a voice like the trumpet tone of God to him: "Thou and thy brothers are free!" Free, free, with the freedom not cherished by the few alone, but for all that had been bound. Free, with the freedom not torn from the secret night, but open to the light of heaven.

When the first call for colored soldiers came, Joshua Leckler hastened down to Boston, and enrolled himself among those who were willing to fight to maintain their freedom. On account of his ability to read and write and his general intelligence, he was soon made an orderly sergeant. His regiment had already taken part in an engagement before the public roster of this band of Uncle Sam's niggers, as they were called, fell into Mr. Leckler's hands. He ran his eye down the column of names. It stopped at that of Joshua Leckler, Sergeant, Company F. He handed the paper to Mrs. Leckler with his finger on the place.

"Mrs. Leckler," he said, "this is nothing less than a judgment on me for teaching a nigger to read and write. I disobeyed the law of my state and, as a result, not only lost my nigger, but furnished the Yankees with a smart officer to help them fight the South. Mrs. Leckler, I have sinned—and been punished. But I am content, Mrs. Leckler; it all came through my kindness of heart—and your mistaken advice. But, oh, that ingrate, that ingrate!"

In the Land of the Free
Sui Sin Far

About the Author   Sui Sin Far (1865–1914) was born Edith Maud Eaton in England to a Chinese mother and an English father. Her family moved to Montreal, Canada, when she was seven years old. As an adult, she lived in the United States and Canada. She was the first person of Chinese ancestry to publish stories in the United States that were focused on Chinese American experiences. Thirty-seven of her stories were collected in the book *Mrs. Spring Fragrance* (1912). When she died in Montreal, the Chinese community erected a monument to her memory.

The Context of the Reading   Immigrants from China arrived in the United States in great numbers between 1849 and 1870. A large percentage of those who emigrated were young males, who hoped to reunite with their families once they gained prosperity.

Many immigrants from China contributed significantly to the growth of the United States. However, partly as a result of an economic depression and the misperception that they took jobs at cheaper wages, these immigrants became victims of racial prejudice. The government was pressured to limit their employment and immigration. After the passage of the federal Exclusion Act of 1882, Chinese nationals who attempted to enter the United States legally were routinely detained for questioning. The examination process often took months and separated family members. The Exclusion Act, renewed in the 1890s, remained in effect until 1943.

"In the Land of the Free" was originally published in 1909 in the magazine *Independent*.

The Language of the Story   The author uses a formal, older form of English, apparently to indicate that the mother is speaking Chinese, not English, to her child.

- □   *thou:* you
- □   *wilt:* will
- □   *thy:* your
- □   *thee:* you
- □   *'Twas:* It was
- □   *'Tis:* It is
- □   *'twill:* it will

1

"**S**ee, little one—the hills in the morning sun. There is thy home for years to come. It is very beautiful and thou wilt be very happy there."

The Little One looked up into his mother's face in perfect faith. He was engaged in the pleasant occupation of sucking a sweetmeat; but that did not prevent him from gurgling responsively.

"Yes, my olive bud; there is where thy father is making a fortune for thee. Thy father! Oh, wilt thou not be glad to behold his dear face. 'Twas for thee I left him."

The Little One ducked his chin sympathetically against his mother's knee. She lifted him on to her lap. He was two years old, a round, dimple-cheeked boy with bright brown eyes and a sturdy little frame.

"Ah! Ah! Ah! Ooh! Ooh! Ooh!" puffed he, mocking a tugboat steaming by.

San Francisco's waterfront was lined with ships and steamers, while other craft, large and small, including a couple of white transports from the Philippines, lay at anchor here and there off shore. It was some time before the *Eastern Queen* could get docked, and even after that was accomplished, a lone Chinaman who had been waiting on the wharf for an hour was detained that much longer by men with the initials U.S.C. on their caps, before he could board the steamer and welcome his wife and child.

"This is thy son," announced the happy Lae Choo.

Hom Hing lifted the child, felt of his little body and limbs, gazed into his face with proud and joyous eyes; then turned inquiringly to a customs officer at his elbow.

"That's a fine boy you have there," said the man. "Where was he born?"

"In China," answered Hom Hing, swinging the Little One on his right shoulder, preparatory to leading his wife off the steamer.

"Ever been to America before?"

"No, not he," answered the father with a happy laugh.

The customs officer beckoned to another.

"This little fellow," said he, "is visiting America for the first time."

The other customs officer stroked his chin reflectively.

"Good day," said Hom Hing.

"Wait!" commanded one of the officers. "You cannot go just yet."

"What more now?" asked Hom Hing.

"I'm afraid," said the customs officer, "that we cannot allow the boy to go ashore. There is nothing in the papers that you have shown us—your wife's papers and your own—having any bearing upon the child."

"There was no child when the papers were made out," returned Hom Hing. He spoke calmly; but there was apprehension in his eyes and in his tightening grip on his son.

"What is it? What is it?" quavered Lae Choo, who understood a little English.

The second customs officer regarded her pityingly.

"I don't like this part of the business," he muttered.

The first officer turned to Hom Hing and in an official tone of voice, said:

"Seeing that the boy has no certificate entitling him to admission to this country you will have to leave him with us."

"Leave my boy!" exclaimed Hom Hing.

"Yes; he will be well taken care of, and just as soon as we can hear from Washington he will be handed over to you."

"But," protested Hom Hing, "he is my son."

"We have no proof," answered the man with a shrug of his shoulders; "and even if so we cannot let him pass without orders from the Government."

"He is my son," reiterated Hom Hing, slowly and solemnly. "I am a Chinese merchant and have been in business in San Francisco for many years. When my wife told to me one morning that she dreamed of a green tree with spreading branches and one beautiful red flower growing thereon, I answered her that I wished my son to be born in our country, and for her to prepare to go to China. My wife complied with my wish. After my son was born my mother fell sick and my wife nursed and cared for her; then my father, too, fell sick, and my wife also nursed and cared for him. For twenty moons my wife care for and nurse the old people, and when they die they bless her and my son, and I send for her to return to me. I had no fear of trouble. I was a Chinese merchant and my son was my son.''

"Very good, Hom Hing," replied the first officer. "Nevertheless, we take your son."

"No, you not take him; he my son too."

It was Lae Choo. Snatching the child from his father's arms she held and covered him with her own.

The officers conferred together for a few moments; then one drew Hom Hing aside and spoke in his ear.

Resignedly Hom Hing bowed his head, then approached his wife. "'Tis the law," said he, speaking in Chinese, "and 'twill be but for a little while—until tomorrow's sun arises."

"You, too," reproached Lae Choo in a voice eloquent with pain. But accustomed to obedience she yielded the boy to her husband, who in turn delivered him to the first officer. The Little One protested lustily against the transfer; but his mother covered her face with her sleeve and his father silently led her away. Thus was the law of the land complied with.

2

Day was breaking. Lae Choo, who had been awake all night, dressed herself, then awoke her husband.

" 'Tis the morn," she cried. "Go, bring our son."

The man rubbed his eyes and arose upon his elbow so that he could see out of the window. A pale star was visible in the sky. The petals of a lily in a bowl on the windowsill were unfurled.

" 'Tis not yet time," said he, laying his head down again.

"Not yet time. Ah, all the time that I lived before yesterday is not so much as the time that has been since my Little One was taken from me."

The mother threw herself down beside the bed and covered her face. Hom Hing turned on the light, and touching his wife's bowed head with a sympathetic hand inquired if she had slept.

"Slept!" she echoed, weepingly. "Ah, how could I close my eyes with my arms empty of the little body that has filled them every night for more than twenty moons! You do not know—man—what it is to miss the feel of the little fingers and the little toes and the soft round limbs of your little one. Even in the darkness his darling eyes used to shine up to mine, and often have I fallen into slumber with his pretty babble at my ear. And now, I see him not; I touch him not; I hear him not. My baby, my little fat one!"

"Now! Now! Now!" consoled Hom Hing, patting his wife's shoulder reassuringly; "there is no need to grieve so; he will soon gladden you again. There cannot be any law that would keep a child from its mother!"

Lae Choo dried her tears.

"You are right, my husband," she meekly murmured. She arose and stepped about the apartment, setting things to rights. The box of presents she had brought for her California friends had been opened the evening before; and silks, embroideries, carved ivories, ornamental lacquer-ware, brasses, camphorwood boxes, fans, and chinaware were scattered around in confused heaps. In the midst of unpacking the thought of her child in the hands of strangers had overpowered her, and she had left everything to crawl into bed and weep.

Having arranged her gifts in order she stepped out on to the deep balcony.

The star had faded from view and there were bright streaks in the western sky. Lae Choo looked down the street and around. Beneath the flat occupied by her and her husband were quarters for a number of bachelor Chinamen, and she could hear them from where she stood, taking their early morning breakfast. Below their dining-room was her husband's grocery store. Across the way was a large restaurant. Last night it had been resplendent with gay colored lanterns and the sound of music. The rejoicings over "the completion of the moon," by Quong Sum's firstborn, had been long and loud, and had caused her to tie a handkerchief over her ears. She, a bereaved mother, had it not in her heart to rejoice with other parents. This morning the place was more in accord with her mood. It was still and quiet. The revellers had dispersed or were asleep.

A roly-poly woman in black sateen, with long pendant earrings in her ears, looked up from the street below and waved her a smiling greeting. It was her old neighbor, Kuie Hoe, the wife of the gold embosser, Mark Sing. With her was a little boy in yellow jacket and lavender pantaloons. Lae Choo remembered him as a baby. She used to like to play with him in those days when she had no child of her own. What a long time ago that seemed! She caught her breath in a sigh, and laughed instead.

"Why are you so merry?" called her husband from within.

"Because my Little One is coming home," answered Lae Choo. "I am a happy mother—a happy mother."

She pattered into the room with a smile on her face.

The noon hour had arrived. The rice was steaming in the bowls and a fragrant dish of chicken and bamboo shoots was awaiting Hom Hing. Not for one moment had Lae Choo paused to rest during the morning hours; her activity had been ceaseless. Every now and again, however, she had raised her eyes to the gilded clock on the curiously carved mantelpiece. Once, she had exclaimed:

"Why so long, oh! why so long?" Then, apostrophizing herself: "Lae Choo, be happy. The Little One is coming! The Little One is coming!" Several times she burst into tears, and several times she laughed aloud.

Hom Hing entered the room; his arms hung down by his side.

"The Little One!" shrieked Lae Choo.

"They bid me call tomorrow."

With a moan the mother sank to the floor.

The noon hour passed. The dinner remained on the table.

3

The winter rains were over: the spring had come to California, flushing the hills with green and causing an ever-changing pageant of flowers to pass over them. But there was no spring in Lae Choo's heart, for the Little One remained away from her arms. He was being kept in a mission. White women were caring for him, and though for one full moon he had pined for his mother and refused to be comforted he was now apparently happy and contented. Five moons or five months had gone by since the day he had passed with Lae Choo through the Golden Gate; but the great Government at Washington still delayed sending the answer which would return him to his parents.

Hom Hing was disconsolately rolling up and down the balls in his abacus box when a keen-faced young man stepped into his store.

"What news?" asked the Chinese merchant.

"This!" The young man brought forth a typewritten letter. Hom Hing read the words:

"Re Chinese child, alleged to be the son of Hom Hing, Chinese merchant, doing business at 425 Clay Street, San Francisco.

"Same will have attention as soon as possible."

Hom Hing returned the letter, and without a word continued his manipulation of the counting machine.

"Have you anything to say?" asked the young man.

"Nothing. They have sent the same letter fifteen times before. Have you not yourself showed it to me?"

"True!" The young man eyed the Chinese merchant furtively. He had a proposition to make and was pondering whether or not the time was opportune.

"How is your wife?" he inquired solicitously—and diplomatically.

Hom Hing shook his head mournfully.

"She seems less every day," he replied. "Her food she takes only when I bid her and her tears fall continually. She finds no pleasure in dress or flowers and cares not to see her friends. Her eyes stare all night. I think before another moon she will pass into the land of spirits."

"No!" exclaimed the young man, genuinely startled.

"If the boy not come home I lose my wife sure," continued Hom Hing with bitter sadness.

"It's not right," cried the young man indignantly. Then he made his proposition.

The Chinese father's eyes brightened exceedingly.

"Will I like you to go to Washington and make them give you the paper to restore my son?" cried he. "How can you ask when you know my heart's desire?"

"Then," said the young fellow, "I will start next week. I am anxious to see this thing through if only for the sake of your wife's peace of mind."

"I will call her. To hear what you think to do will make her glad," said Hom Hing.

He called a message to Lae Choo upstairs through a tube in the wall.

In a few moments she appeared, listless, wan, and hollow-eyed; but when her husband told her the young lawyer's suggestion she became electrified; her form straightened, her eyes glistened; the color flushed to her cheeks.

"Oh," she cried, turning to James Clancy. "You are a hundred man good!"

The young man felt somewhat embarrassed; his eyes shifted a little under the intense gaze of the Chinese mother.

"Well, we must get your boy for you," he responded. "Of course"—turning to Hom Hing—"it will cost a little money. You can't get fellows to hurry the Government for you without gold in your pocket."

Hom Hing stared blankly for a moment. Then: "How much do you want, Mr. Clancy?" he asked quietly.

"Well, I will need at least five hundred to start with."

Hom Hing cleared his throat.

"I think I told to you the time I last paid you for writing letters for me and seeing the Custom boss here that nearly all I had was gone!"

"Oh, well then we won't talk about it, old fellow. It won't harm the boy to stay where he is, and your wife may get over it all right."

"What that you say?" quavered Lae Choo.

James Clancy looked out of the window.

"He says," explained Hom Hing in English, "that to get our boy we have to have much money."

"Money! Oh, yes."

Lae Choo nodded her head.

"I have not got the money to give him."

For a moment Lae Choo gazed wonderingly from one face to the other; then, comprehension dawning upon her, with swift anger, pointing to the lawyer, she cried: "You not one hundred man good; you just common white man."

"Yes, ma'am," returned James Clancy, bowing and smiling ironically.

Hom Hing pushed his wife behind him and addressed the lawyer again: "I might try," said he, "to raise something; but five hundred—it is not possible."

"What about four?"

"I tell you I have next to nothing left and my friends are not rich."

"Very well!"

The lawyer moved leisurely toward the door, pausing on its threshold to light a cigarette.

"Stop, white man; white man, stop!"

Lae Choo, panting and terrified, had started forward and now stood beside him, clutching his sleeve excitedly.

"You say you can go to get paper to bring my Little One to me if Hom Hing give you five hundred dollars?"

The lawyer nodded carelessly; his eyes were intent upon the cigarette which would not take the fire from the match.

"Then you go get paper. If Hom Hing not can give you five hundred dollars—I give you perhaps what more that much."

She slipped a heavy gold bracelet from her wrist and held it out to the man. Mechanically he took it.

"I go get more!"

She scurried away, disappearing behind the door through which she had come.

"Oh, look here, I can't accept this," said James Clancy, walking back to Hom Hing and laying down the bracelet before him.

"It's all right," said Hom Hing, seriously, "pure China gold. My wife's parent give it to her when we married."

"But I can't take it anyway," protested the young man.

"It is all same as money. And you want money to go to Washington," replied Hom Hing in a matter-of-fact manner.

"See, my jade earrings—my gold buttons—my hairpins—my comb of pearl and my rings—one, two, three, four, five rings; very good—very good—all same much money. I give them all to you. You take and bring me paper for my Little One."

Lae Choo piled up her jewels before the lawyer.

Hom Hing laid a restraining hand upon her shoulder. "Not all, my wife," he said in Chinese. He selected a ring—his gift to Lae Choo when she dreamed of the tree with the red flower. The rest of the jewels he pushed toward the white man.

"Take them and sell them," said he. "They will pay your fare to Washington and bring you back with the paper."

For one moment James Clancy hesitated. He was not a sentimental man; but something within him arose against accepting such payment for his services.

"They are good, good," pleadingly asserted Lae Choo, seeing his hesitation.

Whereupon he seized the jewels, thrust them into his coat pocket, and walked rapidly away from the store.

4

Lae Choo followed after the missionary woman through the mission nursery school. Her heart was beating so high with happiness that she could scarcely breathe. The paper had come at last—the precious paper which gave Hom Hing and his wife the right to the possession of their own child. It was ten months now since he had been taken from them—ten months since the sun had ceased to shine for Lae Choo.

The room was filled with children—most of them wee tots, but none so wee as her own. The mission woman talked as she walked. She told Lae Choo that little Kim, as he had been named by the school, was the pet of the place, and that his little tricks and ways amused and delighted every one. He had been rather difficult to manage at first and had cried much for his mother; "but children so soon forget, and after a month he seemed quite at home and played around as bright and happy as a bird."

"Yes," responded Lae Choo. "Oh, yes, yes!"

But she did not hear what was said to her. She was walking in a maze of anticipatory joy.

"Wait here, please," said the mission woman, placing Lae Choo in a chair. "The very youngest ones are having their breakfast."

She withdrew for a moment—it seemed like an hour to the mother—then she reappeared leading by the hand a little boy dressed in blue cotton overalls and white-soled shoes. The little boy's face was round and dimpled and his eyes were very bright.

"Little One, ah, my Little One!" cried Lae Choo.

She fell on her knees and stretched her hungry arms toward her son.

But the Little One shrunk from her and tried to hide himself in the folds of the white woman's skirt.

"Go 'way, go 'way!" he bade his mother.

Eveline

James Joyce

About the Author James Joyce (1882–1941) was born in Dublin, Ireland. Partly because of the difficulty of getting his work published in Ireland, he left his native land in 1904 and began a new life as a prominent literary artist in Trieste, Zurich, and Paris. Joyce's experiments with fiction had a widespread influence on literature worldwide. His novels include *A Portrait of the Artist as a Young Man* (1916) and *Ulysses* (1922).

The Context of the Reading "Eveline" was published in its present form in 1914 in Joyce's collection of stories entitled *Dubliners* (an earlier version of the story had been published in 1904). The story is set in Dublin, Ireland, at the beginning of the 20th century, when 90 percent of its population was Roman Catholic. References to Irish life include the following:

- *blackthorn:* an unlucky tree (in Irish folklore)
- *to keep nix:* to stand guard (idiom)
- *print of the promises made to Blessed Margaret Mary Alacoque:* a list of twelve promises displayed by faithful Catholics in their homes (for example, "I will establish peace in their homes"; "I will comfort them in their afflictions")
- *Derevaun Seraun! Derevaun Seraun!:* James Joyce does not explain what this expression signifies, but some scholars believe that the character who says this is speaking in a distorted form of Gaelic. Its meaning might be "The end of pleasure is pain!" or "The end of song is raving madness!"

At the turn of the century in Ireland, opportunities for women were limited. Middle-class women could maintain social status only through marriage or by entering a convent. But because females greatly outnumbered males, more than half of the marriageable women were unmarried. For single women, jobs were limited mostly to clerking in a store, typing, or dressmaking. The rare educated single woman could become a governess or teacher.

She sat at the window watching the evening invade the avenue. Her head was leaned against the window curtains and in her nostrils was the odour of dusty cretonne. She was tired.

Few people passed. The man out of the last house passed on his way home; she heard his footsteps clacking along the concrete pavement and afterwards crunching on the cinder path before the new red houses. One time there used to be a field there in which they used to play every evening with other people's children. Then a man from Belfast bought the field and built houses in it—not like their little brown houses but bright brick houses with shining roofs. The children of the avenue used to play together in that field—the Devines, the Waters, the Dunns, little Keogh the cripple, she and her brothers and sisters. Ernest, however, never played: he was too grown up. Her father used often to hunt them in out of the field with his blackthorn stick; but usually little Keogh used to keep nix and call out when he saw her father coming. Still they seemed to have been rather happy then. Her father was not so bad then; and besides, her mother was alive. That was a long time ago; she and her brothers and sisters were all grown up; her mother was dead. Tizzie Dunn was dead, too, and the

Waters had gone back to England. Everything changes. Now she was going to go away like the others, to leave her home.

Home! She looked round the room, reviewing all its familiar objects which she had dusted once a week for so many years, wondering where on earth all the dust came from. Perhaps she would never see again those familiar objects from which she had never dreamed of being divided. And yet during all those years she had never found out the name of the priest whose yellowing photograph hung on the wall above the broken harmonium beside the coloured print of the promises made to Blessed Margaret Mary Alacoque. He had been a school friend of her father. Whenever he showed the photograph to a visitor her father used to pass it with a casual word:

—He is in Melbourne now.

She had consented to go away, to leave her home. Was that wise? She tried to weigh each side of the question. In her home anyway she had shelter and food; she had those whom she had known all her life about her. Of course she had to work hard both in the house and at business. What would they say of her in the Stores when they found out that she had run away with a fellow? Say she was a fool, perhaps; and her place would be filled up by advertisement. Miss Gavan would be glad. She had always had an edge on her, especially whenever there were people listening.

—Miss Hill, don't you see these ladies are waiting?

—Look lively, Miss Hill, please.

She would not cry many tears at leaving the Stores.

But in her new home, in a distant unknown country, it would not be like that. Then she would be married—she, Eveline. People would treat her with respect then. She would not be treated as her mother had been. Even now, though she was over nineteen, she sometimes felt herself in danger of her father's violence. She knew it was that that had given her the palpitations. When they were growing up he had never gone for her, like he used to go for Harry and Ernest, because she was a girl; but latterly he had begun to threaten her and say what he would do to her only for her dead mother's sake. And now she had nobody to protect her. Ernest was dead and Harry, who was in the church decorating business, was nearly always down somewhere in the country. Besides, the invariable squabble for money on Saturday nights had begun to weary her unspeakably. She always gave her entire wages—seven shillings—and Harry always sent up what he could but the trouble was to get any money from her father. He said she used to squander the money, that she had no head, that he wasn't going to give her his hard-earned money to throw about the streets, and much more, for he was usually fairly bad of a Saturday night. In the end he would give her the money and ask her had she any intention of buying Sunday's dinner. Then she had to rush out as quickly as she could and do her marketing, holding her black leather purse tightly in her hand as she elbowed her way through the crowds and returning home late under her load of provisions. She had hard work to keep the house together and to see that the two young children who had been left to her charge went to school regularly and got their meals regularly. It was hard work—a hard life—but now that she was about to leave it she did not find it a wholly undesirable life.

She was about to explore another life with Frank. Frank was very kind, manly, open-hearted. She was to go away with him by the night-boat to be his wife and to live with him in Buenos Ayres where he had a home waiting for her. How well she remembered the first time she had seen him; he was lodging in a house on the main road where she used to visit. It seemed a few weeks ago. He was standing at the gate, his peaked cap pushed back on his head and his hair tumbled forward over a face of bronze. Then they had come to know each other. He used to meet her outside the Stores every evening and see her home. He took her to see *The Bohemian Girl* and she felt elated as she sat in an unaccustomed part of the theatre with him. He was awfully fond of music and sang a little. People knew that they were courting and, when he sang about the lass that loves a sailor, she always felt pleasantly confused. He used to call her Poppens out of fun. First of all it had been an excitement for her to have a fellow and then she had begun to like him. He had tales of distant countries. He had started as a deck boy at a pound a month on a ship of the Allan Line going out to Canada. He told her the names of the ships he had been on and the names of the different services. He had sailed through the Straits of Magellan and he told her stories of the terrible Patagonians. He had fallen on his feet in Buenos Ayres, he said, and had come over to the old country just for a holiday. Of course, her father had found out the affair and had forbidden her to have anything to say to him.

—I know these sailor chaps, he said.

One day he had quarrelled with Frank and after that she had to meet her lover secretly.

The evening deepened in the avenue. The white of two letters in her lap grew indistinct. One was to Harry; the other was to her father. Ernest had been her favourite but she liked Harry too. Her father was becoming old lately, she noticed; he would miss her. Sometimes he could be very nice. Not long before, when she had been laid up for a day, he had read her out a ghost story and made toast for her at the fire. Another day, when their mother was alive, they had all gone for a picnic to the Hill of Howth. She remembered her father putting on her mother's bonnet to make the children laugh.

Her time was running out but she continued to sit by the window, leaning her head against the window curtain, inhaling the odour of dusty cretonne. Down far in the avenue she could hear a street organ playing. She knew the air. Strange that it should come that very night to remind her of the promise to her mother, her promise to keep the home together as long as she could. She remembered the last night of her mother's illness; she was again in the close dark room at the other side of the hall and outside she heard a melancholy air of Italy. The organ-player had been ordered to go away and given sixpence. She remembered her father strutting back into the sickroom saying:

—Damned Italians! coming over here!

As she mused the pitiful vision of her mother's life laid its spell on the very quick of her being—that life of commonplace sacrifices closing in final craziness. She trembled as she heard again her mother's voice saying constantly with foolish insistence:

—Derevaun Seraun! Derevaun Seraun!

She stood up in a sudden impulse of terror. Escape! She must escape! Frank would save her. He would give her life, perhaps love, too. But she wanted to live. Why should she be unhappy? She had a right to happiness. Frank would take her in his arms, fold her in his arms. He would save her.

She stood among the swaying crowd in the station at the North Wall. He held her hand and she knew that he was speaking to her, saying something about the passage over and over again. The station was full of soldiers with brown baggages. Through the wide doors of the sheds she caught a glimpse of the black mass of the boat, lying in beside the quay wall, with illumined portholes. She answered nothing. She felt her cheek pale and cold and, out of a maze of distress, she prayed to God to direct her, to show her what was her duty. The boat blew a long mournful whistle into the mist. If she went, to-morrow she would be on the sea with Frank, steaming towards Buenos Ayres. Their passage had been booked. Could she still draw back after all he had done for her? Her distress awoke a nausea in her body and she kept moving her lips in silent fervent prayer.

A bell clanged upon her heart. She felt him seize her hand:

—Come!

All the seas of the world tumbled about her heart. He was drawing her into them: he would drown her. She gripped with both hands at the iron railing.

—Come!

No! No! No! It was impossible. Her hands clutched the iron in frenzy. Amid the seas she sent a cry of anguish!

—Eveline! Evvy!

He rushed beyond the barrier and called to her to follow. He was shouted at to go on but he still called to her. She set her white face to him, passive, like a helpless animal. Her eyes gave him no sign of love or farewell or recognition.

The German Refugee

Bernard Malamud

About the Author   Bernard Malamud (1914–1986) was born in the United States in New York, to Jewish immigrants from Russia. A collection of his stories, *The Magic Barrel* (1958), received the National Book Award, as did his novel *The Fixer* (1966), which also won the Pulitzer Prize.

The Context of the Reading   "The German Refugee" was originally published in 1963. The story is set in New York City in 1939, the year Adolf Hitler's German army invaded Poland, which led to the start of World War II. Before 1939, Jews had been deprived of their rights and were victims of violence; some were able to flee Germany. With the outbreak of the war, Hitler began to exterminate Jews in all countries conquered by his armies. Those who had not escaped were sent to concentration camps. By the end of the war, six million Jews had been systematically murdered, along with millions of others.

Malamud makes several references to Germany and the Nazis:

- *Bauhaus:* pertaining to a 20th-century school of design
- *Weimar Republic* (1919–1933): the German government that was established at the end of World War I and ended with Hitler's dictatorship
- *the Soviet-Nazi non-aggression pact:* the surprise agreement made by the Soviet Union and Germany, supposedly enemies, which left Poland at the mercy of Hitler
- *Brown Shirts:* private army recruited by the Nazis

Malamud also makes references to U.S. history and literature:

- *the Depression:* the severe economic crisis of the 1930s, also known as the Great Depression, which spread to Europe and contributed to the rise of Adolf Hitler in Germany
- *Life on the Mississippi:* autobiographical work by Mark Twain (1835–1910)
- *Leaves of Grass:* collection of poems by Walt Whitman (1819–1892). An excerpt from one of the poems, "Song of Myself," is included in the story.

The Language of the Story   The native languages of the main character, Oskar, are German and Yiddish (a language common to European Jews). His speech reflects his lack of mastery of English. The author deliberately misspells words to show how the character speaks. For example, "Zis" refers to "This," "bezt" to "best," "mistage" to "mistake," "peacogs" to "peacocks."

1

Oskar Gassner sits in his cotton-mesh undershirt and summer bathrobe at the window of his stuffy, hot, dark hotel room on West Tenth Street while I cautiously knock. Outside, across the sky, a late-June green twilight fades in darkness. The refugee fumbles for the light and stares at me, hiding despair but not pain.

I was in those days a poor student and would brashly attempt to teach anybody anything for a buck an hour, althought I have since learned better. Mostly I gave English lessons to recently-arrived refugees. The college sent me, I had acquired a little experience. Already a few of my students were trying their broken English, theirs and mine, in the American market place. I was then just twenty, on my way into my senior year in college, a skinny, life hungry kid, eating himself waiting for the next world war to start. It was a goddamn cheat. Here I was palpitating to get going, and across the ocean, Adolf Hitler, in black boots and a square mustache, was tearing up and spitting out all the flowers. Will I ever forget what went on with Danzig that summer?

Times were still hard from the Depression but anyway I made a little living from the poor refugees. They were all over uptown Broadway in 1939. I had four I tutored—Karl Otto Alp, the former film star; Wolfgang Novak, once a brilliant economist; Friedrich Wilhelm Wolff, who had taught medieval history at Heidelberg; and after the night I met him in his disordered cheap hotel room, Oskar Gassner, the Berlin critic and journalist, at one time on the *Acht Uhr Abenblatt*.* They were accomplished men. I had my nerve associating with them, but that's what a world crisis does for people, they get educated.

Oskar was maybe fifty, his thick hair turning gray. He had a big face and heavy hands. His shoulders sagged. His eyes, too, were heavy, a clouded blue; and as he stared at me after I had identified myself, doubt spread in them like underwater currents. It was as if, on seeing me, he had again been defeated. I had to wait until he came to. I stayed at the door in silence. In such cases I would rather be elsewhere but I had to make a living. Finally he opened the door and I entered. Rather, he released it and I was in. "Bitte,"† he offered me a seat and didn't know where to sit himself. He would attempt to say something and then stop, as though it could not possibly be said. The room was cluttered with clothing, boxes of books he had managed to get out of Germany, and some paintings. Oskar sat on a box and attempted to fan himself with his meaty hand. "Zis heat," he muttered, forcing his mind to the deed. "Impozzible. I do not know such heat." It was bad enough for me but terrible for him. He had difficulty breathing. He tried to speak, lifted a hand, and let it drop like a dead duck. He breathed as though he were fighting a battle; and maybe he won because after ten minutes we sat and slowly talked.

Like most educated Germans Oskar had at one time studied English. Although he was certain he couldn't say a word he managed to put together a fairly decent, if sometimes comical, English sentence. He misplaced consonants, mixed up nouns and verbs, and mangled idioms, yet we were able at once to communicate. We conversed in English, with an occasional assist by me in pidgin-German or Yiddish, what he called "Jiddish." He had been to America before, last year for a short visit. He had come a month before Kristallnacht, when the Nazis shattered the Jewish store windows and burnt all the synagogues, to see if he could find a job for himself; he had no relatives in America and getting a job would permit him quickly to enter the country. He had been promised something, not in journalism, but with the help of a foundation, as a lecturer. Then he

---

Acht Uhr Abenblatt: the name of a German newspaper
†*"Bitte":* "Please"

returned to Berlin, and after a frightening delay of six months was permitted to emigrate. He had sold whatever he could, managed to get some paintings, gifts of Bauhaus friends, and some boxes of books out by bribing two Dutch border guards; he had said goodbye to his wife and left the accursed country. He gazed at me with cloudy eyes. "We parted amicably," he said in German, "my wife was gentile. Her mother was an appalling anti-Semite. They returned to live in Stettin." I asked no questions. Gentile is gentile, Germany is Germany.

His new job was in the Institute for Public Studies, in New York. He was to give a lecture a week in the fall term, and during next spring, a course, in English translation, in "The Literature of the Weimar Republic." He had never taught before and was afraid to. He was in that way to be introduced to the public, but the thought of giving the lecture in English just about paralyzed him. He didn't see how he could do it. "How is it pozzible? I cannot say two words. I cannot pronounziate. I will make a fool of myself." His melancholy deepened. Already in the two months since his arrival, and a round of diminishingly expensive hotel rooms, he had had two English tutors, and I was the third. The others had given him up, he said, because his progress was so poor, and he thought he also depressed them. He asked me whether I felt I could do something for him, or should he go to a speech specialist, someone, say, who charged five dollars an hour, and beg his assistance? "You could try him," I said, "and then come back to me." In those days I figured what I knew, I knew. At that he managed a smile. Still, I wanted him to make up his mind or it would be no confidence down the line. He said, after a while, he would stay with me. If he went to the five-dollar professor it might help his tongue but not his stomach. He would have no money left to eat with. The Institute had paid him in advance for the summer but it was only three hundred dollars and all he had.

He looked at me dully. "Ich weiss nicht wie ich weiter machen soll."*

I figured it was time to move past the first step. Either we did that quickly or it would be like drilling rock for a long time.

"Let's stand at the mirror," I said.

He rose with a sigh and stood there beside me, I thin, elongated, red-headed, praying for success, his and mine; Oskar, uneasy, fearful, finding it hard to face either of us in the faded round glass above his dresser.

"Please," I said to him, "could you say 'right'?"

"Ghight," he gargled.

"No—right. You put your tongue here." I showed him where as he tensely watched the mirror. I tensely watched him. "The tip of it curls behind the ridge on top, like this."

He placed his tongue where I showed him.

"Please," I said, "now say right."

Oskar's tongue fluttered. "Rright."

---

*"Ich weiss nicht wie ich weiter machen soll": "I don't know how I get further into debt."

"That's good. Now say 'treasure'—that's harder."

"Tgheasure."

"The tongue goes up in front, not in the back of the mouth. Look."

He tried, his brow wet, eyes straining, "Trreasure."

"That's it."

"A miracle," Oskar murmured.

I said if he had done that he could do the rest.

We went for a bus ride up Fifth Avenue and then walked for a while around Central Park Lake. He had put on his German hat, with its hat-band bow at the back, a broad-lapeled wool suit, a necktie twice as wide as the one I was wearing, and walked with a small-footed waddle. The night wasn't bad, it had got a bit cooler. There were a few large stars in the sky and they made me sad.

"Do you sink I will succezz?"

"Why not?" I asked.

Later he bought me a bottle of beer.

2

To many of these people, articulate as they were, the great loss was the loss of language—that they could not say what was in them to say. You have some subtle thought and it comes out like a piece of broken bottle. They could, of course, manage to communicate but just to communicate was frustrating. As Karl Otto Alp, the ex-film star who became a buyer for Macy's, put it years later, "I felt like a child, or worse, often like a moron. I am left with myself unexpressed. What I know, indeed, what I am, becomes to me a burden. My tongue hangs useless." The same with Oskar it figures. There was a terrible sense of useless tongue, and I think the reason for his trouble with his other tutors was that to keep from drowning in things unsaid he wanted to swallow the ocean in a gulp: Today he would learn English and tomorrow wow them with an impeccable Fourth of July speech, followed by a successful lecture at the Institute for Public Studies.

We performed our lessons slowly, step by step, everything in its place. After Oskar moved to a two-room apartment in a house on West 85th Street, near the Drive, we met three times a week at four-thirty, worked an hour and a half, then, since it was too hot to cook, had supper at the 72nd Street Automat and conversed on my time. The lessons we divided into three parts: diction exercises and reading aloud; then grammar, because Oskar felt the necessity of it, and composition correction; with conversation, as I said, thrown in at supper. So far as I could see, he was coming along. None of these exercises was giving him as much trouble as they apparently had in the past. He seemed to be learning and his mood lightened. There were moments of elation as he heard his accent flying off. For instance when sink became think. He stopped calling himself "hopelezz," and I became his "bezt teacher," a little joke I liked.

Neither of us said much about the lecture he had to give early in October, and I kept my fingers crossed. It was somehow to come out of what we were doing daily, I think I felt, but exactly how, I had no idea; and to tell the truth, though I didn't say so to Oskar, the lecture frightened me.

That and the ten more to follow during the fall term. Later, when I learned that he had been attempting with the help of the dictionary, to write in English and had produced "a complete disahster," I suggested maybe he ought to stick to German and we could afterwards both try to put it into passable English. I was cheating when I said that because my German is meager, enough to read simple stuff but certainly not good enough for serious translation; anyway, the idea was to get Oskar into production and worry about translating later. He sweated with it, from enervating morning to exhausted night, but no matter what language he tried, though he had been a professional writer for a generation and knew his subject cold, the lecture refused to move past page one.

It was a sticky, hot July and the heat didn't help at all.

3

I had met Oskar at the end of June and by the seventeenth of July we were no longer doing lessons. They had foundered on the "impozzible" lecture. He had worked on it each day in frenzy and growing despair. After writing more than a hundred opening pages he furiously flung his pen against the wall, shouting he could no longer write in that filthy tongue. He cursed the German language. He hated the damned country and the damned people. After that what was bad became worse. When he gave up attempting to write the lecture, he stopped making progress in English. He seemed to forget what he already knew. His tongue thickened and the accent returned in all its fruitiness. The little he had to say was in handcuffed and tortured English. The only German I heard him speak was in a whisper to himself. I doubt he knew he was talking it. That ended our formal work together, though I did drop in every other day or so to sit with him. For hours he sat motionless in a large green velours armchair, hot enough to broil in, and through tall windows stared at the colorless sky above 85th Street, with a wet depressed eye.

Then once he said to me, "If I do not this legture prepare, I will take my life."

"Let's begin, Oskar," I said. "You dictate and I'll write. The ideas count, not the spelling."

He didn't answer so I stopped talking.

He had plunged into an involved melancholy. We sat for hours, often in profound silence. This was alarming to me, though I had already had some experience with such depression. Wolfgang Novak, the economist, though English came more easily to him, was another. His problems arose mainly, I think, from physical illness. And he felt a greater sense of the lost country than Oskar. Sometimes in the early evening I persuaded Oskar to come with me for a short walk on the Drive. The tail end of sunsets over the Palisades seemed to appeal to him. At least he looked. He would put on full regalia—hat, suit coat, tie, no matter how hot or what I suggested—and we went slowly down the stairs, I wondering whether he would ever make it to the bottom. He seemed to me always suspended between two floors.

We walked slowly uptown, stopping to sit on a bench and watch night rise above the Hudson. When we returned to his room, if I sensed he had loosened up a bit, we listened to music on the radio; but if I tried to sneak in a news broadcast, he said to me, "Please, I can not more stand of world misery." I shut off the radio. He was right, it was a time of no good news. I squeezed my brain. What could I sell him? Was it good news to be alive? Who could argue the point? Sometimes I read aloud to him—I remember he liked the first part of *Life on the Mississippi*. We still went to the Automat once or twice a week, he perhaps out of habit, because he didn't feel like going anywhere—I to get him out of his room. Oskar ate little, he toyed with a spoon. His dull eyes looked as though they had been squirted with a dark dye.

Once after a momentary cooling rainstorm we sat on newspapers on a wet bench overlooking the river and Oskar at last began to talk. In tormented English he conveyed his intense and everlasting hatred of the Nazis for destroying his career, uprooting his life after half a century, and flinging him like a piece of bleeding meat to the hawks. He cursed them thickly, the German nation, an inhuman, conscienceless, merciless people. "They are pigs mazquerading as peacogs," he said. "I feel certain that my wife, in her heart, was a Jew hater." It was a terrible bitterness, an eloquence almost without vocabulary. He became silent again. I hoped to hear more about his wife but decided not to ask.

Afterwards in the dark Oskar confessed that he had attempted suicide during his first week in America. He was living, at the end of May, in a small hotel, and had one night filled himself with barbiturates; but his phone had fallen off the table and the hotel operator had sent up the elevator boy who found him unconscious and called the police. He was revived in the hospital.

"I did not mean to do it," he said, "it was a mistage."

"Don't ever think of it again," I said, "it's total defeat."

"I don't," he said wearily, "because it is so arduouz to come back to life."

"Please, for any reason whatever."

Afterwards when we were walking, he surprised me by saying, "Maybe we ought to try now the legture onze more."

We trudged back to the house and he sat at his hot desk, I trying to read as he slowly began to reconstruct the first page of his lecture. He wrote, of course, in German.

4

He got nowhere. We were back to nothing, to sitting in silence in the heat. Sometimes, after a few minutes, I had to take off before his mood overcame mine. One afternoon I came unwillingly up the stairs—there were times I felt momentary surges of irritation with him—and was frightened to find Oskar's door ajar. When I knocked no one answered. As I stood there, chilled down the spine, I realized I was thinking about the possibility of his attempting suicide again. "Oskar?" I went into the apartment, looked into both rooms and the bathroom, but he wasn't there. I thought he might have drifted out to get something from a store and took the opportunity to look quickly around. There was nothing startling in the medicine chest, no pills but aspirin, no iodine. Thinking, for some reason, of a gun, I searched his desk drawer. In it I found a thin-paper airmail letter from Germany. Even if I had wanted to, I couldn't read the handwriting, but as I held it in my hand I did make out a sentence: "Ich bin dir siebenundzwanzig Jahre treu gewesen."* There was no gun in the drawer. I shut it and stopped looking. It had occurred to me if you want to kill yourself all you need is a straight pin. When Oskar returned he said he had been sitting in the public library, unable to read.

Now we are once more enacting the changeless scene, curtain rising on two speechless characters in a furnished apartment, I, in a straightback chair, Oskar in the velours armchair that smothered rather than supported him, his flesh gray, the big gray face, unfocused, sagging. I reached over to switch on the radio but he barely looked at me in a way that begged no. I then got up to leave but Oskar, clearing his throat, thickly asked me to stay. I stayed, thinking, was there more to this than I could see into? His problems, God knows, were real enough, but could there be something more than a refugee's displacement, alienation, financial insecurity, being in a strange land without friends or a speakable tongue? My speculation was the old one; not all drown in this ocean, why does he? After a while I shaped the thought and asked him, was there something below the surface, invisible? I was full of this thing from college, and wondered if there mightn't be some unknown quantity in his depression that a psychiatrist maybe might help him with, enough to get him started on his lecture.

He meditated on this and after a few minutes haltingly said he had been psychoanalyzed in Vienna as a young man. "Just the jusual drek," he said, "fears and fantazies that afterwaards no longer bothered me."

"They don't now?"

"Not."

"You've written many articles and lectures before," I said. "What I can't understand, though I know how hard the situation is, is why you can never get past page one."

He half lifted his hand. "It is a paralyzis of my will. The whole legture is clear in my mind but the minute I write down a single word—or in English or in German—I have a terrible fear I will not be able to write the negst. As though someone has thrown a stone at a window and the whole house—the whole idea, zmashes. This repeats, until I am dezperate."

He said that fear grew as he worked that he would die before he completed the lecture, or if not that, he would write it so disgracefully he would wish for death. The fear immobilized him.

"I have lozt faith. I do not—not longer possezz my former value of myself. In my life there has been too much illusion."

I tried to believe what I was saying: "Have confidence, the feeling will pass."

---

*"Ich bin dir siebenundzwanzig Jahre treu gewesen.": "I am faithful to you as I have been for twenty-seven years."

"Confidenze I have not. For this and alzo whatever elze I have lozt I thank the Nazis."

5

It was by then mid-August and things were growing steadily worse wherever one looked. The Poles were mobilizing for war. Oskar hardly moved. I was full of worries though I pretended calm weather.

He sat in his massive armchair with sick eyes, breathing like a wounded animal.

"Who can write aboud Walt Whitman in such terrible times?"

"Why don't you change the subject?"

"It mages no differenze what is the subject. It is all uzelezz."

I came every day, as a friend, neglecting my other students and therefore my livelihood. I had a panicky feeling that if things went on as they were going they would end in Oskar's suicide; and I felt a frenzied desire to prevent that. What's more, I was sometimes afraid I was myself becoming melancholy, a new talent, call it, of taking less pleasure in my little pleasures. And the heat continued, oppressive, relentless. We thought of escape into the country but neither of us had the money. One day I bought Oskar a second-hand fan—wondering why we hadn't thought of that before—and he sat in the breeze for hours each day, until after a week, shortly after the Soviet-Nazi non-aggression pact was signed, the motor gave out. He could not sleep at night and sat at his desk with a wet towel on his head, still attempting to write his lecture. He wrote reams on a treadmill, it came out nothing. When he slept out of exhaustion he had fantastic frightening dreams of the Nazis inflicting tortures on him, sometimes forcing him to look upon the corpses of those they had slain. In one dream he told me about, he had gone back to Germany to visit his wife. She wasn't home and he had been directed to a cemetery. There, though the tombstone read another name, her blood seeped out of the earth above her shallow grave. He groaned aloud at the memory.

Afterwards he told me something about her. They had met as students, lived together, and were married at twenty-three. It wasn't a very happy marriage. She had turned into a sickly woman, physically unable to have children. "Something was wrong with her interior strugture."

Though I asked no questions, Oskar said, "I offered her to come with me here but she refused this."

"For what reason?"

"She did not think I wished her to come."

"Did you?" I asked.

"Not," he said.

He explained he had lived with her for almost twenty-seven years under difficult circumstances. She had been ambivalent about their Jewish friends and his relatives, though outwardly she seemed not a prejudiced person. But her mother was always a violent anti-Semite.

"I have nothing to blame myself," Oskar said.

He took to his bed. I took to the New York Public Library. I read some of the German poets he was trying to write about, in English translation.

Then I read *Leaves of Grass* and wrote down what I thought one or two of them had got from Whitman. One day, towards the end of August, I brought Oskar what I had written. It was in good part guessing but my idea wasn't to write the lecture for him. He lay on his back, motionless, and listened utterly sadly to what I had written. Then he said, no, it wasn't the love of death they had got from Whitman—that ran through German poetry—but it was most of all his feeling for Brudermensch, his humanity.

"But this does not grow long on German earth," he said, "and is soon deztroyed."

I said I was sorry I had got it wrong, but he thanked me anyway.

I left, defeated, and as I was going down the stairs, heard the sound of someone sobbing. I will quit this, I thought, it has gotten to be too much for me. I can't drown with him.

I stayed home the next day, tasting a new kind of private misery too old for somebody my age, but that same night Oskar called me on the phone, blessing me wildly for having read those notes to him. He had got up to write me a letter to say what I had missed, and it ended by his having written half the lecture. He had slept all day and tonight intended to finish it up.

"I thank you," he said, "for much, alzo including your faith in me."

"Thank God," I said, not telling him I had just about lost it.

6

Oskar completed his lecture—wrote and rewrote it—during the first week in September. The Nazis had invaded Poland, and though we were greatly troubled, there was some sense of release; maybe the brave Poles would beat them. It took another week to translate the lecture, but here we had the assistance of Friedrich Wilhelm Wolff, the historian, a gentle, erudite man, who liked translating and promised his help with future lectures. We then had about two weeks to work on Oskar's delivery. The weather had changed, and so, slowly, had he. He had awakened from defeat, battered, after a wearying battle. He had lost close to twenty pounds. His complexion was still gray; when I looked at his face I expected to see scars, but it had lost its flabby unfocused quality. His blue eyes had returned to life and he walked with quick steps, as though to pick up a few for all the steps he hadn't taken during those long hot days he had lain torpid in his room.

We went back to our former routine, meeting three late afternoons a week for diction, grammar, and the other exercises. I taught him the phonetic alphabet and transcribed long lists of words he was mispronouncing. He worked many hours trying to fit each sound into place, holding half a matchstick between his teeth to keep his jaws apart as he exercised his tongue. All this can be a dreadfully boring business unless you think you have a future. Looking at him I realized what's meant when somebody is called "another man."

The lecture, which I now knew by heart, went off well. The director of the Institute had invited a number of prominent people. Oskar was the first refugee they had employed and there was a move to make the public cognizant of what was then a new ingredient in American life. Two reporters had come with a lady photographer. The auditorium of the Institute was crowded. I sat in the last row, promising to put up my hand if he couldn't be heard, but it wasn't necessary. Oskar, in a blue suit, his hair cut, was of course nervous, but you couldn't see it unless you studied him. When he stepped up to the lectern, spread out his manuscript, and spoke his first English sentence in public, my heart hesitated; only he and I, of everybody there, had any idea of the anguish he had been through. His enunciation wasn't at all bad—a few s's for th's, and he once said bag for back, but otherwise he did all right. He read poetry well—in both languages—and though Walt Whitman, in his mouth, sounded a little as though he had come to the shores of Long Island as a German immigrant, still the poetry read as poetry:

> And I know the spirit of God is the brother of my own,
> And that all the men ever born are also my brothers,
>   and the women my sisters and lovers,
> And that the kelson of creation is love . . .

Oskar read it as though he believed it. Warsaw had fallen but the verses were somehow protective. I sat back conscious of two things: how easy it is to hide the deepest wounds; and the pride I felt in the job I had done.

7

Two days later I came up the stairs into Oskar's apartment to find a crowd there. The refugee, his face beet-red, lips bluish, a trace of froth in the corners of his mouth, lay on the floor in his limp pajamas, two firemen on their knees, working over him with an inhalator. The windows were open and the air stank.

A policeman asked me who I was and I couldn't answer.

"No, oh no."

I said no but it was unchangeably yes. He had taken his life—gas—I hadn't even thought of the stove in the kitchen.

"Why?" I asked myself. "Why did he do it?" Maybe it was the fate of Poland on top of everything else, but the only answer anyone could come up with was Oskar's scribbled note that he wasn't well, and had left Martin Goldberg all his possessions. I am Martin Goldberg.

I was sick for a week, had no desire either to inherit or investigate, but I thought I ought to look through his things before the court impounded them, so I spent a morning sitting in the depths of Oskar's armchair, trying to read his correspondence. I had found in the top drawer a thin packet of letters from his wife and an airmail letter of recent date from his anti-Semitic mother-in-law.

She writes in a tight script it takes me hours to decipher, that her daughter, after Oskar abandons her, against her own mother's fervent pleas and anguish, is converted to Judaism by a vengeful rabbi. One night the Brown Shirts appear, and though the mother wildly waves her bronze crucifix in their faces, they drag Frau Gassner, together with the other Jews, out of the apartment house, and transport them in lorries to a small border town in conquered Poland. There, it is rumored, she is shot in the head and topples into an open tank ditch, with the naked Jewish men, their wives and children, some Polish soldiers, and a handful of gypsies.

Tito's Good-bye

Cristina Garcia

About the Author   Cristina Garcia was born in Havana, Cuba, and grew up in New York City. She has worked as a journalist for *Time* magazine. Her first novel, *Dreaming in Cuban,* was published in 1992 to high acclaim.

The Context of the Reading   "Tito's Good-bye," originally published in 1992, is set in New York City. References to the character's Cuban background include the following:

☐   *sweet plantains:* tropical fruits that resemble bananas
☐   *"coño":* a Spanish curse word; an expression in Spanish suggesting anger or surprise

After a revolution led by Fidel Castro in 1959, Cuba became a Communist state. Since the revolution, hundreds of thousands of Cubans have left the country because of their opposition to the political and economic situation. Most of these people have received asylum in the United States.

In the 1980s and 1990s, thousands of refugees from South America, Central America, and the Caribbean entered the United States illegally. The Immigration and Naturalization Act of 1980 makes it possible for those who can prove they are victims of political persecution to be given legal refuge, but establishing legitimacy is extremely difficult.

Agustin "Tito" Ureña thought at first that the massive heart attack that would kill him in a matter of seconds was just a bad case of indigestion. He had eaten spareribs with pork fried rice, black beans, and a double side order of sweet plantains at a new Cuban-Chinese cafeteria on Amsterdam Avenue the night before and he hadn't felt quite right all day. "Okay, okay, I hear you!" he lamented aloud, rubbing his solar plexus and dropping his fourth pair of antacid tablets in the dirty glass of water on his desk. He remembered with longing the great spits of suckling pigs dripping with fragrant juices back in Cuba, the two inches of molten fat beneath their crispy skins.

"Coño!" Tito Ureña protested as a violent spasm seized his heart then squeezed it beyond endurance. He stood up, suddenly afraid, and with a terrible groan he slumped forward, his arms swimming furiously, and swept from his oversized metal desk a half-eaten bag of candy corn, the citizenship papers of a dozen Central American refugees, his Timex travel clock in its scuffed plastic case, and the stout black rotary telephone he tried in vain to reach.

It was late Friday afternoon and Tito told his secretary to leave after lunch because it had started to snow and she lived in Hoboken, but mostly because he could deduct the eighteen dollars from her weekly pay. His law office, a squalid room over a vegetable market in Little Italy, was convenient to the federal courts downtown, his prime hunting grounds for the illegal immigrants who made up the bulk of his clients. Tito's specialties were self-styled—forging employment records, doctoring birth certificates, securing sponsors, thwarting deportation, applying for political asylum. Only rarely did he achieve the ultimate, the most elusive victory: procuring a legitimate green card.

Tito worked with the poorest of New York City's immigrants, uneducated men and women from the Dominican Republic, Mexico, El Salvador, Peru, Guatemala, Panama. He impressed them with his deliberate, florid Spanish, with the meaningful pauses and throat clearing they had come to expect from important men. In reality Tito Ureña's qualifications, elaborately set out and framed on the wall behind his secondhand executive chair, came from a correspondence school in Muncie, Indiana. This did not deter him, however, from charging many thousands of dollars, payable in monthly installments ("I'm not an unreasonable man," he protested again and again, his arms outstretched, palms heavenward, when his clients balked or appeared uncertain), for his dubious efforts.

Occasionally Tito Ureña would come by small-time jobs for the mob, defending lowlifes fingered to take the rap for their bosses. These cases paid handsomely and required virtually no work. Tito only had to be careful that his "defense" went off without a hitch and the saps went directly to jail. It helped take the pressure off the mob's local operations. Last year, flush with cash from two such cases, Tito bought sixty seconds of air time on late-night Spanish television to advertise his legal services. With his thick mustache and broad reassuring smile, he received over four hundred calls on the toll-free hotline in less than a week. The only trouble was that his wife, who was something of a night owl, also saw him on TV. Haydée called his office, posing as a rich widow from Venezuela, and made an appointment with her husband the following day. It took Tito months to cover his tracks again.

Tito Ureña had been separated from Haydée for nearly sixteen years and in all that time she had steadfastly refused to divorce him. Whenever she located her husband, Haydée managed to wring from him considerable sums of money to maintain, she said, the lifestyle to which she had grown accustomed as a descendant of the Alarcón family, the greatest sugarcane dynasty in Trinidad, Cuba. Tito insisted that Haydée could smell his cash three miles away in her tiny apartment on Roosevelt Island, even on the hottest days of summer when the stench from the East River and all that was buried there would have stopped a bloodhound dead in its tracks with confusion.

For a while Tito skittered from place to place in the vast waterfront complexes of apartment buildings near Wall Street which, during a downturn in the economy, were offering three months' free rent with every two-year lease. Tito rented beige furniture, always beige (he preferred its soothing neutrality), and lived high above the river, face-to-face with the lights of the city in his glass box suites in the sky.

It snowed hard the night Tito Ureña died of a heart attack in his office in Little Italy. Nine inches fell in the space of twelve hours. It continued to snow the next day, blanketing the city's rooftops and fire escapes, its parks and delivery trucks, awnings and oak trees with a deceptive peacefulness, and it snowed the day after that. It snowed on the black veiled hat Haydée had stolen from Bloomingdale's that very afternoon and which she would later come to interpret as a premonition of her husband's death. It snowed on the sliver of concrete she called a balcony, decorated with a life-sized plastic statue of Cinderella. It snowed on Tito's daughter's brick Colonial house in western Connecticut, across from the country club with its own riding stable. Inés Ureña had married a Yale-trained cardiologist the year before and devoted her days to mastering the baroque recipes in *Gourmet* magazine. It snowed especially hard in Prospect Park, near where her older brother, Jaime, had rented a room and plastered his walls with posters of Gandhi, Beethoven, and Malcolm X.

Tito lay dead in his office all weekend as it snowed, well preserved by the freezing temperatures. His mistress, Beatrice Hunt, called him Saturday night from Antigua, where she had returned to visit her family for an extended holiday. She cut her trip short when a policeman, who had found her number in Tito's wallet, called her in St. Johns. Beatrice, dressed in her Sunday finery, went to claim her lover's body at the Manhattan city morgue. After four days, nobody else had come.

If Tito Ureña had had the chance, if he had known that only a few moments remained of his life and that it was neither indigestion nor an incipient ulcer that was causing his gastric discomfort, he might have permitted himself the brief luxury of nostalgia. He would have remembered the warmth of his mother's cheek, smelling faintly of milk, and her face the last time he saw her (Tito was only nine when she died), or the sight of his father's hands—enormous hands with stiff hairs sprouting near the knuckles—stroking the doves that roosted in his study. He would have remembered the girl he loved madly when he was seven years old and in a moment of melancholy would profess to love still.

And since these would be the very last moments of his life, Tito might even have permitted himself the memory of his first glimpse of Haydée at sixteen, riding her thoroughbred, English style, along the road which marked the southern boundary of her father's vast plantation. She was a magnificent sight—so small, so white, a china doll. How afraid he was of breaking her on their wedding night! He would have remembered, too, her belly, swelling with his child, and the pride he felt strolling with her through the Plaza Mayor. This was long before the problems began, long before they'd sent their son to the orphanage in Colorado to save him from the Communists, who, it was rumored, were planning to ship Cuba's children to boarding schools in the Ukraine. Jaime was still healthy and without rancor then, and Tito's daughter, Inés, danced to please him, clapping her dimpled hands.

It was that life that Tito Ureña would have remembered if he had had the opportunity, a life richly marred by ignorance.

But he had no time to reminisce when his heart attack came. No time to save the Salvadorans from deportation or to pick up the dry cleaning Beatrice Hunt had forgotten on Broadway and 74th Street. No time to call his brothers, whom he hadn't seen in five years, or his sister, Aurora, in New Jersey, who'd announced her determination to save his soul. No time to have dinner with his daughter, Inés, estranged from him in her brick Colonial house in western Connecticut (Tito had missed her fancy wedding and she never forgave him). No time to apologize to his son, if he could have even worked up the courage, or to earn enough money to finally keep Haydée happy. No time to visit his father in Cuba or to plant jonquils on his mother's sad grave. No, Tito no longer had time even to hope. When his hour came on that snowy winter afternoon in Little Italy, all Tito had time to do was say *coño*.

Discussion Activities: Fiction

The discussion activities in Chapter 13 are designed to help you become engaged in the processes of reading and responding to the short stories in Chapter 12. They are not meant to be rigid instructions that you must follow. Ideally, the activities will lead you to think through what you have read and to come to your own conclusions about what is significant.

Working with a partner, in a small group, or with the whole class, decide which material to cover and the amount of time to spend on each section. Allow for different responses to the various aspects of the reading.

Write after You Read: Making a Journal Entry

Writing about a story just after reading it may help you remember and reflect on your reading experience. You can explore your response by recording your reactions in a journal entry, adapting the guidelines on page 9. Share what you have written.

Summarizing

In summarizing a short story, you can explain the *plot,* the series of events and thoughts that usually is characterized by a *conflict:* a struggle between two or more opposing forces. The conflict may be *internal* (for example, person versus conscience) or *external* (for example, person versus person, nature, society, or fate). A story may have more than one conflict.

To summarize a story, you can answer questions such as these:

☐ What is happening?

☐ What is the main conflict?

☐ How is the conflict resolved (brought to a conclusion)?

Share your summary with one or more classmates. Discuss the reasons for the differences in your summaries.

Note: Further guidelines for summarizing fiction can be found in Chapter 21.

Analyzing

Analyzing a short story can involve breaking it down into parts to examine the parts and their relationship. Among the elements of a story that you can examine are *setting, character, point of view,* and *images.*

In this section, these elements are divided into categories to help you focus on one element at a time. Within a story, they are interconnected and sometimes inseparable. For example, the setting may be connected to character development: characters' attitudes and behavior may be influenced by the time and place in which they live.

The following suggestions are designed to help you analyze short stories. As you make observations about the various elements of a story, read aloud corresponding passages.

Note: Not every suggestion will apply to every short story you read.

1. Discuss what you learn and find significant about the *setting.* For example, you can focus on the following details:

   □ place: where the story takes place

   □ time: when and over what period of time the story takes place (as revealed, for example, through actual clock or calendar time, through description of light and darkness, or through activities such as eating supper)

   □ social environment: the manners, customs, codes of behavior, and/or socio-economic level of the society

   □ physical environment: nature, objects, buildings, clothing, sounds, and so on

   Note details that offer contrasts with other details (for example, country versus city, poverty versus wealth, light versus darkness, nature versus machine-made products)

2. Discuss what you learn and find significant about the *characters*. For example, you can focus on the following details:

   □ their outward appearance and behavior

   □ their spoken words and inner thoughts

   □ their inner qualities and values

   □ their interaction with one another

   □ their conflicts (internal or external)

   □ the choices they make

   □ the changes they undergo—or do not undergo

   Note ways in which characters are contrasted with each another (for example, characters of different cultures, socioeconomic levels, religions, gender, races, ages, and so on).

3. Discuss what you learn and find significant about the *point of view* (the perspective from which the story is told) and the *narrator* (the person created by the writer to tell the story). For example, you can focus on the following issues:

   □ who is telling the story

☐ whether the narrator is a character in the story or an outside observer

☐ whether the narrator knows everything about every character

☐ whether the narrator has only limited knowledge of the characters

☐ whether the narrator is trustworthy

Discuss why the writer has chosen this point of view and how the story would be different if it were told from another point of view.

Note: The narrator is not the author and may or may not hold or reflect the author's view.

4. Discuss what you find significant about the *images:* mental pictures that carry suggestive or symbolic meanings in addition to their literal, factual meanings. For example, you can focus on the following details:

☐ words or phrases that appeal to your sense of sight, sound, taste, smell, or touch

☐ words or phrases that allow you to imagine, visualize, and recreate physical scenes and sensations

☐ concrete objects or events that might represent something abstract

Note images that provide contrasts with other images (for example, beautiful versus ugly, soft versus hard, sweet versus bitter, soothing versus frightening, fertility versus death).

Interpreting

Interpreting a story can involve discovering a generalization or abstraction drawn from the story's details. Short stories can be interpreted from multiple perspectives, allowing multiple meanings to emerge. Usually they deal with general areas of human experience, for example (1) the nature of humanity or society, (2) the relationships of human beings to the environment, or (3) the question of ethical responsibility.

To interpret a story, you can ask questions such as these:

☐ What abstract idea(s) emerge(s) from the details of the story?

☐ What insight(s) into society does the writer share?

☐ What does the writer observe about human behavior?

☐ What ethical issue(s) does the writer focus on?

Making Connections

Making connections with something outside a story—such as another reading or your own experience—can uncover meanings.

1. Explore similarities and differences between a story and other readings. Identify or read aloud relevant passages. The many comparisons you can make include the following:

☐ Compare the experiences of oppression in "The Ingrate" and "In the Land of the Free," and/or "Still I Rise" (p. 220).

□   Compare the exploration of female experience in "Eveline" and "Still I Rise" (p. 220).

□   Compare the experience of living in another culture in "In the Land of the Free," "The German Refugee," "The School Days of an Indian Girl" (p. 16), and/or "College" (p. 25).

□   Compare the theme of the past in "Tito's Good-bye," "The German Refugee," and/or "The Road Not Taken" (p. 218).

2.   Examine the relationship between a story and your own life. Identify or read aloud relevant passages.

□   Compare similar experiences.

□   Contrast different experiences.

□   Compare and contrast your attitude toward the subject matter with what you perceive to be the writer's attitude.

Getting Creative

The following activities are designed to help you envision scenes from short stories through perspective of film, television, and the theatre. If possible, videotape the scenes you select.

1.   Imagine that your job is to create a filmed advertisement (a "trailer") for a movie based on a short story. Select a short story, and decide which scene or scenes you would select. Explain why you made this selection and how you might film the scene(s).

2.   Assume that you are a reporter for a local television station that has found out what happened to the character(s) in a story and has assigned you the task of reporting on the story. Write a news report describing the incident, including quotations from the story—perhaps in the form of "interviews" with the character(s). The class can divide into three groups to write three different reports.

□   One group can write a report for a television program that sensationalizes its stories.

□   One group can write a report for a television program that gives the personal angle of a story.

□   One group can write a report for a television program that provides straight-forward coverage of its stories.

Each group can plan a way to present the report to the rest of the class (the television audience). Compare the reports, answering questions such as these:

□   Which details of the story are emphasized in each report? Why?

□   Which report most helps you understand the story?

3.   Select and act out scenes, especially those that include dialogue. Different students can read the narration and play the parts of different characters.

CHAPTER 14

Guidelines for Writing about Fiction

Chapter 14 provides guidelines for fulfilling an assignment to write an essay in response to a work of fiction. The strategies in this chapter are designed to help you compose an essay, but they are not meant to be taken as rigid instructions that you must follow. The writing of one student, George Mavros, is included; his completed essay can be found on pages 211–212. George's work was selected as an example; it is not presented as a model to imitate.

SUGGESTED ESSAY ASSIGNMENTS

Select or adapt one of the following topics, or devise your own topic in consultation with your instructor. Use details and quotations from the story or stories to introduce and/or support your ideas (see Chapters 21–23).

1. Write an essay in which you analyze and interpret one story.
2. Write an essay in which you compare and contrast two stories that have similar elements or themes.
3. Write an essay in which you explore a theme or subject that is common to several stories.
4. Write an essay in the form of a letter. Choose among the following possibilities:
   □ a letter from you to the author
   □ a letter from you to one of the characters
   □ a letter from one character to another
   □ a letter from a character to someone outside the story (for example, the author, a friend, or a character in another story)
5. Write an essay in a creative form, for example, a psychiatrist's case study of a patient (character) or a court scene in which lawyers debate an issue raised in one or more stories.

Selecting a Story

The first step in finding and developing a topic can be to reread all the assigned stories to determine which one you want to discuss in depth. A more efficient approach might be to review all of the writing you have done so far in response to the stories: annotations, journal entries, and any notes you have taken during class discussions. If you still cannot decide, discuss the choices with a classmate or with your instructor.

A Student Writer at Work

After reading and discussing several stories with his class, George decided that he would write about James Joyce's "Eveline." He was influenced in this choice by the fact that he couldn't stop thinking about Eveline's life.

George's Journal Entry on "Eveline"

The reading made me think a lot about Eveline's life. She thought that her life was really bad and she had to get away. She thought that she didn't have a life and must find one away from her family. But when the big moment arrived she could not do it. She was afraid to leave her house or she decided that her life wasn't that bad after all. I think that she did not believe in herself enough to make it on her own in a distant country. Frank was not that big a part of her life and he certainly wasn't the reason she ran away. In the last scene, he is shouting at her but she won't even listen to what he is saying: "her eyes gave him no sign of love or farewell or recognition" (p. 185) or "he held her hand and she knew that he was speaking to her" (p. 185). She used Frank as an excuse to get away and she decided to stay. Frank did not matter anymore.

In preparation for their essay assignment, the students in George's class were asked to write an entry on what they thought they would write about in their paper.

George's Journal Entry about His Plan for His Essay:

I think I'll write this essay in the form of a letter to Eveline. I was really challenged by this reading. I would like to do a little deeper thinking about it. For example, the reasons why she wanted to run away, why did she need Frank to run away with, why didn't she ask him to marry her before leaving? I have the feeling that she did not care about him that much, she used him. On the other hand, she was not sure of his intentions and it was also considered a sin by the Catholic Church to run away with someone to whom you are not married. Frank was a sailor and as we know, some sailors have women in every port. We cannot be sure about that, but Eveline should know. She knew him long enough to be aware of his feelings about her. I would like some answers and the only person to give them to me is Eveline.

Rereading to Understand a Story

Reread the story or stories you have selected. Knowing that you will be writing about this selection, read carefully: you will need to present the material as accurately as possible in your essay. One or more of these strategies may be helpful:

1. *Look up unfamiliar words.* Use the Glossary or a dictionary. Write the meaning above the word in the text, or list words and their meanings in a notebook or in a blank, alphabetized address book.

2. *Make additional annotations or double-entry notes.* For example, in the margins, summarize key scenes and record your reactions (see pp. 5–6).

3. *Take notes.* For example, list key scenes or details, and/or copy what you perceive to be significant quotations, then note why you think they are important.

4. *Cluster.* Use a clustering technique (see pp. 80–81) to create a visual pattern of ideas and details from the story.

Selecting Evidence for Critical Analysis of a Story

The evidence that you include in an essay about a story usually is derived primarily from the story itself.

One or more of the following strategies may help you infer meaning from evidence.

1. *Review the guidelines for analyzing a story in Chapter 13.* You can write down responses that may help you develop the essay.

2. *Use one or more of the exploratory strategies described in Chapter 5.* Strategies such as making a list, freewriting, looping, cubing, clustering—and others that you find productive—might help you generate ideas for your essay.

3. *Discuss the story with a classmate or group of friends.* By engaging in conversation about a story, you might find reasons why you interpret as you do and also get some fresh ideas.

Focusing

When you take notes or engage in exploratory writing, you generate ideas to develop your own understanding of a story. When you write an essay, you share your understanding with others, bringing your thoughts into focus for your readers. Each story in this book allows for many possible focal points. The area you focus on depends upon what you find to be significant in the story. (see Guidelines for Developing a Focal Point on pp. 151–152).

Whatever process you undergo to develop a focal point, remember that at this stage, the focus is tentative. As you move through several stages of writing, your thinking may undergo several changes.

Structuring the Entire Essay

A carefully structured essay can help communicate ideas effectively to readers.

The following chart provides an overall view of how such an essay about fiction can be developed. It by no means represents a rigid formula. The various parts of this chart are discussed at length in the sections that follow on the introduction, body, and conclusion of an essay.

Introduction

Focus on a particular topic.
Ask or imply a question about the topic, or make a point about the topic.

↓

Body

Provide supporting points and evidence to develop the topic.
    Details

    Examples

    Quotations

    Explanations

    Experiences

↓

Conclusion

Explore the implications of what you have discussed.

↓

Developing the Introduction

The purpose of an introduction can be to focus on the topic: to tell readers what the essay is about. Such an introduction can serve to involve readers in your interpretation of the story and can include information that will help them understand the direction your essay will take. This is usually accomplished in one or two paragraphs.

You can choose from a variety of approaches to involve readers in the topic at the beginning of your essay. For example, you might do one or more of the following:

☐ Discuss a *general human experience* (such as love and marriage) before you focus on the specific example of that human experience (of love and marriage) in the story.

☐ Discuss a *general philosophical concept* (such as fate, time, death, or good versus evil) before you focus on that concept as it is revealed in the story.

☐ Provide *biographical information* about the author if it is applicable to the development of the story and to the focus of your essay.

    Note: If information is gleaned from sources other than those used in class, you should cite and document the information, following the guidelines in Chapter 24.

☐ Provide *information on the historical period* in which the story is set, if such information would shed light on the meaning of the story.

    Note: If information is gleaned from sources other than those used in class, you should cite and document the information, following the guidelines in Chapter 24.

☐ Begin with a *quotation* from the story or a famous quotation that relates to the topic of your essay.

☐ Include a *definition* of a term that is important to the meaning of the story.

☐ Include a *plot summary* to give an overview of the story before you narrow your discussion to a specific aspect of the story.

The introduction is flexible; its content and form are dependent on your subject matter and individual writing style. But there are features your readers usually will need and expect in an introduction to an essay that analyzes and interprets a work of fiction.

Note: If the following guidelines do not suit your essay, discuss alternatives with your instructor.

GUIDELINES

For Writing an Introduction

An introduction to an essay about a story can accomplish these goals, though not necessarily in this order and not necessarily in separate sentences:

1. Identify the story by *title* (within quotation marks) and *author* (full name).
2. Focus on a particular *topic* (for example, a character, the setting, or an abstract idea such as love), in one of these ways:
   ☐ State directly what point(s) you will support or prove about the topic.
   ☐ Raise or imply one or more questions about the topic.

Developing the Body

The body of the paper is its longest section. In several paragraphs, you supply evidence to support the point(s) you made or answer the question(s) you raised in the introduction.

GUIDELINES

For Developing Body Paragraphs

1. For each paragraph or set of paragraphs, provide at least one supporting point that relates to and expands on the topic that you focused on in the introduction.
2. Within each paragraph, include details, examples, and quotations from the reading that serve as evidence to substantiate the supporting point.
3. Further explain each quotation through interpretive comments (see Chapter 23).

There are many ways to structure the body of an essay. None of the patterns in the following list represents a rigid formula. You may try variations on these structures or devise another structure that suits your topic. You can use the drafting process to experiment with organization; these first attempts can later be revised.

1. Explore a topic by providing relevant evidence from different scenes *chronologically* (in the order in which the scenes occur in the story).

   □ Start at the beginning of the story, and provide evidence to support any points that you make about a topic (for example, about a character or the setting or an abstract idea such as freedom).

   □ Then move through the story, examining one scene at a time. Make a new point about your topic, and provide evidence from each relevant scene.

   □ Continue this process until you reach the end of the story.

2. Explore a topic by providing relevant evidence from different scenes in *order of importance* (according to your view of what is important), not necessarily following the chronology of the story.

   □ Select a scene that you think is significant to your topic. This scene may be in the beginning, the middle, or the end of the story. Provide evidence to support any points you make about a topic (for example, about a character or the setting or an abstract idea such as freedom).

   □ Then move to another scene in the story. You can move forward from the beginning to the middle or end, or backward from the end to the beginning or middle of the story. Make a new point about your topic, and provide evidence from the scene to support it.

   □ Continue this process until you have discussed all relevant scenes.

3. Explore a topic by providing relevant evidence according to a set of *categories* that you determine.

   □ Determine a set of categories according to which you will analyze details of a story. For example, you might divide a discussion of a story into categories such as hope, disillusionment, and discovery, or restrictions, freedom, and consequences of freedom.

   □ In one paragraph or set of paragraphs at a time, expand on and make a point about each category.

   □ Throughout the body of the essay, show how the different categories are connected or follow logically from one another.

4. Explore a topic by *comparing* or *contrasting* a similar topic in two or more stories, by providing relevant evidence from different scenes chronologically, in order of importance, or by creating categories as a basis of comparison. Here are some organizational possibilities (see Synthesizing References to Two or More Readings, pp. 159–160).

   □ Discuss and make points about one story at a time, dividing the body into two sets of paragraphs. The second set of paragraphs can cover the same or similar points covered in the first set; you can show how the stories compare on each point.

□ Discuss one point about the topic at a time, providing evidence from both stories within each paragraph, moving paragraph by paragraph.

□ Discuss similarities first, and then differences (or vice versa).

Developing the Conclusion

The conclusion, usually one to two paragraphs, grows out of the rest of the essay. Having introduced and provided evidence about a topic, now you can explore the implications of what you have discussed. The way your essay begins will to some extent determine how it ends. If in the beginning you state directly what point you will support or prove about a topic, you can expand on that point in the conclusion. If you raise a question about a topic, you can answer the question.

There are many ways to bring your essay to its end. The approaches that you can use for an introduction, such as including historical details, a famous quotation, or a definition (see pp. 207–208) also can be useful for a conclusion. Which approach you choose will depend on your topic and purpose.

If none of the following suggestions suits your purpose, discuss alternatives with your instructor. You may find, for example, that your essay raises more questions than it answers. In that case, perhaps your conclusion should be a series of questions. Or you may see multiple interpretations. In that case, your conclusion can discuss alternative interpretations.

GUIDELINES

For Writing a Conclusion

Show—or raise questions about—the connection between your topic and one or more of the following:

□ The writer's view of society
□ The writer's view of human behavior
□ The historical period in which the story is set
□ A philosophical, ethical, or psychological concept
□ What happens in the real world today

Drafting

Prepare a draft of your essay adapting the guidelines for writing an interim draft on page 53 and for structuring the entire essay on pages 206–210.

Giving and Receiving Feedback

Exchange drafts with one or more classmates, adapting the guidelines for giving and receiving feedback on page 55. Review one another's work by examining (1) what you like about a paper and (2) what you think can be done to strengthen it. Use the feedback form on page 56 and/or the suggestions for summarizing and analyzing fiction on pages 200–202, or raise your own questions.

Revising

You can revise your paper by answering questions such as these (see pp. 57–58 for a fuller discussion):

- ☐ What should I keep?
- ☐ What should I add?
- ☐ What should I delete?
- ☐ What should I change?
- ☐ What should I rearrange?
- ☐ What should I rethink?

Completing

Once you have revised the draft, you can complete the essay by adapting these guidelines:

- ☐ Evaluate the essay as a whole.
- ☐ Proofread and edit the essay (see Chapter 25).
- ☐ Prepare a neat final manuscript to hand in for evaluation (see Chapter 28).

Student Essay

A Letter to Eveline

George Mavros

About the Author   George Mavros wrote the following essay to fulfill an essay assignment for a composition course.
Note: This essay has been edited for publication in this book.

Dear Eveline,

I'm taking the opportunity to write this letter because there are many things about your story that trouble me. I hope that you, more than anyone else, will be able to answer the questions that arose when I read what James Joyce said about you. It is easy for me to judge your life, but I do not think that would be fair since I do not know you at all. However, if you answer my questions you will help me become more objective in my criticism.

I am sure you have had so far a really bad life and you feel that you deserve something better. After all, your mother died when you were young and you had to take care of the entire family and especially your father, who has been really hard on you. It makes perfect sense to me that you wanted to run away and leave it all behind. You certainly have the right to a better life since I believe you did not even have a life so far. Leaving your family is a big decision and I was impressed by your determination to seek freedom away from it.

And then there was Frank. He offered you the chance to escape from all these problems and start something new with him. But I believe that your feelings about him weren't that strong. He was just an excuse to get away. I know this is true because in the end, when he was shouting at you, you did not pay any attention to his cries: "[Your] eyes gave him no sign of love or farewell or recognition" (p. 185). You must admit that you never took Frank seriously and to some extent I understand that. Frank was a sailor and most sailors have girls in every port they visit. You could not have been certain as to whether he would marry you when you arrived in Buenos Aires. That is the reason I would like to ask you why you didn't marry him in Ireland. Running away with him while unmarried would be considered a sin in your Catholic Church, so it seems to me more reasonable to marry first and leave afterwards.

I believe that you thought Frank had no intention of marrying you. You were going to have to make it on your own in Argentina. However, when the big moment arrived I think you were afraid. Were you just scared to leave your house, or did you not believe in yourself enough to make it on your own in a distant country? Your house provided you with security that Frank could not provide you with. I think that he did not treat you very well either. He seemed too aggressive toward you: you "felt him *seize* [your] hand" (p. 185, my emphasis). Perhaps he reminded you of your father and that scared you in the end away from him and the life he offered you.

Your life in Ireland seems to me a little pathetic. You do not have a good job and you spend your time in the house taking care of the household and the family. In the beginning you felt obliged to your mother who asked you before she died to keep the family together. But now it is your chance to live too. I know you want this: you "wanted to live"; you thought: "Why should [I] be unhappy?"; you felt you had a "right to happiness" (p. 185). Of course you do, and that is the reason why you must leave home and become independent. As long as you stay there you will only be limited and depressed. Home may provide security but that is not enough; every person must try to fulfill his or her dreams, and I'm sure yours are not to stay in the same house all your life and watch over your father until he dies.

Eveline, you must start asking yourself, "What do I want from my life?" That is the only way to get away from your past and start over. Maybe not with Frank, who was not the right person to run away with, but even by yourself, provided that you have confidence in your potential. Everyone goes, and you can "go away like the others" (p. 183). Never stop hoping because hope is what keeps us alive.

Write after You Read

Explore your response to "A Letter to Eveline" by recording your reactions in a journal entry, adapting the guidelines on page 9.

ACTIVITY

For Class Discussion

Working with a partner, in a small group, or with the whole class, engage in some or all of the following activities. Decide the order in which to cover the material and the amount of time to spend on each activity. Allow for different reactions to and interpretations of the various aspects of the reading.

1. Share the reactions to "A Letter to Eveline" that you have recorded in your journal entry.

2. Examine the essay closely, using the suggestions for summarizing and analyzing fiction on pages 200–202. ■

POETRY

This unit, Writing from Sources: Poetry, consists of three chapters that can help you fulfill an assignment to compile a poetry anthology. By exploring your reactions to poems, guided by the discussion activities in Chapter 16, you may develop a sense of what you appreciate about poetry. In Chapter 17, guidelines are provided for finding and writing about poems other than those included in this book. A sample student anthology with eight poems is included.

CHAPTER 15

Readings: Poetry

Chapter 15 includes five poems. As you read and reread a poem, you can aim to accomplish the following:

☐ Read the poem aloud

☐ Enter the world of the poem

☐ Reflect on what the poet thinks and feels

☐ Examine your own experience and views

The Reading Selections

The poems in this chapter are complete and unabridged. Written by U.S. poets, they span over one hundred years and deal with personal, philosophical, and political topics.

So that you can have a more direct experience reading the poems, no background material is included other than biographical information about the poets.

When I Heard the Learn'd Astronomer
Walt Whitman

About the Poet   Walt Whitman (1819–1892) was born in New York. Early in his life he worked as a printer, teacher, newspaper editor, and carpenter. His poetry collection entitled *Leaves of Grass* (1855), which he enlarged and revised throughout his life, became one of the most influential volumes of poems in U.S. literary history. It reflects his belief in freedom, individualism, and the great potential of the United States. Among his other collected works is *Drum-Taps* (1865), poetry about the Civil War.

"When I Heard the Learn'd Astronomer" was published in 1865.

When I heard the learn'd astronomer,
When the proofs, the figures, were ranged in columns before me,
When I was shown the charts and diagrams, to add, divide, and
    measure them,
When I sitting heard the astronomer where he lectured with much
    applause in the lecture-room,
How soon unaccountable I became tired and sick,
Till rising and gliding out I wander'd off by myself,
In the mystical moist night-air, and from time to time,
Look'd up in perfect silence at the stars.

"Hope" is the thing with feathers*

Emily Dickinson

About the Poet   Emily Dickinson (1830–1886) was born in Massachusetts and lived there all her life. By her choice, only a few of her poems were published during her lifetime, but she often included them in letters to her friends. After her death, most of her over 1,700 poems were published in collections such as *Poems* (1890) and *Poems: Second Series* (1891); her name and work quickly became famous.

"'Hope' is the thing with feathers" was written in 1861.

"Hope" is the thing with feathers—
That perches in the soul—
And sings the tune without the words—
And never stops—at all—

And sweetest—in the Gale—is heard—
And sore must be the storm—
That could abash the little Bird
That kept so many warm—

I've heard it in the chillest land—
And on the strangest Sea—
Yet, never, in Extremity,
It asked a crumb—of Me.

---

*Dickinson did not give this poem a title; the title given here is taken from the first line.

The Road Not Taken

Robert Frost

About the Poet   Robert Frost (1874–1963) was born in California but spent most of his life in New England. He left college after two years and became a teacher, cobbler, and editor of a weekly newspaper. By 1915 he had become famous as a poet and was later a professor of English at Amherst College. Frost was awarded four Pulitzer Prizes, many honorary degrees, and membership in distinguished academies. In 1961, he was given the honor of reading an original poem at the inauguration of President John F. Kennedy. Among his many volumes of poetry are *West-Running Brook* (1928) and *In the Clearing* (1962).

"The Road Not Taken" was originally published in 1916.

Two roads diverged in a yellow wood,
And sorry I could not travel both
And be one traveler, long I stood
And looked down one as far as I could
To where it bent in the undergrowth;

Then took the other, as just as fair,
And having perhaps the better claim,
Because it was grassy and wanted wear;
Though as for that the passing there
Had worn them really about the same,

And both that morning equally lay
In leaves no step had trodden black.
Oh, I kept the first for another day!
Yet knowing how way leads on to way,
I doubted if I should ever come back.

I shall be telling this with a sigh
Somewhere ages and ages hence:
Two roads diverged in a wood, and I—
I took the one less traveled by,
And that has made all the difference.

Love is not all*

Edna St. Vincent Millay

About the Poet   Edna St. Vincent Millay (1892–1950) was born in Maine. She published her first poems when she was still a child. Her first book of poems, *Renascence and Other Poems* (1917), was published the year she graduated from college. In addition to writing poetry, she wrote stories, plays, and an opera. She won many awards for her poetry, including a Pulitzer Prize. Among her many published works is the poem collection *Fatal Interview* (1931).

"Love is not all" was originally published in 1931.

Love is not all: it is not meat nor drink
Nor slumber nor a roof against the rain;
Nor yet a floating spar to men that sink
And rise and sink and rise and sink again;
Love can not fill the thickened lung with breath,
Nor clean the blood, nor set the fractured bone;
Yet many a man is making friends with death
Even as I speak, for lack of love alone.
It well may be that in a difficult hour,
Pinned down by pain and moaning for release,
Or nagged by want past resolution's power,
I might be driven to sell your love for peace,
Or trade the memory of this night for food.
It well may be. I do not think I would.

---

*The poet did not give this poem a title; the title given here is taken from the first line. The poem is the 30th in a sequence of 52 sonnets published in *Fatal Interview.*

Still I Rise

Maya Angelou

About the Poet   Maya Angelou was born in Missouri and raised in Arkansas. In addition to being a writer, she has been a performer, producer, civil rights activist, and teacher. She focuses much of her work on her African heritage and on the experiences of African Americans. The first volume of her highly acclaimed autobiography is entitled *I Know Why the Caged Bird Sings* (1970). Among her books of poetry is *I Shall Not Be Moved* (1990). In 1993, she was given the honor of reading an original poem at the inauguration of President William Jefferson Clinton.

"Still I Rise" was published in 1978.

You may write me down in history
With your bitter, twisted lies,
You may trod on me in the very dirt
But still, like dust, I'll rise.

Does my sassiness upset you?
Why are you beset with gloom?
'Cause I walk like I've got oil wells
Pumping in my living room.

Just like moons and like suns,
With the certainty of tides,
Just like hopes springing high,
Still I'll rise.

Did you want to see me broken?
Bowed head and lowered eyes?
Shoulders falling down like teardrops,
Weakened by my soulful cries.

Does my haughtiness offend you?
Don't you take it awful hard
'Cause I laugh like I've got gold mines
Diggin' in my own back yard.

You may shoot me with your words,
You may cut me with your eyes,
You may kill me with your hatefulness,
But still, like air, I'll rise.

Does my sexiness upset you?
Does it come as a surprise
That I dance like I've got diamonds
At the meeting of my thighs?

Out of the huts of history's shame
I rise
Up from a past that's rooted in pain
I rise
I'm a black ocean, leaping and wide,
Welling and swelling I bear in the tide.

Leaving behind nights of terror and fear
I rise
Into a daybreak that's wondrously clear
I rise
Bringing the gifts that my ancestors gave,
I am the dream and the hope of the slave.
I rise
I rise
I rise.

Discussion Activities: Poetry

The discussion activities in Chapter 16 are designed to help you become engaged in the processes of reading and responding to poems. They are not meant to be rigid instructions that you must follow. Ideally, the activities will lead you to think through what you have read and to come to your own conclusions about what is significant.

Working with a partner, in a small group, or with the whole class, decide which material to cover and the amount of time to spend on each section. Allow for different responses to the various aspects of the poem.

Write after You Read: Making a Journal Entry

Writing about a poem just after reading it may help you remember and reflect on your reading experience. You can explore your response by recording your reactions in a journal entry, following the guidelines on page 9. Share what you have written.

Summarizing

To summarize a poem, you can ask questions such as these:

☐ What is the subject of the poem?

☐ Who is speaking to whom?

☐ What does the speaker say or feel about the subject?

Share your summary with one or more classmates. Discuss the reasons for the differences in your summaries.

Analyzing

Analyzing a poem can involve breaking it down into parts to examine the parts and their relationship. Among the parts of a poem you can examine are the *speaker*, *subject*, *setting* or *scene*, *character*, and *images*.

In this section, these elements are divided into categories to help you focus on one at a time. Within a poem, they are interconnected and sometimes insep- arable. For example, the setting may be connected to character: the speaker's or characters' attitude and behavior may be influenced by the time and place in which the poem is set; their emotional states can be affected by the physical environment.

The following suggestions are designed to help you analyze poems. As you make observations about the various elements of the poem, read aloud corresponding passages.

Note: Not all of the suggestions will apply to every poem you read.

1. Discuss what you learn and find significant about the *speaker* of the poem. For example, you can focus on the following issues:
   - □ who is speaking
   - □ whether the speaker is directly involved in the events of the poem or is an outside observer
   - □ whether the speaker represents more than a single person (for example, a community, a race, a gender)
   - □ to whom the speaker is directing the words

2. Discuss what you learn and find significant about the *subject* of the poem. For example, you can focus on the following issues:
   - □ the subject the speaker is focusing on
   - □ the reason the speaker might be focusing on this subject

3. Discuss what you learn and find significant about the *setting* or *scene*. For example, you can focus on the following details:
   - □ place: where the events of the poem take place
   - □ time: when and over what period of time the events of the poem take place
   - □ physical environment: nature, objects, animals, rooms, clothing, light, sounds, and so on
   - □ social environment: the manners, customs, codes of behavior, and/or socioeconomic level of the society

   Note details that offer contrasts with other details (for example, country versus city, poverty versus wealth, light versus darkness, nature versus machine-made products)

4. Discuss what you learn and find significant about *characters* (including the speaker) in the poem. For example, you can focus on the following details:
   - □ their outward appearance and behavior
   - □ their spoken words and inner thoughts
   - □ their inner qualities and values
   - □ their interaction with one another
   - □ their conflicts (internal or external)
   - □ the choices they make
   - □ the changes they undergo—or do not undergo

   Note ways in which people are contrasted with one another (for example, people of different cultures, socioeconomic levels, gender, races, and so on).

5. Discuss what you find significant about the *images:* mental pictures that carry suggestive or symbolic meanings in addition to their literal, factual meanings. For example, you can focus on the following details:

   □ words or phrases that appeal to your sense of sight, sound, taste, smell, or touch

   □ words or phrases that allow you to imagine, visualize, and recreate physical scenes and sensations

   □ words or phrases that tap into past experiences and memories

   □ concrete objects or events that might represent something abstract

   Note images that provide contrasts with other images (for example, beautiful versus ugly, soft versus hard, sweet versus bitter, soothing versus frightening, fertile versus barren).

Interpreting

Interpreting a poem can involve inferring a generalization or abstraction from the details of the poem. Poems can be interpreted from more than one perspective, allowing multiple meanings to emerge.

   To interpret a poem, you can ask questions such as these:

   □ What overriding feeling or emotion emerges from the details of the poem?

   □ What abstract idea(s) emerge(s) from the details of the poem?

Making Connections

Making connections between a poem and something outside a poem—such as another reading or your own experience—can help uncover meanings.

1. Explore similarities and differences between a poem and another reading. Identify or read aloud relevant lines. Among the many comparisons you can make are the following:

   □ Compare the experience of learning in "When I Heard the Learn'd Astronomer" and "What True Education Should Do" (p. 3).

   □ Compare " 'Hope' is the thing with feathers" and "Still I Rise."

   □ Compare the speaker in "The Road Not Taken," and Tito Ureña in "Tito's Good-bye" (p. 196).

   □ Compare the speaker in "The Road Not Taken" and the narrator in "Shooting an Elephant" (p. 31).

   □ Compare "Love is not all" and "The Rewards of Living a Solitary Life" (p. 37).

   □ Compare the African American experience in "Still I Rise," "The Ingrate," (p. 168) and/or "Waiting in Line at the Drugstore" (p. 22).

   □ Compare the speaker in "Still I Rise" with the narrator of "The School Days of an Indian Girl" (p. 16) and/or the narrator of "College" (p. 25).

2. Examine the relationship between a poem and your own life experiences.
   - ☐ Compare similar experiences.
   - ☐ Contrast different experiences.
   - ☐ Compare and contrast your attitude toward the subject matter with what you perceive to be the poet's attitude.

CHAPTER 17

Guidelines for Compiling a Poetry Anthology

Chapter 17 provides guidelines for fulfilling an assignment to compile an anthology of poems. This assignment gives you the opportunity to choose poems and to write about them in ways meaningful to you.

The poetry anthology of one student, Francisco Javier Rojo-Alique, can be found on pages 232–239. Francisco's work was selected as an example of what can be accomplished when a student is deeply involved in a poetry project. It is not presented as a model to imitate.

SUGGESTED ASSIGNMENT

Compile an anthology of poems of your own choice. Include the following:

☐ An essay that explains the entire anthology
☐ Individual discussions of several of the poems you have selected
☐ A bibliography

Finding Poems

Poems can found in collections of poetry, which may include poems by only one poet—for example, *The Poetry of Edgar Allan Poe* or *The Poems of Emily Dickinson*—or poems of many different poets. Such collections may be organized by the following categories:

☐ *Theme* (for example, *The War Poets*; *Loving a Woman in Two Different Worlds*)

☐ *Country* (for example, *The American Poetry Anthology*; *Poets of Nicaragua: A Bilingual Anthology*)

☐ *Culture* (for example, *Breaking Silence: An Anthology of Contemporary Asian American Poets*; *Voices from Wah'kon-Tah: Contemporary Poetry of Native Americans*)

☐ *Time period* (for example, *Modern Verse in English: 1900–1950*; *The Random House Book of Twentieth-Century French Poetry*)

☐ *Type* (for example, *The Symbolist Poem*; *The Faber Book of Comic Verse*)

☐ *General category* (for example, *The Norton Anthology of Poetry*; *The World's Greatest Poems*)

There are primarily three ways to find books of poetry in the reference section of the library: through a card catalog, computer file, or index. For general instructions on using these reference sources, see Chapter 19. For specific guidelines on using a computer file to find books of poetry, see the next section in this chapter.

If you need help, speak to a reference librarian.

Using a Computer File to Find Books of Poetry

1. To find *general* poetry collections, use descriptors such as these:

☐ poetry

☐ poetry collections

☐ poetry anthologies

When the file displays a list of books, write down the call numbers for the books you are interested in.

2. To find *specific* collections (for example, collections categorized according to theme, country, culture, time period, or type), use descriptors such as these:

☐ nature poetry

☐ American poetry

☐ Latin American poetry

☐ Turkish poetry

☐ 19th-century poetry

☐ humorous poetry

☐ poetry by women

☐ political poetry

☐ poetry of places—Jerusalem

When the file displays a list of books, write down the call numbers of the books you are interested in.

3. To find poems written by a *particular poet*, type in the poet's last name, then first name.

☐ Hughes, Langston

☐ Baudelaire, Charles

☐ Po, Li

When the file displays a list of books by the poet, write down the call numbers of the books you are interested in.

Using a Poetry Index

Granger's Index to Poetry, a reference work that consists of several volumes, lists anthologies of poetry and indexes poems by (1) author, (2) subject, and (3) title and first line.

Use a card catalog or computer file to find *Granger's* call number.

Finding Books of Poetry in the Library

After you have written down the call numbers of the books you are interested in, follow the directions in Chapter 19 for finding a book in the library.

Once you have found a call number for a certain poetry collection, you might find similar collections on or near the same shelf. For example, you might find books of French poetry shelved together or books written by the same poet shelved together.

Finding Books of Poetry in a Bookstore

In a bookstore, poetry usually is shelved in one of two ways: (1) by poet's name in the literature/fiction section, or (2) in a separate section of poetry anthologies.

Selecting Poems

You may look for poems that you are familiar with but should also read through one or more anthologies until you find unfamiliar poems that capture your attention. Your selection may be determined by a certain category or theme:

☐ Poems about nature, love, friendship, childhood, or any other specific subject(s)

☐ Poems about war or other historical events

☐ Poems by and/or about women

☐ Poems by and/or about men

☐ Poems by and/or about immigrants

☐ Poems by and/or about people of a particular culture or group

☐ Poems by poets of a particular religion (or of different religions)

☐ Humorous poems

You may be able to determine the theme or category only after you have found poems that appeal to you. In other words, read first to find poems that you like. Then look for a connection among the poems.

All of the poems you select should be written in or translated into English. You may include poems from several countries and can include bilingual versions of a poem. The total number of poems will be determined by your instructor and/or class (for example, you may be searching for eight to ten poems).

Recording Bibliographic Information

Once you have selected a poem, photocopy it; or copy it *exactly* as it is written, with the precise spacing, indentation, capitalization, and punctuation. Write down the publication information of the source in which you found the poem; this information will later appear in the bibliography:

☐ Title of book

☐ Author(s) or editor(s)

☐ City of publication

☐ Publisher

☐ Date of publication

☐ Page number(s) on which the poem can be found

Writing about Individual Poems

There are many ways to discuss poems. For example, you can do some or all of the following:

☐ Explain how or where you found the poem.

☐ Share what you like about the poem or what interests you most.

☐ Share what you think or feel as you read the poem.

☐ Share your knowledge of the poet.

☐ Explain how the poem reflects the culture of the country of origin and/or of the poet.

☐ Discuss the significance of the title.

☐ Explore why you find the poem significant.

☐ Analyze the poem (see pp. 222–224).

☐ Interpret the poem (see p. 224).

Note: If you refer to critical, biographical, or historical material taken from other sources, cite and document the sources (see Chapter 24).

Writing an Essay to Introduce the Entire Anthology

The content of an essay that explains your entire anthology depends on the process you have gone through to compile the anthology and the particular poems you have chosen. For example, you can do some or all of the following:

☐ Explain how and where you found the poems.

☐ Explain the organization of the anthology—for example, what the poems have in common.

☐ Discuss your overall reaction to the poems you have selected.

☐ Provide historical background information related to the poems.

☐ Discuss your past experience with poetry—as a reader and/or writer.

Note: If you refer to any critical, biographical, or historical material taken from other sources, cite and document the sources (see Chapter 24).

Preparing a Bibliography

Prepare a bibliography to show from which sources the poems were taken.

Sample citations are included here in the MLA format. The sources should be listed in alphabetical order. For further instructions on the format for the list of sources, see Chapter 24.

Sample citation for a poem in a collection

       poet   *poem*   *source*

Robinson, Edwin Arlington. "Richard Cory." <u>Modern Verse in</u>

                        editors   *city*

    <u>English: 1900–1950.</u> Ed. David Cecil and Allen Tate. New York:

publisher   *date*   *page*

    Macmillan, 1958. 141

Sample citations for more than one poem in the same collection

If you take several poems from the same collection, provide the full bibliographic information for the collection:

Kennedy, X. J., ed. <u>An Introduction to Poetry.</u> 7th ed. Boston:
    Little, 1990.

Also provide a separate citation for each of the poems. Include poet's name, title of poem, editor's name, and page number:

Atwood, Margaret. "All Bread." Kennedy 284.

Thomas, Dylan. "Do Not Go Gentle into That Good Night."
    Kennedy 178–79.

Sample citation for a poem with no title

If a poem has no title, use all or part of the first line as a title:

Millay, Edna St. Vincent. "Love is not all." <u>Collected Sonnets of</u>
    <u>Edna St. Vincent Millay.</u> Ed. Elizabeth Barnett. Rev. ed. New
    York: Harper, 1988. 99.

Sample citation for a poem that has been translated

If a poem has been translated, put the name of the translator right after the title of the poem, preceded by the abbreviation *Trans.:*

Fuertes, Gloria. "Love Which Frees." Trans. Philip Levine. <u>Women</u>
    <u>Poets of the World.</u> Ed. Joanna Bankier and Dierdre Lashgari.
    New York: Macmillan, 1983. 260–61.

Structuring the Entire Anthology

The following chart provides an overall view of how a poetry anthology can be organized. It does not represent a rigid formula.

Table of Contents

↓

Essay explaining the anthology

↓

Poems, with individual discussions of certain poems

↓

Bibliography

Drafting

Prepare a draft of your anthology, adapting the guidelines for writing an interim draft on page 53 and for writing and structuring an anthology on pages 229–231.

Giving and Receiving Feedback

Exchange drafts with one or more classmates, adapting the guidelines for giving and receiving feedback on page 55. Review one another's work by examining (1) what you like about an anthology and (2) what you think can be done to strengthen it.

Revising

You can revise your work by answering questions such as these (see pp. 57–58 for a fuller discussion):

☐ What should I keep?

☐ What should I add?

☐ What should I delete?

☐ What should I change?

☐ What should I rearrange?

☐ What should I rethink?

Completing

Once you have revised the anthology, you can complete it by adapting these guidelines:

☐ Evaluate the anthology as a whole.

☐ Proofread and edit the entire anthology (see Chapter 25).

☐ Prepare a neat final manuscript (see Chapter 28).

Life and Poets, Poets and Life: A Poetry Project

Francisco Javier Rojo-Alique

About the Author   Francisco Javier Rojo-Alique, who was born and raised in Spain, compiled this anthology to fulfill an assignment for a composition course taken in the United States.

Note: This anthology has been edited for publication in this book.

CONTENTS

The present poetry anthology is a collection of poems with one or more aspects of human life as a common topic. I chose the topic of life for this project because it was wide enough to find many poems related to it, and especially because it could embrace almost any other subject in which I might be interested. Looking for poems related to life I could find, then, different points of view on childhood, youth, adulthood, old age. I could find the poets' vision and feelings on love, joy, sadness, suffering, personal relationships, loneliness, friendship, and so on, with none of them expressed in the same way.

My goal was to look for poems in which the subject of life was present. Almost every book of poetry that has been written includes some verses related to human existence, so I had to put some limits on my research. I determined to start by seeking works that I knew best, those written by poets from Spain, my native country. This was not very hard because previously I had decided that, if I found Antonio Machado's "Retrato" ("Portrait") translated into English, it would be part of my anthology. Machado is one of my favorite poets, and his work is familiar to me because I had to write a paper on his vision of love during my senior year in high school. It was easy to find this poem in an English version. I found Juan Ramón Jiménez's "The Last Journey," the second Spanish poem in this project, by turning the pages of a selection of poems from my country. I had read those verses many times, and, when I saw them translated into English, I thought the poem would be the perfect last piece for my anthology.

Now, I wanted to discover new authors, those who wrote in languages different from my native one. I thought that, for this English seminar, it would be preferable to use verses originally written in that language. I am in the United States, so I decided that I would search only for poems by American authors. As Machado and Jiménez were poets from the present century, so would be the others that would appear in my anthology.

I had never read American poetry, and I knew almost nothing about it. I rejected the idea of opening a manual of criticism where it would say "this is the best American poet and this is not." I had absolute freedom to choose my authors, so I considered that it was much better to explore the poems by myself, without being warned about them by any other person's opinion. I borrowed from the library two anthologies of American writers, because I realized that would be an easy way to find works by many different authors in the same book.

The following pages are the results of all this research. The anthology opens with James Reiss's "¿Habla Usted Español?" ["Do You Speak Spanish?"], first published in 1974, in which the poet recalls his childhood. Next is Machado's "Portrait," a summary of the life of the poet until his maturity, written at the beginning of this century. Next, Kenneth Koch, in "Poem for My Twentieth Birthday," published in 1945, reflects on the step from adolescence to adulthood: according to the poet, it is time not to have more dreams for the future, but to start experiencing some realities. Next is Daniel Halpern's "The Ethnic Life," composed in the early seventies, when the "hippie" movement and a strong attraction for the Eastern cultures was still in the mind of many people. I picked this poem because it offered a quite different vision of life. The poem that follows is "Marriage" by William Carlos Williams, published in 1916. As marriage is an important stage in the lives of many people, I thought it was not a bad idea to include a poem on it in my project, although these lines impressed me for other reasons, which I will explain in the poem's introduction. Merrill Moore's "Transfusion" is a vision of the painful side of life: sometimes to continue to live is a great struggle, as this poem shows. A not very optimistic vision of old age is given by Hilda Doolittle in her "The Time of Gold" (1957); and, finally, Juan Ramón Jiménez writes on the topic of death: people pass away, but the world continues being.

Life offers very different aspects, and so the following poems express very different situations, ages, points of view about human existence. Enjoy reading them!

¿Habla Usted Español?*

James Reiss

The Spanish expression *Cuando yo era muchacho*
may be translated: when I was a boy,
as, for example, "When I was a boy I wanted to be
a train driver," or "When I was a boy I was completely unaware of the
    flimsy orchid of life."
It is the kind of expression found in textbooks of the blue breeze
and is more useful, really, than expressions like "Please put the bananas
    on the table, Maria,"
or "Take it easy is the motto of the happy-go-lucky Mexican."
When I was a boy the sun was a horse.
When I was a boy I sang "Rum and Coca-Cola."
When I was a boy my father told me the mountains were the earth's sombreros.†

Portrait (*Retrato*)

Antonio Machado

Antonio Machado (Spain, 1875–1939) is one of my favorite poets, and this is one
of the poems I most like from him. Machado is one of the main figures of what was
called the Spanish Generation of 1898 (Turnbull 406). In that year, Spain lost its
last ultramarine colonies, Cuba and the Philippines, and the whole country was
invaded by a generalized idea of pessimism and the need for regeneration. All
these ideas are present in the literature of the time.

    The following poem is in some way Machado's autobiography. The poet
explains his life up to the moment he is writing: his external appearance, his
political and literary ideas, his expectations for the future.

    My childhood is memories of a patio in Seville
and a sunny yard with lemons turning ripe,
my youth twenty years in lands of Castile,
my story certain matters I don't care to recite.

    I never was a playboy or Don Juan—
you know how shabbily I always dress—
but none of Cupid's arrows came my way
and women found a lodging in my breast.

    The springs that feed my verse are calm and clear
for all my heritage of rebel blood;

---

*¿Habla Usted Español?: Do You Speak Spanish?
†sombreros: hats

I'm neither doctrinaire nor worldly wise—
Just call me in the best sense simply good.

    In my passion for beauty, out of modern aesthetics
I've cut old-fashioned roses in gardens of Ronsard,
but I've no great love for the latest in cosmetics
nor will you find me trilling the stylish airs.

    I'm not impressed by those puffed-up tenors' ballads
or the cricket chorus crooning to the moon.
I've learned to tell the voices from the echoes
and of all the voices listen to only one.

    Call me romantic or classic—I only hope
that the verse I leave behind, like the captain's sword,
may be remembered, not for its maker's art,
but for the virile hand that gripped it once.

    I talk with the man who is always at my side—
one who talks to himself hopes to talk to God sometime—
soliloquizing is speaking with this good friend
who has shown me the way to love of humankind.

    In the end I owe you nothing—you owe me all I've written.
I go about my work, I pay in my own coin
for the clothes upon my back, the roof over my head,
the bread that sustains my life, the bed where I lie down.

    And when the day for the final voyage is here
and the ship that does not return heads down the stream,
I'll be aboard, you'll find me traveling light
and nearly naked like children of the sea.

—Translated by Alan S. Trueblood

Poem for My Twentieth Birthday

Kenneth Koch

Passing the American graveyard, for my birthday
the crosses stuttering, white on tropical green,
the years' quick focus of faces I do not remember . . .

The palm trees stalking like deliberate giants
for my birthday, and all the hot adolescent memories
seen through a screen of water . . .

For my birthday thrust into adult and actual:
expected to perform the action, not to ponder
the reality beyond the fact,
the man standing upright in the dream.

The Ethnic Life

Daniel Halpern

I've been after the exotic
For years: champac
And patchouli in air, distant
Root scents, their smoke
Dazing rooms where dark men
Sit on legs
On rugs.

I ride teak trains
Through the Khyber Pass
Into Pakistan, and speak
Tongues I can't write.

My wife is young,
She turns to me from the East
After prayer—
Her black hair, her
Eurasian face spreading
Below the long eyes
Like Asian night itself.

On summer evenings before the monsoon
I meet my contortionist
Lover from India
Over Campari.
In her room my eyes roll
To paradise, click
Like a pair of Moroccan dice;
The undoing of her spine
Releases me from mine.

In my life
There is no room
for bikinis or Chanel
Or the waxed beauty of the West . . .

For years I've lived simply,
Without luxury—
With the soundness of the backward
Where the senses can be heard.

Marriage

William Carlos Williams

Although he is considered one of the most important modern American poets, I did not know who William Carlos Williams (1883–1963) was until I read this poem. I decided to include "Marriage" in my anthology because I was impressed by how the poet, with an unbelievable economy of words, is able to express so deeply what was his idea of matrimony.

One of the biggest mysteries—or miracles—of human life is, in my opinion, how two different people, with different origins, are able to "become like one," to become a new family. I think that this poem wonderfully expresses this idea.

> So different, this man
> And this woman:
> A stream flowing
> In a field.

Transfusion

Merrill Moore

I have chosen the following poem, originally published in *Poetry* magazine in 1929, because I have found it very original: a scene of a hospital, a blood transfusion, does not seem the "typical" topic to be considered by poets. However, I have found in these verses written by Merrill Moore a dramatic celebration of life: human existence is not made only of joy and happiness. There are difficult moments, and there are also occasions in which existence is threatened, death seems close. The poet expresses in her verses the struggle to survive: when everything seems lost, fresh blood will run through the veins; life will be recovered.

> The scene is set now: in a silent room
> Is Woman exsanguinated on a bed;
>
> Enter the cult in mask and white cloth clad
> Bearing borrowed blood in a red cup
> The first tall foremost priest holds and lifts up;
>
> The arm is cleansed—a needle in the vein,
> Then rosy color fast returns again.

Averted is proximity of doom
And joyous the new blood enters avenues
Of old veins to dispel the bluish hues
On face and finger, joyous as a bride-groom,

The new blood enters in the trembling room
That is the heart's first chamber whence it flows
And does the miracles men say it does.

In Time of Gold

H. D. (Hilda Doolittle)

Now there are gold reflections on the water,
how old am I and how have the years passed?

I do not know your age nor mine, nor when you died;
I only know your stark, hypnotic eyes

are different and other eyes meet mine, amber and fire,
in the changed content of the gazing-glass.

Oh, I am old, old, old and my cold hand
clutches the shawl about my shivering shoulders,

I have no power against this bitter cold,
this weakness and this trembling, I am old;

who am I, why do I wait here, what have I lost?
nothing or everything but I gain this,

an image in the sacred lotus pool,
a hand that hesitates to break

the lily from the lily-stalk and spoil
what may be vision of a Pharaoh's face.

The Last Journey (*El viaje definitivo*)

Juan Ramón Jiménez

I will bring this brief anthology to an end with a poem written by Juan Ramón Jiménez (1881–1958), who was awarded the 1956 Nobel Prize in literature. Jiménez is one of the greatest exponents of lyric poetry of the current century (Turnbull 426). He was born in Moguer, a sunny little town in Andalucia, Spain, which often is his source of inspiration.

I have chosen "The Last Journey" to close this anthology because it refers to the end of life. "What will happen afterwards?" asks the poet himself. He and all the people he met will leave this world, but life will continue. It is sad to think that one is going to lose the landscape, the world one loves so much; but on the other hand, it is a consolation to know that it will be there, that it will continue.

> . . . I shall go away. And the birds will stay
> still singing;
> and my garden will remain, with its tree of green,
> and its white well of water.
> Every afternoon the sky will be blue and placid;
> and the bells will chime as this afternoon
> they are chiming,
> the bells of the old belfry.
> And those will die who once did love me;
> the town will be made over new each year;
> and in that corner of my whitewashed, blossoming garden,
> my nostalgic spirit will wander . . .
> I shall go away; I shall be lonely without hearth
>   and green tree,
> without well of clear water,
> without the sky so blue and placid . . .
> and the birds will remain still singing.

—Translated by Eleanor T. Turnbull

Works Cited

Doolittle, Hilda (H. D.). "In Time of Gold." Hine and Parisi 346–47.

Halpern, Daniel, ed. The American Poetry Anthology. New York: Equinox, 1975.

Halpern, Daniel. "The Ethnic Life." Halpern 132–33.

Hine, Daryl, and Joseph Parisi, eds. The *Poetry* Anthology, 1912–1977: Sixty-five Years of America's Most Distinguished Verse Magazine. Boston: Houghton, 1978.

Jiménez, Juan Ramón. "The Last Journey." Trans. Eleanor L. Turnbull. Turnbull 431.

Koch, Kenneth. "Poem for My Twentieth Birthday." Hine and Parisi 249.

Machado, Antonio. "Portrait." Trans. Alan S. Trueblood. Antonio Machado: Selected Poems. Ed. Alan S. Trueblood. Cambridge, MA: Harvard UP. 1982. 100–101.

Moore, Merrill. "Transfusion." Hine and Parisi 111.

Reiss, James. "¿Habla Usted Español?" Halpern 355.

Turnbull, Eleanor L., ed. Ten Centuries of Spanish Poetry: An Anthology in English Verse with Original Texts from the XIth Century to the Generation of 1898. Baltimore: Johns Hopkins, 1955.

Williams, William Carlos. "Marriage." Hine and Parisi 42.

LIBRARY RESEARCH

This unit, Writing from Sources: Library Research, consists of three chapters that can help you fulfill an assignment to write an essay based on library research. Chapter 18 demonstrates ways to explore a research topic. Chapter 19 provides guidelines for conducting research in the library. Chapter 20 provides guidelines for composing a research essay.

Writing an essay based on research is a complex process that needs time and careful planning. Although undoubtedly you will develop your own way of working, the strategies demonstrated in this unit suggest approaches you can take to fulfill a research assignment. Various stages of research are presented separately to help you focus on one at a time. You will discover as you actually work that the stages often overlap.

To show how the different stages can interact in the development of a research essay, the writing of one student, Yordanka Ivanova, is included. Her completed essay, "The Vietnam War and Public Opinion," can be found on pages 265–270. Yordanka's work was selected as an example; it is not presented as a model to imitate.

CHAPTER 18

Guidelines for Exploring a Research Topic

Chapter 18 provides guidelines for selecting a research topic, developing a research question, and writing an informal research proposal. None of these suggestions is presented as a rigid rule that you must follow.

SUGGESTED ESSAY ASSIGNMENT

Select or adapt the assignment below, or devise your own assignment in consultation with your instructor.

Write an essay in which you reveal your point of view on an issue about which there is a diversity of views. Present various perspectives on the issue, using material gathered primarily through library research. Choose (1) an issue raised in a reading selection in this book or (2) a controversial issue that has recently been covered in the news.

Selecting Potential Research Topics

Many possible research topics emerge from the reading selections in this book. For example, you might want to research a topic related to cross-cultural communication or education or one of the following topics:

- "The School Days of an Indian Girl" by Zitkala-Ša (p. 16): an issue related to the treatment of Native Americans in the United States (for example, English-only Indian schools; removal to reservations) or to Sioux history and culture

- "Waiting in Line at the Drugstore" by James Thomas Jackson (p. 22) and "Still I Rise" by Maya Angelou (p. 220): an issue related to racism in the United States or to African American history and culture

- "College" by Anzia Yezierska (p. 25): an issue related to the immigration of Russian Jews (or any other group's immigration) to the United States (for example, the education of immigrants; discrimination against immigrants; immigrant's contributions to the United States)

- "Shooting an Elephant" by George Orwell (p. 31): an issue related to British imperalism (or any other country's imperialism) or to oppression.

- ☐ "The Ingrate" by Paul Laurence Dunbar (p. 168): an issue related to slavery in the United States (for example, the treatment or education of slaves; the abolitionist movement) or the Civil War (for example, its causes; the role of African American soldiers)

- ☐ "In the Land of the Free" by Sui Sin Far (p. 174): an issue related to Chinese immigration (or any other group's immigration) to the United States (for example, immigration laws; discrimination against immigrants; immigrants' contributions to the United States)

- ☐ "Eveline" by James Joyce (p. 182): an issue related to life at the turn of the 20th century (for example, the opportunities for women; the influence of the Catholic Church in Ireland)

- ☐ "The German Refugee" by Bernard Malamud (p. 186): an issue related to World War II (for example, Germany's treatment of Jews; Hitler's invasion of Poland) or to the status of refugees

- ☐ "Tito's Good-bye" by Cristina Garcia (p. 196): an issue related to Cuba (for example, the turn to Communism; Cuban immigration to the United States) or to illegal immigration

To prepare for an essay on a controversial issue covered recently in the news, you can consult major newspapers and news magazines to find an appropriate topic. From the magazines and/or newspapers, select some issues that interest you. Discuss with your instructor and/or classmates the following questions about each topic.

- ☐ Is this topic controversial? In other words, is there a conflict of opinion about this issue?

- ☐ Is this topic researchable? In other words, will there be enough material in the library to draw from? Are there people on campus or in the community who can share their knowledge of this topic?

A Student Writer at Work

Yordanka looked through the reading selections in her course textbook until she found an area that captured her interest: she wanted to learn more about the Vietnam War, which was the setting of one of the stories she had read.* In the story, an American soldier disobeys orders to shoot villagers. Yordanka thought she would do research so that she could compare this character's feelings with those of actual soldiers.

Writing an Informal Research Proposal

The purpose of an informal research proposal can be to explain to your instructor, and to yourself, how you think you want to proceed in your research. In other words, discuss what you want to learn about your topic.

---

*The story Yordanka read, "Village" by Estela Portillo Tremblay, is not included in this book.

As you move through various stages of this project, your ideas about what you want to learn may change. You can adjust your research accordingly.

A Student Writer at Work

Yordanka went with her class to the library and found an encyclopedia article that provided her with an overview of the topic. She proposed the following research project:

Yordanka's Informal Research Proposal

Reading the story "Village" made me curious to learn more about the war in Vietnam. At first I thought I would focus on American soldiers, but I changed my mind. The *Encylopedia Americana* article that I found divides the subject of the Vietnam War into three categories: (1) Political Aspects of the War, (2) Military Aspects of the War, and (3) Effects of the War on U.S. Society. I would like to narrow my topic to focus on the effects of the war on U.S. society. I know the Vietnam War is a controversial topic even today. I want to know what people feel and why they feel that way.

Formulating a Research Question

Research is often undertaken to find an answer to a question. A research question based on what you want to learn about your topic can guide you in finding sources in the library.

After you have begun doing the actual research, the question may change. Adjust your research accordingly.

A Student Writer at Work

Yordanka formulated her reseach question after reading an encyclopedia article on her topic.

Yordanka's Research Question

Why did the United States become involved in Vietnam, and what was the reaction of the people of the United States?

As you can see, Yordanka's research question actually combined two questions. Her task at this stage was to discover (1) why the United States became involved in Vietnam and (2) how the people of the United States reacted to that involvement. She would now go to the library to find sources to help answer those questions.

CHAPTER 19

Guidelines for Conducting Library Research

Once you know what you want to learn about a research topic, you need to find information that will help you answer your research question. At first you cannot know what you will find or what your answer will be. But, as you gather information, you will increase your knowledge of the topic. At each stage, you will have a better understanding of what you have already found and a better idea of what you still need to discover.

There are many ways to learn more about a subject. The following guidelines can give you some idea of how to proceed. The order or way in which you follow the guidelines will be determined by your topic, your working habits, and your instructor's advice.

Becoming Familiar with the Library

To become familiar with the library, you can do one or more of the following:

☐ Read the library pamphlets and/or take a library tour to learn where and how to find books, magazines, journals, and so on.

☐ Attend a session on how to use the library's computer file.

☐ Learn where the *reference* librarians are. Ask them for help whenever you need it.

Finding Current Information

A library usually keeps current newspapers and magazines in a reading room for several weeks or months before they are filed in a different place. If you have chosen a current topic, try to follow it in newspapers and magazines. In addition to reading news articles, you can look in the editorial sections to see if there is any commentary on the issue you are researching.

For some topics, you will want to look at newspapers and magazines that are less recent. Guidelines for finding those materials are included below.

Determining Subject Headings

Your topic can be described in several ways; in other words, it has different *subject headings* or *descriptors*. Creating a list of possible headings before you begin your search for library sources may be helpful. If you later find that this list is inadequate, check the reference book *Library of Congress: Subject Headings* or the text that explains the library's computer program.

A Student Writer at Work

Yordanka made a list of possible subject headings:
- ☐ Vietnam
- ☐ The Vietnam War
- ☐ The War in Vietnam
- ☐ Vietnam—United States

Finding Books

To find books related to your topic, you can begin with a computer file or card catalog that lists books. Both usually list books alphabetically in several ways: by author, by title, and by one or more subject headings. You may be able to make a computer printout listing books on a given topic.

Note: Since each library uses a particular computer program, you may need help from a librarian to learn how to use the program in your library.

GUIDELINES

For Finding Book Titles

1. Look up in the computer or card catalog the first subject heading on your list. If you do not find books that seem relevant to your topic, go down your list trying out different headings. You may need two descriptors (for example, "Vietnam War—United States") to find the books most closely related to your topic.
2. If you find one or more books related to your topic, copy the name of the author and title, and, most important, the *call number.* (If there are many books on your topic, just write down one or two call numbers; you will find books on similar topics shelved together.) This call number will tell you where the book is shelved in the library. For example, if the number is
DS
559.46
W93
the book is shelved, according to the Library of Congress classification system, with books on the history of Asia, as indicated by the code letters **DS**.

A Student Writer at Work

Yordanka used the library's computer file to find books. The first screen on the computer asked her to choose which database she wanted to use. She typed in the letters that would allow her to search for books in the on-line catalog.

Following the computer's directions to type s = before her subject, she typed: s = Vietnam. The screen that appeared indicated that 1,878 entries had been found, and it listed those entries within 14 categories (see Figure 19-1).

Knowing that she could not search 1,878 entries, Yordanka limited her search by looking down this list of 14 categories and choosing a category that connected the Vietnamese conflict to the United States (line 13):

13 VIETNAMESE CONFLICT 1961 1975—UNITED STATES

She then typed in the line number she had chosen, and a list of book titles appeared on the screen (see Figure 19-2).

Yordanka looked down this list of books, searching for the most recent publications, so that her research would be up to date. She saw that three of the books had been published in 1993 (she was doing her research in the fall of 1994). She decided to type in the line numbers of those books, one by one, and began with line 1678; detailed information about the book appeared on the screen (see Figure 19-3).

From the first few lines of this screen, Yordanka could read the author's name, the book's full title, the city of publication, the name of the publisher, and the date of publication. She also learned in which part of the library the book was shelved, the call number of the book, and that the book was available to be checked out.

```
Search Request: S=VIETNAM                                   Online Catalog
Search Results: 1878 Entries Found                          Subject Guide
-------------------------------------------------------------------------
LINE: BEGINNING ENTRY:                                      INDEX RANGE:
  1    VIETNAM                                                 1 -   135
  2    VIETNAM--FOREIGN RELATIONS--UNITED STATES             136 -   270
  3    VIETNAM--HISTORY--1945 1975                           271 -   405
  4    VIETNAM--POLITICS AND GOVERNMENT--1945 1975           406 -   540
  5    VIETNAMESE CONFLICT 1961 1975                          541 -   675
  6    VIETNAMESE CONFLICT 1961 1975                          676 -   810
  7    VIETNAMESE CONFLICT 1961 1975--CALIFORNIA--BERKELEY    811 -   945
  8    VIETNAMESE CONFLICT 1961 1975--ECONOMIC ASPECTS--UNITED ST   946 - 1080
  9    VIETNAMESE CONFLICT 1961 1975--LITERATURE AND THE WAR 1081 - 1215
 10    VIETNAMESE CONFLICT 1961 1975--PERSONAL NARRATIVES AMERICA 1216 - 1350
 11    VIETNAMESE CONFLICT 1961 1975--POETRY                 1351 - 1485
 12    VIETNAMESE CONFLICT 1961 1975--PUBLIC OPINION--UNITED STAT 1486 - 1620
 13    VIETNAMESE CONFLICT 1961 1975--UNITED STATES          1621 - 1755
 14    VIETNAMESE CONFLICT 1961 1975--UNITED STATES          1756 - 1878
-------------------------------------------------------------------------
STArt over          Type number to begin display within index range
HELp
OTHer options

NEXT COMMAND:
```

Figure 19-1

```
Search Request: S=VIETNAM                                    Online Catalog
Search Results: 1878 Entries Found                           Subject Index
----------------------------------------------------------------------------
        VIETNAMESE CONFLICT 1961 1975--UNITED STATES
1676    OUR OWN WORST ENEMY <1968>  (OL)
1677    OUR VIETNAM NIGHTMARE <1965>  (OL)
1678    PAPER SOLDIERS THE AMERICAN PRESS AND THE VI <1993>  (OL)
1679    PEACE DENIED THE UNTIED STATES VIETNAM AND T <1975>  (OL)
1680    PEOPLE VS PRESIDENTIAL WAR <1970>  (OL)
1681    PLANNING A TRAGEDY THE AMERICANIZATION OF TH <1982>  (OL)
1682    POLEMICS AND PROPHECIES 1967 1970 <1970>  (OL)
1683    POLEMICS AND PROPHECIES 1967 1970 <1972>  (OL)
1684    PRESIDENTS POLITICS AND INTERNATIONAL INTERV <1969>  (OL)
1685    PRESIDENTS WAR THE STORY OF THE TONKIN GULF <1971>  (LL)
1686    PRESIDENTS WAR THE STORY OF THE TONKIN GULF <1971>  (OL)
1687    REALITIES OF VIETNAM A RIPON SOCIETY APPRAIS <1968>  (OL)
1688    RECEPTIONS OF WAR VIETNAM IN AMERICAN CULTUR <1993>  (OL)
1689    RED THUNDER TROPIC LIGHTNING THE WORLD OF A <1993>  (OL)
---------------------------------------------- CONTINUED on next page  ---
STArt over           Type number to display record      <F8>  FORward page
HELp                 GUIde                               <F7>  BACk page
OTHer options        PRInt

NEXT COMMAND:
```

Figure 19-2

```
Search Request: S=VIETNAM                                    Online Catalog
BOOK - Record 1678 of 1878 Entries Found                    Brief View
----------------------------------------------------------------------------
Author:         Wyatt, Clarence.
Title:          Paper soldiers : the American press and the Vietnam War / by
                   Clarence Wyatt.
Published:      New York : W.W. Norton, 1993.

Subjects:    S=Vietnamese Conflict, 1961-1975--Press coverage.
                United States--Politics and government--1963-1969.
----------------------------------------------------------------------------
LOCATION:            CALL NUMBER:               CIRC/ORD STAT:
Library Stacks       DS559.46 .W93 1993         Not checked out


---------------------------------------------- Page 1 of 1  -----------
STArt over           LONg view       PRInt          <F6>  NEXt record
HELp                 INDex                           <F5>  PREvious record
OTHer options        GUIde

NEXT COMMAND:
```

Figure 19-3

Yordanka then wrote down the call number (DS 559.46 .W93) and went to search for the book.

GUIDELINES

For Finding and Selecting Books

1. Find the bookshelves that hold books beginning with the code letters (for example, **DS**); then search for the numbers following the code letters (for example, **559.46**) and then the final code (for example, **.W93**), until you find your book.
2. Skim the book to see if its information is helpful. Check the table of contents at the beginning, and read the first few lines of several chapters.
3. *Important*: Keep a list of the books that you may use in your research. Record author or editor's name, title, publisher, year of publication, and call number. One efficient way to keep track of sources is to record each source on a 3-by-5 inch lined index card (see Figure 19-4).

Finding Lists of Magazine or Journal Articles

To find magazine articles other than current ones that you can find in the reading room of the library, use *periodical indexes*. These indexes, available both on computer file and in bound volumes in the reference section of the library, list articles published on a variety of subjects.

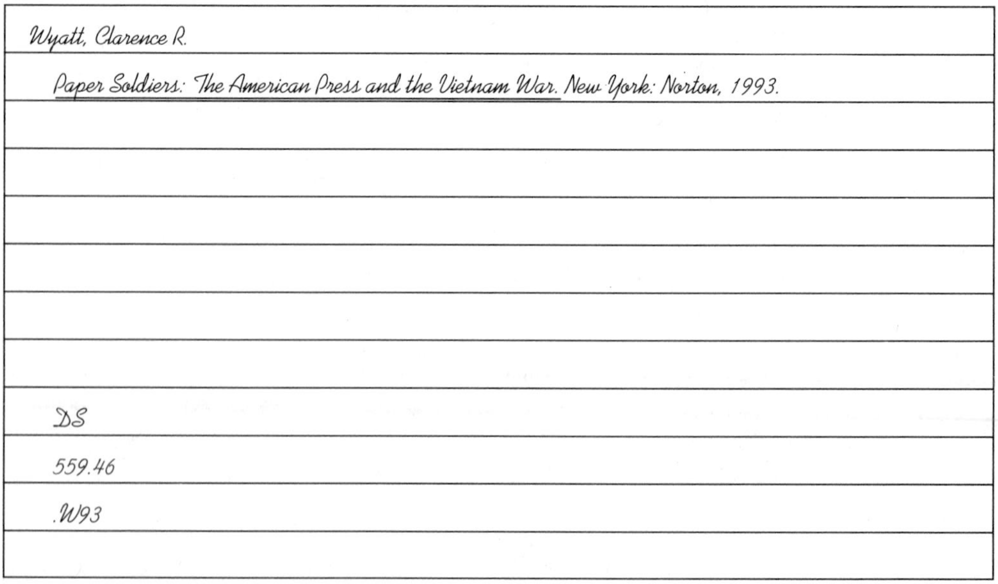

Wyatt, Clarence R.

Paper Soldiers: The American Press and the Vietnam War. New York: Norton, 1993.

DS

559.46

.W93

Figure 19-4

The most general index in book form is the *Readers' Guide to Periodical Literature*, which lists many magazines. This and other similar reference works are organized by year (for example, articles published in 1994) and are arranged alphabetically. Explanations of the abbreviations the indexes use can be found at the beginning of each volume.

Specialized indexes list (1) journal articles written in a scholarly way for specialized and academic audiences, or (2) articles on scholarly topics written in a way that is understandable to nonspecialists.

Examples of specialized indexes include the following:

Applied Science and Technology Index

Art Index

Business Periodicals Index

Education Index

Environment Index

Humanities Index

PAIS (Public Affairs Information Service Bulletin)

Social Sciences Index

Some of the articles you find through a specialized index may be too difficult to read. A number of periodicals in various fields are considered authoritative yet are accessible to nonspecialists. The following list may help you; a reference librarian may provide other titles in your area of investigation.

Psychology
American Psychologist

Psychology Today

International Relations
Current History

Far East Economic Review

Foreign Policy

The Nation

World Press Review

Education
Chronicle of Higher Education

Clearing House

Educational Leadership

Phi Delta Kappan

Political Science
American Political Science Review

Journal of the History of Ideas

Journal of International Affairs

Public Opinion Quarterly

Western Political Quarterly

Science

American Scientist

Bioscience

Discover

National Geographic

Science

Science News

Scientific American

Space World

Sociology

American Journal of Sociology

International Journal of Comparative Sociology

A Student Writer at Work

Yordanka used the computer file to find an article related to her topic. She first selected the database that would allow her to search the Humanities, Social Science catalog. Then she selected her subject and typed: s = Vietnam. The next screen that appeared on the computer indicated that 1,080 entries had been found; these entries were divided into 14 categories (see Figure 19-5).

Knowing that she could not search 1,080 entries, Yordanka narrowed the search by selecting the category that she felt was most closely connected with her topic:

```
Search Request: S=VIETNAM                          Humanities, Social Science
Search Results: 1080 Entries Found                            Subject Guide
-----------------------------------------------------------------------------
LINE:  BEGINNING ENTRY:                                        INDEX RANGE:
 1     VIETNAM                                                    1 -    78
 2     VIETNAM--ECONOMIC CONDITIONS                              79 -   156
 3     VIETNAM--ECONOMIC POLICY                                 157 -   234
 4     VIETNAM--FOREIGN RELATIONS--CHINA                        235 -   312
 5     VIETNAM--FOREIGN RELATIONS--JAPAN                        313 -   390
 6     VIETNAM--FOREIGN RELATIONS--UNITED STATES                391 -   468
 7     VIETNAM--POLITICS AND GOVERNMENT                         469 -   546
 8     VIETNAMESE--CHILDREN--GREAT BRITAIN                      547 -   624
 9     VIETNAMESE WAR 1957 1975                                 625 -   702
10     VIETNAMESE WAR 1957 1975--AMERICANS MISSING IN ACTION    703 -   780
11     VIETNAMESE WAR 1957 1975--LITERATURE AND THE WAR         781 -   858
12     VIETNAMESE WAR 1957 1975--PERSONAL NARRATIVES            859 -   936
13     VIETNAMESE WAR 1957 1975--PSYCHOLOGICAL ASPECTS          937 -  1014
14     VIETNAMESE WAR 1957 1975--PSYCHOLOGICAL ASPECTS         1015 -  1080
-----------------------------------------------------------------------------
STArt over        Type number to begin display within index range
HELp
OTHer options

NEXT COMMAND: 13
```

Figure 19-5

```
13  VIETNAMESE WAR 1957 1975—PSYCHOLOGICAL ASPECTS
```

She typed in line 13 and looked through the list of articles, but none of the titles captured her interest. She then typed in line 14 to find more article titles related to the same topic of psychological aspects. She scrolled through that list until she found a subcategory (VIETNAMESE WAR 1957 1975—SOCIAL AS-PECTS) that attracted her attention (see Figure 19-6).

From this list of article titles, Yordanka selected the article that most interested her and that had been published most recently. When she typed in line 1049, detailed information about the article appeared on the next screen (see Figure 19-7).

From the first few lines of this screen, Yordanka could read the title of the article (The ghosts of Vietnam), the name of the magazine in which it was published (The Economist), the volume number of the magazine (327), the page number on which the article could be found (32), and the date the magazine was published (Jun 5 '93).

Yordanka then wrote down this information and used the computer file to find the call number for the bound volumes of *The Economist*.

Finding Lists of Newspaper Articles

To find newspaper articles on a particular topic, use a newspaper index, which may be available both on computer file and in bound volumes (for example, *The New York Times Index;* see Figure 19-8).

The library may subscribe to several newspapers, including some from other countries. Through a computer file or at the reference desk, you can learn which

```
Search Request: S=VIETNAM                      Humanities, Social Science
Search Results: 1080 Entries Found                          Subject Index
---------------------------------------------------------------------------
     VIETNAMESE WAR 1957 1975--REPARATIONS
1043   EUROPE TO HASSLE USA OVER AGENT ORANGE <1984>  (SS)

     VIETNAMESE WAR 1957 1975--SECRET SERVICE
1044   GENERAL EDWARD G LANSDALE AND THE FOLKSONGS <1989>  (HU)
1045   WESTMORELAND VS CBS <1984>  (HU)
1046   WHY WESTMORELAND GAVE UP <1985>  (HU)

     VIETNAMESE WAR 1957 1975--SOCIAL ASPECTS
1047   COMMEMORATING THE UNWON WAR ON NOT REMEMBERI <1989>  (SS)
1048   DEBRIDING VIETNAM THE RESURRECTION OF THE WH <1988>  (SS)
1049   GHOSTS OF VIETNAM <1993>  (SS)
1050   PEOPLES QUITE APART AMERICANS SOUTH VIETNAME <1990>  (HU)
1051   POST VIETNAM SYNDROME NEUROSIS OR SOCIOSIS <1985>  (SS)
1052   SOCIAL IMPACT OF WAR <1991>  (SS)
-------------------------------------------------- CONTINUED on next page  ----
STArt over          Type number to display record      <F8>  FORward page
HELp                GUIde                               <F7>  BACk page
OTHer options       PRInt

NEXT COMMAND:
```

Figure 19-6

```
Search Request: S = VIETNAM                  Humanities, Social Science
WILSON RECORD 1049 of 1080 Entries Found            Brief View
-----------------------------------------------------------------------
ARTICLE TITLE:  The ghosts of Vietnam.

CITATION:       The Economist  327:32 Jun 5 '93

SUBJECTS:       Vietnamese War, 1957-1975--Social aspects.
                United States--Military policy.




------------------------------------------------ Page 1 of 1 -----------
STArt over          HOLdings          GUIde          <F6>  NEXt record
HELp                LONg view         PRInt          <F5>  PREvious record
OTHer options       INDex
Held by library--type HOL for holdings information.
NEXT COMMAND:
```

Figure 19-7

Summary of article related to Yordanka's research →

Date, page number: column number →

Sulzberger comments on N Vietnam's new strategy of parallel mil campaigns and negotiations, Mr 10,IV,14:3; T Wicker says Amer pub opinion seems to be moving to conclusion that war is creeping disaster that mil means cannot salvage; cites indications of trend; notes statements and actions by McCarthy, R F Kennedy, Rockefeller, Nixon and several Sens, Mr 10,IV,15:5; E O Reischauer says US is bogged down in seemingly endless war and should take new look at Asian policy; says it may be too early to judge full significance of new stage of war, but psychological effects will outweight mil; says psychological impact on US has been heavy; says US has lost war in terms of original objectives; discusses new approach to US relationship to Asia; illus, Mr 10,VI,p23; Nixon indicates he will stand firm on pledge that new Adm would end war, but continues to resist pressure to explain how he or any other Repub Pres would achieve objective, int; says explanation of implementation of pledge would fatally weaken his bargaining position if he became Pres; mentions USSR is possible key to securing settlement; says it would be dangerous to answer question whether Gen Eisenhower's techniques in Korea might provide pattern for future diplomacy in Vietnam; makes other comments, Mr 11,1:4; Sec Rusk to testify on Adm policy before Sen Foreign Relations Com; results of NH primary said to have possible effect on pendig decisions about war, Mr 11,1:6; hundreds of anti-Communist S Vietnamese open what they describe as major movement for unity and sense of natl purpose; call for nationwide austerity program to strengthen nation for all-out war on Vietcong: make other proposals; rival unity front is being formed by another group; some pol figures in both groups noted, Mr 11,12:3;

Excerpt from *New York Times Index*, 1968. Subject heading: VIETNAM.

Figure 19-8

newspapers your library subscribes to. Current newspapers are available in the periodical or reading room. Less recent newspapers are stored on microfilm. Microfilm machines give you access to these older newspapers.

Finding Articles in the Library

Once you have a list of articles that you think will help you in your research, you need to find those articles in the library.

GUIDELINES

For Finding Articles in the Library

1. Check the list of library holdings at the reference desk or the computer file to see if the library carries the magazines or newspapers you are interested in and to see how these materials are stored.
2. Use the computer file or card catalog to find the call number for the volume that contains the magazine (older magazines are bound together in large volumes). Some magazines and most newspapers are stored on microfilm or microfiche.
3. If the article you are searching for is in a bound volume, find the volume on the library shelf, and look for the article by date and page number.
4. If the article you are searching for is on microfilm or microfiche, go to the microfilm area, and ask the librarian for help in finding the article and using the microfilm or microfiche machine.
5. *Important*: Keep a list of or photocopy the articles that you may use in your research. Record authors' name, title of article, name of publication, volume number and date of publication, and page number(s) on which the article can be found.

Evaluating Sources

Initially, you will be reading to discover whether or not the library sources are appropriate for your topic. The first step can be to preview and skim the reading.

GUIDELINES

For Previewing and Skimming a Source

Preview an article or book chapter for a few minutes, to gain a general idea of its topic and organization.

1. Read the title and subtitle, if there is one.
2. Read the abstract (summary at the beginning), if there is one.
3. Read the first and last paragraphs.
4. Read the first sentence of every paragraph.
5. Look at any photographs, illustrations, or graphs.

Then skim the reading: read quickly to get an idea of the general content.

Before you spend a lot of time working with a source, try to determine how reliable it is. Even though you are not an expert, you can use several criteria to evaluate each source.

GUIDELINES

For Evaluating a Source

The answers to the following questions may help you determine if you have found a reliable source.

1. *Is the information up to date?* Though an older publication may provide background information, it may be outdated; that is, some of the information may no longer be valid. Check the date of publication.
2. *What is the publication's bias?* Check on the purpose and intended audience of a source by using a reference book that evaluates periodicals (for example, *Magazines for Libraries* or *Standard Periodical Directory*) or by asking your instructor or a reference librarian.
3. *What is the author's expertise on the subject?* Check on the expertise of the author by reading the description of the author accompanying the article or book, if there is one; by consulting an index that discusses authors' achievements and credentials (for example, the *Biographical Index* or *Current Biography*); or by asking your instructor or a reference librarian.
4. *Is the article well researched?* Skim the article or book to find evidence that the author has done research.

Summarizing an Article or Chapter

Once you have selected a topic, it can be useful to clarify the issue for yourself and your instructor. One way to accomplish that goal is to summarize an article or book chapter that explains the complexity of the issue.

In summarizing newspaper or magazine articles, you might aim to report both the events and their significance by answering questions such as these:

□ What has happened?

□ What might the newspaper or magazine want its readers to know or to learn?

To summarize a book chapter, adapt the guidelines for summarizing in Chapter 21. Hand in a photocopy of the article or book chapter with your summary.

Taking Notes

The goal of taking notes can be to record specific information and ideas that you might be able to use in your research essay. As with all other aspects of research, the way you take notes is dependent on your material and your working style.

For example, you may want to keep notes on lined index cards, in a notebook, or on a word processor; or you may want to photocopy articles in the library so that you can later annotate the texts.

For Taking Notes

1. Indicate the source of the notes (for example, author, title).
2. Indicate the page number(s) of the selection.
3. Summarize the selection.
4. List key ideas and evidence.
5. Record your own opinions in response to what you read.
6. Raise any questions you have about what you read.

   Note: Use quotation marks when you copy exact wording.

A Student Writer at Work

Yordanka took notes on lined index cards, especially to record important quotations and facts.

Writing a Progress Report

After taking numerous notes from several sources, it can be a good idea to stop and assess what you have accomplished. One way to do that is to write a *progress report* that summarizes what you have done and learned and that indicates what you still need to discover. The report can be written as a journal entry or letter to your instructor. You can use this opportunity to ask for help or advice.

A Student Writer at Work

At this stage, Yordanka had searched in the library and found several sources on Vietnam that she found useful for her research.

Progress Report on Yordanka's Research

   I have two books and two articles so far. One of the books is very useful because it contains many different articles about the Vietnam War and gives many different views of the war.

1. The Vietnam War: Opposing Viewpoints by William Dudley and David Bender (Editors), St. Paul, Minnesota, Greenhaven Press, 1990. This book has many articles that give different viewpoints about the war. The articles are in pairs, so that one side of an issue is discussed and then another. What I like is that some of the readings are original documents dating back to the time of the war. So far I have read a speech by Secretary of

State John Foster Dulles given in 1954 and a speech by Senator Thomas Dodd given in 1965. The book also explains some of the history of the war.

2. Paper Soldiers: The American Press and the Vietnam War by Clarence R. Wyatt, New York, W. W. Norton & Company, 1993. This book is mostly about how the press covered the war. I don't think I will read the whole book. There are one or two chapters that give important information about the attitudes of Americans toward the war.

3. "The Ghosts of Vietnam," The Economist, June 5, 1993, page 32. This article talks about the pain of the Vietnam veterans and how some of them still feel bitter.

4. "How to Bandage a War," by Laura Palmer, The New York Times Magazine, November 7, 1993, pages 36, 38–43, 68, 72–73. This is a really sad and shocking article about the nurses' experiences in Vietnam. Some of them suffer from the same stress as the soldiers.

CHAPTER 20

Guidelines for Composing a Research Essay

Perhaps the hardest part of research is deciding how to combine and organize all the material you have gathered. Many researchers enjoy the process of finding sources and of learning more about their subject, but feel enormous anxiety when faced with the task of putting it all together to make sense to others. If you feel that anxiety, you are not alone.

Creating a Preliminary Outline

Since there is so much material involved in research writing, a preliminary outline might be useful to help you organize the information. You may change the order or content of the outline as you continue to work on your paper.

A Student Writer at Work

Yordanka looked over her notes and made a list of different areas of the issue that she would cover. She then made a mental outline of the material.

Preliminary Outline for Yordanka's Research Essay

I. Introduction
II. Historical information about Vietnam
III. Patriotism
IV. Peace movement
V. End of war
VI. Conclusion

GUIDELINES

For Creating a Preliminary Outline

1. Reread your notes.
2. Find the major areas of the subject that you want to present in your paper.
3. Create categories or codes to label those areas.
4. Organize the categories into headings for a preliminary outline.

Structuring the Entire Essay

A well-structured essay enables you to communicate ideas effectively to readers. The following chart provides an overall view of how such a research essay can be developed. It by no means represents a rigid formula. The various parts of this chart are discussed in the sections that follow.

Introduction
☐ Explain the issue you are researching.
☐ Ask or imply a question about the issue, or make a point about the issue.

↓

Body
☐ Present supporting points and evidence related to various perspectives on the issue.

Explanations	Facts
Details	Opinions
Examples	Theories
Quotations	Experiences
Statistics	

↓

Conclusion
Answer the question you raised, expand on the point you made in the introduction, and/or raise new questions.

Developing the Introduction

The purpose of an introduction can be to focus on your topic and to tell readers what the essay is about. You can open your essay in a variety of ways, for example, relating a case study, quoting a passage, defining a term, stating an important fact, or providing historical background information. As you draft the paper, you can experiment with different openings. But there are features that your readers usually need and expect in the introduction to a research essay.

Note: If the following guidelines do not suit your essay, discuss alternatives with your instructor.

For Writing an Introduction

An introduction to a research essay usually accomplishes these goals:

1. Explain the issue you are researching
2. Focus on a particular topic by asking or implying a research question or by making a point about the issue

A Student Writer at Work

After drafting and receiving feedback on her essay, Yordanka eventually developed an introduction that began with background information about the Vietnam War. Then she explained diverse attitudes toward the war and finally focused on the main point of her research.

Introduction to Yordanka's Research Essay

Vietnam, a country in Asia that not many Americans had heard of before the year 1959, became a second "home" for many of them for the next fourteen years. One-tenth of young soldiers' lives were spent there, precious years of their early twenties, filled with constant fears that they would never see America again or survive at all. These soldiers had a destiny to serve their country during the years of the Vietnam War.

Background information about the war

The Vietnam War was the bloodiest of all; many thousands of American soldiers were killed, maimed, and mutilated. No better description can be found to illustrate the trauma than a citation from a veteran's vivid story, in this case a nurse whose daily experience was not to fight on the battlefield but to work behind the "stage":

> ... "he is going to be O.K.," she replies. ... As she begins to unwind the field dressing, all the blood she has been pumping into the soldier suddenly pours out over her. Blood and brains, the whole back of his head, are lying in her hands. Calmly, she puts his head together and secures it neatly with a clean dressing. (Palmer 38)

Quotation used to reveal the horror of war

Vietnam overwhelmed many Americans and challenged their patriotic feelings. Americans' point of view underwent crucial changes and reached both extremes, from a necessary support of the government's decision to a desperate desire to end this prolonged war. The Vietnam War was a war more painful than other wars, a war that scarred the nation and left it sore until today.

Focal point of the research

Developing the Body

In several paragraphs in the middle of the essay, you can present material that provides various perspectives on the issue. You do not necessarily have to support one viewpoint over the other. But you can show readers that you understand the issues well.

GUIDELINES

For Writing Body Paragraphs

1. Categorize the evidence you have gathered about your research topic (for example, all the material that provides historical background information, or all the evidence *in favor of* something versus all the evidence *against* something).

2. Combine and integrate material from different sources (see Synthesizing References to Two or More Readings, p. 159). Ex. p. '60-1

   □ Within each paragraph or set of paragraphs, provide at least one supporting point that relates to and expands on the topic that you focused on in the introduction.

   □ Within each paragraph or set of paragraphs, provide evidence (for example, details, examples, quotations, statistics) to substantiate the supporting point.

3. Identify your sources clearly (see Chapter 24).

There are several ways to organize the body of a research essay. None of the following suggested patterns represents a rigid formula. You may try variations on these structures or devise another structure that is better suited to your topic. You can use the drafting process to experiment with organization; your early efforts can be revised later.

Note : Include historical background information first if it is necessary for an understanding of the topic.

1. *Present one viewpoint at a time.*

   □ *First half*: Present what you perceive to be the weaker set of viewpoints first. In several paragraphs, explain this view, and include the reasons and evidence used to support it. (You do not need to evaluate this view here. Just present this point of view as fairly as possible.)

   □ *Second half*: Present the other set of viewpoints. In several paragraphs, explain this view, and include the reasons and evidence used to support it. You can organize this section so that it refutes the weaker set of viewpoints presented earlier. You will thus be evaluating the first set of points.

2. *Present and then evaluate opposing viewpoints, one at a time.*

   □ *First section*: Present what you perceive to be the weaker set of viewpoints. In several paragraphs, explain this view, and include the reasons and evidence used to support it.

□ *Second section*: Evaluate this weaker set of viewpoints. In one or more paragraphs, explain what you perceive to be the strengths and weaknesses of this view.

□ *Third section*: Present what you perceive to be the stronger set of viewpoints. In several paragraphs, explain this view, and include the reasons and evidence used to support it.

□ *Fourth section*: Evaluate this stronger set of viewpoints. In one or more paragraphs, explain why you believe this is the stronger view.

3. *Present opposing viewpoints together.* In one or more paragraphs, discuss one aspect of the issue. Then show how various sides view that aspect. You can do this without evaluating a side. Repeat this procedure for each aspect you want to discuss.

4. *Present and evaluate opposing viewpoints together.* In one or more paragraphs, discuss one aspect of the issue. Then show how various sides view that aspect. Then evaluate each viewpoint, showing what you perceive to be the strengths and weaknesses of each side. Repeat this procedure for each aspect you want to discuss.

A Student Writer at Work

In the final draft of her essay, Yordanka began the body with historical background information and an explanation of how the United States became involved in Vietnam. Then she began to present different points of view about the war. She began with the pro-war view and then showed how attitudes began to change. Paragraphs 9 through 11, the point at which she moved from one point of view to the other, are reprinted here.

Paragraphs 9, 10, and 11 of Yordanka's Research Essay

Indeed, it was honor! Inspired patriots felt they had to *Pro-war view* prove themselves, and many volunteered for the sake of their country. According to statistics, the average age of these youths was nineteen, a much younger age than in any other war; for example, in World War II, the average age was twenty-six (Gelman 148; Palmer 38). Their patriotic feelings were understandable, given that they were born in a country whose First Amendment of the Constitution guarantees freedom in almost all respects. In 1964, Senator Barry Goldwater said:

> No responsible world leader suggests that we should withdraw our support from Vietnam. . . . we need the dedication and the courage to face some hard and unpleasant facts. . . . we must have the will to win that war. (Dudley and Bender 31)

This was the attitude of almost all Americans back home, supported by the national leaders, but no one knew what was really happening on the battlefield.

Up to 1968, there had been many defeats for the U.S. Army, but the American public had not been told the full truth about them (Zaroulis and Sullivan 150). From that point on, President Johnson reinforced the armed forces with air force and navy reservists. In January of that year, the Tet Offensive took place, in which guerrillas from North Vietnam attacked thirty-four provincial centers, sixty-four district towns, and every major city in the South. This surprise attack cost the lives of thousands of soldiers; and it was also documented, published, and shown through the media in the States, causing the public to change its opinion about the war (Zaroulis and Sullivan 150).

Transition to an antiwar view

Consequently, the number of people raging against the war not only grew steeply, but a peace movement was spreading all over the United States (Zaroulis and Sullivan 149). Supporters of peace aimed their disapproval toward rising taxes, the inevitable and unpopular draft, and the lack of a prospect for a solution. Important leaders in the peace movement were Senator Robert F. Kennedy, who was running for president, and Martin Luther King, Jr., who preached against the unfairness of a "class army," for which mostly African Americans were drafted since they didn't have the means to afford college (Zaroulis and Sullivan 108). As a result of the public's dissatisfaction, Johnson decided not to seek another term in office.

Antiwar view

Developing the Conclusion

The conclusion grows out of the rest of the essay. Having introduced and provided evidence about an issue, now you can make a final statement about your topic, revealing your own perspective.

The way your essay ends will to some extent be determined by how it began. If your introduction raises a question, your conclusion can answer the question. If your introduction directly states a point about a topic, your conclusion can expand on that point.

Although you have to come to some conclusion about the topic, you do not have to prove anything. If you are writing about a controversial issue, for example, you may have found that all sides of the issue have reasonable evidence to support their views or that all sides have contradictions. Therefore, in your conclusion, you can either choose a side or explain why you are unable to choose a side. You may also raise new questions.

There are many ways to bring an essay to its end. The approaches used to introduce an essay (for example, quoting a passage, relating a case study, defining a term, stating an important fact, providing historical background) also can be useful for a conclusion. Which approach you choose will depend on your topic and purpose.

GUIDELINES

For Writing a Conclusion

In bringing your essay to a conclusion, you can use one or more of these strategies:

1. Evaluate the various perspectives, if you have not already done so.
2. Suggest solutions to a problem.
3. Discuss future consequences if no solution is found.
4. Suggest avenues for further research.
5. Raise questions about the topic.
6. Discuss the effect that your research/writing experience has had on your outlook on your topic.

Drafting

Prepare a draft of your research essay, adapting the guidelines for writing an interim draft on page 53 and for structuring the entire essay on pages 264–269.

Receiving Feedback: Presenting an Oral Report

Presenting your research orally to the class may help you shape your ideas. A good time to do that can be after you have written an interim draft. By then you will have done substantial research but can still benefit from comments and questions from classmates.

GUIDELINES

For Presenting Research Orally

Prepare a 10- to 15-minute oral presentation of your research topic by adapting these guidelines:

1. Prepare a one-page outline of your interim draft. The outline can be a list of headings or a more detailed list of major points and evidence.
2. Plan to explain these points to your listeners:

    □ Background of the subject you are researching
    □ Your research question
    □ Various perspectives on the issue
    □ Explanation of your own perspective on the issue

3. On the day your presentation is due, hand out copies of the outline to class members, and report on your research.
4. Leave time to answer questions. If you do not have an answer to a question, you can just tell the class you will do further research.
5. Take notes on class comments to record helpful suggestions.

Giving and Receiving Feedback: Sharing a Written Draft

One way to receive feedback on your draft is to provide copies for one or more classmates to review. If this process is used, adapt the guidelines for giving and receiving feedback on page 55 and the suggestions for summarizing and analyzing an essay on pages 145–146, or raise your own questions.

Revising

You can revise your paper by answering questions such as these (see pp. 57–58 for a fuller discussion):

☐ What should I keep?

☐ What should I add?

☐ What should I delete?

☐ What should I change?

☐ What should I rearrange?

☐ What should I rethink?

Completing

Once you have revised the draft, you can complete the essay by adapting these guidelines:

☐ Evaluate the essay as a whole.

☐ Proofread and edit the essay (see Chapter 25).

☐ Prepare a neat final manuscript (see Chapter 28).

Student Research Essay

The Vietnam War and Public Opinion
Yordanka Ivanova

About the Author   Yordanka Ivanova wrote the following research essay to fulfill an assignment for a composition course. In earlier sections in this unit, you can see how she selected and developed her topic.
Note: This essay has been edited for publication in this book.

Vietnam, a country in Asia that not many Americans had heard of before the year 1959, became a second "home" for many of them for the next fourteen years. One-tenth of young soldiers' lives were spent there, precious years of their early twenties, filled with constant fears that they would never see America again or survive at all. These soldiers had a destiny to serve their country during the years of the Vietnam War.

The Vietnam War was the bloodiest of all; many thousands of American soldiers were killed, maimed, and mutilated. No better description can be found to illustrate the trauma than a citation from a veteran's vivid story, in this case a nurse whose daily experience was not to fight on the battle field but to work behind the "stage":

> . . . "he is going to be O.K.," she replies. . . . As she begins to unwind the field dressing, all the blood she has been pumping into the soldier suddenly pours out over her. Blood and brains, the whole back of his head, are lying in her hands. Calmly, she puts his head together and secures it neatly with a clean dressing. (Palmer 38)

Vietnam overwhelmed many Americans and challenged their patriotic feelings. Americans' point of view underwent crucial changes and reached both extremes, from a necessary support of the government's decision to a desperate desire to end this prolonged war. The Vietnam War was more painful than other wars, a war that scarred the nation and left it sore until today.

Historical Background

After Communists came to power in China in 1949, the United States developed a foreign policy aimed against the spread of Communism in Asia (Dudley and Bender 18). With such a policy, Americans engaged in the Korean War beginning in 1950, and before long, there was a new conflict waiting impatiently. Early in Dwight D. Eisenhower's presidency (1953–1961), a turmoil in regard to the same part of the world, called Indochina, drew America's attention. As a territory of France, Indochina issued a declaration of independence that France refused to acknowledge. Especially in Vietnam, which was one of the three countries comprising Indochina, rebellious political movements began to take place, supported by the newly powerful forces of Communist China and the Union of Soviet Socialist Republics. The United States supported its ally, France, financially and militarily. In 1954, Ho Chi Minh and his Communist followers defeated France, forcing the French government to give up any claims and return to its homeland. Vietnam was divided into two governments: Communist North Vietnam and anti-Communist (nationalistic) South Vietnam. War soon broke out in South Vietnam as the Communists tried to overthrow the government.

U.S. Involvement in Vietnam

One should ask the next question: Why did the United States continue to stay involved in Vietnam? The answer is not so simple and not very convincing either. Many Americans nowadays cannot believe they served their country for reasons as unclear as these were.

The United States was a member of the Southeast Asian Treaty Organization (SEATO) and had given its word to help South Vietnam in its development and to proceed with scheduled elections. The United States, as a great power, was watching over this development with "a sense of kinship with those everywhere who yearn for freedom" (Dulles 20). Because of previous experiences with Communism, Americans had created an image of it as a moral evil, and such a strong opinion had always stimulated the nation. Deep inside, hatred and a spontaneous feeling of responsibility had arisen to help any victim of this evil. Furthermore, another reason for the U.S. involvement, according to Secretary of State John Foster Dulles, was that

> the United States would take a grave view of any future overt military Chinese Communist aggression in relation to the Pacific or Southeast Asia area. Such an aggression would threaten island and peninsular positions which secure the U.S. and its allies.
>
> If such overt military aggression occurred, that would be a deliberate threat to the United States itself. (21)

Lastly, the area where Vietnam is situated was called the "rice bowl," which refers to the natural resources growing there. It was in Vietnam's best interest not to be occupied by a Communist nation. Overall, as President Eisenhower said, it was an area of "transcendent importance" (Dulles 22).

It was to be an easy and a quick war; in fact the term "limited war" was applied in the beginning to describe it, meaning limiting the military involvement, advice which history contradicted. Statistics show that by 1962, 4,000 troops had been sent; by 1965, there were air strikes almost daily; in 1966, U.S. soldiers numbered 200,000; and the peak year was 1969, when the number of military troops reached over a half million (Dudley and Bender 13–14). The war's demands kept increasing by great numbers under Lyndon Johnson's presidency, whose goal was to maintain the commitment and win this war once and forever. However, it became complicated because it was a guerrilla war. Nobody could distinguish the enemy from the innocent people, and the U.S. Army was not prepared for that (Gelman 149).

The War and American Patriotism

Nevertheless, the commitment to Vietnam remained an issue of great importance that did not escape the minds of U.S. leaders, as the words of Congressman Russell Long show:

> We have more than 200,000 men there. We have at stake our national honor. We are committed to resisting Communist aggression. (Dudley and Bender 29)

Indeed, it was honor! Inspired patriots felt they had to prove themselves, and many volunteered for the sake of their country. According to statistics, the average age of these youths was nineteen, a much younger age than in any other war; for example, in World War II, the average age was twenty-six (Gelman 148; Palmer 38). Their patriotic feelings were understandable, given that they were born in a country whose First Amendment of the Constitution guarantees freedom in almost all respects. In 1964, Senator Barry Goldwater said:

> No responsible world leader suggests that we should withdraw our support from Vietnam. . . . we need the dedication and the courage to face some hard and unpleasant facts. . . . we must have the will to win that war. (Dudley and Bender 31)

This was the attitude of almost all Americans back home, supported by the national leaders, but no one knew what was really happening on the battlefield.

The Antiwar Movement

Up to 1968, there had been many defeats for the U.S. Army, but the American public had not been told the full truth about them (Zaroulis and Sullivan 150). From that point on, President Johnson reinforced the armed forces with air force and navy reservists. In January of that year, the Tet Offensive took place, in which guerrillas from North Vietnam attacked thirty-four provincial centers, sixty-four district towns, and every major city in the South. This surprise attack cost the lives of thousands of soldiers; and it was also documented, published, and shown through the media in the States, causing the public to change its opinion about the war (Zaroulis and Sullivan 150).

Consequently, the number of people raging against the war not only grew steeply, but a peace movement was spreading all over the United States (Zaroulis and Sullivan 149). Supporters of peace aimed their disapproval toward rising taxes, the inevitable and unpopular draft, and the lack of a prospect for a solution. Important leaders in the peace movement were Senator Robert F. Kennedy, who was running for president, and Martin Luther King, Jr., who preached against the unfairness of a "class army," for which mostly African Americans were drafted since they didn't have the means to afford college[1] (Zaroulis and Sullivan 108). As a result of the public's dissatisfaction, Johnson decided not to seek another term in office.

In the following year, on October 15, 1969, a different type of anti-war movement had reached its peak, with a great number of people participating in it. "Teach-ins," rallies, parades, and church services had all gathered on that day to mark Moratorium Day, the largest antiwar demonstration in the nation's history (Zaroulis and Sullivan 269). Teach-ins were activities at colleges where groups of students had gathered to hold a massive discussion on the subject. In 1969 alone, there were 221 major demonstrations at 101 colleges, involving 40,000 students.

Later on in the year, disturbing rumors began to circulate about the brutal conduct of American troops in Vietnam. In November, a newspaper reporter had published a story about My Lai, a small Vietnamese village where American soldiers had slaughtered civilians the year before (Zaroulis and Sullivan 294). That shocked and outraged the American public, and few people believed any longer that "we must do what we are doing to honor the commitments," as President Johnson had claimed (qtd. in Larson and Larson 34). The public was not acting as a listener but rather as a speaker, and opposite points of view were now everywhere supported by documents as well.

> The true fact is that the United States has had no obligation to South Viet-Nam or anyone else under the SEATO treaty to use its own armed forces in the defense of South Viet-Nam. (Larson and Larson 35)

The U.S. Involvement Comes to an End

In his campaign for the presidency, Richard Nixon claimed he had a "secret plan" to put an end to the war. When he took office in January 1969, he said, "I am not going to end up like LBJ,[2] holed up in the White House afraid to show my face. I'm going to stop that war" (Wyatt 191). But actually he had no plan. It wasn't until months later that he adopted a new policy that he called "Vietnamization," which stated that the United States should help the Vietnamese fight the war but not fight the war for them. The policy was designed to satisfy the impatient and frustrated public who cared for nothing but to see the bright light of the ending. But the public's pessimism had grown to the extreme, and that pessimism was reflected in the statement of an American official in Saigon:

> "As usual, we've been guilty of self-delusion," the offical lamented. "Vietnamization was to be the theme upon which we were going to slide out of this mess. And nobody wants to recognize the fact that Vietnamization does not reflect the reality on the ground." (Wyatt 196)

Nevertheless, this policy soon resulted in the gradual withdrawal of U.S. troops. On July 31, 1973, Congress had voted to end all bombing and

---

[1]These peace leaders were both assassinated in this same year, 1968.
[2]*LBJ:* Lyndon Baines Johnson

to ban any future military moves. With the slow withdrawal of the U.S. Army, South Vietnam had revealed its weakness; and on April 30, 1975, the capital city, Saigon, fell into the hands of the Communists.

Effects of the War

Officially it was over, but not in the minds of many of the survivors, whose painful memories never seem to have healed. Reliving bad experiences in their dreams and ordinary lives, veterans have suffered from postwar traumas, which psychologists have referred to as signs of post-traumatic stress disorder (PTSD). The symptoms are much the same, going beyond the "battle fatigue" of earlier wars: long spells of depression; sudden, explosive bursts of rage; insomnia; repeated war nightmares; emotional separation from loved ones; obsessive memories; the feeling of being in danger; and flashbacks of battlefield experiences (Gelman 149). These symptoms showed up after five, ten, and as many as fifteen years after the soldiers had come home and afflicted at least 470,000 men, which was 15% of those who served in the war; approximately 7,000 women, mostly nurses, were also victims (Gelman 147).

As to the whole nation, the Vietnam War had destroyed the national sense of innocence and, thus, its faith in itself and its leaders. Many actions were regretted and, inside their hearts, Americans will never forgive some of the government's mistakes:

> They [the armed forces] declared that they would never again go willingly to war without clear political aims; that when they did go to war for such aims they would do so with overwhelming force; and they would discover, in advance, how they were supposed to get out of a job once they had started it. ("The Ghosts of Vietnam")

Needless to say, in the Vietnam War, the government had failed in all these points.

The public is also not going to forgive the government for drafting nineteen-year-old youths who were barely equipped to deal with the pain, anger, atrocity, hatred, barbarous acts, and the guilt they had to face. They went to fight believing they were going to do something worthwhile, but once there, and after being mistreated when they returned home, they experienced "moral confusion" (Gelman 149).

To end this research, I would like to quote from an article that reflects the mood of most of the soldiers leaving the war:

> . . . everything had mattered in Vietnam, but afterward life seemed meaningless. (Palmer 40)

Works Cited

Dodd, Thomas J. Speech delivered to the U.S. Senate. Washington, 23 Feb. 1965. Rpt. as "The U.S. Must Maintain Its Commitments." Dudley and Bender 27–32.

Dudley, William, and David Bender, eds. The Vietnam War: Opposing Viewpoints. St. Paul: Greenhaven, 1990.

Dulles, John Foster. Speech delivered to the Overseas Press Club of America. New York, 29 Mar. 1954. Rpt. as "The U.S. Must Stop Communist Expansion." Dudley and Bender 19–22.

Gelman, David. "Treating War's Psychic Wounds." Newsweek 29 Aug. 1988, Rpt. as "Vietnam Veterans Suffer from Psychological Problems." Dudley and Bender 146–151.

"The Ghosts of Vietnam." The Economist 5 June 1993: 32.

Larson, Don R., and Arthur Larson. Excerpt from Vietnam and Beyond. Durham: Duke University Rule of Law Research Center, 1965. Rpt. as "The U.S. Has No Binding Commitments." Dudley and Bender 33–36.

Palmer, Laura. "How to Bandage a War." The New York Times Magazine 7 Nov. 1993: 36+.

Wyatt, Clarence R. Paper Soldiers: The American Press and the Vietnam War. New York: Norton, 1993.

Zaroulis, Nancy, and Gerald Sullivan. Who Spoke Up? American Protest Against the War in Vietnam, 1963–1975. Garden City, New York: Doubleday, 1984.

Academic Writing Conventions

Part Three consists of four chapters that demonstrate academic ways of writing about what you read.

Chapter 21 provides general guidelines for summarizing both nonfiction and fiction works. Chapter 22 explains the purpose and process of paraphrasing an author's words. Chapter 23 offers suggestions for selecting and incorporating quotations from the reading into your own writing. Chapter 24 focuses on various ways to cite and document sources.

It is impossible to learn everything in these four chapters before you begin to write about what you read. Your instructor may work with certain chapters or sections in class at various points in the semester. You may also refer to various sections on your own, just before or after you begin writing. Slowly, over the course of the semester, you can become more familiar with the entire unit.

CHAPTER 21

Summarizing

Summarizing is a process of condensing, or shortening, a reading selection while preserving its overall meaning. Reasons to create a summary may include the following:

☐ To explore your understanding of a reading

☐ To demonstrate your understanding of a reading

☐ To establish the ideas that you will discuss

☐ To inform a reader (for example, when you summarize a source that the reader has not read)

A Student Writer at Work

In the first paragraph of her essay, "Is Creativity Suppressed by Knowledge?" (p. 163), Sophia Skoufaki includes a brief summary of the reading selection to which she is responding.

Sophia's Summary

In his essay, "We Should Cherish Our Children's Freedom to Think," Kie Ho supports the American system of education. He expresses disappointment with the Indonesian way of teaching that he had experienced. As he points out, American schools tend to teach students how to develop their creativity more, rather than try to stuff their heads with knowledge. Ho always had to memorize things and to acquire as much knowledge as he could from books, while his son in California learned practical things through experience. Ho admires the approach of his son's school. But I hesitate to endorse it.

Sophia's purpose here is to introduce the reading selection she will be discussing in her essay and to establish the ideas in the reading that she will be evaluating and analyzing.

Just as there are different purposes for summarizing, there are different approaches to summarizing. The following guidelines offer suggestions for developing summaries of various types of reading selections in this book, both *nonfiction* (essays, articles) and *fiction* (short stories).

Summarizing Nonfiction

Your primary goal in summarizing nonfiction (texts other than short stories, novels, poems, plays) can be to uncover what you perceive to be the writer's stance toward the subject. To summarize, then, you need to distinguish between main ideas and secondary details.

Summarizing Passages That Contain Direct Statements of a Main Idea

In short passages and in some complete essays, a main idea may be clearly stated, for example, in the following paragraph from May Sarton's "The Rewards of Living a Solitary Life" (p. 37):

> For me the most interesting thing about a solitary life, and mine has been that for the last twenty years, is that it becomes increasingly rewarding. When I can wake up and watch the sun rise over the ocean, as I do most days, and know that I have an entire day ahead, uninterrupted, in which to write a few pages, take a walk with my dog, lie down in the afternoon for a long think (why does one think better in a horizontal position?), read and listen to music, I am flooded with happiness.

The first sentence of this paragraph can be said to contain its main idea. A one-sentence summary of this paragraph could be:

> *Living alone is a joyful experience in that it becomes more fulfilling as time passes.*

Note that many details of the paragraph have been left out of the summary: the author's twenty years of a solitary life, her watching the sun, writing, walking with her dog, lying down, reading, listening to music, and so on. Most of these details are included in the paragraph to *illustrate* what Sarton means by "rewarding." But they are secondary to the idea expressed in the one-sentence summary.

Summarizing Passages by Combining Ideas

Though some passages or entire essays contain direct statements of main ideas, more often you must search through the reading, looking at several important ideas and examples. To write a summary, you then need to combine those ideas, to establish what the entire passage is about. Sometimes you can be fooled by a first sentence that appears to be the main idea of the passage, but a careful reading will reveal that another idea emerges later on. This can happen, for example, when you read the following paragraph from Kie Ho's "We Should Cherish Our Children's Freedom to Think" (full text on pp. 125–127):

> There's no doubt that American education does not meet high standards in such basic skills as mathematics and language. And we realize that our youngsters are ignorant of Latin, put Mussolini in the same category as Dostoevski, cannot recite the Periodic Table by heart. Would we, however, prefer to stuff the developing little heads of our children with hundreds of geometry problems, the names of rivers in Brazil and 50 lines from *The*

Canterbury Tales? Do we really want to retard their impulses, frustrate their opportunities for self-expression?

A first reading of this paragraph might suggest that Ho's main point is that American education does not meet high standards in certain basic skills. He includes details in the second sentence that reveal that this is true. But in the third sentence, he questions the alternatives. And in the final sentence, he suggests that the alternative educational program might prevent opportunities for self-expression. If only the first sentence were used to summarize this passage, the meaning of the passage would be distorted. By combining the idea in the first sentence with the idea in the last sentence, a one-sentence summary that preserves the meaning could be as follows:

> *Although American education does not meet high standards in certain basic skills, it does provide valuable opportunities for self-expression.*

This summary, one of many possible sentences, presents two ideas: (1) that Ho acknowledges the weak standards of American education and (2) that Ho approves of the values of American education. The summary is carefully constructed to show the relationship between the ideas. The first clause is a dependent (subordinate) clause (subordinated by the word *although*), showing that this idea is less important to Ho. The second clause is an independent (main) clause, showing that this is the main point Ho makes. Note that other details in the paragraph are omitted: ignorance of Latin, names of rivers in Brazil, and so on. These details illustrate what Ho means, but they are secondary to the main idea of the paragraph.

Summarizing Fiction

Writers of fiction rarely state main ideas directly within a story. What readers can summarize is the *plot*: the series of events and thoughts in a story that usually is characterized by a conflict: a struggle between two or more opposing forces. The conflict may be internal (for example, person versus conscience) or external (for example, person versus person, person versus nature, person versus society, or person versus fate). A story may have more than one conflict.

To summarize a plot, you can determine what you believe are the key events or happenings in the story and identify the conflict(s). In a plot summary, there are primarily four important features:

1. *It should be brief.* Try to summarize the plot in a few sentences, or in only one or two sentences.

2. *It should be accurate.* Use the facts as they are presented in the story.

3. *It should contain the most important details.* Your goal is to tell what is happening in the story, to identify what you perceive to be the main conflict.

4. *It should be primarily in your own words.* Retell the story in your own words. Of course, some of the original words of the story must remain, such as the names of characters and places. But you can replace many of the words from the original text.

Identifying a Source

In academic writing assignments, you are expected to identify the sources you use (see also pp. 298–301). You need to refer to writers by name, to give them credit for their ideas. If you are summarizing an entire reading selection, you can initially include the title of the selection.

Indicating the Author and Title: Introductory Phrases

You can choose among many different introductory phrases to indicate the author and title. For example, you can say:

- ☐ (The author) states in (this reading selection) that. . . .
- ☐ (The author), in (this reading selection), shows that. . . .
- ☐ In (this reading selection), (the author) writes that. . . .
- ☐ As (the author) says in (this reading selection), . . .
- ☐ The main idea of (the author's reading selection) is that. . . .

Note: See also Introducing Quotations, page 289–290.

Introducing an Author's Ideas: Verbs

Many verbs and verb phrases can be used to introduce an author's ideas, depending on what you perceive to be the intention of the author and on your emphasis. The following verbs and verbal phrases, listed alphabetically, are among those most commonly used. Check a thesaurus and dictionary of usage, if necessary, to determine which verb or verb phrase to select.

acknowledge	discuss	observe
admit	doubt	point out
advise	emphasize	proclaim
advocate	endorse	propose
affirm	establish	question
allude to	examine	reason
argue	explain ✓	recognize
ask	explore	recommend
assert	expose	remark
assume	express	reveal
believe	feel	say
bring to light	find	show ✓
caution	focus on	state
claim	give credence to	stress
concede	highlight	suggest
concentrate on	identify	think
conclude	illustrate ✓	uncover
condone	imply	underline
confess	indicate	underscore
contend	insist	unveil
convey	intimate	voice
declare	maintain	write ✓
disclose	note	

Introducing an Author's Ideas: Verb Tense

When you refer to an author's ideas, it is conventional to use the present tense. This use of tense acknowledges that the author's ideas continue to exist even though the author has finished writing about them.

EXAMPLE

☐ May Sarton *begins* her essay "The Rewards of Living a Solitary Life" by retelling the experience of a male friend who was surprised that he had enjoyed being alone in a museum.

Introducing an Author's Ideas: Author's Name

The first time you refer to an author, you can include the full name. After that, you can refer to the author by the surname only:

EXAMPLE

☐ *May Sarton* begins her essay "The Rewards of Living a Solitary Life" by retelling the experience of a male friend who was surprised that he had enjoyed being alone in a museum. She then shares her own experiences with solitude. *Sarton* maintains that living alone is a joyful experience in that it becomes more fulfilling as time passes.

GUIDELINES

For Summarizing a Reading Selection

1. Reread the selection carefully.

   ☐ Determine what you perceive to be the significance of each idea and example.
   ☐ Note the way ideas and examples are linked to other ideas or examples.

2. Decide what you are going to include in your summary and what you are going to leave out.
3. Group the essential information, ideas, and details that you have selected in an order that shows the relationships among the ideas and facts. This does not necessarily have to be the order in which they are presented in the reading selection.
4. Create a sentence—or several sentences, as long as the summary is considerably shorter than the original—that reveals what you think the whole selection is about. You might try to do this orally first, as if you were telling a friend what you just read. Then write down your words.
5. Identify author (and title, if you are summarizing an entire essay or story).

ACTIVITY

Writing Summaries

Working alone, with a partner, or in a small group, summarize in one sentence each of the following passages in one of these ways:

1. Select and rewrite in your own words a direct statement of what you perceive to be the main idea from the passage.

2. Combine ideas to create one main idea.

3. Infer an idea from details.

A

Loneliness is most acutely felt with other people, for with others, even with a lover sometimes, we suffer from our differences of taste, temperament, mood. Human intercourse often demands that we soften the edge of perception, or withdraw at the very instant of personal truth for fear of hurting, or of being inappropriately present, which is to say naked, in a social situation. Alone we can afford to be wholly whatever we are, and to feel whatever we feel absolutely. That is a great luxury!

> *May Sarton, fifth paragraph of*
> *"The Rewards of Living a Solitary Life"*
> *(full text on pp. 37–39)*

B

"If a man does not keep pace with his companions, perhaps it is because he hears a different drummer." This thought by Thoreau strikes a chord in so many people that it has become part of our language. We use the phrase "the beat of a different drummer" to explain any pace of life unlike our own. Such colorful vagueness reveals how informal our rules of time really are. The world over, children simply "pick up" their society's time concepts as they mature. No dictionary clearly defines the meaning of "early" or "late" for them or for strangers who stumble over the maddening incongruities between the time sense they bring with them and the one they face in a new land.

> *Robert Levine and Ellen Wolff, first paragraph of*
> *"Social Time: The Heartbeat of Culture"*
> *(full text on pp. 84–91)*

C

There are many viewpoints regarding the practice of intercultural communication but a familiar one is that "people are people," basically pretty much alike; therefore increased interaction through travel, student exchange programs, and other such ventures should result in more understanding and friendship between nations. Others take a quite different view, particularly those who have done research in the field of speech communication and are fully aware of the complexities of interpersonal interaction, even *within* cultural groups. They do not equate contact with communication, do not believe that the simple experience of talking with someone insures a successful transfer of meanings and feelings. Even basic commonalities of birth, hunger, family, death, are perceived and treated in vastly different ways by persons with different backgrounds. If there *is* a universal, it might be that each has been so subconsciously influenced by his own cultural upbringing that he assume that the needs, desires, and basic assumptions of others are identical to his own.

LaRay M. Barna, first paragraph of
"Intercultural Communication Stumbling Blocks"
(full text on pp. 75–83)

D

Of all the common practices in our schools, doubtless the most tyrannical and indefensible is our insistence on attempting to evaluate students' performance through a system of grades or "marks." The harm done by this practice is incalculable, but we persistently cling to it in spite of its obvious unworkability. Every person who has ever gone to school can cite numerous instances of unfairness and injustice caused by grading systems and practices, but for some strange reason we seem to assume it to be necessary and intrinsic to the process of formal education.

Arthur E. Lean, first paragraph of
"The Farce Called 'Grading'"
(full text on pp. 130–134)

CHAPTER 22

Paraphrasing

Paraphrasing is a process of restating a reading passage in your own words while preserving what you perceive to be the writer's intended meaning and tone. This process is similar to translating; but unlike translating, paraphrasing does not involve changing words from one language to another. Instead, when you paraphrase, you write in the same language, translating someone else's ideas into your own words.

The Purposes of Paraphrasing

Paraphrasing can be a useful process for reading because it enables you to record ideas in a written form that you can understand and remember. For example, you can paraphrase for these purposes:

- ☐ To annotate
- ☐ To make double-entry notes
- ☐ To take notes

Paraphrasing also can be a useful process for clarifying meaning in essay writing. When you write essays in which you write about readings, you usually paraphrase for these purposes:

- ☐ To refer to the reading at different points in your essay
- ☐ To indicate to readers exactly which of the authors' ideas you are responding to
- ☐ To clarify an author's ideas

When you paraphrase a passage to include it in your own essay, you can take an idea or example from the reading to introduce or support an idea you want to discuss in your paper. You might incorporate the paraphrased passage into your own sentence.

Whether the paraphrase is alone or incorporated, you should in some way identify the source on which the paraphrase is based (see Identifying a Source, pp. 275–276, and Avoiding Plagiarism, p. 295).

Occasionally, you might want to use the author's exact words (see Quoting, pp. 287–293).

The Process of Paraphrasing

Paraphrasing is not a simple process. You can rarely translate word by word. First of all, some basic words often must remain, for example, names, indefinite articles, pronouns, and prepositions. Furthermore, even though you need to look up unfamiliar words in order to paraphrase, using a thesaurus or dictionary to substitute words can sometimes create sentences that are nonsensical or more difficult to understand than the original:

EXAMPLE

■ Sentence from the eighth paragraph of LaRay M. Barna's "Intercultural Communication Stumbling Blocks" (p. 79):

Learning the language, which most foreign visitors consider their only barrier to understanding, is actually only the beginning.

■ Word-by-word paraphrase of Barna's sentence:

Acquisition of knowledge of human or written speech, which the majority of alien guests or newcomers think their alone of its kind obstacle to comprehension, is in fact but the commencement.

Obviously, this is not an acceptable paraphrase, since it does not clarify the meaning of the original passage.

■ A clearer paraphrase of Barna's sentence:

In spite of what most international travelers think, language is not the only factor preventing full communication.

Determining Meaning and Tone

As a paraphraser, you need to be flexible if what you produce is to be clear and accurate. A good approach can be to follow these guidelines to determine meaning:

□ Think about what the writer is really saying.

□ Observe how the passage fits into the entire reading selection.

When you paraphrase, think not only about the meaning of the passage but also its tone. For example, if the writer is sarcastic or funny or angry or compassionate, your paraphrase should reflect that sarcasm, humor, anger, or compassion. Again, knowing how a passage fits into an entire text can help you determine tone.

□ Look for clues in the title.

□ Look for clues in the way the writer introduces the reading selection.

□ Look for clues in the words the writer has chosen. (Are there any words or phrases that surprise or shock or please you? If so, they are probably reflective of the tone.)

Capture the tone in your paraphrase.

EXAMPLE

■ Third sentence of May Sarton's "The Rewards of Living a Solitary Life" (p. 37):

> For him it proved to be a shock nearly as great as falling in love to discover that he could enjoy himself so much alone.

■ Paraphrase of Sarton's sentence:

> He was surprised and delighted when he realized that he could find pleasure in solitude.

This paraphrase captures the meaning as well as the tone of Sarton's words. The writer of the paraphrase knows from reading her entire essay that Sarton believes that being alone is worthwhile. The words *surprised and delighted* reveal the positive connotation of the word *shock*. The paraphraser uses the words *delighted* and *pleasure* to reveal the positive nature of the experience.

A paraphrase that does not capture the tone of the passage might look like this:

■ Paraphrase of Sarton's sentence that does not capture the tone:

> He nearly had a stroke when he realized that he liked being by himself.

Here the paraphraser turns the word *shock* into something negative by comparing it to a *stroke*. The expression *nearly had a stroke* is also too conversational compared to Sarton's more literary use of the language. This paraphrase does not accurately reflect the author's attitude and writing style.

Incorporating Paraphrases into Your Own Sentences

When you include a paraphrase of a reading passage in your own essay, integrate it smoothly with your own writing so that your ideas will be easy to follow.

GUIDELINES

For Incorporating Paraphrases

To incorporate paraphrases, you can use one or more of these strategies:

1. Introduce the paraphrase by mentioning the writer's name and using a verb that indicates the writer's approach to the topic (see Identifying a Source, pp. 275–276).
2. Change a writer's first person viewpoint to the third person. For example, "I argue that" can become *He argues that.*
3. Use words in the sentence to show your own view of the paraphrased material (for example, *I agree with Neusner that . . .* ; *Lean overstates the case when he argues that . . .*). (See also pp. 289–290.)
4. Check to see that the grammar and punctuation of the sentence help make sense of what you are saying.

EXAMPLE

The following example shows how one student paraphrased a sentence from LaRay M. Barna's "Intercultural Communication Stumbling Blocks" (p. 75) and integrated it into his own sentence. Note that he preserves Barna's idea even as he expresses it in his own words.

■ Barna's sentence:

The first [stumbling block] is so obvious it hardly needs mentioning—*language*. (p. 78)

■ Student's paraphrase of Barna's sentence:

The basic problem that an international student faces, as Barna correctly says, is the language.

Analysis of the Paraphrase

☐ The order of the sentence is preserved.

☐ The word *basic* is substituted for *first* and allows for the deletion of the phrase *so obvious it hardly needs mentioning*.

☐ The word *problem* is substituted for the implied *stumbling blocks*.

☐ The paraphrase is then integrated into the student's sentence. He is careful to indicate that this idea came from Barna's essay by mentioning her name. By using the expression *correctly*, he shows that he agrees with Barna.

ACTIVITY

Analyzing Paraphrases

Working alone, in a small group, or with the whole class, analyze these student paraphrases of sentences from "Intercultural Communication Stumbling Blocks" by LaRay M. Barna (p. 75).

1. Barna's sentence:

Learning the language, which most foreign visitors consider their only barrier to understanding, is actually only the beginning. (p. 79)

Student's paraphrase of Barna's sentence:

However, as Barna points out, language is not the only problem a foreigner will face.

2. Barna's sentence:

Stereotypes are stumbling blocks for communicators because they interfere with objective viewing of stimuli. (p. 80)

Student's paraphrase of Barna's sentence:

According to Barna, stereotypes create communication barriers because they cause people to make biased judgments about each other.

Note that Barna herself paraphrases other authors whose work she has read. For example, on page 137 she incorporates a paraphrase into her own sentence:

> Stereotypes help do what Ernest Becker says the anxiety-prone human race *must* do, and that is to reduce the threat of the unknown by making the world predictable. ■

Changing Direct Speech to Indirect Speech

To report what was said in a text (*direct speech*) without using the exact words that were used by the speaker, you can turn the passage into *indirect speech*.

GUIDELINES

For Changing Direct to Indirect Speech

A number of adjustments need to be made when you change direct to indirect speech, which include the following:

1. Do not use quotation marks.
2. Change first person pronouns (for example, *I*, *me*, *we*, *us*, *my*, *our*) to third person (*he*, *she*, *they*, *them*, *his*, *hers*, and so on).
3. Shift the verb tense to the past, unless the information is still true at the moment of writing. You may need to move the verb tense further into the past from the tense used by the speaker (for example, from *am* to *was*; from *will* to *would*; from *went* to *had gone*).
4. Change expressions related to time to match the new verb, for example:

   □ from *today* to *that day*
   □ from *yesterday* to *the day before* or *the previous day*
   □ from *tomorrow* to *the next day*, *the following day*, or *a day later*
   □ from *next week* to *the following week*, *the next week*, or *a week later*

5. If you change a question to a statement, eliminate the question mark and change the subject/verb word order (for example, from "*When will they return?*" to *He doesn't know when they will return.*).

EXAMPLE

The following example shows one way to turn direct speech into indirect speech and then to paraphrase it.

■ Passage from reading selection:

> Back home in California, I never need to look at a clock to know when the class hour is ending. The shuffling of books is accompanied by strained expressions that say plaintively, "I'm starving. . . . I've got to go to the bathroom. . . . I'm going to suffocate if you keep us one more second." (*Levine & Wolff*, pp. 85–86)

■ Passage in indirect speech:

> Back home in California, Levine never needed to look at a clock to know when the class hour was ending. The shuffling of books was accompanied by strained expressions that said plaintively that the students were starving, they had to go to the bathroom, and they were going to suffocate if he kept them one more second.

■ Passage in indirect speech, paraphrased:

> Levine says that at his own university in California he did not need to consult a clock to realize that the class was coming to an end. Combined with the noise of their books being closed, the faces of his students told him that they were hungry, had to use the toilet, and were going to suffocate if he did not let them go in the next second.

GUIDELINES

For Paraphrasing

After selecting a passage that you plan to refer to in your own essay, put the passage into your own words. In adjusting the writer's words, you can rearrange word order, turn longer sentences into shorter ones, make two sentences out of one, or select only a key idea from a long sentence.

1. Look up the definitions of unfamiliar words.
2. Think about what the writer really means.
3. Use one of these strategies to find your own words to rephrase the passage:

   ☐ Cover up the passage, and write from memory.
   ☐ Take notes on the passage. Then cover up the passage, and write the paraphrase from your notes.
   ☐ Work word by word, substituting synonyms. Then rewrite the substitute passage so that it makes sense.

4. Reread the original passage to make sure that you have preserved meaning and tone. Revise your paraphrase if necessary.
5. Incorporate the paraphrase into your own sentence (see pp. 281–282).

ACTIVITY

Evaluating Paraphrases

Each of the following sentences is taken from reading selections in this book. Each sentence is followed by a paraphrase. Working alone, with a partner, or in a small group, read each sentence, and then examine each paraphrase. Determine whether the paraphrase preserves the original meaning and tone (if necessary, read the entire reading selection). If it does not, rewrite the paraphrase.

1. Original sentence:

What was my little sorrow to the centuries of pain which those stars had watched?

*Anzia Yezierska, from
"College," page 30*

Paraphrase:

My unhappiness was unimportant when compared with the suffering that the world has always known.

2. Original sentence:

People from different cultures inhabit different nonverbal sensory worlds.

*LaRay M. Barna, from
"Intercultural Communication Stumbling Blocks," page 79*

Paraphrase:

There are diverse ways of speaking in other countries.

3. Original sentence:

Solitude is the salt of personhood. It brings out the authentic flavor of every experience.

*May Sarton, from
"The Rewards of Living a Solitary Life," page 39*

Paraphrase:

If you sprinkle sodium chloride on yourself, you will really taste what it's like to be alone.

4. Original Sentence:

I perceived in this moment that when the white man turns tyrant it is his own freedom that he destroys.

*George Orwell, from
"Shooting an Elephant," page 34*

Paraphrase:

At this very moment Orwell realized that a slaveholder, in certain aspects, is deprived of personal liberty himself. ■

ACTIVITY

Paraphrasing

Paraphrase the following passages, adapting the guidelines on page 284.

1. In spite of the staggering amount of incontrovertible evidence that grading not only does not accomplish its purpose but in reality inhibits and injures the educative process, we obstinately continue with this perverted practice.

   *Arthur E. Lean, from
   "The Farce Called 'Grading,'" page 132*

2. The belief that self-esteem is a pre-condition to learning is now dogma that few teachers question.

Randy Moore, from
"Grades and Self-Esteem," page 136

3. There are many viewpoints regarding the practice of intercultural communication but a familiar one is that "people are people," basically pretty much alike; therefore increased interaction through travel, student exchange programs, and other such ventures should result in more understanding and friendship between nations. Others take a quite different view, particularly those who have done research in the field of speech communication and are fully aware of the complexities of interpersonal interaction, even *within* cultural groups.

LaRay M. Barna, from
"Intercultural Communication Stumbling Blocks," page 76

4. Like historical friends, our crossroads friends are important for *what was*—for the friendship we shared at a crucial, now past, time of life.

Judith Viorst, from
"Friends, Good Friends—and Such Good Friends," page 67

CHAPTER 23

Quoting

When you write about a reading selection, you may want to use the exact words of the writer. In quoting, as in paraphrasing, you take material from the reading to introduce or support a point you want to discuss. Quoting also enables you to enrich your writing by adding the distinctive flavor of another writer's words.

Selecting a Quotation

Although quotations serve an important purpose in an essay, too many quotations can break the flow of your discussion. Readers are primarily interested in learning how you view or make sense of the material. Most of your essay will be written in your own words as you evaluate, analyze, or interpret a reading selection.

An important first step in selecting a quotation is deciding whether to paraphrase or to quote. The following guidelines can help you make that decision.

GUIDELINES

For Selecting a Quotation

Before you decide to use a quotation, ask yourself this question: why am I quoting rather than paraphrasing this passage? If your answer is one of the following statements, then include the quotation in your essay:

- ☐ The author's words are so impressive or so clever that to put them in my own words would lessen their impact.
- ☐ The author's words are so precise that to put them in my own words would change their meaning.
- ☐ The author's words are so concise that I would need twice as many words to paraphrase the passage.

Note: In academic writing, you are expected to indicate the page number from which a quotation is taken.

QUOTING

A Student Writer at Work

In her essay "Is Creativity Suppressed by Knowledge?" (p. 163), Sophia Skoufaki includes several quotations from the reading selection she is responding to: "We Should Cherish Our Children's Freedom to Think" by Kie Ho (p. 125). Some of those quotations and an explanation of Sophia's purpose in selecting them are discussed here.

Quotations in Sophia's Essay

In this excerpt from her second paragraph, Sophia includes quotations to introduce Ho's ideas:

He asks why so many people complain about the American education system, since "America is the country of innovation" (p. 126). This innovativeness is tied to the fact that the public schools provide children with the opportunity to be creative:

> I think I found the answer on an excursion to the Laguna Beach Museum of Art, where the work of schoolchildren was on exhibit . . . they had transformed simple paper lunch bags into, among other things, a waterfall with flying fish. (p. 126)

In this excerpt from her third paragraph, Sophia includes quotations to introduce ideas of Ho's that she disagrees with:

However, I don't agree that this is the best way to educate students. Ho wonders if we would "prefer to stuff the developing little heads of our children with hundreds of geometry problems, the names of rivers in Brazil, and 50 lines from *The Canterbury Tales* (p. 126). He believes that by asking them to acquire much knowledge and take memorization seriously, we really "retard" the impulses of students and "frustrate their opportunities for self-expression" (p. 126). While I agree that experimentation, free expression of one's self and creativity, and innovation are important, I don't think that by learning geography, history, and math or by studying literature, students underdevelop their impulses.

In this excerpt from her fourth paragraph, Sophia uses a quotation from Ho's essay for the purpose of supporting her own criticism of Ho's view:

> Isn't it sad that Ho's son thought that "Buenos Aires was Spanish for good food—a plate of tacos and burritos, perhaps" (p. 126) and that that doesn't sound strange to Ho?

ACTIVITY

Selecting a Quotation

Read the following passage, the opening paragraphs of Sydney J. Harris's essay "What True Education Should Do" (full text on pp. 3–4). Then, (1) read the statements following the passage, and (2) search through the passage to find at least one quotation that can introduce or verify each statement.

> When most people think of the word "education," they think of a pupil as a sort of animate sausage casing. Into this empty casing, the teachers are supposed to stuff "education."
>
> But genuine education, as Socrates knew more than two thousand years ago, is not inserting the stuffings of information *into* a person, but rather eliciting knowledge *from* him; it is the drawing out of what is in the mind.

QUOTING

"The most important part of education," once wrote William Ernest Hocking, the distinguished Harvard philosopher, "is this instruction of a man in what he has inside of him."

And, as Edith Hamilton has reminded us, Socrates never said, "I know, learn from me." He said, rather, "Look into your own selves and find the spark of truth that God has put into every heart, and that only you can kindle to a flame."

1. Harris creates an unusual analogy to explain how most people view education.
2. According to many people, the purpose of education is to fill students with knowledge.
3. Some scholars' concept of education has focused on the student rather than the teacher. ■

Incorporating Quotations into an Essay

Once you have decided to use a quotation, you should try to incorporate it into your essay in such a way that your essay doesn't have a choppy, unnatural rhythm. Otherwise, it may appear to readers that the quotation has just been dropped into the essay for no reason.

GUIDELINES

For Incorporating Quotations

To incorporate quotations, you can use one or more of these strategies:

1. Introduce or in some way lead into the quotation so that readers know whose words are being quoted or can understand why the quotation is important.
2. Comment on the quotation after you have included it so that readers understand its connection to other points made in the paper.
3. Insert *ellipses* (three spaced periods: . . .) if you delete any words from the original quotation.
4. Use *brackets* [ ] to add words to or to substitute words for those in the original quotation.

Introducing Quotations

There are a variety of ways to introduce a quotation, as demonstrated below (see also Identifying a Source, pp. 275–276). An introductory phrase or verb can tell readers something about your reason for including the quotation.

EXAMPLES

■ Revealing the author's point of view
  □ According to (the author), ". . ."
  □ As (the author) says, ". . ."
  □ (The author) claims that ". . ."
  □ ". . . ," admits (the author).

QUOTING

- □ In (the essay), (the author) concludes that ". . ."
- □ ". . .," remarks (the author), ". . ."
- □ The following quotation reveals (the author)'s bias: ". . ."
- □ Unlike most professors, (the author) believes that ". . ."
- □ (The author) is opposed to the idea that ". . ."
- □ (The author) is in favor of the idea that ". . ."
- □ (The author) is concerned about " . . ."

■ Showing complete agreement with the author

- □ I agree with (the author)'s point that ". . ."
- □ Like (the author), I believe that ". . ."
- □ (The author) is correct when he/she says, ". . ."
- □ (The author)'s view that ". . ." is valid.
- □ (The author) is wise to argue that ". . ."
- □ It is true, as (the author) states, that ". . ."
- □ My own experience has shown that ". . ."

■ Showing complete disagreement with the author

- □ In my opinion, (the author)'s view that ". . ." is wrong.
- □ When (the author) argues that ". . .," his/her reasoning is flawed.
- □ (The author) is unwise to claim that ". . ."
- □ It is not a question of ". . ." but of . . .
- □ (The author)'s notion that ". . ." is untrue.
- □ I disagree with (the author)'s idea that ". . ."

■ Showing partial agreement with the author

- □ (The author)'s point that ". . ." is only partly true.
- □ (The author)'s argument that ". . ." has some merit but is not convincing.
- □ To say, as (the author) does, that ". . ." is true, but the point is irrelevant to the issue.
- □ I agree with (the author)'s point that ". . .," but not with the idea that . . .
- □ (The author)'s view that ". . ." may be true for some, but not for all.
- □ While I agree with (the author) that ". . .," I don't believe that . . .

A Student Writer at Work

The following excerpts from Sophia's essay "Is Creativity Suppressed by Knowledge?" (p. 163) show how she integrated quotations into her own sentences by first introducing them.

Sophia's Introductions of Quotations

In introducing these quotations, Sophia is careful to make clear that the idea is Ho's (not Sophia's) and to indicate exactly where the quotation can be found (the page number):

> He believes that by asking them to acquire much knowledge and take memorization seriously, we really "retard" the impulses of students and "frustrate their opportunities for self-expression" (p. 126).

In introducing the following quotation, Sophia reveals her attitude toward its content:

> It is not flattering at all for America that "our youngsters . . . put Mussolini in the same category as Dostoevski" (p. 126).

Commenting on Quotations

Obviously, what you say after you have included a quotation depends upon your purpose and subject matter. The important point to remember is that readers may not understand why a quotation is included unless you tell them. The following examples show the types of comments you can make.

EXAMPLE

- ☐ Explain what the quotation means by paraphrasing it (for example, *The author means that . . . ; In other words, . . .*).

- ☐ Expand on the quotation: add details or facts or ideas that reveal its truth or significance (for example, *This point is significant because . . . ; Moreover, . . .*).

- ☐ Explain the connection between the quotation and what has already been said (for example, *This statement reflects [the author]'s stated desire to . . . ; This point contradicts [the author]'s earlier point that . . .*).

- ☐ Refer to one important word or phrase in the quotation, and explain its significance (for example, *The word ". . ." is significant because . . . ; [The author] emphasizes ". . ." because . . .*).

- ☐ Explain your position in relation to the quotation: you might agree, disagree, or partially agree with the point made in the quotation (for example, *My experience confirms that [the author]'s viewpoint is valid; Contrary to what [the author] implies, . . . ; It may be true that . . . , but . . .*).

A Student Writer at Work

After introducing a quotation from the essay by Kie Ho, Sophia commented on the quotation by explaining her position in relation to it.

Sophia's Comment on a Quotation

He believes that by asking them to acquire much knowledge and take memorization seriously, we really "retard" the impulses of students and "frustrate their opportunities for self-expression" (p. 126). While I agree that experimentation, free expression of one's self and creativity, and innovation are important, I don't think that by learning geography, history, and math or by studying literature, students underdevelop their impulses.

In "International Communication Stumbling Blocks" (p. 75), LaRay M. Barna quotes from her own outside reading, comments on the quotation, expands on it, and shows its connection to her research.

> As Frankel says, "To enter into a culture is to be able to hear, in Lionel Trilling's phrase, its special 'hum and buzz of implication.'" This brings in *nonverbal areas* and the second stumbling block. People from different cultures inhabit different nonverbal sensory words. Each sees, hears, feels, and smells only that which has some meaning or importance for him.

In fact, the single quotation marks around the expression 'hum and buzz of implication' reveal that Frankel has quoted Trilling (see Quotation Marks, pp. 367–369).

Using Ellipses to Delete Words

Ellipses (three spaced periods*) can be helpful if you want to delete some words from the middle of a quotation, as long as you don't change the writer's intended meaning.

There are primarily two reasons to use ellipses:

1. Delete words from a quotation to make the quotation shorter or to select the part of the quotation that comes right to the point you want to emphasize.

EXAMPLE

> *Original:* Yes; most teachers try to be fair and accurate, but all the time they know—at least, those who are honest with themselves know—that they are attempting the impossible.
>
> *Arthur E. Lean, from*
> *"The Farce Called 'Grading,'" page 133*
>
> *Altered:* Lean believes that "most teachers try to be fair and accurate, but . . . know . . . that they are attempting the impossible" (p. 133).

2. Delete words to make a quotation fit logically into your own sentence.

EXAMPLE

> *Original:* We'll improve students' self-esteem most by helping and motivating our students to exceed *higher* standards.
>
> *Randy Moore, from*
> *"Grades and Self-Esteem," page 137*
>
> *Altered:* Moore argues that teachers can "improve students' self-esteem most by helping and motivating . . . students to exceed *higher* standards" (p. 137).

*If the deleted words include a period at the end of a sentence, use four periods.

Note: Ellipsis is necessary only if you omit words from the *middle* of a quotation you have integrated into your own sentence. It is not necessary to use ellipsis if you omit words from the beginning or from the end of the quotation.

EXAMPLE

Original: Yes; most teachers try to be fair and accurate, but all the time they know—at least, those who are honest with themselves know—that they are attempting the impossible.

Arthur E. Lean, from
"The Farce Called 'Grading,'" page 133

Acceptable: Lean believes that ". . . most teachers try to be fair and accurate . . ." (p. 133).

Preferable: Lean believes that "most teachers try to be fair and accurate" (p. 133).

Using Brackets to Add Words

If you need to add words to or substitute words in a quotation, put the additional or changed expression within brackets.

Note: Use brackets **[ ]**, not parentheses **( )**, for this purpose.

1. Add words to help clarify a potentially confusing quotation.

EXAMPLE

Original: In a foreign land they increase our feeling of security . . . .

LaRay M. Barna, from
"Intercultural Communication Stumbling Blocks," page 80

Altered: Barna explains that "in a foreign land they [stereotypes] increase our feeling of security" (p. 80).

Alternative: Barna explains that "in a foreign land [stereotypes] increase our feeling of security" (p. 80).

2. Substitute words to make a quotation fit smoothly into your own sentence, as long as you don't change meaning. You may use brackets, for example, to change verb tenses or to change pronouns to nouns.

EXAMPLE

Original: Our final measurement, the average time it took postal clerks to sell one stamp, turned out to be less straightforward than we expected.

Robert Levine with Ellen Wolff, from
"Social Time: The Heartbeat of Culture," page 90

Altered: The final measurement of Levine's research team "turned out to be less straightforward than [they] expected" (p. 90).

Combining Paraphrase and Quotation

In your essay writing, you may include a mixture of quotation and paraphrase. If you borrow any uniquely expressed phrases or recognizable expression from a writer, even two words, you should put the words within quotation marks. Otherwise, ideas taken from the reading should be paraphrased.

EXAMPLE

Original: Special-interest friends. These friendships aren't intimate, and they needn't involve kids or silverware or cats. Their value lies in some interest jointly shared.

Judith Viorst, from
"Friends, Good Friends—and Such Good Friends," page 66

Paraphrase and Quotation: According to Viorst's definition, "special-interest friends" are characterized by a common activity (p. 66).

ACTIVITY

Integrating Quotations

Working alone, with a partner, or in a small group, practice integrating quotations into a written text. Select an appropriate quotation from the source below (passage A), and insert it logically into the paragraph taken from a student essay (passage B). Guidelines for punctuating quotations can be found on pages 367–369.

Passage A

The fifth stumbling block is *high anxiety*, separately mentioned for the purpose of emphasis. Unlike the other four (language, illusive nonverbal cues, preconceptions and stereotypes, and the practice of immediate evaluation), the stumbling block of anxiety is not distinct but underlies and compounds the others. The presence of high anxiety/tension is very common in cross-cultural experiences because of the uncertainties present.

LaRay M. Barna, from
"Intercultural Communication Stumbling Blocks," page 81

Passage B

Anxiety is the last problem that Barna mentions in her article. Many foreign students get scared because they do not know what to expect. During my first month in America, I did not dare talk to anybody. I often had a stomachache before I went to school. Every time a teacher asked me a question, my legs got so shaky and my voice cracked. I was afraid that other students might laugh at my English when I mispronounced some words. Every day I tried to figure out what other people were saying, but it seemed so hopeless. By the end of the day when I got home, I felt so exhausted; I felt like I had been jogging for ten miles or more.

P. C.

Follow the same instructions for the next two paragraphs.

QUOTING

Passage C

> When I was 12 in Indonesia, where education followed the Dutch system, I had to memorize the names of all the worlds' major cities, from Kabul to Karachi. At the same age, my son, who was brought up a Californian, thought that Buenos Aires was Spanish for good food—a plate of tacos and burritos, perhaps. However, unlike his counterparts in Asia and Europe, my son had studied *creative* geography. When he was only 6, he drew a map of the route that he traveled to get to school, including the streets and their names, the buildings and traffic signs and the houses that he passed.
>
> Disgruntled American parents forget that in this country their children are able to experiment freely with ideas; without this they will not really be able to think or to believe in themselves.

Kie Ho, from
"We Should Cherish Our Children's Freedom to Think," page 126

Passage D

> Some societies value creativity; they encourage and fertilize their children's thinking. In their schools, teachers do not tell students what to think but rather let them create their own ideas and provide them with opportunities to express them. As a result of this system, children are like pumpkins who are free to carve themselves as they imagine. Each pumpkin is completely different. However, there is a danger to this approach.

P. P. ■

Avoiding Plagiarism

When you incorporate material from other sources into your own text, whether through summary, paraphrase, or quotation, you have an obligation to cite the source of that material. You must give credit to another writer for ideas and information by accurately identifying the source.

To omit proper identification of borrowed material is to commit *plagiarism*, the serious offense of presenting someone else's material as your own. Discovery of deliberate plagiarism can lead to severe penalties ranging from failure in a course to expulsion from school.

GUIDELINES

For Avoiding Plagiarism

Plagiarism is the act of using another person's ideas or expressions without acknowledging the source. Here are several ways to avoid plagiarism:

1. When you use the exact words of a writer, make clear that the words are being reprinted from another source. Use quotation marks for short quotations, or set off a long quotation in the body of your text (see Quotation Marks, pp. 367–369).
2. When you paraphrase a writer's words, identify the writer (see pp. 281–282).
3. Never hand in a paper written by someone else and present it as your own.
4. Never have anyone write any part of your paper.
5. Cite your sources (see the following examples).

Note: Students who do not understand the conventions of using sources may commit plagiarism unintentionally. Instructors understand that unintentional plagiarism can occur. However, it is your responsibility to learn the conventions of academic writing to avoid plagiarism in the first place.

EXAMPLES *of Acceptable Citations*

The following examples show three ways to integrate material from a source into an essay.

■ Original passage

Another deterrent to an understanding between persons of differing cultures or ethnic groups is the *tendency to evaluate*, to approve or disapprove, the statements and actions of the other person or group rather than to try to completely comprehend the thoughts and feelings expressed.

LaRay M. Barna, from
"Intercultural Communication Stumbling Blocks," page 80

■ Direct quotation

In her article "Intercultural Communication Stumbling Blocks," LaRay M. Barna explains that the tendency to judge others is a "deterrent to an understanding between persons of differing cultures or ethnic groups" (p. 80).

■ Paraphrase

According to LaRay M. Barna, one reason that people from different ethnic and cultural backgrounds have difficulty communicating is that they tend to judge one another.

■ Paraphrase and quotation

According to Barna, the *"tendency to evaluate"* creates a communication barrier between people of different ethnic and cultural backgrounds (p. 80).

EXAMPLES *of Plagiarism*

The following examples demonstrate plagiarism.

■ Original passage

Another deterrent to an understanding between persons of differing cultures or ethnic groups is the *tendency to evaluate*, to approve or disapprove, the statements and actions of the other person or group rather than to try to completely comprehend the thoughts and feelings expressed.

LaRay M. Barna, from
"Intercultural Communication Stumbling Blocks," page 80

■ Plagiarism

> Barna believes that the tendency to evaluate is a deterrent to an understanding between persons of differing cultures or ethnic groups.

This sentence is an example of plagiarism because there are no quotation marks to identify the direct quotation "deterrent to an understanding between persons of differing cultures or ethnic groups." Also, the page number is missing.

■ Plagiarism

> I believe that one reason that people from different cultural and ethnic backgrounds have difficulty communicating is that they tend to judge rather than try to understand one another.

This sentence is an example of plagiarism because there is no acknowledgment that the idea comes from another source that the student has read. The writer, who read Barna's article, should have included Barna's name and/or the title of the article, for example, by saying, *I agree with Barna, who says that one reason that people from different cultural and ethnic backgrounds have difficulty communicating is that they tend to judge rather than try to understand one another.*

QUOTING

CHAPTER 24

Citing and Documenting Sources

When you incorporate material from other sources into your own text, whether through summary, paraphrase, or quotation, you have an obligation to cite (mention) the source of that material. You must give credit to another writer for ideas and information by documenting (accurately identifying) your sources. Documentation legitimizes your use of the material and allows reader access to the sources. To omit this documentation is to commit *plagiarism*, the serious offense of presenting someone else's material as one's own.* (For guidelines on avoiding plagiarism, see pp. 295–297.)

In this chapter, documentation rules are presented in two formats, that of the American Psychological Association (APA) and that of the Modern Language Association (MLA). These rules cover instructions for (1) documenting research sources within your text and (2) including a list of research sources (a bibliography) at the end of your text. Your instructor will tell you which format to use. In other college courses, you may be expected to use other formats.

Documenting within Your Text

In your academic writing, you often draw on knowledge that you have gained from numerous sources. By including references to the words of these sources, you reveal that you are aware of previous thinking and writing on the subject and that you are adding to that previous work. Your writing is building on a base of knowledge.

Deciding What to Document

Once you refer to sources, you need to decide what to document. The following list may help you make that decision.

You should document the following borrowed material:

- ☐ Every quotation
- ☐ Every diagram, chart, or picture
- ☐ Any statistics
- ☐ All ideas, opinions, facts, and theories that you did not know before you began the research

*For a discussion of situations in which such documentation may not be necessary, see page 64.

☐ Any information that may not be common knowledge to your reading audience

The last item in the previous list is the most problematic, for it is difficult to decide what an audience's shared common knowledge is, especially if the audience represents a culture different from your own. Here are several guidelines for determining what might be familiar to your reading audience:

☐ If you yourself were aware of the fact or idea before reading the material, you may assume that this is common knowledge. An exception to this guideline might be that the fact or idea is common knowledge to you because of your cultural background, but is not common knowledge to your readers if they have a different cultural background.

☐ If several of the sources you have consulted mention the same fact or idea without having documented it, you may assume that this fact or idea is part of common knowledge.

Note: If you are not sure whether something is common knowledge to an academic audience, check with your instructor.

Another problem that you might have in documenting sources is that you may have some prior knowledge of your subject—from your own past reading or studying, for example—that you are unable to identify accurately because you no longer remember the exact source. If that is the case, it is wise to include a footnote to your instructor explaining the general source of information. Then your instructor will understand why there is no formal documentation.

Formats for In-Text Documentation: APA and MLA

The following guidelines are designed to help you document sources in your paper. Two formats are demonstrated. Your instructor will tell you which format to follow.

APA In-Text Format

The APA format is widely used in social science books and journals. The author and date (and the page number, for a quotation) are given in the body of the paper. The author-date citations must match a list of references attached at the end of the paper.

1. *If your in-text reference includes the author's name, place only the year of publication within parentheses.*

    According to Wyatt (1993), the new president of the United States had no plan to end the Vietnam War when he first took office in 1969.

2. *If your in-text reference does not contain the author's name, place the author's last name and the year of publication of the source within parentheses. Put a comma between the name and the year.*

    In his campaign for president, Richard Nixon claimed he had a plan to end the Vietnam War, but actually he had no plan (Wyatt, 1993).

3. *If you use a quotation, include the page number(s). Use a* p. *for one page and* pp. *for more than one page. Note the punctuation in each of the following examples:*

In his campaign for president, Richard Nixon claimed he had a "secret plan" to put an end to the Vietnam War, but actually he had no plan (Wyatt, 1993, p. 191).

Wyatt (1993) claims that, although candidate Richard Nixon said he had a "secret plan" to put an end to the Vietnam War, actually he had no plan (p. 191).

Wyatt claims that, although candidate Richard Nixon said he had a "secret plan" to put an end to the Vietnam War, actually he had no plan (1993, p. 191).

4. *If your source does not list an author's name, place all or part of the title (inside quotation marks) within parentheses along with the year of publication. Place a comma between title and year.*

Many actions were regretted and, inside their hearts, Americans will never forgive some of the government's mistakes ("The Ghosts of Vietnam," 1993).

5. *If your source was reprinted from another source, include both dates of publication, beginning with the earliest date.*

The United States, as a great power, was watching over this development with "a sense of kinship with those everywhere who yearn for freedom" (Dulles, 1954/1990, p. 20).

6. *If the same point or statistic appears in more than one source, you can place both sources, in alphabetical order, within the same parentheses, separated by a semicolon.*

According to statistics, the average age of these youths was nineteen, a much younger age than in any other war; for example, in World War II, the average age was twenty-six (Gelman, 1988; Palmer, 1993).

7. *If you need to add explanatory information in a footnote, type a superscript numeral slightly above the line in your text. Then create a separate footnote page, with the word* Footnotes *at the top center, and number the notes in the order in which they are mentioned in the text.*

8. *If you want to cite a personal communication, such as an interview or letter, include the first initial(s) and last name of the communicator and provide as exact a date as possible.*

C. Sadow (personal communication, October 21, 1994)

(C. Sadow, personal communication, October 21, 1994)

MLA In-Text Format

The MLA format is a form of documentation used primarily in the humanities. It is similar to the APA format. One major difference is that in APA format, the year of publication is supplied, whereas in MLA format it is not. Another difference is that in MLA format the page number is supplied for either a paraphrase or a quotation, whereas in APA format the page number is supplied only for quotations. The citation must match a list of works cited, attached at the end of the paper.

Note: A sample student research essay using this format can be found on page 265.

1. *If your in-text reference includes the author's name, place only the page number(s) of the source in parentheses.*

> According to Wyatt, the new president of the United States had no plan to end the Vietnam War when he first took office in 1969 (191).

2. *If your in-text reference does not contain the author's name, place the author's last name and the page number(s) of the source in parentheses. Do not include year, punctuation, or p. for page number.*

> In his campaign for president, Richard Nixon claimed he had a plan to end the Vietnam War, but actually he had no plan (Wyatt 41).

3. *If your source does not list an author's name, place all or part of the title (inside quotation marks) within parentheses along with the page number(s). Omit the page number if you are citing a one-page article.*

> Many actions were regretted and, inside their hearts, Americans will never forgive some of the government's mistakes ("The Ghosts of Vietnam").

4. *If the same point or statistic appears in more than one source, you can place both sources in alphabetical order within the same parentheses, separated by a semi-colon.*

> According to statistics, the average age of these youths was nineteen, a much younger age than in any other war; for example, in World War II, the average age was twenty-six (Gelman 148; Palmer 38).

5. *If you need to add explanatory notes, type a superscript numeral slightly above the line in your text. Match the numeral to the notes, which can appear either at the end of the text, as endnotes, or at the bottom of relevant pages, as footnotes.*

Preparing the Bibliography

A bibliography—a list of the research sources you consulted—should be placed at the end of an essay. By glancing at the list, readers can see how recent, reliable, and thorough the research is. In addition, they can use the list as a resource if they wish to locate the sources themselves.

Sample page of references in APA format*

References

Dodd, T. J. (1990). The U.S. must maintain its commitments. In W. Dudley & D. Bender (Eds.), <u>The Vietnam War: Opposing viewpoints</u> (pp. 27–32). St. Paul: Greenhaven Press. (Original speech delivered in 1965)

Dudley, W., & Bender, D. (Eds.). (1990). <u>The Vietnam War: Opposing viewpoints.</u> St. Paul: Greenhaven Press.

CITING AND DOCUMENTING SOURCES

---

*A list of these sources in MLA format can be found on pages 269–270.

Dulles, J. F. (1990). The U.S. must stop Communist expansion. In W. Dudley & D. Bender (Eds.), The Vietnam War: Opposing viewpoints (pp. 19–22). St. Paul: Greenhaven Press. (Original speech delivered in 1954)

Gelman, D. (1990). Vietnam veterans suffer from psychological problems. In W. Dudley & D. Bender (Eds.), The Vietnam War: Opposing viewpoints (pp. 146–151). St. Paul: Greenhaven Press. (Reprinted from Newsweek, August 29, 1988)

The ghosts of Vietnam. (1993, June 5). The Economist, 327, 32.

Larson, D. R., & Larson, A. (1990). The U.S. has no binding commitments. In W. Dudley & D. Bender (Eds.), The Vietnam War: Opposing viewpoints (pp. 33–36). St. Paul: Greenhaven Press. (Reprinted from Vietnam and beyond, Durham: Duke University Rule of Law Research Center, 1965)

Palmer, L. (1993, November 7). How to bandage a war. The New York Times Magazine, 36, 38–43, 68, 72–73. Section VI

Wyatt, C. R. (1993). Paper soldiers: The American press and the Vietnam War. New York: W. W. Norton & Company.

Zaroulis, N., & Sullivan, G. (1984). Who spoke up? American protest against the war in Vietnam, 1963–1975. Garden City, New York: Doubleday & Company, Inc.

You are not expected to memorize the rules for citations. Use the following guidelines as a reference when you are making your own list of sources. Note the indentation, punctuation, and capitalization, as well as the order in which the publication information is given.

GENERAL GUIDELINES

For Creating a Bibliography: APA and MLA

1. Put the list at the end of your research essay.
2. At the top of the page, title the bibliography *References* (if you are using the APA format) or *Works Cited* (if you are using the MLA format).
3. Double-space throughout.
4. Start the first line of each entry at the margin; indent the second and subsequent lines five spaces.
5. Put the author's last name first, followed by a comma and then the first initial (APA) or first name (MLA).
6. Put the list in alphabetical order, according to the last name of each author.

   □ If a work lists no author, alphabetize according to the first letter of the title.
   □ If the title begins with *A, An,* or *The*, alphabetize according to the second word in the title.

CITING AND DOCUMENTING SOURCES

Bibliographic Forms for Books

GENERAL GUIDELINES

For Books: APA Format

Bibliographic entries for books follow this order:

1. *Author(s)* (last name first, then first initial)
2. *Year of publication* (in parentheses)
3. *Title* (underlined or in italics; capitalize only the first word, the first word after a colon, and proper nouns)
4. *City of publication* (give the name of state too, if city is not well known)
5. *Publisher*

All of this information can be found at the beginning of the book.

GENERAL GUIDELINES

For Books: MLA Format

Bibliographic entries for books follow this order:

1. *Author's name* (last name first; if there is more than one author, put first name first for second and third authors).
2. *Book title* (underlined; capitalize all words, except prepositions, conjunctions, and articles).

   Exception: Capitalize a preposition, conjunction, or article if it is the first word of the title or the first word after a colon.
3. *City of publication* (give the name of state too, if city is not well known)
4. *Publisher* (use shortened form—only the first surname of company names, such as *Harcourt* for *Harcourt Brace Jovanovich, Inc.*, or *Norton* for *W. W. Norton and Co., Inc.* Use *UP* in place of *University Press*, for example, *Oxford UP.*)
5. *Year of publication*

All of this information can be found at the beginning of the book.

Forms for Specific Types of Books: APA and MLA

The APA and MLA formats for specific types of books are shown together. Whichever format you use, carefully follow the capitalization and punctuation.

A book by one author

APA

Wyatt, C. R. (1993). Paper soldiers: The American press and the Vietnam War. New York: W. W. Norton & Company.

MLA

Wyatt, Clarence R. Paper Soldiers: The American Press and the Vietnam War. New York: Norton, 1993.

A book by two authors

APA

Larson, D. R., & Larson, A. (1965). Vietnam and beyond. Durham: Duke University Rule of Law Research Center.

MLA

Larson, Don R., and Arthur Larson. Vietnam and Beyond. Durham: Duke, 1965.

A book by three or more authors

APA

Quirk, R., Greenbaum, S., Leech, G., & Svartvik, J. (1985). Comprehensive grammar of the English language. London: Longman, Inc.

MLA

Quirk, Randolph, Sidney Greenbaum, Geoffrey Leech, and Jan Svartvik. A Comprehensive Grammar of the English Language. London: Longman, 1985.

A book with an editor

APA

Cozic, C. P. (Ed.). (1992). Education in America: Opposing viewpoints. San Diego: Greenhaven Press.

MLA

Cozic, Charles P., ed. Education in America: Opposing Viewpoints. San Diego: Greenhaven, 1992.

A book with two or more editors

APA

Samovar, L. A., & Porter, R. E. (Eds.). (1988). Intercultural communication: A reader. (5th ed.). Belmont, CA: Wadsworth Publishing Company.

MLA

Samovar, Larry A., and Richard E. Porter, eds. Intercultural Communication: A Reader. 5th ed. Belmont, CA: Wadsworth, 1988.

A book other than the first edition

APA

Rosenblatt, L. M. (1983). Literature as exploration. (4th ed.). New York: Modern Language Association.

MLA

Rosenblatt, Louise M. Literature as Exploration. 4th ed. New York: MLA, 1983.

A book with a corporate (agency, association) author

APA

Commission on the Humanities. (1980). <u>The humanities in American life: Report of the commission on the humanities</u>. Berkeley: University of California Press.

MLA

Commission on the Humanities. <u>The Humanities in American Life: Report of the Commission on the Humanities</u>. Berkeley: U of California P, 1980.

A translation

APA

Calvino, I. (1986). <u>The uses of literature</u> (P. Creagh, Trans.). San Diego: Harcourt Brace Jovanovich. (Original work published 1982)

MLA

Calvino, Italo. <u>The Uses of Literature</u>. Trans. Patrick Creagh. San Diego: Harcourt, 1986.

An article or chapter in a book*

APA

Fisher, G. (1988). International negotiation. In L. A. Samovar & R. E. Porter (Eds.), <u>Intercultural communication: A reader</u>. (5th ed.) (pp. 193–200). Belmont, CA: Wadsworth Publishing Company.

MLA

Fisher, Glen. "International Negotiation." <u>Intercultural Communication: A Reader</u>. 5th ed. Ed. Larry A. Samovar and Richard E. Porter. Belmont, CA: Wadsworth, 1988. 193–200.

A speech published in a book

APA

Dulles, J. F. (1990). The U.S. must stop Communist expansion. In W. Dudley & D. Bender (Eds.), <u>The Vietnam War: Opposing viewpoints</u> (pp. 19–22). St. Paul: Greenhaven Press. (Original speech delivered in 1954)

MLA

Dulles, John Foster. Speech delivered to the Overseas Press Club of America. New York, 29 Mar. 1954. Rpt. as "The U.S. Must Stop Communist Expansion." <u>The Vietnam War: Opposing Viewpoints</u>. Ed. William Dudley and David Bender. St. Paul: Greenhaven, 1990. 19–22.

*If you cite two or more articles from the same book, you can use a system of cross-reference. List the book itself, and cross-reference individual articles to that citation by mentioning only editor(s) and page number(s). Example in the MLA format:
Fisher, Glen. "International Negotiation." Samovar and Porter 193–200.
Samovar, Larry A., and Richard E. Porter, eds. <u>Intercultural Communication: A Reader</u>. 5th ed. Belmont, CA: Wadsworth, 1988.
Stewart, Lea P. "Japanese and American Management: Participative Decision Making." Samovar and Porter 182–185.

An article in an encyclopedia

APA

Butwell, R. (1992). Vietnam War. In <u>Encyclopedia Americana</u> (Vol. 28, pp. 112–112h). Danbury, CT: Grolier Inc.

MLA

Butwell, Richard. "Vietnam War." <u>Encyclopedia Americana</u>. 1992.

Bibliographic Forms for Articles in Periodicals

GENERAL GUIDELINES

For Articles in Periodicals: APA Format

Bibliographic entries for articles follow this order:

1. *Author's name* (if there is one—last name first, then first initial)
2. *Date of publication* (in parentheses):

   ☐ Full date: year, month, and day (for weekly magazines and for newspapers)
   ☐ Month and year (for monthly magazines)
   ☐ Year (for quarterly and monthly journals)

3. *Title of the article*
4. *Name of the periodical* (underlined or in italics)
5. *Volume number of a journal* (underlined or in italics)
6. *Inclusive page numbers of the article*

GENERAL GUIDELINES

For Articles in Periodicals: MLA Format

Bibliographic entries for articles follow this order:

1. *Author's name* (if there is one—last name first; for successive authors, put first name first)
2. *Title of the article* (within quotation marks)
3. *Name of the periodical* (underlined or in italics)
4. *Date of publication*

   ☐ Full date: day, month, and year (for weekly magazines and for newspapers)
   ☐ Month and year (for monthly magazines)
   ☐ Volume number and the year (in parentheses) for quarterly and monthly journals

5. *Inclusive page numbers of the article.*
   Exception: When the article is not printed on consecutive pages, write only the first page number and a plus sign (for example, 22 +).

APA and MLA formats for specific types of periodicals are shown together. Whichever format you use, carefully follow the capitalization and punctuation.

Forms for Scholarly Journals: APA and MLA

Scholarly journals are periodicals that contain articles (especially research reports) written by experts and scholars in a field for other experts and scholars in the field. These journals are available primarily in libraries.

General form

APA

Krupnick, C. G. (1985). Women and men in the classroom: Inequality and its remedies. On Teaching and Learning: Journal of the Harvard Danforth Center, 1, 18–25.

MLA

Krupnick, Catherine G. "Women and Men in the Classroom: Inequality and Its Remedies." On Teaching and Learning: Journal of the Harvard Danforth Center 1 (1985): 18–25.

A book review

APA

Finkle, S. (1991). [Review of the book What is English?]. College Composition and Communication, 42, 504–506.

MLA

Finkle, Sheryl. Rev. of What Is English?, by Peter Elbow. College Composition and Communication 42 (1991): 504–06.

Forms for Magazines: APA and MLA

Most magazines are popular periodicals whose articles are written by reporters or writers for the general public. Other magazines are periodicals whose articles are written by experts and scholars for the general public. These periodicals can be found in libraries and often at newsstands.

An article from a weekly magazine without a volume number

APA

Alter, J., & Moreau, R. (1995, June 26). Binding up old wounds. Newsweek, 34–35.

MLA

Alter, Jonathan, and Ron Moreau. "Binding Up Old Wounds." Newsweek 26 June 1995: 34–35.

An unsigned article from a weekly magazine with a volume number

APA

The ghosts of Vietnam. (1993, June 5). The Economist, 327, 32.

MLA

"The Ghosts of Vietnam." The Economist 5 June 1993: 32.

An article from a monthly magazine

APA

Lapham, L. H. (1992, January). Who and what is American? Harper's Magazine, 284, 43–49.

MLA

Lapham, Lewis H. "Who and What is American?" Harper's Magazine Jan. 1992: 43–49.

An editorial

APA

Nationalities, nations, and nationalism [Editorial]. (1990, April 28). America, 162, 419.

MLA

"Nationalities, Nations, and Nationalism." Editorial. America 28 Apr. 1990: 419.

Forms for Newspapers: APA and MLA

An article from a newspaper

APA

Bonner, R. (1994, July 18). U.N. says help for a million is needed. New York Times, pp. 1, A7.

MLA

Bonner, Raymond. "U.N. Says Help for a Million Is Needed." New York Times 18 July 1994: 1+.

An unsigned article from a newspaper

APA

Bitter reminder of a lethal World War II tragedy. (1994, July 18). New York Times, p. A10.

MLA

"Bitter Reminder of a Lethal World War II Tragedy." New York Times 18 July 1994: A10.

An editorial

APA

Two million refugees. (1994, July 20) [Editorial]. New York Times, p. A18.

MLA

"Two Million Refugees." Editorial. New York Times 20 July 1994: A18.

A letter to the editor

APA

Jeffries, A. B. (1994, July 20). Schools can't give students what they don't get at home [Letter to the editor]. New York Times, p. A18.

MLA

Jeffries, Andrea Black. "Schools Can't Give Students What They Don't Get at Home." Letter. <u>New York Times</u> 20 July 1994: A18.

Bibliographic Forms for Personal Communication: APA and MLA

A personal interview

APA

> *Note:* Personal communications are not included in an APA reference list. They are cited in text only (see p. 300).

MLA

Sadow, Catherine. Personal interview. 21 Oct. 1994.

The Editing Process

Errors are expected and understood as a natural result of the process of writing. Most errors have logical causes, and you may be able to learn from your mistakes by examining why you have made them.

Dealing with error is a slow and time-consuming process, requiring that you closely read and reread your writing and refer to other sources such as a usage handbook or dictionary. Therefore, it is best to focus on these processes at a later stage in your writing, after you have developed and organized ideas.

Part Four consists of four chapters that are designed to help you take a critical look at your own writing.

Chapter 25 provides general guidelines for finding and correcting errors. Chapter 26 presents several categories of common sources of error. Chapter 27 is a handbook for correcting error, with examples drawn from the readings in this book. Chapter 28 provides manuscript forms for final copy.

CHAPTER **25**

Proofreading and Editing

The goal of *proofreading* (reading to look for mistakes) and *editing* (the actual correcting of error) is to produce a paper whose meaning is clear. Since errors can shift a reader's attention away from your meaning, you want to remove any errors that prevent someone from understanding what you are saying.

Though proofreading and correcting can be tedious processes, they are important procedures, for they help you prepare a clearly expressed and comprehensible paper to hand in for evaluation. A neat presentation that reveals an attempt to edit out mistakes is also a courtesy to your reader. It reflects well on your effort to strengthen your writing.

Proofreading

There are many ways to proofread. You may want to use only one or all of the following suggestions.

GUIDELINES

For Proofreading

1. *Read for error only. Read your paper primarily to find mistakes.*

2. *Read your paper aloud.* Read your paper to someone else, or read aloud to yourself as if someone were listening. If you hesitate as you read your own writing, the reason may be that you have come across an error.

3. *Learn the rules.* Review your previously corrected essays to find commonly made errors. Then consult a handbook to find the rules to correct three or four of those errors. Then look at your most recent draft, searching for those particular errors, and correct them. You may find it easier to remember the rule once you have applied it to your own writing.

4. *Let someone else proofread your paper.* You might find it helpful to have a friend proofread the paper, but *only to point out and discuss the reasons for your mistakes.* By going through this process, you may learn how to find and correct errors in your writing.

Observing Conventions for Writing about Sources

Because several of the assignments in this book ask you to make direct references in your essays to what you have read, there are specific areas on which you need to focus. The following guidelines present some of the most common conventions for writing about sources.

GUIDELINES

For Proofreading and Editing References to Reading

If you have used quotations:

1. Reread the original statements of the author.
2. Check to see that you have copied the passage *exactly* as it was written originally. This means that your essay should contain the exact words, the exact spelling, and the exact punctuation that you find in the original.
3. Make sure that the quotation you have selected is logically integrated into your own writing, that credit is given to the author, and that you have included the correct page number(s) within parentheses.
4. Consult pages 367–369 for instructions on punctuating quotations.

If you have summarized, paraphrased, or quoted:

Check to see that all references have been properly documented within the paper. (Consult Part 3.)

If your paper requires a list of sources (bibliography):

Review the forms (consult pp. 301–309 on preparing the list of sources), and make sure that your sources are listed correctly and alphabetically and that they are punctuated accurately.

Editing

Your instructor may mark errors in your paper, for example, by underlining them. Your task is then to make corrections. The following guidelines may help you in that process.

GUIDELINES

For Editing

1. When you receive a paper marked for error, correct every error you can without asking for help.
2. Take time with the instructor or another student to go over any markings you do not understand.
3. Attempt to understand the causes of your error (see Chapter 26).
4. Use the Handbook for Correcting Errors (Chapter 27) to help you correct some errors that you cannot correct on your own.
5. Ask for help if you do not know how to correct an error.

CHAPTER 26

Causes of Error

Some errors are simply mistakes made through carelessness, and usually they can be corrected by careful proofreading. Other errors have more complex causes.

This chapter presents several categories of common causes of errors. By studying these categories, you may come to a clearer understanding of why you make certain errors. You can understand that there is logic behind your errors and that making errors is a natural process.

Interlingual Transfer

Interlingual ("between languages") transfer is characterized by interference from another language. In other words, you apply a rule or sound of a familiar language (another language you speak or have studied) in place of the correct rule or sound in English. Errors may then occur in spelling, word order, verb tense, word endings, use of articles, agreement of adjectives and nouns, and so on.

EXAMPLE

In a draft of his essay "Barriers" (p. 59), Rolando wrote:

Even so, I am giving it a *tray*.

■ *Rolando's explanation:*

"This is a problem of pronunciation. I wrote *tray* instead of *try* because I was trying to get the right English sound [the long vowel sound i]. To get that sound in Spanish, you need to write *ay*. So when I looked at the word *tray*, a voice inside my head said *try*."

■ Correction of error:

Even so, I am giving it a *try*.

EXAMPLE

Rolando wrote:

Is hurting my pride.

■ **Rolando's explanation:**

"I forgot to put 'It' at the beginning of the sentence. That's because in Spanish, you don't always have to use the subject pronoun. You can tell by the verb form what the subject is."

■ **Correction of error:**

It is hurting my pride.

Overgeneralization

Overgeneralization is characterized by the inappropriate application of a language rule. In other words, you apply a rule you have learned about the language in place of the correct rule. Errors may then occur in punctuation, spelling, word order, verb tense, articles, and so on.

EXAMPLE

In an essay (not appearing in this book), Angela wrote:

It does not *solves* or *prevents* any problems.

■ **Angela's explanation:**

"I was thinking that the word *it* is third person singular and so it needed a third person singular verb. I added *-s* to *solve* and *prevent* to make them third person singular. I forgot that *does* already had the *-s* ending."

■ **Correction of error:**

It does not *solve* or *prevent* any problems.

EXAMPLE

In an essay (not appearing in this book), Caroline wrote:

Like Robert Levine, I learned *that,* "*ideas* of time and punctuality vary considerably from place to place."

■ **Caroline's explanation:**

"I didn't use the correct rule to punctuate the quotation. I used the rule that says that a comma is used to introduce a quotation. When I looked up the rules to discover why the teacher marked the error, I realized that I did not need the comma before the quotation because a comma should not follow [the subordinator] *that.*"

■ Correction of error:

Like Robert Levine, I learned *that "ideas* of time and punctuality vary considerably from place to place."

Reliance on Incorrect Patterns

A writer can come to rely on often-used word, phrase, or sentence patterns without realizing that they are incorrect. Errors can occur in at least two ways: you use a pattern in the wrong context, or you use a word or phrase that doesn't exist.

EXAMPLE

In an essay that included a description of the process of creating a sculpture (not appearing in this book), Efrat wrote:

When I get to a point where I am stuck and don't know how to go on with the work, I use the following strategy: Since usually I am too close, physically and emotionally, to the work, I try to get away from it, and to do something else like go for a walk or visit an art show. After a while I know *what is the best way I want to continue.*

■ Efrat's explanation:

"I used the forms *what is the best way* and *I want to continue* together in my sentence. I didn't know that it couldn't be used in this way. It sounded fine because it is a familiar expression to me. I always use it when I speak."

■ Correction of error:

After a while I know *the best way to continue.*

EXAMPLE

In an essay (not appearing in this book), Al wrote:

Pressure is like a *tumid* in the brain.

■ Al's explanation:

"I was surprised that the teacher underlined this error. I thought the word 'tumid' was correct. But the problem was that I never pronounced the word correctly."

■ Correction of error:

Pressure is like a *tumor* in the brain.

Appeal to Authority

Appeal to authority occurs when a learner seeks help from an outside source, such as a bilingual dictionary, or a thesaurus, or a native speaker. In other words, when you do not know a particular form or word, you look it up in a dictionary or ask someone. Errors can occur when the form or word you decide on is not accurate.

EXAMPLE

In an essay (not appearing in this book), Sam wrote:

I agree with as well as *contradict* some of his ideas.

■ **Sam's explanation:**

"I didn't want to keep using the same words, *agree* and *disagree*, again and again in my paper. So I looked up the word *disagree* in the thesaurus. I used the synonym *contradict*, but it wasn't the correct substitute. I had to go back and forth in the thesaurus and the dictionary to find the right word."

■ **Correction of error:**

I agree with some of his ideas but *reject* others.

EXAMPLE

In an essay (not appearing in this book), George wrote:

I was a little bit frightened in the beginning that I would flunk out of the school, but my grades quickly *reassured* my confidence.

■ **George's explanation:**

"I wanted to say that my grades made me feel better. But I didn't know how to say it in a sophisticated way. My roommate told me I could say, *my grades were reassuring.* But when I wrote the sentence, I wanted to express the idea that my *confidence* had changed *quickly.* I used a form of my roommate's word, but I used it incorrectly."

■ **Correction of error:**

I was a little bit frightened in the beginning that I would flunk out of the school, but my grades quickly *bolstered* my confidence.

Risk Taking

Risk taking is a way of getting around English-language rules, forms, or words that you have not yet learned or mastered. In other words, when you want to say something but don't know how to say it, you say whatever you can and hope for the best. For example, you take risks when you make up an expression because you do not know or cannot think of a correct one. Taking risks can be a useful strategy for a writer, even if it produces error.

EXAMPLE

Angela wrote:

> These complaints have *brought up* the attention of social scientists and researchers.

- ■ Angela's explanation:

> "I used the expression 'brought up' because I just couldn't think of the correct expression in English. I knew the instructor would know what I meant and tell me the correct words."

- ■ Correction of error:

> These complaints have *come to* the attention of social scientists and researchers.

EXAMPLE

In an essay (not appearing in this book), Miltos wrote:

> I couldn't believe that the author was right in what he was saying, so I started analyzing his points to find where his reasoning *leaked.*

- ■ Miltos's explanation:

> "I was thinking that the author's argument had holes in it. I mean, that his reasoning leaked out like water leaks out of a pail with holes in it. I wasn't sure if it was the right word, but I decided to try it and see."

- ■ Correction of error:

> I couldn't believe that the author was right in what he was saying, so I started analyzing his points to find where his reasoning *failed.*

The preceding list of categories does not, of course, cover all possible errors. Other causes exist. For example, errors may result from direct translation of a phrase or sentence from another language into English. Errors can also be the product of misleading, incomplete, or misinterpreted explanations given by textbooks and instructors. You can examine your own writing to find causes of errors not discussed in this book.

ACTIVITY

Finding Causes of Errors

You might find it helpful to keep a written record of your errors and their causes in a notebook. Adapt these guidelines for identifying causes of error in your own writing.

- ☐ Look through your own writing to find errors. These can be errors marked by someone else or errors that you find on your own.

☐ When you find an error, underline the sentence that contains the error, or rewrite the sentence in your notebook.

☐ Explain or speculate on why you made the error.

☐ Correct the error, asking for help if necessary.

CHAPTER 27

A Handbook for Correcting Errors

This handbook for correcting errors can be used in a number of ways. You may consult it as you are editing your work. You and your classmates may consult it during in-class group editing sessions. You and your instructor may refer to it together during a conference.

The handbook does not contain all of the rules that govern standard English grammar and punctuation. Rather, only some commonly troublesome areas have been selected for discussion. Most of the examples are taken from the readings in this book. The authors and page numbers are identified so that you can see how the language works in context.

Perhaps the most important message of the handbook is to allow for flexibility in your writing. In many cases, alternatives are provided to show various ways to write sentences. Decisions concerning grammar and punctuation are not dependent only on rules and principles. The knowledge shared between the writer and reader as well as the intention of the writer play important roles in determining which forms are used.

Sentence Boundaries

At times, even though you intend to, you may not produce a complete sentence. At other times, you may not know how to punctuate a sentence because you do not fully understand how its parts fit together.

Such sentence errors may interfere with a reader's understanding, and therefore need to be corrected. The following information may help you remember acceptable boundaries for written sentences.

The Basic Sentence

I am black.

James Thomas Jackson, from
"Waiting in Line at the Drugstore," page 22

The fundamental unit of communication in English is the sentence and it has at least two parts: *subject* and verb†* (**S + V**). The first three words of James Thomas Jackson's essay, reprinted in the box above, constitute a sentence. Note that the sentence begins with a capital letter and ends with punctuation (a sentence must end in a period, question mark, or exclamation point).

□□□	**Sentence**	
Subject	Verb	
I	*am*	black.

The Independent Clause

> I am black. I am a writer and I want to place full credit where it belongs for the direction my life has taken: on a photography studio and a drugstore on Main Street in Houston, Texas.
>
> *James Thomas Jackson, from*
> *"Waiting in Line at the Drugstore," page 22*

Every sentence you write should have at least one *independent clause* (IC), which contains a subject and verb combination. A sentence can contain more than one independent clause, as in James Thomas Jackson's second sentence (see the next box.) Note that the two clauses are connected by the word *and;* the general "formula" for this sentence is **IC + IC.**

□□□	**Independent Clauses**					
Subject	Verb			Coordinator	Subject	Verb
I	*am*	a	writer	*and*	*I*	*want . . .*

The independent clause may be part of a larger sentence, but if it is removed from the sentence, it can stand alone (independent) as a complete sentence.

Subject	Verb	
I	*am*	a writer.

---

*An exception to this rule is a command, in which the subject is understood but not always stated. For example, the command *Be still* (Yezierska, p. 26) omits *You: (You) be still.*

†The verb must be complete. For example, the word *going* is part of a complete verb only when it is combined with an auxiliary form: *am going, have been going,* and so on.

Subject	Verb	
I	*want*	to place full credit where it belongs . . .

The Dependent Clause

> I am lonely when I am overtired, when I have worked too long without a break, when for the time being I feel empty and need filling up.
>
> *May Sarton, from*
> *"The Rewards of Living a Solitary Life," page 39*

A *dependent clause* (DC) has a subject and verb combination (**S + V**) but is introduced by a subordinating word. The subordinating word signals that the dependent clause needs to be attached to an independent clause (it *depends* on an independent clause) in order to be part of a complete sentence. In other words, a dependent clause alone is not considered a complete sentence.

May Sarton's sentence, reprinted in the previous box, begins with an independent clause (IC) that is followed by three dependent clauses; the general "formula" for this sentence is **IC DC, DC, DC.**

□□□ **Independent Clause**		
Subject	Verb	
I	*am*	lonely

□□□ **Dependent Clauses**		
Subordinating Word	Subject	Verb
when	*I*	*am*	overtired,
when	*I*	*have worked*	too long . . . ,
when . . .	*I*	*feel*	empty . . .

A sentence can also begin with a dependent clause. The introductory dependent clause is usually followed by a comma.

> As I entered the classroom, I saw young men and girls laughing and talking to one another without introductions.
>
> *Anzia Yezierska, from*
> *"College," page 27*

The sentence in the preceding box begins with a dependent clause that is followed by an independent clause; the general "formula" for this sentence is **DC, IC.**

▫▫▫	**Dependent Clause**		
Subordinating Word	Subject	Verb	
As		*I*	*entered* the classroom,

▫▫▫	**Independent Clause**	
Subject	Verb	
I	*saw*	young men and girls . . .

The Relationship between Clauses

Three kinds of words or word groups are used to show how clauses relate to one another; in this book, they are referred to as *coordinators, transitions,* and *subordinators.* These words show how the ideas discussed in one clause are linked to the ideas in another clause.

Coordinators

The words in the following box can be used to coordinate (make equal in importance) clauses. Because they are *coordinating,* not *subordinating* words, they do not create dependent clauses.

▫▫▫	**Words That Can Coordinate Clauses**
Coordinator	**Purpose**
and	To indicate the *addition* of an idea or example
but⎫ yet⎭	To indicate the *difference* or *contrast* between one thing and another
for	To indicate the *cause* or *reason* for something
or ⎫ nor⎭	To indicate an *alternative* or a *condition*
so	To indicate the *effect* or *result* of something

Examples of Coordinators between Clauses

Note that the coordinator always comes right at the beginning of a clause.

☐ He wears a mask, *and* his face grows to fit it. (Orwell, p. 34)

☐ Most students are quite satisfied with the teaching on their campus, *but* the pressure to get good grades diminishes their enthusiasm (Boyer, p. 94)

☐ Besides, legally I had done the right thing, *for* a mad elephant has to be killed, like a mad dog, if its owner fails to control it. (Orwell, p. 36)

Coordinators can also begin a sentence. When they do, they show the relationship between the new sentence and the previous sentence.

Examples of Coordinators That Begin Sentences

☐ I am lonely when I am overtired, when I have worked too long without a break, when for the time being I feel empty and need filling up. *And* I am lonely sometimes when I come back home after a lecture trip, when I have seen a lot of people and talked a lot, and am full to the brim with experience that needs to be sorted out. (Sarton, p. 39)

☐ I wanted to write just of women friends, but the women I've talked to won't let me—they say I must mention man-woman friendships too. *For* these friendships can be just as close and as dear as those that we form with women. (Viorst, p. 68)

☐ The parents mean well; they are trying to steer their sons and daughters toward a secure future. *But* the sons and daughters want to major in history or classics or philosophy—subjects with no "practical" value. (Zinsser, p. 141)

☐ "This college has a good reputation. *So,* I knew the classes were going to be hard." (Student quoted in Boyer, p. 94)

Transitions

The following box shows a partial list of words that act as transitions: passages from one idea to another. These transitional words can be used to link two independent clauses. They enable readers to refer back to what has just been said and to predict what will follow. Because they are *transitional*, not *subordinating* words, they do not create dependent clauses.

☐☐☐ **Words That Make Transitions from One Independent Clause to Another**	
Function	Transitional Words
To indicate the *addition* of an example or an idea	also, in addition, furthermore, moreover, besides, in fact
To supply an *example* to support a generalization	for example, for instance, e.g.
To indicate the *order* in which events occur or ideas are presented	first, next, then, lastly, finally, in conclusion, initially, at first, earlier, subsequently, later, meanwhile
To indicate the *cause* or *reason* for something	the reason is that, for this reason
To indicate the *effect* or *result* of something	therefore, thus, as a result, consequently, accordingly
To indicate the *difference* or *contrast* between one thing and another	however, nevertheless, on the contrary, in contrast, on the other hand

Function	Transitional Words
To indicate the *similarity* between one thing and another that was already mentioned	similarly, likewise, in the same manner, in the same way, along the same lines
To contrast or to indicate the *continuation* of an idea or experience	still
To indicate the *consequence* of not doing something	otherwise
To indicate a *restatement* or *clarification* of an idea	in other words, that is, i.e.
To indicate *concession to* or *agreement with* an idea	admittedly, of course
To indicate *emphasis* on a certain idea	indeed, certainly, above all, after all
To indicate an *explanation* of something	in this case

Examples of Transitional Words

The following examples show some ways that transitional words are used. Note how the words in italics relate to the previous sentence and can help readers make a transition from one idea or example to another. Note also that a transition does not have a fixed position in a sentence (unlike a coordinator, which always comes right at the beginning of a clause).

☐ When people of different cultures interact, the potential for misunderstanding exists on many levels. *For example,* members of Arab and Latin cultures usually stand much closer when they are speaking to people than we usually do in the United States, a fact we frequently misinterpret as aggression or disrespect. *Similarly,* we assign personality traits to groups with a pace of life that is markedly faster or slower than our own. We build ideas of national character, *for example,* around the traditional Swiss and German ability to "make the trains run on time." (Levine & Wolff, pp. 86–87)

☐ On a related matter, we frequently were struck by the competitive climate in the classroom. Since as a democracy we are committed to equality of opportunity, and since in a vital society we need some way of bringing talent forward, we use, both on and off the campus, the calculus of competition to stimulate ambition and achievement. We must do this, or else we lack essential leadership in all areas of life.

However, if democracy is to be well served, cooperation is essential too. (Boyer, pp. 99–100)

☐ But the pressure on students is severe. They are truly torn. One part of them feels obligated to fulfill their parents' expectations; *after all,* their parents are older and presumably wiser. Another part tells them that the expectations that are right for their parents are not right for them. (Zinsser, p. 142)

ACTIVITY

Reacting to Unnecessary Transitional Words

Too many words used to connect clauses can be distracting to readers and often are not necessary. Compare the following paragraphs. Paragraph A is reproduced exactly as Anzia Yezierska wrote it (see page 30). Paragraph B has been rewritten to include several transitional expressions (in italics). Discuss your reaction to A and then to B.

☐ Are any or all of the transitional expressions helpful? distracting? Why?

☐ Why do you think the author did not include these expressions in the first place?

A

Darkness and stillness washed over me. Slowly I stumbled to my feet and looked up at the sky. The stars in their infinite peace seemed to pour their healing light into me. I thought of the captives in prison, the sick and the suffering from the beginning of time who had looked to these stars for strength. What was my little sorrow to the centuries of pain which those stars had watched? So near they seemed, so compassionate. My bitter hurt seemed to grow small and drop away. If I must go on alone, I should still have the silence and the high stars to walk with me.

B

Darkness and stillness washed over me. Slowly I stumbled to my feet and looked up at the sky. *First,* the stars in their infinite peace seemed to pour their healing light into me. *Then* I thought of the captives in prison, and in addition the sick and the suffering from the beginning of time who had looked to these stars for strength. What was my little sorrow to the centuries of pain which those stars had watched? So near they seemed, so compassionate. My bitter hurt *therefore* seemed to grow small and drop away. If I must go on alone, I should still have the silence and the high stars to walk with me. ■

Subordinators

A subordinating word introduces a dependent clause. By subordinating (making grammatically lower in importance), a subordinating word shows the relationship between a dependent clause and an independent clause in the same sentence.

Subordinators are placed in three types of dependent clauses: adverbial, adjective, and noun, which are discussed in the sections that follow. Lists of subordinators can be found in boxes on pages 328–329, 331–332, and 334.

Adverbial Clauses

Adverbial clauses typically answer these questions about the independent clause:

☐ *Time* (When?)

☐ *Place* (Where?)

☐ *Condition* (Under what circumstances?)

☐ *Unexpected result* (In spite of what?)

- □ *Opposition* (In contrast to what?)
- □ *Reason* (Why? Because of what?)
- □ *Purpose* (Why? For what?)
- □ *Degree* (To what extent?)
- □ *Manner* (How?)

The box that follows includes many of the words that can be used to create dependent adverbial clauses.

□□□ **Subordinating Words That Introduce Dependent Clauses**	
Relationship between Independent and Dependent Clauses	Subordinators
Time (When?)	*after* (subsequent to the time) *as* (at the same time; when; while) *as long as* (for all the time) *as soon as* (immediately after) *before* (prior to the time) *by the time* (before a specific time) *once* (after; quickly after) *since* (from that time to now) *so long as* (during all that time) *until* (up to that moment in time) *when* (at the time) *whenever* (every time; at any time that) *while* (during the time) *the first* (or *second* or *last* or *next*) time
Place (Where?)	*everywhere* (all places) *where* (at *or* in the place) *wherever* (anyplace that)
Condition (Under what circumstances?)	*as long as* (only if) *even if* (whether or not) *except that* (if it were not for the fact that) *in case* (if this circumstance should happen) *in the event that* (if this circumstance should happen) *if* (under this circumstance; on condition that; whether) *on condition that* (under only one circumstance) *once* (under this circumstance) *only if* (under only one circumstance) *provided that* (only if) *so long as* (only if) *unless* (if . . . not) *when* (under this circumstance; on condition that) *whenever* (under this circumstance; on condition that) *whether or not* (regardless of circumstances)

Relationship between Independent and Dependent Clauses	Subordinators
Unexpected Result (In spite of what?)	*although* *even though* *despite the fact that* *in spite of the fact that* *regardless of the fact that* *though* } (contrary to expectation)
Opposition (In contrast to what?)	*whereas* *while* } (in opposition to)
Reason (Why? Because of what?)	*because* (for the reason that) *as* *as a result of the fact that* *as long as* *because of the fact that* *due to the fact that* *inasmuch as* *on account of the fact that* *since* *so long as* *in view of the fact that* } (because) *now that* (because now)
Purpose (Why? For what?)	*if* *in order that* *so that* *in the hope that* } (to fulfill the purpose)
Degree (To what extent?)	*as far as* *insofar as* *so far as* } (to the extent that)
Manner (How?)	*as if* *as though* } (in such a way as to suggest that)

Examples of Subordinators in Sentences

Note that in these examples, the subordinator (for example, *as soon as, wherever*) comes right at the beginning of a dependent clause. Two versions of each sentence are provided so that you can see that an entire dependent adverbial clause can appear either before or after an independent clause. A comma usually follows a dependent adverbial clause that introduces a sentence.

☐ *As soon as I comprehended a part of what was said and done,* a mischievous spirit of revenge possessed me. (Zitkala-Ša, p. 20)

☐ A mischievous spirit of revenge possessed me *as soon as I comprehended a part of what was said and done.*

☐ I felt *if I could only look a little bit like the other girls on the outside,* maybe I could get in with them. (Yezierska, p. 28)

☐ *If I could only look a little bit like other girls on the outside,* I felt, maybe I could get in with them.

☐ Curiously enough, *although men and women do react to the friendship experience differently,* their desires for companionship are of similar intensity. (Block, p. 72)

☐ Curiously enough, their desires for companionship are of similar intensity *although men and women do react to the friendship experience differently.*

☐ *Because they have been exposed to sex roles that are constraining and dysfunctional,* men have allowed themselves precious few options for friendship. (Block, p. 73)

☐ Men have allowed themselves precious few options for friendship *because they have been exposed to sex roles that are constraining and dysfunctional.*

Typical Errors with Adverbial Clauses

Because the rules for clauses are complex, writers sometimes make errors when creating sentences that include adverbial clauses. The following sentences show a typical error (next to the word *No*) and a corrected form (next to the word *Yes*).

1. Unnecessary *but* (in independent clause) used with a subordinating word indicating contrast or unexpected result (in dependent clause)

   No: Curiously enough, *although* men and women do react to the friendship experience differently, *but* their desires for companionship are of similar intensity.

   Yes: Curiously enough, although men and women do react to the friendship experience differently, their desires for companionship are of similar intensity. (Block, p. 72)

2. Unnecessary *of* following *despite*

   No: Despite of the fact that she tried very hard, she made no new friends.
   Yes: Despite the fact that she tried very hard, she made no new friends.
   Alternative: In spite of the fact that she tried very hard, she made no new friends.

So . . . That and Such . . . That Clauses of Result

The expressions *so . . . that* and *such . . . that* indicate that something expressed in the independent clause leads to or should lead to the result expressed in the *that* clause.

□□□　　　*So . . . That* and *Such . . . That* Clauses of Result

---

so . . . that (with adjectives or adverbs and with the quantity words *much, many, few,* and *little*)

- □ And suddenly, I got *so wild with rage that* I seized the hurdle and right before their eyes I smashed it to pieces. (Yezierska, p. 29)
- □ "I spend *so much time studying that* I don't have a chance to learn anything." (Harris, p. 4)

Note: The word *that* may sometimes be omitted:

- □ For a minute when I entered the dean's grand office, I was *so confused* I couldn't even see. (Yezierska, p. 29)

---

such a . . . that (with singular nouns)
such . . . that (with plural and noncountable singular nouns)
According to Boyer, there is *such a difference between the way male and female students participate in the classroom that* instructors should make changes in the way they run discussions. (Excerpt from student essay)

Adjective Clauses

Adjective clauses provide information about a noun or pronoun in another clause. The box that follows shows subordinating words that introduce dependent adjective clauses. The noun phrase in the other clause is underlined.

□□□　　　**Subordinating Words That Introduce Adjective Clauses**

Noun or Pronoun	Subordinator	Sample Sentence
A person	who	I know a <u>student</u> *who wants to be an artist.* (Zinsser, p. 142)
	whom	In her home anyway she had shelter and food; she had <u>those</u> *whom she had known all her life* about her. (Joyce, p. 183)
	whose	I know countless <u>students</u> *whose inquiring minds exhilarate me.* (Zinsser, p. 141)
	that	"The best teachers I know are <u>those</u> *that really care about their students.*" (Student quoted in Boyer, p. 94)
A thing	that	But to play a <u>sport</u> *that I cannot master* is becoming a pain. (Niella, p. 60)

Noun or Pronoun	Subordinator	Sample Sentence
	which	What was my little sorrow to the <u>centuries of pain</u> *which those stars had watched?* (Yezierska, p. 30)
	whose	The <u>essay</u> "Shooting an Elephant," *whose author is George Orwell,* provides insight into the effects of imperialism. (Excerpt from student essay)
A time	when	It takes a while, as I watch the surf blowing up in fountains at the end of the field, but the <u>moment</u> comes *when the world falls away. . . .* (Sarton, p. 39)
A place	where	Finally I fired my two remaining shots into the <u>spot</u> *where I thought his heart might be.* (Orwell, p. 36)
A reason	why	"The <u>reason</u> *why certain foreigners may think that Americans are superficial*—and they are, Americans even recognize this—is that they talk and smile too much." (Student quoted in Barna, p. 77)

Punctuating Adjective Clauses to Reflect Meaning

Punctuation can change the meaning of certain adjective clauses.

> Americans who remember the "good old days" are not alone in complaining about the educational system in this country. Immigrants, too, complain, and with more up-to-date comparisons.
>
> *Kie Ho, from*
> *"We Should Cherish Our Children's Freedom to Think," page 125*

Observe the independent clause in the first sentence in the box above:

1. *Americans . . . are not alone in complaining about the educational system in this country.*

This part of the sentence suggests that all Americans complain about the educational system in this country. But Ho has included a dependent clause in the sentence that specifically identifies which Americans he is referring to (underlined):

2. *Americans <u>who remember the "good old days"</u> are not alone in complaining about the educational system in this country.*

By adding this clause, Ho indicates that he is not talking about all Americans, but only about those Americans who remember the "good old days."

Note what happens, however, when commas surround the dependent clause:

3. *Americans, who remember the "good old days," are not alone in complaining about the educational system in this country.*

By using commas to set off the dependent clause from the independent clause, example 3 returns to the meaning of example 1, the independent clause: *all* Americans complain about the educational system (and all of them remember the "good old days"), which is not what Ho intended to say.

Typical Errors with Adjective Clauses

Because the rules for adjective clauses are complex, writers sometimes make errors when creating sentences that include these clauses. The following sentences show a typical error (next to the word *No*) and a corrected form (next to the word *Yes*).

1. Unnecessary pronoun

   No: Americans *who* remember the "good old days" *they* are not alone in complaining about the educational system in this country.

   Yes: Americans *who* remember the "good old days" are not alone in complaining about the educational system in this country. (Ho, p. 125)

2. Unnecessary preposition

   No: There was in them that sure, settled look of those who belong to the world *in which* they were born *in*.

   Yes: There was in them that sure, settled look of those who belong to the world *in which* they were born. (Yezierska, p. 26)

3. Missing preposition

   No: I was no longer in a tropical zone, and this realization now entered my life like a flow of water dividing formerly dry and solid ground, creating two banks, *one which* was my past—so familiar and predictable that even my unhappiness then made me happy now just to think of it—the other my future, a gray blank, an overcast seascape on which rain was falling and no boats were in sight.

   Yes: I was no longer in a tropical zone, and this realization now entered my life like a flow of water dividing formerly dry and solid ground, creating two banks, *one of which* was my past—so familiar and predictable that even my unhappiness then made me happy now just to think of it—the other my future, a gray blank, an overcast seascape on which rain was falling and no boats were in sight. (Jamaica Kincaid, from "The Poor Visitor")

4. Unnecessary comma before clause introduced by *that*

   No: Each language has a vocabulary of time, *that* does not always survive translation.

   Yes: Each language has a vocabulary of time *that* does not always survive translation. (Levine & Wolff, p. 88)

Noun Clauses

Noun clauses function like nouns. The box that follows provides subordinating words that introduce noun clauses.

□□□	**Noun Clauses**	
Subordinating Word	**Function of Clause**	**Sample Sentence (Noun Clause in Italics)**
that	Subject	*That Jackson benefited from a discriminatory situation* <u>is</u> ironic. (Excerpt from student essay)
	Subject after *it*	<u>It</u> was obvious *that the elephant would never rise again,* but he was not dead. (Orwell, p. 36)
	Object of verb	He <u>thinks</u> *that an artist is a "dumb" thing to be.* (Zinsser, p. 142)
	Restated subject or object	The <u>belief</u> *that self-esteem is a precondition to learning* is now dogma that few instructors question. (Moore, p. 136)
how, what, when, where, who, which why, (-ever) whether	Subject	*How a country paces its social life* <u>is</u> a mystery to most outsiders, one that we're just beginning to unravel. (Levine & Wolff, p. 87)
	Object of verb	Then for a little while the house feels huge and empty, and I <u>wonder</u> *where my self is hiding.* (Sarton, p. 39)
	Object of preposition	When you tossed on our desks writing <u>upon</u> *which you had not labored,* we read it and even responded as though you earned a response. (Neusner, p. 12)

ACTIVITY

Identifying Clauses

Identify the independent and dependent clauses in each of the following sentences.

1. There's no doubt that American education does not meet high standards in such basic skills as mathematics and language. (Ho, p. 126)

2. If I were an employer I would rather employ graduates who have this range and curiosity than those who narrowly pursued safe subjects and high grades. (Zinsser, p. 141)

3. Students themselves are so conditioned to grading that they soon become willing dupes of the system. (Lean, p. 134)

4. Individuals of either sex who have a trusted friend to whom they can express thoughts, feelings and opinions honestly are less likely to report symptoms of depression and loneliness than those who do not have the benefit of this experience. (Block, p. 71)

5. When you tossed on our desks writing upon which you had not labored, we read it and even responded, as though you earned a response. (Neusner, p. 12) ■

ACTIVITY

Correcting Errors in Use of Clauses

Locate and correct errors in the use of clauses in the following sentences. The page number on which the correctly formed sentence can be found is indicated in parentheses.

1. The few who achieve complete insight and acceptance, they are outstanding by their rarity. (p. 76)

2. Even though self-disclosure is an infrequent occurrence, but it is clear that men desire others with whom to share problems and personal experiences. (p. 71)

3. He thinks, that an artist is a "dumb" thing to be. (p. 142)

4. We have many prepackaged excuses for our failures, which some are partly valid and others that are self-delusion. (p. 135)

5. Perhaps she would never see again those familiar objects from which she had never dreamed of being divided from. (p. 183) ■

Sentence Fragments

A *sentence fragment* is a group of words that is punctuated like a sentence but that does not qualify as a sentence because of at least one of these reasons:

1. It lacks an independent clause.
   □ When there is no longer a place that is yours in the world. (Saint-Exupéry, p. 336)
   □ And who, by her presence puts us in touch with an earlier part of ourself, a part of ourself it's important never to lose. (Viorst, p. 67)
   □ That, suddenly alone, he would discover that he bored himself, or that there was, quite simply, no self there to meet? (Sarton, p. 37)

2. It lacks a subject-verb combination.
   □ Especially that kind of waiting. (Jackson, p. 23)
   □ And my waits at the counter? (Jackson, p. 24)

☐ Worse than being an outcast. (Yezierska, p. 30)

Sentence fragments are sometimes used deliberately by experienced writers for emphasis or to express a theme. The following activity may help you understand how a writer can use a fragment for a specific purpose.

ACTIVITY

Finding and Determining the Purpose of Sentence Fragments

Working with a partner or in a group, have one student read the following passage aloud. Then find the two sentence fragments, and discuss what purpose they serve.

> Looking down on those swarming highways I understood more clearly than ever what peace meant. In time of peace the world is self-contained. The villagers come home at dusk from their fields. The grain is stored up in the barns. The folded linen is piled up in the cupboards. In time of peace each thing is in its place, easily found. Each friend is where he belongs, easily reached. All men know where they will sleep when night comes. Ah, but peace dies when the framework is ripped apart. When there is no longer a place that is yours in the world. When you know no longer where your friend is to be found. Peace is present when man can see the face that is composed of things that have meaning and are in their place. Peace is present when things form part of a whole greater than their sum, as the divers minerals on the ground collect to become the tree.
>
> But this is war.

> *Antoine de Saint-Exupéry, from*
> Flight to Arras. *Translated by L. Galantière*
> ∎

Turning Sentence Fragments into Sentences

A sentence fragment is an error when a writer creates one unintentionally. Since such a fragment has no purpose, it should become part of a full sentence. The following box shows three ways to achieve that goal.

☐☐☐   **Turning Sentence Fragments into Sentences**

---

1. Add a subject and/or a verb (to complete the subject-verb combination) if it is missing.
   Sentence fragment:
   All the while going to the drugstore each morning.
   Complete sentence:
   All the while I kept going to the drugstore each morning. (Jackson, p. 24)

2. Connect a fragment to the preceding sentence as a dependent clause.
   Sentence fragment (underlined):
   She pointed out my place in line. Where I had to stand with the rest like a lot of wooden soldiers.
   Complete sentence:
   She pointed out my place in line, where I had to stand with the rest like a lot of wooden soldiers. (Yezierska, p. 28)

3. Integrate a fragment into the preceding (or following) sentence.
   Sentence fragment (underlined):
   I picked up the food. <u>And wheeled back to the studio—slowly.</u>
   Complete sentence:
   I picked up the food and wheeled back to the studio—slowly. (Jackson, p. 24)
   Sentence fragment (underlined):
   <u>For example, the guy across the hall.</u> Yesterday he asked me to turn down my stereo.
   Complete sentence:
   Yesterday, for example, the guy across the hall asked me to turn down my stereo. (Niella, p. 61)

ACTIVITY

Turning Sentence Fragments into Sentences

Find the sentence fragments in the following sets of sentences, taken from student essays. Then turn them into complete sentences.

1. I was pleased by the warm greeting I received from my American sponsor. Whom I had also known from my previous job in Vietnam.

2. I disagree with Moore's argument that instructors' focus on self-esteem is connected to the problem of underprepared students. Is much more complex than that.

3. Neusner and Zinsser both discuss college students, but they reveal different attitudes toward them. Especially when it comes to the issue of how hard they work.

4. Ho argues that freedom to think is an important component of education. And that creativity is crucial as well. ∎

ACTIVITY

Identifying Sentence Fragments

Look through your own writing to see if you have created sentence fragments unintentionally. If you find such a fragment, turn it into a complete sentence. If you have used a fragment deliberately, explain its purpose.
Note: Fragments should be used sparingly, if ever. ∎

Punctuation between Clauses

Punctuation between clauses provides readers with clues as to how the ideas in the clauses relate to one another and how the words in the sentence are grouped together.

To see how punctuation between clauses functions, observe these two independent clauses (ICs), taken from a sentence in Zitkala-Ša's "The School Days of an Indian Girl" (p. 18):

1. *my spirit tore itself in struggling for its lost freedom*
   all was useless

   A common error is to combine two clauses in a sentence with no punctuation between them, so that the reader does not know know where to pause:

2. *My spirit tore itself in struggling for its lost freedom all was useless.*

   Another common error is to combine two independent clauses in a sentence with only a comma between them when a comma is not considered strong enough punctuation:

3. *My spirit tore itself in struggling for its lost freedom, all was useless.*

   To learn various ways to punctuate this sentence, see the box that follows.

☐☐☐   **Punctuation between Clauses**

In this box, you can observe several ways to punctuate these two clauses to reflect emphasis and meaning:

☐ my spirit tore itself in struggling for its lost freedom
☐ all was useless

Note: **IC** refers to independent clause; **DC** refers to dependent clause.

1. To give equal emphasis to both statements, place *a period* between the two independent clauses. The "formula" = **IC. IC.**

   My spirit tore itself in struggling for its lost freedom. All was useless.

2. To show a close link between the two statements, place *a semicolon* between the two clauses. The "formula" = **IC; IC.**

   My spirit tore itself in struggling for its lost freedom; all was useless.

3. To give relatively equal emphasis to both statements, place *a comma,* and then *a coordinator* (see p. 324) between the two clauses. The "formula" = **IC, coordinator IC.**

   My spirit tore itself in struggling for its lost freedom, but all was useless.

4. To indicate the relationship between the clauses and to emphasize the second statement, use *a subordinator* (see p. 327) to turn the first independent clause into a dependent clause, and then *a comma.* The "formula" = **DC, IC.**

   Although my spirit tore itself in struggling for its lost freedom, all was useless.

5. To indicate the relationship between the clauses and to emphasize the first statement, use *a subordinator* (see p. 327) to turn the second independent clause into a dependent clause (a comma is usually not necessary); the "formula" = **IC DC.**

   My spirit tore itself in struggling for its lost freedom although all was useless.

6. Use a transition to indicate the relationship between the two statements: place *a semicolon,* then *a transition* (see p. 325), and then *a comma* between the clauses. The "formula" = **IC**; transition, **IC**.

My spirit tore itself in struggling for its lost freedom; however, all was useless.

or

Place *a period* between the two clauses. Begin the second clause with *a transition* (see p. 325), followed by *a comma.* The "formula" = **IC**. Transition, **IC**.

My spirit tore itself in struggling for its lost freedom. However, all was useless.

or

Place *a period* between the two clauses. Place *a comma,* and then *a transition* at the end of the second clause. The "formula" = **IC**. **IC**, transition.

My spirit tore itself in struggling for its lost freedom. All was useless, however.

or

Place *a period* between the two clauses. Place *a transition,* with *commas* on each side, between the subject and the verb of the second clause.

My spirit tore itself in struggling for its lost freedom. All, however, was useless.

ACTIVITY

Punctuating between Clauses

Punctuate in various ways each of the following sentences, taken from student essays.

1. He would break everything down into pieces and start from scratch he would then build on that slowly so that I would understand.
2. In the past, Americans had a tendency to think that English was the only language worth knowing and that foreigners were forced to learn it so they did not even try to learn another language.
3. However, the fact is that I am not a supernatural being, I could not take the stress.
4. My decision to apply early to college was meant to lighten the burden, unfortunately the three essays and several short questions added to my unbearable load.

ACTIVITY

Punctuating Your Own Clauses

Look through your own writing to examine punctuation between clauses. The following formulas (discussed in the preceding box) may help you make decisions about punctuation.

1. **IC**. **IC**.
2. **IC**; **IC**.

3. IC, coordinator IC.
4. DC, IC.
5. IC DC.
6. IC; transition, IC.
7. IC. Transition, IC.
8. IC. IC, transition.   ■

Subject-Verb Agreement

> Good teaching is at the heart of the undergraduate experience.
>
> *Ernest L. Boyer, from*
> *College: The Undergraduate Experience in America*
>
> Pupils are more like oysters than sausages.
>
> *Sydney J. Harris, from*
> *"What True Education Should Do," page 4*

Verbs in English agree with their subjects in number. That is, if the subject is singular, the verb is singular; if the subject is plural, the verb is plural.

□□□	**Subject-Verb Agreement**	
Singular Subject	Singular Verb	
Good teaching	*is*	at the heart of the undergraduate experience.
Plural Subject	Plural Verb	
Pupils	*are*	more like oysters than sausages.

Deciding Whether a Verb Should Be Singular or Plural

Unfortunately, making verbs agree with their subjects is not as easy as it may first appear. The grammatical singular or plural form of the subject is not the only factor. The intention of the writer and current usage may also play a role.

The following sentences show whether to use a singular or plural verb in these cases.

1. When the subject is *everybody* or *everyone, anybody* or *anyone, somebody* or *someone, nobody* or *no one, every* + *noun, each* (+ noun), *one of the* + plural noun

Singular verb:

□ *Everyone is* right! (Moore, p. 136)

☐ *Each sees, hears, feels,* and *smells* only that which has some meaning or importance for him. (Barna, p. 79)

☐ *One of the few rights* that America does not proclaim *is* the right to fail. (Zinsser, p. 140)

2. When the subject is *who, which,* or *that*

Singular verb, if the word it refers to is singular:

Every *person* who *has* ever gone to school can cite numerous instances of unfairness and injustice caused by grading systems and practices, but for some strange reason we seem to assume it to be necessary and intrinsic to the process of formal education. (Lean, pp. 130–131)

Plural verb, if the word it refers to is plural:

Yes; most teachers try to be fair and accurate, but all the time they know—at least *those* who *are* honest with themselves know—that they are attempting the impossible. (Lean, p. 133)

3. When the subject is a collective noun

Singular verb, if the writer thinks of the people as one unit:

The faculty *takes* pride in its educational achievements.

Plural verb, if the writer thinks of the people as separate individuals:

We the faculty *take* no pride in our educational achievements with you. (Neusner, p. 11)

Note: Nouns that fit into the category of collective nouns include *audience, class, committee, couple, crowd, faculty, family, government, group, party, public, staff,* and *team.*

4. When the subject is composed of two or more nouns joined by *either . . . or, neither . . . nor,* or *not only . . . but also*

Singular verb, if the subject closest to it is singular:

Neither the students *nor* the *professor is* to blame.

Plural verb, if the subject closest to it is plural:

Neither the professor nor the *students are* to blame.

5. When the subject is *enough* or *none*

Singular verb, if the reference is to one item:

Enough has been said.

Plural verb, if the reference is to more than one item or person:

Enough are here to start the meeting.

Note: Current usage provides a choice of singular or plural verb when *none* is followed by *of:*

☐ *None of* these exercises *was giving* him as much trouble as they apparently had in the past. (Malamud, p. 189)

☐ *None of* these exercises *were giving* him much trouble.

6. When the subject is *there*

Singular verb, if the reference is singular:

> If *there is a universal*, it might be that each has been so subconsciously influenced by his own cultural upbringing that he assumes that the needs, desires, and basic assumptions of others are identical to his own. (Barna, p. 76)

Plural verb, if the reference is plural:

> *There have been* successful *attempts* to eliminate marks. (Lean, p. 134)

7. When the subject is an expression of quantity with the word *of*

Singular verb, if it is followed by a noncountable noun (see box on p. 357)

> *Some of* the *advice* he gave *is* inadequate.

Plural verb, if it is followed by a plural noun

> *Some of* the authors *have experienced* discrimination.

8. When the subject includes the expression *number of*

Singular verb, if the expression is *the number of* (indicating a specific amount):

> The number of students who take French 210 *is* eighteen.

Plural verb, if the expression is *a number of* (meaning *some* or *several*)

> To some extent, this is nothing new: *a* certain *number of* professors *have* always *been* self-contained islands of scholarship and shyness, more comfortable with books than with people. (Zinsser, p. 143)

9. When the subject is an infinitive (*to* + verb), gerund (simple form of verb + *-ing*), or dependent noun clause (see p. 334)

Singular verb:

☐ *To err is* human. (Robert Frost, from "The White-tailed Hornet")

☐ *Learning* the language, which most foreign visitors consider their only barrier to understanding, *is* actually only the beginning. (Barna, p. 79)

☐ *That James Thomas Jackson benefited from a discriminatory situation is* ironic. (Excerpt from student essay)

10. When the subject is a book or essay title

Singular verb:

> "Intercultural Communication Stumbling Blocks" by LaRay M. Barna *includes* students' own testimonies.

11. When the subject combines an expression of quantity or amount and a plural noun referring to time, money, weight, or distance

Singular verb:

> *Six months is* a long time to be away from home.

12. When the subject is a noun that ends in *-s* but is considered singular

Singular verb:

> The *news is* bad."

Note: Nouns that fit into this category include:

- ☐ Countries (for example, the United States)
- ☐ Stores (for example, Sears)
- ☐ Institutions (for example, the United Nations)
- ☐ Fields of study that end in *-ics* (for example, economics)

13. When the subject is a percentage

Plural verb:

- ☐ More than *30% of* U.S. 17-year-olds *don't know* that Abraham Lincoln wrote the Emancipation Proclamation. (Moore, p. 135)
- ☐ Almost *two-thirds say* they are under great pressure to get high grades; about *one third feel* it is difficult to get good grades and "still really learn something." (Boyer, p. 94)

Pronoun Agreement

> Americans who remember "the good old days" are not alone in complaining about the educational system in this country. Immigrants, too, complain, and with more up-to-date comparisons. Lately I have heard a Polish refugee express dismay that his daughter's high school has not taught her the difference between Belgrade and Prague. A German friend was furious when he learned that the mathematics test given to his son on his first day as a freshman included multiplication and division. A Lebanese boasts that the average high-school graduate in his homeland can speak fluently in Arabic, French and English. Japanese businessmen in Los Angeles send their children to private schools staffed by teachers imported from Japan to learn mathematics at Japanese levels, generally considered at least a year more advanced than the level here.
>
> *Kie Ho, from*
> *"We Should Cherish Our Children's Freedom to Think," page 125*
>
> Our public education certainly is not perfect, but it is a great deal better than any other.
>
> *Kie Ho, from*
> *"We Should Cherish Our Children's Freedom to Think," page 127*

Pronouns agree in number (singular or plural) and gender (masculine, feminine, or neuter) with the nouns and noun phrases they replace. They should clearly refer to the words they replace.

The examples in the box that follows show nouns and pronouns taken from the passages by Kie Ho reprinted in the preceding box.

□□□ Pronoun Agreement

Singular Noun   **Singular Pronoun**

A German friend   was furious when   *he*   learned . . .

Plural Noun   **Plural Pronoun**

Japanese businessmen   in Los Angeles send   *their*   children . . .

                             Masculine Noun   **Masculine Pronoun**

. . . the mathematics test given to his   *son*   on   *his*   first day

---

Feminine Noun   **Feminine Pronoun**

. . . his *daughter's*   high school has not taught   *her*   the difference . . .

         Neuter Noun   **Neuter Pronoun**

Our public *education* certainly is not perfect, but *it* is a great deal better . . .

Selecting the correct pronoun is sometimes dependent on the writer's intended meaning, for example, with collective nouns:

□□□ Pronoun Agreement with Collective Nouns

The collective noun can refer to the unit as a whole:
The *faculty* takes pride in *its* educational achievements.
The collective noun can refer to the individuals in the unit:
We the *faculty* take no pride in *our* educational achievements with you.
(Neusner, p. 11)
Note: Nouns that fall into this category include *audience, class, committee, couple, crowd, faculty, family, government, group, party, public, staff,* and *team.*

When the subject of the sentence is *each, one, everybody* or *everyone, somebody* or *someone, anybody* or *anyone, nobody,* or *no one* (indefinite pronouns) , selecting the appropriate pronoun involves knowing whether the subject is masculine, feminine, or either.

□□□	**Pronoun Agreement When the Subject Is an Indefinite Pronoun**

Male subject:	*Each* expressed *his* ideas.
Female subject:	*Each* expressed *her* ideas.
Male and female subject:	*Each* expressed ideas.

Deciding Whether a Pronoun Should Be Singular or Plural

Selecting a pronoun can be tricky because it can depend upon other words in the sentence or how close the pronoun is to the word it refers to. The following examples may help you make a decision about whether the pronoun should be singular or plural.

1. When the words the pronoun refers to are joined by *and*

Plural pronoun:

   If Jacob Neusner *and* William Zinsser were to meet, *they* would have an interesting debate about college life.

2. When the words the pronoun refers to are joined by *or* or *nor*

Singular pronoun:

   If Randy Moore *or* Arthur Lean were to enter our classroom, *he* would probably discuss *his* views on grading.

3. When the subject consists of or two or more nouns joined by *either . . . or, neither . . . nor,* or *not only . . . but also*

Singular pronoun, if the noun closer to the pronoun is singular:

   Not only the students *but also* the *professor* found *his* attention wandering.

Plural pronoun, if the noun closer to the pronoun is plural:

   Not only the professor *but also* the *students* found *their* attention wandering.

Avoiding Sexist Use of Language

Using the masculine pronoun to refer to human beings in general was common practice before the 1980s. You may notice its use in readings in this book that were originally published before 1980. The use of the masculine pronoun to refer to all human beings is now considered sexist by most readers and editors.

The following examples show ways to avoid a sexist pronoun. Discuss the most acceptable ways with your instructor.

1. Use the alternatives *he or she (him or her; his or hers).*

Previous practice:

   Each person's culture, *his* own way of life, always seems right, proper, and natural. (Barna, 1976, p. 80)

Current practice:

> Each person's culture, *his or her* own way of life, always seems right, proper, and natural.

2. Turn the reference into a plural form.

Previous practice:

> No self-respecting *teacher* ever *rests* peacefully the night after turning in a set of grades, for *he knows* that the "system" has made *a charlatan* of *him* and *he* goes to bed hating *himself* for it. (Lean, 1976, p. 133)

Current practice:

> No self-respecting *teachers* ever *rest* peacefully the night after turning in a set of grades, for *they know* that the "system" has made *charlatans* of *them* and *they* go to bed hating *themselves* for it.

3. Rewrite the sentence to avoid pronouns with gender.

Previous practice:

> Each sees, hears, feels, and smells only that which has some meaning or importance for *him*. (Barna, 1976, p. 79)

Current practice:

> Each sees, hears, feels, and smells only that which has some *personal* meaning or importance.

4. Use a plural pronoun to refer back to indefinite pronouns such as *each* or *everyone*, even though there is a singular verb.
  Note: This usage is controversial.

Previous practice:

> If there is a universal, it might be that *each has been* so subconsciously influenced by *his* own cultural upbringing that *he assumes* that the needs, desires, and basic assumptions of others are identical to *his* own. (Barna, 1976, p. 76)

Current (controversial) practice:

> If there is a universal, it might be that *each has been* so subconsciously influenced by *their* own cultural upbringing that *they assume* that the needs, desires, and basic assumptions of others are identical to *their* own.

ACTIVITY

Identifying Errors of Pronoun Agreement

Look through your own writing to search for errors of pronoun agreement. If you find any, correct them based on the previous guidelines. ∎

Verb Tenses

Tense is concerned with time, but not in any simple way. It is possible, for instance, to use a present tense to express a future time, as the example in the box below shows.

"Right now I'm going to take a long walk."

Student quoted in
"College Pressures," page 138

The Presents

Simple Present

The simple present is used primarily in four ways, as illustrated in the box below.

□□□   **Uses of the Simple Present**

States of being (as opposed to actions) that exist at the moment of writing:
> I *remember* that it was a cloudy, stuffy morning at the beginning of the rains. (Orwell, p. 33)

Note: Verbs that fit into this category include *appreciate, believe, care, desire, dislike, doubt, envy, fear, hate, imagine, know, like, love, mean, mind, need, prefer, recognize, remember, seem, suppose, think, trust, understand, want.* These verbs are rarely used in the progressive form.

Habits or routines:
> Students themselves *are* so *conditioned* to grading that they soon become willing dupes of the system. (Lean, p. 134)

Universal truths or permanent situations:
> Even within our own country, of course, ideas of time and punctuality *vary* considerably from place to place. (Levine & Wolff, p. 86)

Author's ideas (see also p. 276):
> In "Grades and Self-Esteem," Randy Moore *argues* that self-esteem is not a "prepackaged handout"; it must be earned (p. 136).

Present Progressive

The present progressive tense is formed by *be (am, is, are)* + verb + *-ing*.

□□□   **Uses of the Present Progressive**

Activities and situations that are in progress at the present moment and will probably continue:
    Educators and linguists *are improving* methods of learning a second language. (Barna, p. 82)

Temporary activities and situations that are in progress at the present moment:
    Then for a little while the house feels huge and empty, and I wonder where my self *is hiding.* It has to be recaptured slowly by watering plants, perhaps, and looking again at each one as though it were a person, by feeding the two cats, by cooking a meal. (Sarton, p. 39)

Present Perfect

The present perfect tense is formed by *have* (abbreviation: *'ve*) + past participle.

□□□   **Uses of the Present Perfect**

Activity or situation repeated in the past that still affects the present and is likely to be repeated in the future:
    We *have had* this asinine practice of grading in schools for so long that we unconsciously assume it to be necessary to the learning process, but this is a manifestly false assumption. (Lean, p. 133)

Activity or situation just completed that still affects the present moment:
    Is that B− an estimate? No, indeed; when the reports come out, when the averages and grade-points are computed, when the failures are determined, when you are called in and told that you*'ve flunked* out of school, there is no room for estimates—this is a very <u>absolute</u> decision. (Lean, p. 133)

Completed activity or situation that occurred at an unspecified time in the past and that might continue:
    There *have been* successful attempts to eliminate marks. (Lean, p. 133)

Words That Often Accompany Perfect Forms: Since *and* For

The words *since* and *for* are often used with present perfect or past perfect forms to indicate the beginning point or span of an event.

□   Use *since* to indicate the beginning point of the event.

    Since the rise of the women's movement, sex-role behavior *has come* under close scrutiny. (Block, p. 70)

□   Use *for* to indicate the entire span of the event.

We *have had* this asinine practice of grading in schools *for so long* that we unconsciously assume it to be necessary to the learning process, but this is a manifestly false assumption. (Lean, p. 133)

Note: With perfect forms, the word *for* (not *since*) is always used with words referring to quantity of time (for example, *for a long time, for many years, for five weeks*).

Present Perfect Progressive

The present perfect progressive tense is formed by *have been* + verb + *-ing*.

□□□ **Use of the Present Perfect Progressive**

Activity in progress over a period of time in the past and continuing into the present:
Professor Levine *has been studying* cross-cultural attitudes toward punctuality and pace of life for several years. (Excerpt from student essay)

Note: The present perfect (*has studied*) could be used in this case without changing the writer's intended meaning, but it would not emphasize that the activity is still going on, as the progressive form does.

The Pasts

Simple Past

The simple past tense is formed by the simple form of the verb + *-ed* and has many irregular forms.

□□□ **Use of the Simple Past**

Activities and situations completed in the past:
I *was* eighteen then and a drop-out, but I *was* deep into the wonderful world of literature and life. (Jackson, p. 24)

Activities and situations finished in the past that happened only one time:
A year passed, and I *discovered* a black library branch at Booker T. Washington High. (Jackson, p. 24)

Past Progressive

The past progressive tense is formed by *be (was, were)* + verb + *-ing.*

□□□ **Use of the Past Progressive**

Unfinished, temporary activity in progress in the past that overlapped with another past activity:

As I started forward practically the whole population of the quarter flocked out of the houses and followed me. They had seen the rifle and *were* all *shouting* excitedly. . . . (Orwell, p. 33)

Past Perfect

The past perfect tense is formed by *had* + past participle.

□□□ **Uses of the Past Perfect**

Activity or situation completed in the past prior to another past event:

As soon as I saw the dead man I sent an orderly to a friend's house nearby to borrow an elephant rifle. I *had* already *sent* back the pony, not wanting it to go mad with fright and throw me if it smelt the elephant. (Orwell, p. 33)

Note: The past perfect is the form used for the action that happened first.

Past Perfect Progressive

The past perfect progressive is formed by *had been* + verb + *-ing.*

□□□ **Uses of the Past Perfect Progressive**

Completed activity or situation that was in progress over a period of time in the past:

In my purse was the money I *had been saving* from my food, from my clothes, a penny to a penny, a dollar to a dollar, for so many years. (Yezierska, pp. 25–26)

Note: The past perfect form (*had saved*) could have been used in this case without changing the writer's essential meaning, but it would not emphasize that the saving took place over a long period of time, as the progressive form does.

Activity in progress over a period of time in the past that overlapped with another past activity:

I turned to some experienced-looking Burmans who had been there when we arrived, and asked them how the elephant *had been behaving.* They all said the same thing: he took no notice of you if you left him alone, but he might charge if you went too close to him. (Orwell, p. 35)

Note: The past perfect form (*had behaved*) would not be appropriate here, because it would relate to a moment in time and not reflect the writer's concern with the behavior over time.

The Futures

There are many ways to express the future in English.

□□□   **Expressing the Future**

Present progressive: plan of action for the future
     He is taking a train to Washington, D. C., tomorrow.

Simple present: anticipated or scheduled event
     The class meets at six o'clock this evening.

Note: This form is used with verbs such as *start, begin, finish,* and *arrive, depart, leave.*

Be going to: intention or plan
     "Right now *I'm going to* take a long walk." (Student quoted in Zinsser, p. 138)

Be to: obligation
     He is to be in class at 2:30 sharp.

Be about to: action on the verge of happening
     He *was about to* start the class when the fire started.

Simple Future

The simple future tense is formed by *will* (abbreviation: *'ll*) + the simple form of a verb.

□□□   **Use of the Simple Future**

Activity or situation that will take place in the future in response to some prior activity/situation:
     We *'ll improve* students' self-esteem most by helping and motivating our students to exceed <u>higher</u> standards. (Moore, p. 137)

Future Progressive

The future progressive tense is formed by *will be* + verb + *-ing.*

□□□   **Use of the Future Progressive**

Temporary action that will be in progress in the near future:
     They will be driving to work at 8 A.M. tomorrow.

Future Perfect

The future perfect tense is formed by *will have* + past participle.

□□□ **Use of the Future Perfect**

Action that will be completed prior to a specific future time:
    We'll improve students' self-esteem most by helping and motivating our students to exceed <u>higher</u> standards. Only then *will* our students *have accomplished* something meaningful and *will* we *have excelled* at our work. (Moore, p. 137)

Future Perfect Progressive

The future perfect progressive is formed by *have been* + verb + *-ing*.

□□□ **Use of the Future Perfect Progressive**

An activity in progress until another time or event:
    I will have been writing for three hours by the time the class starts.

Figure 27-1 shows the relationship of several tenses on a time line. You may find this helpful in determining which verb tenses to use in your writing. You can design a time line for your own essay.

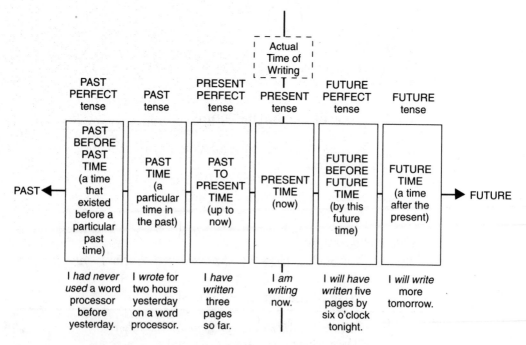

Figure 27-1 Time Relationship of Several Verb Tenses

ACTIVITY

Examining Verb Tenses in Your Own Writing

Look through your own writing to examine the verb tenses. Look closely at the various actions or situations you have described in relation to the time at which you are writing. Decide whether the verb tense used reflects accurately what you want to say. ■

Modal Auxiliaries

Modal auxiliaries, used with the simple form of the verb, add meaning to the verb. Most modals have two functions: a social function and a logical function. These functions are illustrated below. They are followed by some other meanings of modals that do not fit into these categories.

Social Functions of Modals

Modals serve three functions in situations that require that something be communicated from one person to another: (1) to make requests, (2) ask permission, or (3) give advice.

1. Making requests

□□□	**Request**		
will	would	can	could

EXAMPLE

Early one morning the sub-inspector at a police station the other end of town rang me up on the 'phone and said that an elephant was ravaging the bazaar. *Would I please come and do something about it?* (Orwell, p. 32)

The use of the word *would* (rather than *will*) in this case is required by the past sequence of tenses. If *could* were used instead of *would,* the person making the request might be asking Orwell, "Are you willing to do this?" The word *would* makes the request a bit more polite, as if the speaker were asking Orwell, "Is it possible for you to do this?"

2. Asking or giving permission

□□□	**Permission**		
might	may	could	can

> A chaperon must have noticed my face, and she brought over one of those clumsy, backward youths who was lost in a corner by himself. How unwilling were his feet as she dragged him over! In a dull voice, he asked, *"May I have the next dance?"* his eyes fixed in the distance as he spoke. (Yezierska, p. 30)

The use of *may* instead of *can* (or *could*) usually indicates a formal relationship between the speaker and listener. *Might* is the most polite and formal way to ask for permission.

3. Giving advice or suggestions

The modals in the box entitled Advice or Suggestions are listed according to the approximate degree of authority or sense of urgency employed by the writer. For example, the word *might* is an indirect way to make a suggestion.

□□□ **Advice or Suggestions**	
	Degree of Authority or Urgency Increases
might could should ought to have to had better must will	↓

> Teachers *should* learn each student's name and make sure to use names frequently, so that all students know they are recognized members of the class. (Catherine G. Krupnick, from "Women and Men in the Classroom: Inequality and Its Remedies")

In this example, the word *should* indicates less authority and urgency than if the writer had used the word *must*. Use of *must* instead of *should* would have indicated an even more authoritative tone and/or that the issue needs even more immediate attention.

Logical Functions of Modals

Modals can function to indicate the probability of something. To determine whether something is probable, a writer draws conclusions or predicts from whatever evidence is available.

The modals in the following box entitled Conclusion or Deduction are listed according to the writer's degree of certainty. For example, the word *must* indicates a greater degree of certainty than the word *might*.

□□□ **Conclusion or Deduction**	
	Degree of Certainty Increases
can, could, might may should must would will	

EXAMPLE

One reason for the long delay in tackling the widespread failure to achieve understanding across cultures *might* be that it is not readily apparent when there has been miscommunication at the interpersonal level. (Barna, p. 77)

If Barna had used *must,* she would have been indicating that she was more certain about the reason that she is providing. The degrees differ when negative words are used, however, as the box below reveals.

The modals in the following box entitled Conclusions or Deductions (with *Not*) are listed according to the writer's degree of certainty about the statement being made. For example, the words *could not* indicate greater certainty than the words *may not.*

□□□ **Conclusion or Deduction (with *Not*)**	
	Degree of Certainty Increases
might not may not should not must not cannot, could not, will not	

EXAMPLE

I rounded the hut and saw a man's dead body sprawling in the mud. He was an Indian, a black Dravidian coolie, almost naked, and he *could not have been* dead many minutes. The people said that the elephant had come suddenly upon him round the corner of the hut, caught him with its trunk, put its foot on his back and ground him into the earth. (Orwell, p. 33)

If Orwell had used *may not* instead of *could not,* he would have been indicating less certainty about the amount of time that had passed since the man died.

The modals in the following box entitled Prediction are listed according to the degree of probability of the event.

□□□ **Prediction**	
	Degree of Probability Increases
could, might, may should will	↓

EXAMPLE

In the United States today, we are reminded of the exact hour of the day more than ever, through the little symphonies of beeps emanating from people's digital watches. As they become the norm, I fear our sense of precision *may* take an absurd twist. The other day, when I asked for the time, a student looked at his watch and replied, ''Three twelve and eighteen seconds.'' (Levine & Wolff, p. 89)

If Levine and Wolff had used *will* instead of *may,* they would have been indicating a stronger sense of what the future holds.

Note: The word *should* is not appropriate in this context. *Should* indicates prediction based on reliable evidence, which is nevertheless offered only tentatively (for example, *If there's no traffic jam on the bridge, we should be home in half an hour*). Levine and Wolff do not base their prediction on solid evidence.

Other Meanings of Modals

Meaning	Modal	Example
Ability	be able to can	Only 11% of eighth-graders in California's public schools *can* solve seventh-grade math problems. (Moore, p. 135)
Desire	would like to	I *would like to* meet the president of the United States.
Offer *(question)*	would (you) like to	When I finally did get there during business hours, the clerk was more interested in discussing relatives in America. *Would* I *like to* meet his uncle in Cincinnati? (Levine & Wolff, p. 90)

| *Preference* | would prefer to
would rather | *Would* we, however, *prefer to* stuff the developing little heads of our children with hundreds of geometry problems, the names of rivers in Brazil and 50 lines from <u>The Canterbury Tales</u>? (Ho, p. 126) |

Articles

Each time a writer writes a noun in English, a decision is made concerning the use of articles. Should it be *a* (or *an*)? Should it be *the*? Should the article be omitted?

Several factors determine the use of articles. They include:

1. Whether the noun is countable or noncountable (see box that follows)

2. Whether the noun is singular or plural

3. Whether the writer believes the noun refers to something that is familiar or unfamiliar to the reader

4. Whether the statement that contains the noun is general or specific

5. Whether the noun has a modifier (word that describes or limits the meaning of the noun)

6. Whether the noun acts to classify a person or thing or is representative of the category it is in

7. Whether the noun is part of an idiom

□□□   **Noncountable Nouns**

Noncountable nouns, which typically do not form plurals and can only be counted indirectly (for example, *two pieces of furniture,* not *two furnitures*), include words such as these:

Groups of items (for example, equipment, furniture, homework, machinery, money)

Substances without a fixed shape (for example, air, blood, coffee, grass, meat, milk, smoke, steam, tea, water)

Abstractions (for example, advice, confidence, happiness, information, knowledge)

Recreation (for example, baseball, chess, football, soccer, tennis)

Fields of study (for example, biology, economics, history, mathematics, politics)

General activities, in gerund form (for example, driving, studying, traveling, walking)

Natural phenomena (for example, darkness, fog, heat, sunshine, weather)

Because there are so many factors, it is impossible to memorize all the rules for using articles. Two basic rules may be easy to remember:

□ Plural nouns never take *a* or *an*.

□ A singular, countable noun must have an article *(a, an,* or *the),* even if an adjective precedes the noun *(a beautiful day),* unless there is a determiner* other than the article *(that beautiful day).*

To show how articles can function in context, the opening lines of James Thomas Jackson's essay "Waiting in Line at the Drugstore" (pp. 22–23) are analyzed in the following section. Although many categories emerge, they do not represent all possible uses of articles.

Note: Each sentence is numbered. On pages 359–362, nouns taken from the passage are matched with the sentence number in parentheses.

---

[1]I am black. [2]I am a writer and I want to place full credit where it belongs for the direction my life has taken: on a photography studio and a drugstore on Main Street in Houston, Texas.

[3]When I was thirteen, I dropped out of school, bought a bike for $13 (secondhand and innately durable) and went to work as a messenger for the Owl Foto Studio. [4]Each day we processed film which I picked up as raw rolls on my three routes. [5]That was great: a bike and job are supreme joys to a thirteen-year-old.

[6]The Owl Studio, on a nondescript street named Brazos (very Texan), was located in a white stucco building that blended unobtrusively into the rest of the neighborhood, which was mostly residential. [7]The area was predominantly white, and though it did not smack of affluence, it was not altogether poverty stricken either. [8]Six blocks away was the drugstore, where I had to go first thing each morning for coffee, cakes, doughnuts, jelly rolls, milk, cigarettes, whatever—anything the folks at the Owl wanted. [9]My trip amounted to picking up "breakfast" for a crew of six: three printer-developers, one wash-dry man, the roll-film man and the foreman. [10]The drugstore was the biggest challenge of my young life. [11]Being thirteen is doubtless bad enough for white male youths, but for blacks—me in particular—it was pure dee hell. [12]Going to this drugstore each morning was part of my job; it was required of me. [13]With my dropping out of school and all, my parents would have whipped my behind till it roped like okra if I had tried to supply them with reasons for not wanting to go. [14]So, I gritted my teeth and, buoyed by the power of my Western Flyer, rode on down there.

James Thomas Jackson, opening paragraphs of
"Waiting in Line at the Drugstore," pages 22–23.

---

*Determiners (other than articles) fall into these categories:
Possessives (for example, his, Maria's)
Demonstratives (for example, that, those)
Indefinite quantity words (for example, any, each, more, some)
Numerals (for example, two, 50)

No Article

1. Use no article with a noun that in the context of the passage has a noncountable sense.

   film (4)*
   affluence (7)
   coffee (8)
   milk (8)
   picking up (9)
   breakfast (9)
   hell (11)
   okra (13)
   wanting (13)

   Note: Noncountable nouns sometimes can be used with *the* if the noun has a modifier, or is followed by *of* + noun. In the following example (the first two sentences of an essay by Simon Ortiz entitled "The Language We Know"), the writer uses the word *language* in its noncountable sense, both with and without an article:

   > What would I be without *language?* My existence has been determined by *language,* not only *the* spoken but *the* unspoken, *the* language of speech and *the* language of motion.

2. Use no article with a plural, countable noun that the writer uses to represent a general category of things or people.

   rolls (4)
   joys (5)
   cakes (8)
   doughnuts (8)
   jelly rolls (8)
   cigarettes (8)
   white male youths (11)
   blacks (11)
   reasons (13)

   Note: Plural countable nouns can be used with *the* if the writer makes a specific reference or modifies the noun. In the following example (taken from a research article entitled "The Cross-Cultural Student: Lessons in Human Nature"), the authors use a plural countable noun both without and with an article:

   > Many East Asians we interviewed had come to feel that *Americans* lacked spiritual values. . . . And, in a surprising way, *the Americans* in Taiwan expressed approximately the same sentiment about their hosts.

---

*The number in parentheses refers to the sentence number of the passage above from James Thomas Jackson.

3. Use no article with a singular or plural noun that has another determiner.*

> *Each day (4)*
> *my three routes (4)*
> *Six blocks (8)*
> *each morning (8)*
> *My trip (9)*
> *three printer-developers (9)*
> *one wash-dry man (9)*
> *each morning (12)*
> *my dropping out (13)*
> *my parents (13)*
> *my behind (13)*
> *my teeth (14)*
> *my Western Flyer (14)*

In cases where the noun is known to the reader or has been referred to previously by the writer, the numeral could be preceded by the article *the*. For example, if Jackson were to refer to distance between the studio and the drugstore again, he could refer to it as *the six blocks*.

4. Use no article with a noun used in certain idioms.

> *place credit where (2)*
> *drop out of school (3, 13)*
> *go to work (3)*

Other common idioms that lack an article include the following:

> At college, school, work, home
> By bus, train, plane
> Go to school, church, bed
> Have faith in
> Have fun
> Make friends with
> Play soccer (or any other ball game)
> Take advantage of
> Take care of
> Take notice of
> Take part in
> Take pride in

A or An

1. Use *a* or *an* with a singular, countable noun that refers to something or someone that was not previously referred to by the writer, if the writer assumes or knows that the reader cannot identify which thing or person the writer is thinking of.

> *a photography studio (2)*
> *a drugstore (2)*

*See definition of determiner in the footnote on page 358.

a bike (3)
a nondescript street (6)
a white stucco building (6)
a crew (9)

2. Use *a* or *an* with a singular, countable noun that the writer uses to classify a person or thing or to represent a whole group of which it is a member.

a writer (2)
a messenger (3)
a bike (5)
(a) job (5)
a thirteen-year-old (5)

Note: A singular, countable noun can also be used with *the* when the writer's intention is to classify or to make the noun representative of other members of its group. In the following example, the writer is not referring to specific people that she knows or has previously introduced but rather is generalizing about the types of people she mentions:

The foreign visitor to the United States nods, smiles, and gives affirmative comments, which *the* straightforward, friendly American confidently translates as meaning that he has informed, helped, and pleased the newcomer. (Barna, p. 77)

The

1. Use *the* with a singular or plural noun that refers to something that was previously referred to (not necessarily with the exact same word) by the writer and that the writer therefore knows is now familiar to the reader.

the neighborhood (6)
The area (7)
the drugstore (8, 10)

Note: The article *the* can also be used in situations where the writer has not previously referred to what the noun represents but knows or assumes the reader is familiar with it. In the following example, the writer assumes his readers know what the days after World War II were like:

During *the* hectic post–World War II days I was pressed into service to teach Freshman Composition (Expository Writing) at a large university. There were more than a hundred sections of this course, each with a maximum of twenty-five students. (Lean, p. 131)

2. Use *the* with a singular or plural, countable or noncountable noun that is followed by a modifier. This noun may or may not have been previously referred to.

the direction my life has taken (2)
the rest of the neighborhood (6)
the power of my Western Flyer (14)

Note: A countable noun followed by *of* + noun can take *a, an*, or *the,* depending on the writer's intention. In the following example, the writer chooses *an* to indicate that the noun is not the only one of its kind:

> In other words, we wanted to devise *an* objective study of a controversial issue on which almost everyone has an opinion. (Catherine G. Krupnick, from ''Women and Men in the Classroom: Inequality and Its Remedies'')

3. Use *the* with a singular or plural countable noun that the writer knows is unique (the only one that exists).

> *the Owl Foto Studio (3)*
> *The Owl Studio (6)*
> *the folks at the Owl (8)*
> *the roll-film man (9)*
> *the foreman (9)*

Note: A singular countable noun that is unique to the writer can also be used with *a.*

4. Use *the* with a singular or plural, countable or noncountable noun that is preceded by a superlative.

> *the biggest challenge (10)*

Note: For special uses of articles, such as with names of places, consult a grammar handbook.

ACTIVITY

Identifying Errors in the Use of Articles

Check each noun in your essay to determine whether it needs *a/an, the,* or no article.

Punctuation

Punctuation is a tool writers use to help readers understand how to read their sentences. Though there are many principles that govern punctuation, how a sentence is punctuated is often dependent on a writer's style or intended meaning. For example, read this sentence and then explain what it means:

> A woman without her man is lost.

Now discuss how the meaning of the sentence is changed when the punctuation is changed:

> A woman: without her, man is lost.

Punctuation can be changed further to reflect the writer's style or emphasis. Discuss the effect of the following changes:

> **1.** A woman without her man is lost.
> A woman, without her man, is lost.

A woman without her man is lost!
A woman without her man is lost?

2. A woman: without her, man is lost.
A woman: Without her, man is lost!
A woman—without her, man is lost.
A woman. Without her, man is lost.

Many of the following guidelines for punctuation exist to help readers avoid misreading of sentences. Your guiding principle in determining which mark of punctuation to choose should be to find a way to transmit your ideas as clearly as possible to readers.

Note: In addition to the following, guidelines for punctuating can be found on pages 332–333 and 338–339.

The Period .

Periods are used in these situations:

1. At the end of statements and commands or requests:

   I pressed my face against the earth. (Yezierska, p. 30)

2. After indirect questions:

   I don't know what time it is.

3. After deliberate sentence fragments:

   Worse than being an outcast. (Yezierska, p. 30)

4. After abbreviations:

   Mr. Leckler was a man of high principle. (Dunbar, p. 168)

The Question Mark ?

Question marks are used in these situations:

1. After direct questions:

   What do our time judgments say about our attitude toward life? (Levine & Wolff, p. 88)

2. At the end of doubtful statements:

   A woman without her man is lost?

3. After deliberate sentence fragments:

   And my waits at the counter? (Jackson, p. 24)

The Exclamation Point !

Exclamation points are used after emphatic or emotional statements, phrases, words, or expressions:

That burning day when I got ready to leave New York and start out on my journey to college! (Yezierska, p. 25)

The Comma ,

A comma is used to indicate a natural division or slight pause in a sentence. Commas usually are used in the following situations:

1. To separate three or more items (words, phrases, or clauses) in a series:

   I see four kinds of pressure working on college students today: economic pressure, parental pressure, peer pressure, and self-induced pressure. (Zinsser, p. 140)

The comma before the word *and* may be omitted if the writer feels it is not necessary for clarity:

   We complain endlessly that students don't know anything, don't *want* to know anything, can't write well and can't think critically. (Moore, p. 135)

The word *and* may be omitted from the end of the series, usually when the writer wants to create a more dramatic effect:

   As we drove along, someone would single out to me a famous building, an important street, a park, a bridge that when built was thought to be a spectacle. (Jamaica Kincaid, from "The Poor Visitor")

2. Between two independent clauses linked by a coordinator (*and, but, for, or, nor, so, yet*)

   I heard a man's voice at one end of the hall, and I looked around to see him. (Zitkala-Ša, p. 19)

The comma before the coordinator may be omitted if the writer feels it is not necessary for clarity:

   I am a writer and I want to place full credit where it belongs for the direction my life has taken: on a photography studio and a drugstore on Main Street in Houston, Texas. (Jackson, p. 22)

A semicolon may be used instead of a comma if the writer feels it is necessary for clarity or emphasis:

   The communication cut-off caused by immediate evaluation is heightened when feelings and emotions are deeply involved; yet this is just the time when listening with understanding is most needed. (Barna, p. 80)

3. Following introductory elements:

   □ Dependent clause:

   As I entered the classroom, I saw young men and girls laughing and talking to one another without introductions. (Yezierska, p. 27)

The comma may be omitted if the writer feels it is not necessary for clarity:

   As soon as I saw the dead man I sent an orderly to a friends' house nearby to borrow an elephant rifle. (Orwell, p. 33)

☐ Phrase:

> Back home in California, I never need to look at a clock to know when the class hour is ending. (Levine & Wolff, p. 85)

The comma may be omitted if the writer feels it is not necessary for clarity:

> All the while I kept going to the drugstore each morning. (Jackson, p. 24)

☐ Transitional or adverbial words:

> Typically, school guidelines are couched in terms of learning skills, rather than the content of learning. For example, school guidelines might say, "First graders develop map skills" and "learn about plants." (Hirsch, p. 129)

4. To set off interrupting transitional or explanatory elements:

> There are times, of course, when lecturing is necessary to convey essential issues and ideas and also to handle large numbers of students. (Boyer, p. 99)

5. To set off ending elements:

> With another human being present vision becomes double vision, inevitably. (Sarton, p. 37)

Note: Another writer might have placed on comma between *present* and *vision,* for clarity:

> With another human being present, vision becomes double vision, inevitably.

The Semicolon ;

A semicolon links two closely related clauses. It also indicates a major division in a sentence, marking a stronger pause than is indicated by a comma. Semicolons usually are placed as follows (see also pp. 338–339):

1. Between two independent clauses:

> The parents mean well; they are trying to steer their sons and daughters toward a secure future. (Zinsser, p. 141)

2. Between two independent clauses joined by a transitional or adverbial expression; the expression is followed by a comma:

> One part of them feels obligated to fulfill their parents' expectations; after all, their parents are older and presumably wiser. (Zinsser, p. 142)

The comma after the transitional expression may be omitted if the writer does not find it necessary for clarity:

> There are many viewpoints regarding the practice of intercultural communication but a familiar one is that "people are people," basically pretty much alike; therefore increased interaction through travel, student exchange programs, and other such ventures should result in more understanding and friendship between nations. (Barna, p. 76)

3. Between independent clauses, if one or both clauses contain a comma, even if the clauses are linked by a coordinator (*and, but, for, nor, or, so, yet*):

> Her father was not so bad then; and besides, her mother was alive. (Joyce, p. 182)

A comma may be used instead of a semicolon if the writer feels the semicolon is not necessary for clarity:

> How they made me laugh, and I wondered what sort of parents I must have had, for even to think of such words in their presence I would have been scolded severely, and I vowed that if I ever had children I would make sure that the first words out of their mouths were bad ones. (Jamaica Kincaid, from "The Poor Visitor")

4. Between items in a series if the items contain internal commas:

> Don't worry about learning, thinking or communicating; the important thing is to feel good about ourselves. (Moore, p. 136)

The Colon :

A colon introduces explanatory items and lists. It marks a major break in a sentence and directs attention to what follows it. Colons can be used in at least three situations:

1. To link independent clauses when the subsequent clause explains or expands on the first:

> To some extent this is nothing new: a certain number of professors have always been self-contained islands of scholarship and shyness, more comfortable with books than with people. (Zinsser, p. 143)

2. To set off a listing or series of items:

> In another newspaper I wrapped up my food for the journey: a loaf of bread, a herring, and a pickle. (Yezierska, p. 25)

3. To introduce a full-sentence quotation:

> Robert T. Oliver phrases it thus: "If we would communicate across cultural barriers, we must learn what to say and how to say it in terms of the expectations and predispositions of those we want to listen." (Barna, p. 83)

The Apostrophe '

An apostrophe indicates possession or the omission of one or more letters in a word.

1. To indicate possession:

   □ Add *'s* to form the possessive of singular nouns and pronouns:

   > As you envision tomorrow's international society, do you wonder who will set the pace? (Levine & Wolff, p. 91)

   > Everyone's opinion has equal value! (Moore, p. 136)

   □ Add *'s* to form the possessive of plural nouns that do not end in *-s*:

They had none of that terrible fight for bread and rent that I always saw in New York people's eyes. (Yezierska, p. 26)

☐ Add ' to form the possessive of plural nouns ending in *-s* or *-es*:

Contrary to proponents' claims, emphasizing all-purpose mental skills to "prepare children for the 21st century" is not new. (Hirsch, p. 129)

☐ Add 's to the last word in a compound noun or pronoun:

James Thomas Jackson tells his story from a thirteen-year-old's perspective.

☐ Add 's only to the last item to indicate joint possession (one item shared by two people):

Levine and Wolff's article is titled "Social Time: The Heartbeat of Culture."

☐ Add 's to each item to indicate individual possession (two separate items):

Leans's and Moore's essays deal with the subject of grading.

2. To indicate omission of a letter:

There's no doubt that American education does not meet high standards in such basic skills as mathematics and language. (Ho, p. 126) [contraction of *There is*]

Quotation Marks " "

Quotation marks are used to indicate the beginning and end of a quotation. In many of the following examples, the number within parentheses refers to the page number from which the quotation is taken.

1. Title

Use double quotation marks (" ") to enclose titles of essays, articles, stories, poems, and chapters.

In "The Rewards of Living a Solitary Life," May Sarton maintains that living alone is a joyful experience in that it becomes more fulfilling as time passes.

2. Direct Quotation

Use double quotation marks (" ") to enclose a direct quotation.

According to Sarton, "loneliness is most acutely felt with other people" (p. 39).

3. Quotation within a Quotation

Use single quotation marks (' ') to enclose a quotation within a quotation.

Robert Levine tells of his experience in Brazil when he rushed to be on time to teach a class, only to hear "gentle calls of 'Hola, professor' and 'Tudo bem, professor?' from unhurried students" (p. 84).

4. Placement of Period

Place a period *after* the page number, when the page number is included within parentheses at the end of a sentence.

May Sarton finds that living alone has become "increasingly rewarding" (p. 39).

Place a period *before* the end quotation mark if there is no need for the page number (for example, when the title of an essay is mentioned).

May Sarton reveals her attitude toward being alone in the title of her essay "The Rewards of Living a Solitary Life."

5. Placement of Comma

Place a comma *before* the end quotation mark.

The grading system is "tyrannical and indefensible," according to Arthur E. Lean (p. 130).

Use commas to set off explanatory phrases that interrupt a quotation; include an extra set of quotation marks.

"Every person who has ever gone to school," Lean argues, "can cite numerous instances of unfairness and injustice caused by grading systems" (pp. 130–131).

Use a comma to separate an opening quotation from the part of the sentence that follows:

America "is still the country of innovation," insists Ho (p. 126).

Note: A comma is not necessary if the quotation is blended into your own sentence:

Use a comma to introduce a short quotation.

Moore says, "self-esteem is *earned*" (p. 136).

Note: Do not use a comma if the quoted statement follows the word *that*:

Moore argues that "self-esteem is *earned*" (p. 136).

6. Placement of Semicolon, Colon, and Dash

Place semi-colon (;) and colon (:) and dash (—) *after* the end quotation mark.

Lean argues that schools should "eliminate marks"; that idea is more easily suggested than implemented (p. 134).

7. Placement of Question Mark and Exclamation Point

Place question marks (**?**) and exclamation points (**!**) *before* the end quotation marks if the quotation itself is a question or an exclamation.

Kie Ho asks, "If American education is so tragically inferior, why is it that this is still the country of innovation?" (p. 126).

Note: If your own words follow a quotation that ends in a question mark or exclamation point, you do not need to add a comma.

"If American education is so tragically inferior, why is it that this is still the country of innovation?" asks Kie Ho (p. 126).

Place question marks and exclamation points *after* the end quotation mark, if your own sentence is a question or exclamation.

> Is it really possible, as Lean suggests, to "eliminate marks"? (p. 134).

8. Long Quotation

Set off a lengthy quotation (more than four or five lines) with a colon, and with no quotation marks (unless there is a quotation within the quotation), by *indenting five spaces* from the left margin. Double-space throughout.

> To prove his point that the grading system is unfair, Arthur Lean provides the example of an experiment in which a panel of mathematics teachers graded students' work in geometry:
>
> > Student papers in plane geometry were graded by these expert teachers, each using an identical copy so as to eliminate any persuasive effect of extraneous factors such as neatness. The result was, of course, that the grades assigned to exactly the same paper ranged all the way from the 90s down to the 40s and 50s. (p. 131)
>
> What is unexpected about this study—to readers, if not to Lean—is that mathematics tests do not have clear right-or-wrong answers.

Note: If the long quotation is an incomplete sentence, use ellipses to show that words are omitted at the beginning or at the end.

9. Lines of Dialogue

Quote multiple lines of dialogue as they appear on the page, with different lines of dialogue beginning on different lines. Double-space throughout.

> "Just here. If Josh knew how to read and write and cipher—"
>
> "Mr. Leckler, are you crazy!"
>
> "Listen to me, my dear, and give me the benefit of your judgment. This is a very momentous question. As I was about to say, if Josh knew these things, he could protect himself from cheating when his work is at too great a distance for me to look after it for him."
>
> "But teaching a slave—" (p. 169)

Note: If multiple lines of dialogue include narration, place double quotation marks at the beginning of each new paragraph but only at the end of the entire quotation. Use single quotation marks to enclose lines of dialogue.

> "'Well, of course, it's just as you think best,' said his wife.
>
> "'I knew you would agree with me,' he returned. 'It's such a comfort to take counsel with you, my dear!' And the generous man walked out onto the veranda, very well satisfied with himself and his wife, and prospectively pleased with Josh." (p. 169).

Parentheses ( )

Parentheses may be used for these purposes:

1. To enclose comments or explanations that interrupt the main thought:

There appears to be a very strong relationship (see chart) between the accuracy of clock time, walking speed and postal efficiency across the countries we studied. (Levine & Wolff, p. 89)

2. To expand on an idea:

But according to Hall, in many Mediterranean Arab cultures there are only three sets of time: no time at all, now (which is of varying duration) and forever (too long). (Levine & Wolff, p. 88)

3. To indicate documentation of sources:

Isn't it sad that Ho's son thought that "Buenos Aires was Spanish for food—a plate of tacos and burritos, perhaps" (126) and that that doesn't sound strange to Ho? (Skoufaki, p. 164)

Brackets [ ]

Brackets are used to indicate words you have added to quoted material to clarify it (see also p. 293):

Barna explains that "they [stereotypes] increase our feeling of security" in a foreign land (p. 80).

Ellipses . . .

Ellipses are a series of three spaced dots used to indicate that material has been omitted from a quotation. Four dots are used if a period is included in the omission. (See also pp. 292–293.)

Moore argues that teachers "can improve students' self-esteem most by helping and motivating . . . students to exceed *higher* standards" (p. 137).

The Hyphen -

A hyphen is used for these purposes:

1. To divide multisyllable words when there is no more room on the line:

Many of the readings have made me reconsider what education should be.

2. To join compound words:

That was great: a bike and job are supreme joys to a thirteen-year-old. (Jackson, p. 22)

The Dash —

A dash marks an emphatic or abrupt break. It can replace a colon, semicolon, comma, or parentheses in some of their uses, for example:

1. To expand on an idea or add details:

The intellectual faculties developed by studying subjects like history and classics—an ability to synthesize and relate, to weigh cause and effect, to see events in perspective—are just the faculties that make creative leaders in business or almost any general field. (Zinsser, p. 142)

2. To indicate an interruption in the expression of an idea:

> She is a free spirit on a campus of tense students—no small achievement in itself—and she deserves to follow her muse. (Zinsser, p. 142)

3. To set off a final item, for emphasis:

> I picked up the food and wheeled back to the studio—slowly. (Jackson, p. 24)

Note: A dash typed on a regular typing keyboard consists of two consecutive hyphens (--).

Underlining or Italics

Underline or put in italics titles of newspapers, magazines, movies, and books. (One way to remember whether to underline or to use quotation marks is this rule of thumb: underline the longer works; use quotation marks with the shorter works.)

> The essay ''The Rewards of Living a Solitary Life'' was originally published in the *New York Times*.

> The article ''Social Time: The Heartbeat of Culture'' was originally published in *Psychology Today*, a monthly magazine that makes research findings accessible to a nonprofessional audience.

> ''College'' is the title of a chapter in Anzia Yezierska's book *Bread Givers*.

> ''Don't Worry, Be Happy'' is a song on the album entitled *Simple Pleasures*.

Many punctuation marks are actually pause or stop symbols, telling the reader when to rest. These rest symbols represent progressively longer pauses:

,	—	;	:	.
comma	dash	semicolon	colon	period

ACTIVITY

Punctuating Sentences

Working in pairs or in a small group, punctuate the following sentences. First, punctuate each sentence two times, so that two meanings emerge. Then, use various forms of punctuation on each sentence to reflect a different writing style or emphasis. Refer to a dictionary to look up vocabulary words, if necessary.

1. A woman without her man is lost
2. See the elephant eat Maria
3. Give the bird to my cousin Sylvia
4. She said hold it softly
5. I can can can but I cant cant can you
6. That that is is that that is not is not

ACTIVITY

Identifying and Correcting Punctuation Errors

Look through your own writing to search for punctuation errors. Using the guidelines for punctuation, check to see if you have logically punctuated your sentences.   ■

CHAPTER 28

Manuscript Form for Final Copy

After you have revised and edited your paper, you can write or type the final copy for presentation to the instructor. The way your paper looks can have a positive or negative psychological effect on the reader.

Whether a paper is handwritten or typewritten, it will usually include these features:

☐ Your name

☐ The course name and number

☐ The instructor's name

☐ The due date

☐ The title of the essay

The pages should be numbered and stapled together.

The guidelines that follow are for handwritten, typewritten, and computer-generated papers. They are not meant to be rigid instructions that you must follow. Adapt them to suit your project.

GUIDELINES

For a Handwritten Paper

1. Write on white, $8\frac{1}{2}$- by 11-inch lined paper.
2. Use a pen.
3. Write neatly and legibly.
4. Write on only one side of the paper.
5. Indent each paragraph.
6. If you find errors after the paper is finished, you can put a line through the error(s) and then handwrite the correction in the space above, or use white correction fluid to cover the error(s) and then handwrite the correction.

GUIDELINES

For a Typewritten Paper

1. Use $8\frac{1}{2}$- by 11-inch unruled paper of good quality. (Do not use onionskin paper or erasable bond.)
2. Use a fresh ribbon.
3. Double-space.
4. Leave at least 1-inch margins all around.
5. Indent each new paragraph five spaces.
6. After you have typed, check for typographical errors.
7. If you find an error after your paper is finished, use white correction fluid to cover the error, and then neatly handwrite or type the correction.

GUIDELINES

For a Computer-Generated Paper

1. Use white paper.
2. Use a ribbon that produces clear copy.
3. Set the printer to double-space.
4. Set the top and side margins at 1 inch; set the bottom margin at $1\frac{1}{4}$ inches.
5. Use an unjustified right margin.
6. Set the page-length setting at 66 lines.
7. Set the default tab stop at five spaces in from the left margin, to indent your paragraphs.
8. Instruct the printer to number the pages.
9. Select the print mode that produces the best copy.
10. Use a style or spell-checker program, if you have one.
11. Proofread carefully to check for errors that may have occurred as a result of deleting or moving text.

Glossary

A

abash: make ashamed or uneasy
accountable to: responsible for
accrue: increase; accumulate
ad infinitum **(Latin):** to infinity; without end or limit; endlessly
admonish: remind of a responsibility or obligation; caution; warn
ad nauseam **(Latin):** to nausea; to the point of disgust
adversity: misfortune; state of hardship
affiliative: tending to make close connections (with people)
air: quality that seems to surround someone; aura
albeit: even if; even though; although; notwithstanding
alleged: supposed; being described as but not proved to be
alluring: attractive and desirable; tempting; fascinating
ambivalent: uncertain; indecisive as to which course to follow; holding opposing feelings toward someone or something
amicably: in a friendly way
anti-Semite: one who discriminates against or is hostile or prejudiced toward Jews
anxiety-prone: tending to feel uneasy or fearful about the future
apathetic: feeling or showing a lack of interest or emotion
apostrophize: speak as if to an imaginary person
apt to: likely to; having a natural tendency to
apt: quick to learn or understand
ardor: passion; intense affection; eagerness; enthusiasm
arrant: complete; thorough; absolute
articulate: express clearly; give words to
asinine: utterly stupid or silly
assert: put forward boldly, forcefully, or confidently; affirm; claim
attribute to: consider as resulting from, caused by, or belonging to

B

bait: torment with insults and ridicule; trick; trap; tease
balm: substance that is healing or soothing
barbiturates: sedatives; drugs having a tranquilizing effect
batting .666: baseball term measuring a batter's performance, indicating success 66% of the time
beckon: send for; signal to come; summon; call
beef (slang): complaint
bereaved: suffering from the loss of a loved one
beset with: troubled with; attacked from all sides
bethought to: caused (oneself) to; reminded (oneself) to
bliss: extreme happiness; ecstasy
blithe: carefree; lighthearted
blue-collar: related to those involved in manual labor

bondage: condition of a slave; servitude

brash: bold; shameless; impetuous

bread (in idiom): to *break bread with* means to *share a meal with*

brim: uppermost edge (of a cup)

brink (in idiom): *on the brink of* means *at the point at which something is about to begin*

buck (informal): dollar

buoyed by: inspired by; uplifted by

burner (in idiom): to *move to the back burner* means to *put aside; delay; give lower priority to*

C

cabalistic: having a secret or hidden meaning

cajole: urge with gentle appeals; persuade with flattery

calculating: tricky; crafty; coldly scheming or conniving

calculus: method of analysis or calculation

calibrate: measure; adjust by comparison with a standard

candor: frankness; openness and sincerity

charlatan: person who makes fraudulent claims to knowledge

chattel: slave

chemistry: mutual attraction; rapport

chord (in idiom): to *strike a chord* means to *cause a familiar emotional feeling or response*

chronic: lasting for a long period of time

chuck up (British idiom): quit

cipher: solve arithmetic problems; calculate

circuitous: indirect; taking a roundabout course

clacking: making an abrupt, sharp sound

clamoring: making loud, insistent demands

cling to: remain emotionally attached to; hold on to

codified: reduced to a system of rules and regulations; arranged

coerce: force to think or act in a certain way

cognizant of: aware of; fully informed about

complementary: supplying mutual needs

comply with: obey

confiding (adj): trusting

congruent: corresponding in kind; having agreement

conjurer: magician

conspicuous: easy to notice; attracting attention by being unusual

constable (British): police officer

constrain: confine; keep (someone) within close bounds; inhibit

convene: bring together for an official purpose

conventional: customary; conforming to established practice

conviction: strong belief

cope with: deal with successfully

couched in: worded in a certain manner; phrased

counsel (in idiom): to *take counsel with* means to *get advice from*

cowed: frightened; intimidated

crack (in idiom): to *crack a book* means to *open a book (and read it)*

creek (in idiom): *up the creek* means *in a difficult position*

cretonne: heavy, colorfully printed fabric used for curtains

crucified: put to death by being nailed to a cross; as if nailed to a cross

crucifix: image or figure of Jesus Christ nailed on the cross

cutthroat: cruel; merciless or relentless (in competition)
cynicism: scornful, bitterly mocking attitude; contempt; distrust

D

darn: mend by weaving thread or yard
defenses: means or methods of defending or protecting (oneself)
degrade: reduce in worth or value; expose to dishonor
delivery: manner of speaking
delude: deceive; mislead
denominate: designate
deprive of: keep from possessing (something)
designate: indicate; give a name to
despot: ruler with absolute power
deter: prevent or discourage
diffused: softened; made less brilliant; become spread out
digress: turn from the main subject
dilute: lessen the force of strength of; weaken
dire: warning of terrible consequences
disciple: one who accepts or follows a teacher or doctrine
disclosure: revelation; process of revealing or uncovering
disconsolate: cheerless; gloomy; dejected
discrepancy: inconsistency; disagreement between facts
discretion: ability to decide what is proper; cautious judgment
dismiss: reject; put aside
dispense: deal out in parts; distribute; give out
disperse: move away in different directions; vanish
disquieting: troubling
distress: trouble; anxiety; suffering; condition of being in need
diverge: go in different directions; draw apart from a common point
docile: submissive (to training); easily taught
dogma: authoritative principle; doctrine
dolt: person regarded as stupid
dormant: lying asleep or as if asleep; inactive
dovetail: connect or combine precisely or harmoniously
drek (Yiddish slang): trash
dumb down: rewrite for a less intelligent audience
dupe: easily deceived person; person who functions as the tool of another person or power
durable: lasting; able to continue for a long time in the same state

E

earnest: showing deep sincerity or seriousness
edge (in idiom): to *have an edge on* means to *have an advantage over* or to *have a margin of superiority*
elated: proud and joyful
elicit: draw out; bring out
elusive: resisting capture; hard to grasp
emanate from: come from
emancipation: freeing from oppression or slavery
embers: small glowing pieces of coal or wood, as in a dying fire
endemic: natural; native; peculiar to a particular area
enervating: weakening; destroying the vitality of
entitlement: right
ephemeral: lasting only for a very brief time
epitome: concise summary

erudite: learned; possessing deep knowledge
estranged: emotionally removed or separated; alienated
ethnocentric: believing that one's own culture is superior
exhort: urge by strong argument or advice
expense (in idiom): *at the expense of* means *at the risk of*
explicit: fully and clearly expressed; readily observable
extraneous: irrelevant; unrelated to the topic; inessential
extremity: grave danger, necessity, or distress; moment at which death or ruin is near
ever and anon (idiom): time after time; now and then

F

fanciful: imaginative; ideal
fatalistic: accepting the belief that all events are predetermined and therefore unchangeable
felony: serious crime such as murder, rape, or burglary
fervent: showing great emotion; intense in feeling
fetching: very attractive
fetter: chain or shackle for ankle or foot
fierce (informal): *something fierce* means *cruelly; violently*
finger (v) (slang): inform on; designate, especially as an intended victim
firsthand: received from the original source
flock (v): move as a group (like birds)
florid: ornate; flowery; flashy or showy
flush: cause something to glow
fly pages: front pages of a book
formality: established social rules, customs, or ceremonies; conventions of dignified behavior
formidable: arousing fear; difficult to defeat
fortnightly: happening once in two weeks
founder: fail completely; collapse
fractured: broken; disrupted or destroyed; abused or misused
fray: fight; heated dispute
frenzied: frantic; characterized by nervous activity; crazed
fugitive: one who escapes
furtive: secret, in such a way as to express hidden motives
futile: having no useful result; useless; ineffective

G

gale: very strong wind; breeze; sweet-smelling shrub
gallows humor: humorous treatment of a serious situation
garish: loud and flashy; gaudy; showy in a tasteless or vulgar way
garrulous: excessively talkative; given to trival and tedious talking
gentile: one who is not of the Jewish faith; Christian
gnaw: bite; chew on; eat away
granted (in idiom): to *take for granted* means to *underestimate the value of* or to *assume to be true or available when required*
gregarious: sociable; seeking or enjoying the company of others
grim: gloomy; dismal; rigid
grit: clamp (one's teeth) together
ground: foundation for an argument, belief, or action
guardedness: tendency to be cautious, restrained, or self-protective
guru: guide in spiritual matters; recognized leader; influential supporter of a movement or idea
guts (slang): courage; audacity
gyve: fetter or chain for the leg

H

handcuffed: restrained with handcuffs; ineffective; impotent
harrowing: extremely distressing; agonizing; tormenting
harsh: disagreeable to the senses, especially the sense of hearing
hassle: trouble; bother; fight; argument
haughtiness: pride; scornful and condescending attitude
havoc: widespread destruction; disorder; chaos
hitch: obstacle; obstruction; delay
hoops (in idiom): to *jump through hoops* means to *undergo a rigorous trial or examination*
hound: pursue; hunt for, as with dogs

I

idly: as a way of passing time; while not occupied
illusion: false belief; condition of being deceived by false perception; erroneous perception of reality
impassive: revealing no emotion; expressionless
impeccable: perfect; without flaws
imperative: having the authority to command control
imperialism: policy of extending a nation's authority by acquiring territory or establishing power over other nations
impound: seize in legal custody; take legally
impregnable: impossible to challenge successfully; incapable of being entered
inclined to: have a preference for; have a tendency toward
incongruity: lack of harmony; lack of agreement; inconsistency
inconspicuous: not readily noticeable; not prominent
incontrovertible: unquestionable; impossible to disprove
indefatigable: tireless; having a great capacity for hard work
indiscreet: lacking caution; not careful to avoid errors of judgment
inevitable: impossible to avoid or prevent; certain
infamous: known well for something negative
infinitesimal: immeasurably small; so small as to be insignificant
inflation: inappropriate increase that hides real value
inflection: alteration in pitch or tone of voice
inflict: impose, as if by force, cause to suffer
inhalator: respirator; device that supplies oxygen for breathing
inhibit: hold back; restrain
iniquitous: wicked; immoral; unjust; sinful
innately: characteristically; from birth or origin; naturally
innumerable: too numerous to be counted; incalculable
in saecula saeculorum **(Latin):** forever and ever
insurmountable: impossible to overcome or conquer
intangible: incapable of being seen, heard, or touched; not definable
integral: essential or necessary for completeness
integrity: honesty; uprightness of character; devotion to a strict moral or ethical code
in terrorem **(Latin):** as a warning
intervene: come between two things, to stop or alter something
intimate: make known indirectly; hint
intrinsic: relating to the essential nature of something; inherent
introvert: person who turns inward; person who is not outgoing

J

jargon: specialized language
jeer: speak or shout in a mocking way; abuse vocally; taunt
jockey: maneuver to gain an advantage
jostle: come in rough contact while moving; push or shove

K

keen: having a sharp edge; having intellectual quickness; sensitive
kelson: piece of wood fastened to a boat for additional strength
kin: relatives; family
kindle: build a fire; ignite; cause to glow; arouse

L

labyrinth: maze; confusing network of paths
laden: weighed down (with a load); burdened
lament: express sorrow or regret; grieve
latent: dormant; undeveloped but capable of normal growth under the proper conditions; not visible; hidden
latterly: lately; recently; not long ago
lay for (idiom): wait to attack
learn'd: learned; possessing or demonstrating profound knowledege
life (in idiom): *for the life of me* means *though trying hard*
lingering: slowness in leaving; staying; reluctance to leave
lingo: dialect; slang; specialized language
listless: lacking energy; inattentive; indifferent
lorry: truck for carrying heavy loads
lowlife: person of low social status or moral character
lustily: strongly; with energy; powerfuly

M

magnate: powerful or influential person, especially in business
mangled: ruined or spoiled through incompetence; mutilated
manifest: clearly apparent; obvious
manumission: freedom from slavery; emancipation
marginally: even within a lower standard; even of limited quality
markedly: noticeably; in a clearly evident manner
marred: damaged; spoiled; impaired
materialistic: excessively interested in the physical comforts of life
meager: scant; deficient in quantity; barely sufficient
mediocre: of only moderate quality; ordinary; average
melancholy: sadness; depression of the spirits; gloom
mentor: wise and trusted teacher or counselor
merit: earn; deserve
midwife: person who is trained to assist women in childbirth
milquetoast: one who has a meek, timid, unassertive nature
minatory: threatening
miry: swampy; muddy
mission: effort to spread a certain kind of teaching; effort to provide help for needy people
missionary: person who attempts to convert others to a particular set of principles; person sent to do religious or charitable work in a territory or foreign country
moccasined: wearing soft leather shoes
molten: melted
momentous: of utmost importance; of outstanding consequence
monkeyshines (slang): tricks (like a monkey's)
muse (n): guiding spirit; source of (artistic) inspiration
muse (v): consider thoughtfully; mediate on

N

nag: torment persistently, as with anxiety
negligible: not significant enough to be worth considering
neophyte: novice; recent convert; beginner
niche: special place or position suited to a person's abilities

nimble: quick, light, or agile in movement; clever
nonchalant: casual; unconcerned; indifferent
nondescript: not distinctive enough to be described; having no individual character
nose out (idiom): defeat by a narrow margin
nudge: push gently
nurturant: characterized by providing loving care and attention

O

obscure: little known
obsolescence: uselessness; process of losing usefulness
obstacle: something that stands in the way; barrier
okra: a tall tropical plant, often used in soups or stews
onset: beginning; start
opportune: suited or right for a particular purpose
oppress: weigh heavily on; overwhelm
opt: make a choice or decision
orderly: soldier assigned to attend a superior officer
organic: constituting an integral part of a whole; close to nature
oriented: adapted mentally to a situation; placed in relation to the points of the compass
outcast: one who has been excluded from or rejected by a society
overexert: make too much effort

P

paddy: rice; field where rice is grown
palpitations: trembling or shaking; irregular, rapid heartbeats
pant: yearn; gasp with desire
paraphernalia: equipment; things used in a particular activity
parley: have a discussion, especially with an enemy
parlous: dangerous; perilous; mischievous
passive: inactive; not responsive; inert; not mentally active
pat: contrived
Patagonians: original inhabitants (known as giants) of a region in southern Argentina and Chile
pathology: departure or deviation from a normal condition; scientific study of the nature of disease
pathos: quality that arouses feelings of pity or tenderness
patter: move with quick, light steps
pauper: one who is extremely poor
peculation: stealing of money or goods; embezzlement
peer: equal; companion
perch: sit on an elevated place; rest on a branch (like a bird)
perforce: by necessity; by force of circumstance
persistent: refusing to give up or let go; continuing to exist
perverted: corrupt; deviating from what is correct; distorted
petty: of small importance; trivial; marked by narrowness of mind
pin down (idiom): fix or establish clearly; force to give a firm opinion or precise information
pine: grieve; mourn; yearn
plagued: afflicted, as if with a disease
plunge: throw (oneself) into an activity or situation; descend steeply; move downward violently
plunge (in idiom): to *take the plunge* means to *begin an unfamiliar adventure, especially after hesitating*
ponder: weigh in the mind with care; consider carefully

poring over: reading or studying carefully and attentively
potent: powerful; possessing strength
premise: proposition upon which an argument is based
press into (idiom): force into (such as service in the army)
pretext: excuse; strategy intended to conceal something
privy to: made a participant in knowledge of something private
procure: get by special effort; obtain
productivity: quality of producing favorable or useful results
profess: claim; pretend
proponent: one who argues in support of something; advocate
prospective: anticipated
prostrate: lying with one's face to the ground; brought low in mind and spirit (by an outside force)
proverbial: widely referred to; famous
proximity: closeness; nearness
pulling to (informal): attractive to
pun: play on words (e.g., on different meaning of similar words)
purport: present the false appearance of being or intending

Q   **quay:** wharf where ships are loaded and unloaded

R   **random (in idiom):** *at random* means *unsystematically*
ranged: arranged in a particular order; classified
rap (slang): to *take the rap* means to *accept punishment* or to *take the blame for an offense or horror*
rascal: dishonest, unscrupulous person; mischievous person
ravage: bring heavy destruction on; destroy violently
reams: very large amount
reassure: restore confidence or courage to; encourage
recidivistic: having a tendency to return to a previous pattern of behavior, especially a tendency to return to criminal behavior
reckon (informal): think; assume
reckoning (in idiom): *day of reckoning* means *time when something must be paid back* or *time to settle accounts (with God)*
regalia: fine clothes; distinctive symbols of any society
reigning: predominant; prevalent
release: liberation from suffering; relief from debt
relentless: steady and persistent; indifferent to the pain of others
relevant: having a connection to the subject or issue at hand
relinquish: give up; abandon; surrender
remedial: intended to correct or improve deficient skills
replete with: filled with; abundantly supplied with
reprehensible: deserving blame or criticism
reprobate: unprincipled, immoral person
reproving: voicing disapproval of; finding fault with
residential: limited to places where people live
resignedly: accepting something as inevitable; giving up (a position); submitting oneself passively
resolute: firm; determined; unwavering; having a fixed purpose
resonant: having a stimulating effect beyond the initial impact; strong and deep in tone; continuing to sound in the ears or memory
resplendent with: splendid or dazzling in appearance
responsive: readily reacting to suggestions, influences, or appeals

restrain: hold back; control; restrict
revellers: people who engage in merry festivities or celebrations
rivet: fasten; fix directly
roster: list of names, especially of military personnel
roundabout: indirect
rudimentary: elementary; relating to the basic facts

S

sag: sink; settle from pressure or weight; lose vigor or firmness
sanitary: freed from unhealthy filth; hygienic
sap (slang): foolish, stupid person
sassiness: brash behavior; impertinent disrespect; impudence
savor: taste or smell with pleasure; appreciate fully; enjoy
scandal: publicized incident that brings about disgrace or offends the moral sensibilities of society
scheming: tending to make secret or devious plans
scrutiny: close, careful examination or study; critical inspection
scurry: go with light, running steps
secondhand: not direct from the original source; received or borrowed from another; previously used; not new
selective: tending to make a choice from several possibilities while excluding other choices
senility: mental and physical deterioration characteristic of old age
serenity: calmness; tranquility
shallow: lacking depth of intellect, emotion, or knowledge
sheer: absolute; total
shingled: cut short and close to the head
shorn (past participle of *shear*): cut or clipped
shuck: cast off; remove the husk (of corn) or shell from
shuffle: mix the order of papers or cards
siesta: rest or nap after the midday meal
sine qua non **(Latin):** necessity
singular: beyond what is ordinary or usual
sissy (informal): weakling; boy or man regarded as effeminate; person regarded as timid or cowardly
slipshod: careless; sloppy
slobber: let saliva or liquid spill out from the mouth; drool heavily
slogan: phrase expressing the aims of an organization or endeavor
smack of (idiom): suggest; give an indication of
smattering: superficial knowledge; very small, scattered amount
sneering: scornful; contemptuous
solicitous: expressing care or concern; extremely careful
soliloquy: act of speaking to oneself; monologue
song and dance (informal): interesting or entertaining statement or performance unrelated to the subject at hand
sore: causing misery, sorrow, or distress; angry or offended
spar: buoy; float moored in water to guide navigators
speculation: conclusion, opinion, or theory reached by guessing
spic-and-span: immaculately clean; spotless; looking as if new
split (slang): departed; left quickly
squabble: noisy argument, usually about a trivial matter
squalid: dirty and neglected; morally repulsive
squander: spend wastefully or extravagantly

squirm: twist about in a wriggling motion, like a snake
staggering: overwhelming; causing great astonishment or dismay
stigmatize: characterize as disgraceful or shameful
street-smart (informal): aware of how to survive in an often hostile urban environment
stricken: suffering from
stride: single long step
strode (past tense of *stride*): took long steps
subtle: so slight as to be difficult to detect or see; not obvious
succinct: clear and precise; concise
suffice: satisfy needs; be enough
summon: request to appear; call
sundries: small articles; miscellaneous items
supplicant: beggar; one who humbly asks or prays for something
surge: swelling motion, like a wave
susceptible to: easily or likely to be influenced or affected by
swamp (v): burden; overwhelm; cover with (as if with water)
sway: swing back and forth; bend to one side; influence; incline toward change

T

tackle: deal with; undertake to solve
telling: revealing
tempo: characteristic rate or rhythm of an activity; pace
tenacity: tendency to hold persistently to something
thorn: something that causes sharp pain or discomfort
throng: large group of people gathered closely together; crowd
together (slang): unified and harmonized
tonic: refreshing or restorative agent or influence
tormented: tortured; agonized; distorted
tottering: unsteady
tractable: easily managed or controlled; obedient
trail the pack: lag behind (an opponent) in a competition
transcribe: represent letters or words in the corresponding characters of another alphabet; transliterate
transgress: commit an offense by violating a law or rule
treadmill: monotonous task or set of tasks seeming to have no end
tremulous: marked by trembling or shaking; timid; fearful
trod (past tense of *tread*): walked on or over; pressed beneath the feet
trudge: walk in a heavy-footed way; walk wearily
truism: self-evident truth
turmoil: state of extreme confusion or agitation; disturbance

U

unaccountable: inexplicable; impossible to account for
undermine: weaken slowly; wear away at the base
unnerving: causing to lose one's nerve or courage
unobtrusive: not readily noticeable; inconspicuous; not prominent
unswerving: without turning aside; steady
uppity (informal): assuming airs beyond one's assigned place in society
utter (adj): complete; absolute

V

vacillate: hesitate; swing indecisively from one course of action or opinion to another
venerate: regard with great respect; revere
vengeance: infliction of punishment in return for a wrong committed; retribution
venture (v): expose to danger or risk; express at the risk of criticism or denial

versatile: capable of doing many things competently; changeable
viable: capable of success or continuing effectiveness
vindicate: clear of blame or doubt; justify; prove the worth of
virtually: almost but not quite; nearly; practically
vista: distant view or prospect

W

waddle: walk clumsily with the body tilting from side to side
wan: unnaturally pale, as from distress, weariness, or unhappiness
whereupon: after which; in consequence of which
whither: to what place
whopping : exceptionally large
wistful: melancholic; thoughtfully sad; full of wishful yearning
withstand: oppose with force or resolution; resist successfully
woe: deep distress or misery; wretchedness
worked over (slang): beat up; had physical damage inflicted
wot (archaic): knows
wreak: inflict or bring about
wretched: miserable; in a state of misfortune

(Acknowledgments continued)

George Orwell, "Shooting an Elephant" from *Shooting an Elephant and Other Essays* by George Orwell. Copyright © The estate of the late Sonia Brownell Orwell and Martin Secker and Warburg Ltd. Reprinted by permission of Harcourt Brace & Company.

May Sarton, "The Rewards of Living a Solitary Life." *The New York Times* Op-Ed (April 8, 1974) Copyright © 1974 by the New York Times Company. Reprinted by permission.

May Sarton, Excerpt from "Moving In," from *Collected Poems 1930–1993 May Sarton,* published in 1993 by W.W. Norton & Company, Inc. Copyright © 1993 by May Sarton. Reprinted by permission of Russell & Volkening, Inc. and A.M. Heath & Company Limited as agents for the author.

Don Koberg and Jim Bagnall, "How to Criticize Painlessly . . . How to Accept Criticism." Copyright © Crisp Publications, Inc. 1200 Hamilton Court, Menlo Park, California 94025; 800-442-7477. Reprinted by permission.

Judith Viorst, "Friends, Good Friends—and Such Good Friends." Copyright © 1977 by Judith Viorst. Originally appeared in *Redbook.* Reprinted by permission of the author.

Joel D. Block, "Myth, Reality and Shades of Gray: Comparing Same-Sex Friendships." *Friendships,* Copyright © 1980 by Joel D. Block. Reprinted with the permission of Simon & Schuster, Inc. and Collier Associates, P.O. Box 21361, West Palm Beach, Florida 33416, USA.

LaRay M. Barna, "Intercultural Communication Stumbling Blocks." Copyright © 1976 by LaRay Barna. From *Intercultural Communication: A Reader* by Larry A. Samovar and Richard E. Porter, Wadsworth Publishing Co., Inc. 1976. Reprinted by permission of the author. Professor Barna teaches at Portland State University, Portland, Oregon.

Robert Levine, with Ellen Wolff, "Social Time: The Heartbeat of Culture." Reprinted with permission from *Psychology Today* magazine. Copyright © 1985. (Sussex Publishers, Inc.).

Ernest L. Boyer, "Creativity in the Classroom" from *College: The Undergraduate Experience in America* by Ernest L. Boyer. Copyright © 1987 by The Carnegie Foundation for the Advancement of Teaching. Reprinted by permission of HarperCollins Publishers, Inc.

E.D. Hirsch, "Teach Knowledge, Not 'Mental Skills' " *The New York Times* (September 4, 1993). Copyright © 1993 by The New York Times Company. Reprinted by permission.

Arthur E. Lean, "The Farce Called 'Grading'" from *And Merely Teach: Irreverent Essays on the Mythology of Education.* Copyright © 1976 by the Board of Trustees of Southern Illinois University. Reprinted by permission of the publisher.

Randy Moore, "Grades and Self-Esteem" from *The American Biology Teacher,* vol. 55, no. 7 (October 1993). Reprinted with permission of Randy Moore.

William K. Zinsser, "College Pressures" from the *Blair & Ketchum's Country Journal,* Vol. VI, No. 4, April 1979. Copyright © 1979 by William K. Zinsser. Reprinted by permission of the author.

James Joyce, "Eveline" from *Dubliners* by James Joyce. Viking Press 1964. Courtesy of Random House UK Limited and the estate of James Joyce.

Bernard Malamud, "The German Refugee" from *Idiots First* by Bernard Malamud. Copyright © 1963 by Bernard Malamud. Copyright renewed © 1991 by Ann Malamud. Reprinted by permission of Farrar, Straus & Giroux, Inc.

Cristina Garcia, "Tito's Good-bye" from *Iguana Dreams: New Latino Fiction.* Copyright © 1992 by Cristina Garcia. Reprinted by permission of Cristina Garcia.

Emily Dickinson, "Hope" from *The Complete Poems of Emily Dickinson* edited by Thomas H. Johnson. Published by Little, Brown and Company in association with Harvard University Press.

Robert Frost, "The Road Not Taken" from *The Poetry of Robert Frost,* ed. Edward Connery Lathem. Copyright © 1962 by Robert Frost. Copyright © 1969 by Holt, Rinehart and Winston, Inc. Copyright © 1975 by Lesley Frost Ballantine. Reprinted by permission of Henry Holt and Company, Inc.

Edna St. Vincent Millay, "Sonnet XXX" of *Fatal Interview* from *Collected Poems,* HarperCollins. Copyright © 1931, 1950 by Edna St. Vincent Millay and Norma Millay Ellis. Reprinted by permission of Elizabeth Barnett, literary executor.

Maya Angelou, "Still I Rise." From *And Still I Rise* by Maya Angelou. Copyright © 1978 by Maya Angelou. Reprinted by permission of Random House, Inc. and Virago Press Limited.

James Reiss, "*¿Habla Usted Español?*" Copyright © 1974 by James Reiss. Reprinted by permission of The Ecco Press, Inc. 100 W. Broad Street, Hopewell, New Jersey, 08525.

Antonio Machado, "Portrait," from *Antonio Machado: Selected Poems,* trans. by Alan S. Trueblood, Cambridge, MA.: Harvard University Press. Copyright © 1982 by the President and Fellows of Harvard College. Reprinted by permission of the publishers.

Kenneth Koch, "Poem for My Twentieth Birthday," from *The* Poetry *Anthology: 1912–1977* by Daryl Hine and Joseph Parisi, eds. Houghton-Mifflin (1978). Copyright © 1995 by Kenneth Koch. Reprinted by permission of the author.

Daniel Halpern, "The Ethnic Life." Copyright © 1970, 1972 by Daniel Halpern. Reprinted by permission of Curtis Brown, Ltd.

William Carlos Williams, "Marriage," from *William Carlos Williams: CollectedPoems: 1909–1939,* Volume 1. Copyright © 1938 by New Directions Publishing Corp. Reprinted by permission of New Directions Publishing Corp. and Carcanet Press, 406–408 Corn Exchange Bldgs., Manchester M43BQ England.

Merrill Moore, "Transfusion," from *Poetry* magazine (1929). Reprinted in *The* Poetry *Anthology: 1912–1977: Sixty-Five Years of America's Most Distinguished Verse Magazine,* Daryl Hine and Joseph Parisi, eds. Houghton-Mifflin Company (1978). Reprinted by permission.

Hilda Doolittle, "In Time of Gold," from *Hilda Doolittle: Collected Poems, 1912–1944.* Copyright © 1982 by the Estate of Hilda Doolittle. Reprinted by permission of New Directions Publishing Corp. and Carcanet Press, 406–408 Corn Exchange Bldgs., Manchester M43BQ England.

Juan Ramón Jiménez, "The Last Journey," trans. Eleanor L. Turnbull, from *Ten Centuries of Spanish Poetry: An Anthology in English Verse with Original Text.* Copyright © 1955. Reprinted by permission of The Johns Hopkins University Press.

Antoine de Saint-Exupéry, excerpt from *Flight to Arras,* translated by Lewis Galantière. Copyright © 1942 by Harcourt Brace & Company. Reprinted by permission of the author and the publishers: Harcourt Brace & Company and William Heinemann Ltd.

Excerpts from *The New York Times Index,* 1968. Copyright © 1968 by The New York Times Company. Reprinted by permission.

Index